Teaching Resistance

Radicals, Revolutionaries, and Cultural Subversives in the Classroom

Edited by John Mink

D1572263

Teaching Resistance: Radicals, Revolutionaries, and Cultural Subversives in the Classroom
Edited by John Mink
© 2019 the respective authors
This edition © 2019 PM Press.

ISBN: 978-1-62963-709-9
Library of Congress Control Number: 2019933019

Cover by John Yates / www.stealworks.com
Cover illustration by Miriam Klein Stahl / www.miriamkleinstahl.com
Interior design by briandesign

10 9 8 7 6 5 4 3 2 1

PM Press
PO Box 23912
Oakland, CA 94623
www.pmpress.org

Printed in the USA.

This book is dedicated to my darling companion
Megan March—for so much indispensable guidance,
and without whom this project would never have happened.
to my mother—a dedicated teacher's aid/para and SPED teacher
who had a wicked sense of humor shot through with deep, deep love.
and to my father—a wily old commie and lifelong anti-fascist
who taught social studies for over thirty years in East Oakland,
and who warned me never to become a teacher.
Sorry, pop, but that's mob life for ya.

All royalties/author profits for this book will be donated to
Teachers 4 Social Justice, who I hope continue to stir the pot and
make us all confront uncomfortable truths for as long as possible.

Contents

INTRODUCTION   1

School Is a Riot   6
by Melissa Merin

From These Classroom Windows We Can See the Confederacy   25
by dwayne dixon

How Schools Can Address Racism   30
by Kadijah Means

The Legacy of Trauma   38
by Lindsay McLeary

Resistance in the Palestinian Classroom   51
Mike Corr interviews Murad Tamini

Safe(r) Spaces and Future Cops   57
by Frankie Mastrangelo

**The Dissent of Consent: An Educator's Experience Teaching
Sexual Violence Prevention**   64
by Sarah Orton

Interview with Miriam Klein Stahl   78
interviewed by John Mink

Koko Lepo: Kindergarten and the Struggle in Belgrade, Serbia   92
by Frederick Schulze

What Prison Teaching Can Teach Us   101
by Lena Tahmassian

Cops Out of Our Schools!   110
by John Mink

Becoming a Teacher in Bavaria: Making Up and Finding Leeway within Structural Conservatism   116
by E. Schmuse

Personal Pedagogy   124
by Jessica Mills

Community College Is Totally Punk Rock   132
by Michelle Cruz Gonzales

Insurgent Pedagogies: Decolonization Is for All of Us   144
by Natalie Avalos

Radical Inclusion and Special Education   158
by Stephen Raser

Neurotypicals and the Rest of Us   167
by Ash Tray

Interview with Alice Bag   173
interviewed by John Mink

Our Students Are Radical *Because* They Live in the Real World   185
by Mimi Thi Nguyen

Talking to ESL Students about Anti-Black Racism   190
by Ian McDeath

Interview with Martin Sorrondeguy   207
interviewed by John Mink

False Equivalencies and the Resurgent Far Right in a Messy, Violent World   233
by John Mink

Guide for Youth Protestors   239
by Jessalyn Aaland

Building the Movement to Stop Trump: Lessons from an Anti-Fascist Civil Rights Educator in Berkeley   256
   by Yvette Felarca

The Big Takeover of New Orleans   267
   by Roburt Knife

Letters from the Educational Battle Lines in Oklahoma (AKA Everywhere, USA)   282
   by Taylor McKenzie

Notes on an Anarchist Pedagogy   290
   by Ron Scapp

The People and Teachers Unite against the State and Neoliberalism in Oaxaca   312
   by Scott Campbell

Maximumrocknroll Radio's "Teaching Resistance" DJ Slot   324
   by John Mink

Who Punk Forgot   331
   by Christiana Cranberry

Problem Posing in the ESL Classroom   339
   by Ruth Crossman

Lesson Plans for Community Self-Defense in a Time of Resurgent Neofascism   347
   by John Mink

Navigating Spaces   352
   by Mike Friedberg

ABOUT THE AUTHORS   355

ACKNOWLEDGMENTS   363

Introduction

Misfits, outsiders, radicals, and marginalized people have always had a conflicted relationship with education. On one hand, they recognize that school is an oppressive institution. It is a potentially dangerous environment that is forced upon them as kids. Then, when they finally finish or escape it, they are pressured into often ruinously expensive higher education. On the other hand, education has also been an escape valve for people who are otherwise stuck in grim or disadvantaged life situations, helping provide them with structure and intellectual skills that have the potential to improve their lives and those of others.

Although the institutions of education are historically problematic and often oppressive, students who have experienced them as "outsiders" understand the importance of learning from teachers who have developed radical notions of what education is and how it works. Sometimes these students become teachers themselves, helping subvert the educational institutions or finding alternatives outside of them. In recent decades, one of the most subversive, transgressive, and misunderstood global subcultures—punk—has seen many of its consummate "outsider" adherents become teachers. This makes sense, given that a large percentage of punks embrace radical idealism, strong personal ethics, and intellectualism. These teachers retain their punk identity, or at least acknowledge the significant role of the subculture in their radicalization.

I am an activist, a fairly new teacher, and a punk. I play in bands and participate in the DIY- and DIT-oriented subculture. Coming to teaching as a politically radical punk, I was not interested in being a one-way fount of information and judgment to my students. Rather, I was hopeful about the potential to explore different approaches to classroom practice—universally reciprocal and justice-oriented, respectful, and centering of a wide array of life experiences; equitable and committed to diversity and demarginalization on a deep level, critical thought–oriented and self-reflective, counter-hierarchical, and antiauthoritarian; intersectionally feminist, decolonizing, and liberatory.

Unsurprisingly, I found there was little real support for such goals in the state credentialing process I was required to undergo. Many of these kinds of ideas are reflected in the rhetoric found in modern teacher training programs, representing a belated acknowledgment by collegiate academies of the newfound visibility of some very hard-fought (and often deeply contentious) radical concepts. This superficial rhetoric, however, is contradicted when it comes to how teachers are trained in actual practice, and the structural nature of many educational institutions results in problematic norms of instruction and learning being perpetuated by default.

In his seminal 1979 book *Subculture: The Meaning of Style*, Dick Hebdige draws from Althusser's theories on unconscious ideology to describe how broader social divisions, processes, and hierarchies are replicated in schools, from the physical structure of campuses separated into "traditional" arts and sciences divisions (further divided by specific subject) to the act and shape of classroom instruction itself:

> The hierarchical relationship between teacher and taught is inscribed in the very lay-out of the lecture theatre where the seating arrangements—benches rising in tiers before a raised lectern—dictate the flow of information and serve to "naturalize" professorial authority. Thus, a whole range of decisions about what is and what is not possible within education have been made, however unconsciously, before the content of individual courses is even decided.
>
> These decisions help to set the limits not only on what is taught, but on how it is taught.[1]

Seemingly intractable structures such as these, physical and otherwise, can carry strong (sub)conscious connotations of support for a

---

1   Dick Hebdige, *Subculture: The Meaning of Style* (London: Routledge, 1979), 12–13.

status quo that is often harmful to marginalized people and groups, recasting the well-meaning educator into a role that perpetuates injustice. My own student teaching assessments and pedagogy courses were undertaken in two liberal-leaning institutions that have been repeatedly excoriated by the reactionary right-wing outrage crowd for their reputed leftist "extremism." In these institutions, I was struck by how much pressure was placed on teachers to maintain a veneer of "neutrality" and "lack of bias." Of course, neither of these positions truly exist in a broader society. We cannot separate ourselves from our learned, unconscious frames of reference, implicit biases, and positionality in the world—things our students see in us even when we don't. Many diverse perspectives can and should be considered in any classroom setting, and an open-minded, accepting teacher who is also transparent about their own worldview helps to set a standard of honesty for the entire class. But the pressure to conform to a model of purported neutrality serves the purpose of perpetuating some of the most harmful aspects of the status quo, continuing to effectively marginalize many student identities and stifle critical dissent.

Fortunately, we live in a world where insurgent pushback against rotten institutions and injustice is growing stronger. There are many genuine radicals among teachers. Under the weight of administrative, parental, and social pressures (including the threat of doxxing by reactionaries), these teachers must often learn to be quite creative in teaching students to ask a more challenging set of questions, in fighting to push back against the oppressive status quo, and in using subversion to reinvent education from within by putting new and transgressive ideas into practice. As an aspirational radical and student teacher coming from a subculture/community that is used to being defined as "outsider" and consistently needs to create its own spaces, I wanted to connect with and learn from others who knew how to radicalize and subvert teaching pedagogy; those who treated their students as equals. I needed to learn from those who thought more like me.

The "Teaching Resistance" column, which this book is drawn from, began in January 2015, the month I got my teaching credential. It ran monthly in the infamous politically and culturally insurgent punk magazine *Maximumrocknroll* (aka MRR, est. 1982). I started the column on the suggestion of Megan March, my life partner and bandmate in Street Eaters, who had the idea after hearing me repeatedly bemoan the lack of a network and skill share for all the radical, punk-affiliated teachers I was meeting on tour and wanted to learn from. Although "Teaching Resistance" was born in a punk context, it was designed to be a platform for subversive educators of many stripes to share their innovative ideas and to draw attention to important issues around education. All of the authors in this book are personally dedicated to a deeply intersectional fight against oppression, lifting up transformative social justice ideals through direct action in their own classrooms and a wide array of other educational contexts.

In this book, you will find stories that directly document and reflect on classroom teaching practice, personal journeys in education, a little bit of theory, crucial labor struggles, and the challenges educators and students face in a wider world that is increasingly hostile to radical thought and to marginalized people in general. There are also several long-form interviews with iconic figures in punk and education that dive deeply into the backgrounds and motivations of these fascinating individuals.

The powerful, diverse voices in the column have given me countless insights and have been a major component in my education as a radical teacher, lessons hard to come by in institutional settings. I hope it can do the same for you, whether you are a teacher of any kind, a student, or a curious person who wants a greater understanding of how education can be used to center often marginalized voices, question and subvert the dominant narratives, rethink classroom structures and methods, and hopefully make the world a slightly better place.

> **I celebrate teaching that enables transgressions—a movement against and beyond boundaries. It is that movement which makes education a practice of freedom.**
> —bell hooks, *Teaching to Transgress*

One of the most consistent undercurrents in this book is that of intersectionality. This often misunderstood but absolutely crucial concept, theorized in 1989 by feminist scholar and critical race theorist Kimberlé Crenshaw, involves the understanding that any system of power that confers advantages or disadvantages on one group over another group (and among individuals within those groups) requires analysis of how these different categories—such as race, gender, sexuality, and class—are interdependent and overlapping, as are the power systems that generate such discriminations.

An effective approach to radical pedagogy recognizes that an intersectional lens is vital to understanding the "big picture," and that keeping various types of oppression in separate, discrete categories makes it much easier for the structural forces (and their agents) driving such oppression to prevent people from finding solidarity in their struggles, keeping resistance diffuse and myopic and thus cutting effective opposition off at the knees. Intersectionality's wide scope does not, however, require its advocates to eschew a specific focus or rhetorical emphasis on their individual struggles and battles with systems of oppression. In contrast, the intersectional lens encourages ever more crucial and detailed focus on the deep, underlying problem(s), with one eye always trained on the wider context—the "big picture."

The following essay is intersectional as fuck, to put it mildly, but it is also centered on wrangling with what is inarguably a primary concern for teachers: the long, difficult battle to combat racism in the United States, a chronic, historic cancer that is directly reflected in the fundamental structures and failures of the American school system. It is by **Melissa Merin**, known to some as Shakes, who has worked for many years with kids in a variety of counseling and teaching roles at public schools in the San Francisco Bay Area.

School Is a Riot

by Melissa Merin

> External control, are you gonna let 'em getcha?
> Do you wanna be a prisoner to the boundaries they set ya?
> You say you wanna be yourself, by christ, you think they'll let ya?
> They're out to getcha getcha getcha getcha getcha getcha.
> —Crass, "Big A Little A"

A GUIDE TO THIS CHAPTER

1. You're going to see u.s./usa/america in lower case. Stylistically, I find that it causes people to pause and wonder: Why the lack of capitalization? As a practice, I believe that it is one small step in un-essentializing america and american values and power, a minor subversion of sorts.

2. I cite about seventeen different radical writers, educators, and general badasses. You mighta heard of Noam Chomsky or Pedro Noguera, but a lot of these folks are largely unknown outside of academia related to education. This is largely because unless someone has produced something fit for mass consumption, we are trained to believe it's unattainable, unrelatable, elitist, or simply not for us. I challenge us to think beyond what capitalism teaches us is good or worthy. When you see these citations, imagine the words "incomparable badass scholar" or "decolonial educator" or something to that effect. I'll add a small guide to these folk at the end.

3. Footnotes are either exciting or intimidating. I like to think of them as a statement that just won't fit in (parenthesis). They're not

critical to understanding what I'm trying to get at here, but they're interesting and might lead you to some things you didn't know.
4.   STPP = school-to-prison pipeline; STCP = school-to-confinement pathways

★

On the eve of the twenty-fifth anniversary of the L.A. riots, my social media was saturated with tomes dedicated to the notorious urban revolt. The riots left human and economic casualties and devastation in their wake, and yet they also revitalized a revolutionary sentiment that seemed to lie dormant for so many years for so many people after the apex of the Civil Rights Movement. This anniversary called me to remember my young self in 1992 and to recollect, in particular, how the L.A. riots were catalysts that allowed me to draw clear lines from my early experiences with covert and overt racism to my nascent introductions to radical thought and waking. It wasn't just that Rodney King coulda been me. It was that in so many ways I'd been experiencing a different kind of beating from the first time I entered a schoolyard. The images of folks destroying buildings that seemed concretely impenetrable were affirming and exciting to my young mind, because, as terrifying as it was to see block after block engulfed in flame, I knew that those burning buildings would later become empty charred lots, and then what? The possibilities seemed endless. I hoped I could bring that fire to school with me from middle school through high school and into college(s).

Decades later, I find it important to continue to link my political awakenings and my experiences in school. Though I was never a model student, I have managed to stay connected to institutional education in one way or another. Once in a while, I attempt to reconcile my distrust and outright rebellion toward education with my understanding that school is necessary, and yet doesn't necessarily need to be an "evil." It is within the framework of critical race theory that I find the most success in uniting my love of education and my never-ending quest for collective liberation from racist and heterosexist capitalist oppression. From this place of desire, I enter education as an educator and see as my responsibility as a punker, an antiauthoritarian, and a Black human in america to hone my practice in order to build and perpetuate transformative, restorative practices at the elementary school/early childhood education level. That's where most of us begin our more formal educational journeys.

The year before the riots, when I watched the beating of Rodney King on television so casually reported and with so little context, I felt a familiar rage. The grainy moving image of him lying on the ground surrounded by bright lights and uniformed officers beating him again and again felt familiar. I identified with his brutalization. He was trapped, alone, and vulnerable. The military agents of the state had dehumanized him and all anyone could do was watch. I was only twelve and a half and had already had at least half a dozen encounters with police officers, none of them good. Though I knew I'd been targeted in each interaction, and though I was aware that it was because I was Black, I didn't realize until Rodney King was writhing on the side of the road, surrounded, that they could *rise to that specific level of brutality*. I didn't realize that I had been smoldering.

The riots that followed the acquittal of the officers who beat King reflected the frequent and spontaneous inner explosions I experienced in my early adolescence, and the utter annihilation on the landscape seemed to be a reckoning to me. The news reported the riots as a tragedy, and that's how we talked about them at home, but secretly I saw them as revelatory—a fervent call for the destruction of oppression. A burned-out building was an indictment of capitalism, of racism. In the year following the beating, a sort of hopelessness burrowed inside of me. Nothing and no one was safe. However, a year later, as I watched L.A. burning on the nightly news, I felt almost relieved. The riots were seventy long miles away from me, yet they felt dangerously—inspiringly—close.

In our current epoch of protest, rebellion, and riot, it is not uncommon to see or hear folks in radical left circles quote Martin Luther King Jr. from 1968, when he declared that "riots are the language of the unheard." King was making the point that one can't condemn folks engaged in riotous behavior without also condemning the conditions and actions that preceded them. I believe this is true, and I believe that is why the L.A. riots spoke to me so deeply. This notion of the unheard, however King intended it to be interpreted, is analogous to children in early childhood education settings who are often misinterpreted, pathologized, and misunderstood, and whose voices are rarely heard or valued. Adding to this quandary is the slippery slope of "school discipline." Though the root of discipline is literally to instruct (a disciple is a student), through the ages and especially in western educational institutions, discipline is synonymous with punishment and is usually informed by a teacher's interpretation of a student's behavior.

Educational policy centered around discipline on local, state, and federal levels generally asks educators to look at the behavior of the students, while the mirror rarely faces in toward the institution and the adults inside, who are often the source and cause of *student* suffering. Kids like the kid I once was are suffering in our institutions, and when kids are suffering, their behavior tells us. I want to be clear here: I am not saying that all kids who misbehave are suffering nor am I saying that all suffering is due to all teachers. I am also not saying that all *misbehavior* is problematic. I do not believe in absolutes, especially those concerning kids and education. I am making the argument that often an educator's perceptions of a child combined with their ideas of what discipline is or is not can exacerbate stressors for students, and that their behavior is often a good indicator not only of "problems at home" but of foundational problems in the classroom and school.

Shawn Ginwright works around healing and transformational justice with urban youth in the Bay Area. He writes, "suffering is the internal consequence of oppression. Suffering is the result of the psycho-spiritual injury resulting from oppression."[1] There are degrees to suffering, as in most things. The damage caused by daily microaggressions causes suffering. Witnessing the brutalizing of people who look like you causes suffering. Worrying constantly about your safety and well-being causes suffering. Being made aware of your difference in the world as a negative causes suffering. Suffering accrues incrementally, and as it does it draws in more alarming terms: violence, crime, trauma, and abuse. As we take in these terms, we also necessarily distance ourselves from them so that we may alleviate the potential damage that suffering will cause. Suffering occurs in many realms of human existence. It persists especially in education.

CONCRETE

The way that I entered education is similar to the way many folks in the u.s. do. I went to kindergarten, learned how to write letters with monkey

---

1   Shawn Ginwright, *Hope and Healing in Urban Education: How Urban Activists and Teachers Are Reclaiming Matters of the Heart* (New York: Routledge, 2016).

tails and wanted to draw and play all day. School is also where I learned about racism and sexism and homophobia, though not because I had radically transformative teachers. School is where I learned to internalize those things, to hide aspects of my interior life to make everyone else comfortable, and, more importantly, to avoid the ridicule and abuse to which I was subject by students and teachers alike. School is where I learned to internalize punishment; where I discovered an inner voice that relayed messages that declared I wasn't good enough for anything although I could read and write for comprehension at an early age and was relatively "bright." All I ever wanted to do was to learn and get better at it and be smarter and to understand everything, including my own brain, yet school is where I learned how to sabotage my own potential. Elaborating on the work of Dr. Carol Dweck, Zaretta Hammond breaks down the four critical elements that imprint learning mindsets in the schema of a learner, building either "fixed" or "growth" mindsets. In her work on cultural responsiveness in education, Hammond explains that microaggressions/assaults play a vital role in imprinting a "fixed" mindset on a young learner.[2] I understood from a very early age that shit just wasn't going to be fair for me. I just knew it, the way most kids knew it. But it wasn't because I didn't get an ice cream cone, or because I had to stop playing and do school work. It wasn't fair because no matter who was talking in class, I was always called out the loudest; because if there was a conflict and I was involved, the assumption was that I caused it; because life is sometimes outlandish when you're a kid, but adults rarely believed me when I told my versions of what happened. In *The First R: How Children Learn Race and Racism*, Van Ausdale and Feagin present astounding evidence confirming what I and many children of color growing up in the u.s. intrinsically know; children know about race and racism and experience it deeply. In their authoritative study, the authors noted that children operate and understand racialization in three distinct social worlds; the first is categorized as adult to adult interaction that encodes "racial-ethnic distinctions and concepts . . . essential for social life." The second world occurs as child to adult interaction, where kids take in the coded racial meanings and images they digest from adults without expressly letting the adults know what they

---

2   Zaretta Hammond, *Culturally Responsive Teaching and the Brain* (Thousand Oaks, CA: Corwin, 2015), 110–13.

understand. The third and likely most important and impressionable world exists among children to the exclusion of adults, where children experiment and interact with the dynamic information gleaned from the other two worlds.[3] Having worked with young children for over two decades, I recognize that kids, like adults, have skewed perceptions of what happens, when, and why. I am quite aware of the trouble that I was responsible for and the mischief that I created. I was naturally a very curious, inventive, and inquisitive kid, and like many kids I yearned for social connection and meaningful relationships. However, it was within Van Ausdale's and Feagin's category of the third social world that I most often found myself, usually alone and working against experimentation with racialized power by other (usually white) kids. In this third world, the concept of fairness continued to elude me.

A child's world is rarely a democratic one. There were many instances where my treatment by other students and the teachers was categorically unfair. Third grade is when this notion became concrete for me. In third grade, I punched a kid and broke his nose and got suspended. I punched a kid who called me a nigger. I punched a kid because after he called me a nigger. I asked him what a nigger was, because I didn't really know, and I thought we were friends, and he said, "You!" and everybody laughed. I punched that kid, because I didn't know what a nigger was, but I knew that when he said that and the kids laughed, there was nothing I could do or say that would stop that laughter, and with their laughter they were threatening my life.

There were no protocols for understanding what was happening to me. Van Ausdale and Feagin remind us that "As a group, children are not socially naive and inexperienced, but develop complex social skills for dealing with a variety of people and situations that they are likely to encounter throughout their lives."[4] The white boy who called me a nigger denied it vehemently to anyone who would listen, to the point of tears. Given my young reputation, the teachers and the principal did not believe that the boy had actually called me a nigger or that a punch in the nose was the appropriate way to handle it *even if he had*. A study out of Yale revealed that teachers in early childhood education "show

---

3   Debra Van Ausdale and Joe R. Feagin, *The First R: How Children Learn Race and Racism* (Oxford: Rowman & Littlefield, 2001), 173–74.
4   Ibid., 195.

a tendency to more closely observe [B]lack students . . . when challenging behaviors are expected." The study also found that while having
the low expectation that Black students will present more problem
behaviors [B]lack teachers "hold [B]lack students to a higher standard of
behavior," possibly demonstrating "a belief that [B]lack children require
harsh assessment and discipline to prepare them for a harsh world."[5]
Though the Yale study focused more on the disparate discipline policies focused on young boys, the work of Kimberlé Crenshaw, Monique
Morris, and Connie Wun, among others, highlights that these disparities occur for Black female students at astoundingly high rates as well,
and that pushout and confinement often take different forms than
"school-to-prison." Connie Wun notes that discipline and punishment
in schools is rooted in "foundational anti-[B]lack logic" that unnecessarily punishes Black girls for being Black. She writes, "consciously or
unconsciously—[B]lack girls are rendered vulnerable to racialized and
gendered forms of discipline and punishment."[6] In my case the school
chose to eject me for a period of time. *Even though the white boy had
called me a nigger,* in the perspective of my teacher and the principal, I
was expected to have behaved with more restraint—civilized and "lady-
like." Calling a Black girl a nigger was not considered violent, yet the
boldness of this particular moment created a laceration that I carry to
this day. No repairs were made, no conversations had, and there was
never an attempt to understand why I had done what I'd done. There
was a victim and a perpetrator, and I was the latter. I went home for two
days and returned to the same classroom with the same kids and the
same teachers and the same sense that inside that building I was always
going to be in danger. Following this incident, I would be suspended
four more times in third grade alone. This situation mirrored countless
others, in and out of school, where I could find no authority figure to
hear what I had to say or to take my concerns or inquiries seriously. By
purposefully being left out of equitable opportunities to discuss issues
and problem solve, I was inadvertently taught another skill: question

---

5   "Implicit Bias May Help Explain High Preschool Expulsion Rates for Black Children,"
    Yale News, September 27, 2016, accessed June 8, 2019, https://news.yale.edu/2016/09/27/
    implicit-bias-may-explain-high-preschool-expulsion- rates-black-children.
6   Connie Wun, "Unaccounted Foundations: Black Girls, Anti-Black Racism, and
    Punishment in Schools," *Critical Sociology* 42, nos. 4–5 (July 2016): 1–14, accessed
    June 8, 2019, http://www.usprisonculture.com/blog/wp-content/uploads/2015/02/
    Black-Girls-Anti-Black-Racism-and-Punishment-in-Schools.Wun_.pdf.

authority at all times. By the end of third grade, I was highly literate, skilled in math, and quite honestly didn't give a fuck about what anyone anywhere had to tell me about anything.

I highlight this incident and my general turmoil in the third grade because it directly connects to my growing judiciousness. The ways in which I was experiencing racism profoundly affected my worldview, and as my capacity for empathy deepened, my sense of justice began to extend to other folks, and my worldview became broader. It also began to dawn on me that the adults around me could not adequately address or repair the wounds that constant microassaults inflicted on me and people like me, especially in the world of education; indeed, many adults would commit a number of these microassaults.

Being a lover of learning meant that I worked very hard to find things that would help me to describe what was happening, but school was never the place for that. School is where I experienced damage but not where I learned how to analyze or cope with or combat it. Noam Chomsky reminds us that as far as school is concerned:

> The important thing is to be able to obey orders, and to do what you're told and to be where you're supposed to be. . . . [T]he institutional role of the schools for the most part is just to train people for obedience and conformity.[7]

Chomsky is not saying this in order that we may eschew education entirely—he is after all an accomplished intellectual who has spent his entire adult life embedded in academia. Here, he is making a broader point about discipline, in particular what discipline looks like and means within the institution of school. Chomsky counterposes the mission of traditional discipline to that of independence of mind and spirit, noting that education is largely useless/serves only to indoctrinate if it doesn't mean anything to the students who are on the receiving end of the learning. He states, "just reading does you no good: you only *learn* if the material is integrated into your own creative processes somehow. . . . And there's nothing valuable about that" (emphasis added).[8] The dominant narrative says that school is where you learn

---

7   Noam Chomsky, *Understanding Power: The Indispensable Noam Chomsky* (New York: New Press, 2002), 236–37.

8   Ibid, 235.

the things that are important, but my experience has taught me how rarely that is true, especially for Black kids. Pedro Noguera sums it up brilliantly when he writes of discussing education with other Black men:

> We all attended public schools, but each of us felt that we had suc-
> ceeded in spite of, and not because of, the schools we attended. . . .
> [W]e threw out the possibility that the only thing that spared us
> the fate of so many of our brethren was luck—not getting caught
> for past indiscretions and not being in the wrong place at the
> wrong time.[9]

Somewhere in the morass of adult voices were pleas to me to "do better" and some version of how I needed "more discipline," and though I'd looked up the word and attempted to contextualize it many times, I still didn't know what they meant when they told me that I needed it. What I knew was that there would be deprivation and there would be punishment—both of which I would have to learn to avoid.

I find the works of Damien Sojoyner and the work of Daniel Solorzano and Dolores Delgado Bernal instructive as I consider and reconfigure ideas around discipline and equity in schools. They propose "transformational resistance" in their work, noting that many Black and Brown students arrive at school sites with an alertness that brings them to specific points of rebellion and release throughout their educational careers. These rebellions become classified as disciplinary problems; however, in light of the ongoing suppression of student life and iden-tity in public schools, it is fair to say, as Sojoyner might, that these acts of rebellion qualify as *forms of political resistance*. In January 2009, in Oakland, California, undisciplined and militant political resistance drew the nation's attention to the endemic and systemic problem of police violence. The rebellions that raged for days (and were resparked in the subsequent weeks and months) set a new tone for demonstrat-ing against racist oppression and would be followed by later rebellions in New York, Ferguson, South Carolina, and Baltimore, among myriad other places. Various adults, from politicians to teachers to "community leaders," called for calm, called rioters thugs and outside agitators and saw no point to the destruction the rebellions left. Others saw these

---

9   Pedro A. Noguera, *The Trouble with Black Boys . . . and Other Reflections on Race, Equity, and the Future of Public Education* (San Francisco: Jossey-Bass, 2008), 20.

rebellions as acts of principled defiance against a system designed to promulgate racist oppression. If the streets of Oakland were one giant classroom, then the smashed windows of banks and Footlocker were the desks upended by students of the streets who had taken in one too many indignities while simply trying to survive. Whose ideas of discipline are more valuable? And who gets to decide?

K. Wayne Yang, in the article "Discipline or Punish? Some Suggestions for School Policy and Teacher Practice," defines punishment as "retribution for an offense, an exclusionary act by which students are removed from the opportunity to learn; it is harm inflicted . . . through which outside regulation becomes internalized subjectivity."[10] Yang goes on to define discipline as "an act of rigorous physical or mental training, a practice of will that can lead paradoxically to docile compliance or emancipatory possibilities."[11] Yang emphasizes that punishment masked as discipline in schools relies on exclusion from participation. This type of exclusion correlates with lower achievement and higher pushout rates. Yang also notes that punishment in public schools is revealed along lines of race, gender, and class, which is to say, it's fairly obvious who the targets of school punishment are. Yang writes, "furthermore, this racially disproportionate punishment and preference is not invisible to our students. They are collectively impacted by the culture of removal—even if they themselves are not punished."[12] So-called zero tolerance policies negatively impact everybody, as even students who "don't fit the demographic profile for punishment" see themselves as "always being available for punishment."[13] More damningly, however, these students begin to believe that some are more deserving of punishment than others. This reinforces and perpetuates the cycles of exclusion, as all students grow into adults who are conditioned to believe that Black people are more deserving of punishment; some of these students grow up to be teachers, principals, store clerks, cops, judges. . .

---

10 K. Wayne Yang, "Discipline or Punish? Some Suggestions for School Policy and Teacher Practice," *Language Arts* 87, no. 1 (September 2009): 49, accessed March 30, 2019, https://escholarship.org/uc/item/8ss5t567.

11 Ibid.

12 Ibid., 52.

13 Ibid., 53.

FIRE

> [T]he anger built up through experience and the quotidian strug-
> gles against dehumanization every [B]rown or [B]lack person lives
> simply because of skin color. This other kind of anger in time can
> prevent, rather than sponsor, the production of anything except
> loneliness.
>
> You begin to think, maybe erroneously, that this other kind
> of anger is really a type of knowledge: the type that both clari-
> fies and disappoints. It responds to insult and attempted erasure
> simply by asserting presence, and the energy required to present,
> to react, to assert is accompanied by visceral disappointment: a
> disappointment in the sense that no amount of visibility will alter
> the ways in which one is perceived.[14]

In high school, I was the only Black student in my grade for a while
and only one of about five Black people altogether. Not even the jani-
tors were Black. I was tallish, tomboyish, loudish, and strong. I had
an awkward body and a beautifully masculine face that everyone felt
entitled to comment on, constantly. By then, I'd learned that fistfighting
with people who threatened my sense of self, my spirit, or my well-being
would not be tolerated by the adults who held my future in their hands,
so I made it a mission to become smarter and better in the hopes that
I would begin to feel worthy of my own humanity.

By all accounts I was a fairly run-of-the-mill to average student.
My growing "attitude problem" kept me from being moved forward in
math, and I internalized that, believing I simply couldn't do it. Though
I stayed ambivalent about school, my desire to learn continued to grow.
I sought out random books in libraries and bookstores that I would
spend hours perusing, looking for the right title or topic, anything that
would jump out at me. In conjunction with books and magazines, I
consumed a broad variety of music that not only informed my spiritual
well-being but nourished my intellect. I taught myself how to play guitar.
I became involved with youth organizing groups, taggers, troublemak-
ers, gangsters, and punk subcultures. I maintained a B/C average.

I listened to Bikini Kill and the Dead Kennedys and X-Ray Spex and
Sepultura. I brooded along to Tori Amos and Nina Simone. I smoked

---

14 Claudia Rankin, *Citizen: An American Lyric* (Minneapolis: Graywolf Press, 2014).

cigarettes and weed after school. I read Malcolm X and classic literature when I was alone—*Wuthering Heights* was my shit! My favorite writers were Hemingway, Audre Lord, and William Butler Yeats. I was weird and out of place anywhere that I went. Had it not been for my desire to learn more and be better, I would not have discovered a love of myself—a love rooted in my Black skin and my kinky hair and my strong body—and my weirdness and out of place–ness might have destroyed me.

Between my disparate interactions with school and the racist and heterosexist world we interact with in america, it's no wonder that my path to the academy was so divergent. In conversations with friends and colleagues, I frequently tell them that I believe I am lucky and that there are privileges that I had access to which kept me from being confined or destitute (sometimes by very narrow margins). The common dialogue among those of us who made it or made it out about not being in the wrong place at the wrong time is an endless echo for us, one which we rarely get to turn down or tune out. For however lucky I was, there are many more who are not as lucky. Students who are suspended and/or expelled from school are more than twice as likely to be incarcerated than students who have never been suspended. Black youth are disproportionately suspended and expelled from public schools at exorbitant rates: in 2003, in grades K-12 (kindergarten through twelfth grade), 20 percent of Black students were suspended across the country, and 5 percent were expelled, compared to 9 percent and 1 percent, respectively, for white students, and the numbers continue to trend negatively.

These statistics are critical to the overall understanding of race and equity so necessary in today's educators and vital to conversations about race and equity in america. I spent many hours (which add up to days) in and out of hallways and principal's offices, exited for infractions so slight as dropping a pencil and not picking it up fast enough, talking too loudly during class discussion time, and "talking back," which really means speaking without permission. In theory, I was prime fodder for the epic pipeline. However, there are problems with consistently drawing connections between school discipline and the school-to-prison pipeline. Sojoyner explains that when considering this pipeline, policy frequently fails to address the historical development of public schools in that "the structure of public education is responding to the actions taken by Black students that are perceived to threaten the status quo."[15] What this means for education policy is that while institutions routinely focus on discipline and behavior, they consistently ignore what Sojoyner terms the "ethos of anti-Blackness" that the very core of american public education and approaches to discipline center around, while simultaneously driving the "deficient" behaviors of Black kids. This creates a seemingly impenetrable bind; how can Black kids "succeed" in a system that requires that you either dispense of your dignity and your identity or that you believe that you deserve to be disrespected, undervalued, and mistreated? When the institution is designed to deal with you only as a problem, it becomes an ethical quandary: Stay or go? In my case, I opted to hang on by a very thin rope, understanding that, from time to time, I would need to collaborate with this system to avoid being sucked beneath it.

I cannot pretend to begin to approach curriculum policy with any sort of authoritative mind nor would I want to. I've worked in many classrooms and alongside many teachers and administrators, but I am not a classroom teacher. I've always been more effective working with kids on areas that help develop their academic, intellectual, social, and emotional skills without constraints like Common Core or teaching to tests. I find our methods of educating kids to be antiquated, colonial, and problematic. This being said (and unlike many folks in my field), I do not buy into the popular campaign year narrative that says that our schools are failing. I believe that neoliberal policy is failing and that the colonial educational strategy has been a failure for some time, but I don't believe that education itself can fail.

Let me back up for just a moment. In 1992, the beauty and hope I saw in the L.A. riots was not predicated on a nihilist excitement for destruction. In the burning and the crumbling concrete ruins, I saw potential. I saw *hope*. I wasn't from the place that was on fire but my people were, and I held hope for them and, by proxy, for all of us. When I consider urban kids with "discipline problems" or "behavior issues," I think about the teenagers riding up and down Broadway Street in Oakland on their scrapers while their peers danced on police cars next to Laney College; I hear them yelling the familiar chant, "*Whose*

---

15   Damien Sojoyner, "Black Radicals Make for Bad Citizens: Undoing the Myth of the School to Prison Pipeline," *Berkeley Review of Education* 4, no. 2 (January 2013): 241–63, accessed June 16, 2019, https://escholarship.org/uc/item/35c207gv

streets? Our streets!" I imagine them organizing in their schools and their neighborhoods. I imagine their potential for transformative resistance. When I say that I don't believe the "education is failing" hype, it's because I think it's impossible to destroy *education*. Education is merely the process by which one learns. I do, however, think it's necessary to destroy the paradigm that says there is only one way forward for young kids in education.

New teachers, seasoned teachers, former teachers, and soon-to-be teachers will all tell you that dealing with kids' difficult behavior is probably the most challenging aspect of their jobs. Often they will blame students' behavior for their inability to pass tests or grade levels. We institute policies like Response to Intervention (RTI) or Multi-Tiered Systems of Supports (MTSS) in the hopes that these alone will be magic fixes, but I propose something bolder than more policy: I propose we torch our expectations of good and bad behavior, of discipline, of punishment, of order, that instead we look at our classrooms and our schools and recognize, as Connie Wun points out, that "the spectacle of punishing [B]lack bodies is ingrained in the 'dreams and desires' of the U.S. racial society and its citizens."[16] I propose that educators—current and future—be taught in unequivocal terms that our system of education exists to keep order, to keep subordinate Black and Brown and Indigenous bodies, to enable poverty to proliferate and capitalism to thrive. But, whoa, this is heavy. Where do we start? I think that we need to approach education from the standpoint that we are here to make things better, and to do so we need to embark on a journey of betterness. I introduce betterness as a way of thinking about a world that is rooted in the destruction of the racist and patriarchal ideals that subjugate women and queer folk and people of color—and white folk as well; betterness is a standard of existence that includes an equitable distribution of resources and an understanding of the complex and nuanced rules that govern our lives; betterness means always outdoing what was done before, which means not ever settling into compromises made out of necessity (some modern examples of such compromises would be suffrage, the Civil Rights Movement, second wave feminism, and Barack Obama's presidency—these compromises were necessary and also not nearly enough to end oppression). Betterness is ever flexible, always

---

16 Wun, "Unaccounted Foundations," 4.

growing, always building. I break this down, because I feel it's necessary to redefine the terms, to up the ante, as it were. I think it's crucial, as educators, to take important risks, and even sometimes reckless ones, to interrupt the giant miasma of oppression that still colors our society, because education to me is nearly synonymous with liberation, and redefining terms on our own terms is a means toward collective liberation and toward betterness in the future.

Betterness as a process begins and proliferates inside of communities and works best when communities are united and aligned. In the world we currently inhabit here in america, community is often a loose concept that is devalued or destroyed altogether by the need to create and maintain material possessions and capital. People don't have time to build, nurture, and grow their communities. We speak of communities in terms of ethnic groupings or queer groupings, but here again I think it important to redefine the terms, so I add "radical" to community. Radical community here is defined as a group of people who intentionally come together and are unified toward common goals outside of acquiring property and material wealth. Those goals can be food, shelter, self-governance, public education—all of these things and more happen toward a common purpose, which is betterness. Betterness is what we build and who we become out of the ashes of oppressive institutions like public education. If you made it this far, then you clearly have some investment in education regardless of its form. I write this with the hope that some of you out in the broader punk community will at least skim this and take the following message to heart: school is a *riot*. If we work hard and with intention and a great deal of critical inquiry, we can make education do and be and say what we want and need it to.

RIOTOUS REFERENCES

Noam Chomsky is an old head. He's a linguist, educator, anarchist, and kind of a genius. He is never a light read.

Kimberlé Crenshaw is the lawyer and radical Black feminist who brought you the concept of intersectionality. She is also a hard-core critical race theorist and scholar. She has been championing equity, anti-racism, and actual feminism since before mp3s.

Carl Crozier is a Black man who wrote a book about the history of racially motivated riots in the u.s., beginning with and centering around the 1992 L.A. Riots. If you need a primer on these riots from a refreshingly nonacademic perspective, get his book *Some of My Heroes Died in the Riots* (New York: Page Publishing, 2016).

Dolores Delgado Bernal is a feminista advocate for Latinx folks in the education matrix. Her work studies *resistance* in education and transformative modes of education.

Carol Dweck is far more establishmentarian than most of these other authors. She wrote and developed the theory behind "growth mindset," which has been horribly misunderstood and haphazardly applied ever since. Her original work around mindset is definitely worth a read.

Christopher Emdin is an urban hip-hop educator and radical theorist who uses hip-hop pedagogies to inform his educational worldview. I can't say enough about how dope he is. Read *For White Folks Who Teach in the Hood . . . and the Rest of Y'all Too* (Boston: Beacon Press, 2016). It's critical.

Shawn Ginwright has done all kinds of educating that focuses on Black youth in educational settings, healing in urban environments, and hope over defeatism.

Zaretta Hammond is here to remind you that hard science and sociology coexist. Her book *Culturally Responsive Teaching and the Brain: Promoting Authentic Engagement and Rigor among Culturally and Linguistically Diverse Students* (Thousand Oaks, CA: Corwin, 2015) and her blogs show again and again how racism and implicit bias affect the brain and thus the classroom. She also makes brain science accessible.

Monique W. Morris is a journalist, an activist, and a mother who wrote a timely book, *Pushout: The Criminalization of Black Girls in Schools* (New York: New Press, 2016), which focuses on Black girls and their (our) systematic exclusion (pushout) from educational institutions. She coined the term school-to-confinement pathways (STCP).

Pedro Noguera is a longtime educator and sociologist whose work largely focuses on cultural competency and the so-called achievement gap. I hate and reject the achievement gap, *and* Noguera's work is vital to understanding how it continues to undermine Black and Brown kids in education.

Damien Sojoyner is one of those badasses who really needs more airtime. A scholar and educator, he focuses on Black futures and the problematic school-to-prison pipeline (STPP) in an effort to destroy and rebuild education in our images.

Daniel Solorzano is an incredible and humble force for Chicanx/Latinx studies, women's studies, and critical race theory in education. His work examining transformational *resistance* should be required reading for all educators.

Debra Van Ausdale and **Joe R. Feagin** study the littler folks. They wrote an informative book, *The First R: How Children Learn Race and Racism* (Oxford: Rowman & Littlefield, 2001).

Connie Wun works hard to destroy the realms of anti-Blackness and violence against women of color. She approaches education from a Transformative Justice perspective and teaches educators how to do better.

K. Wayne Yang is a decolonial/anti-colonial scholar and educator whose work focuses on critical pedagogies, culture, and school disciplinary practices.

The next essay is by **dwayne dixon**, writer of the zine *Astronaut Etiquette*. He is an anthropology professor at University of North Carolina, where he is widely noted for his powerful, conversational and student-centered teaching practice. dixon is also an active member of Redneck Revolt (https://www.redneckrevolt.org/), an anti-racist, anti-fascist community defense formation that advocates for broad working-class solidarity and very explicit rejection of structural racism/white supremacy.

Redneck Revolt is well-known for its members who arrive at protests openly armed. This strategy has proven extremely effective in shitstorms like the fascist "Unite the Right" rally in Charlottesville on August 12, 2017, the largest convergence of far-right and white nationalist/white supremacist organizations in recent U.S. history. On the evening before the main rally, over three hundred torch-wielding white supremacists marched across the University of Virginia campus to Confederate statues and then to St. Paul's Memorial Church, where a community prayer meeting to resist racism was being led by Dr. Cornel West and local faith leaders. A relatively small number of armed Redneck Revolt members (including dixon) provided a community defense bulwark against this violent mob of white supremacists (who had already committed several acts of violence that night), protecting groups of unarmed churchgoers from violence, helping them to their cars, and generally serving as security, leading West to later remark that without the anti-fascists' help at that moment they could have been "crushed like cockroaches."

On August 14, two days after the "Unite the Right" rally (which culminated in the murder of Heather Heyer by a fascist who plowed his car into a crowd of people), the people of Durham helped with a nighttime takedown of the Confederate statue in front of the Durham courthouse. On the August 18, eleven people who had been arrested over that action were scheduled to be arraigned in court, and almost two thousand people showed up in support and in response to a rumored KKK rally. The Durham Freedom Fighters bloc, of which dixon is a member, came armed to help with community defense in the event that KKK members brought violence. In the aftermath, dixon was arrested, along with two comrades, and charged with two counts related to the (fully permitted) open carry weapon he brought with him that day. After a legal battle and trial that lasted several months, he was entirely acquitted of all charges in late February 2018. He urges support for the Durham folks still facing trial for bringing down the Confederate memorial (see http://doitlikedurham.org/ for updates and how to support).

dwayne dixon is writing today on some of the many challenges and joys of teaching at this point in history. He was charged with participating in a mass demonstration in August 2018 at University of North Carolina, during which the Confederate statue "Silent Sam" (erected in 1913) was taken down by protestors. As of this writing (late 2019), many of the legal charges against dwayne and other participants in the protest have been dismissed, but some are still pending, while "Silent Sam" has not been reerected (yet).

From These Classroom Windows We Can See the Confederacy

by dwayne dixon

> So how many times must Rome burn
> Before the crucial lesson of history is learned?
> Power kills, destroy everything that power builds
> —Antischism, "Elements of Oppression"

The white supremacist memorial to the Confederate soldiers enlisted from the student population of the University of North Carolina was dedicated on June 3, 1913, by Confederate Army veteran Julian Carr. In his dedication speech, he famously boasted of "horse-whipp(ing) a negro wench until her skirts hung in shreds" only two months after the Confederate surrender at Appomattox and just a hundred yards from the statue's present place of honor on the UNC campus. "Silent Sam," as the statue of the soldier is known, was yet another symbol intended to dominate public space with the official, monumentalized power of resurgent white supremacy sanctioned and enforced through local segregationist laws collectively known as "Jim Crow." The monument was dedicated the very year President Wilson would institutionalize white supremacy even further by segregating all federal offices and workplaces. The bronze soldier, towering over the green space between grand academic buildings, cocked rifle in his hand, continued the violent work of maintaining white power initially undertaken by the Confederate veterans who returned defeated but determined to preserve a brutal racial social order. In his speech, Julian Carr explicitly connected the statue to the Confederate soldiers who, "during the four years immediately succeeding the war" through "their courage and steadfastness saved the very life of the Anglo-Saxon race in the South."[1] The statue is a testament to this racist violence in "saving" the white race and a mute sentry watching over public space with the dead eyes of the slavers' foot soldiers. From our classroom on the second floor of Graham Memorial Hall, I and my undergraduate students can clearly see Silent Sam, erect and permanent as ever, being watched over by an endless rotation of (almost exclusively white) campus and Chapel Hill police. The serial ironies are not lost on us, of police protecting property that is in itself a celebration of white men fighting to preserve their property in the form of humans—slaves. Throughout class my gaze drifts out upon the unmoving, intractable statue amidst a shifting, frenetic moment when the white supremacy it commemorates and assures sees its foot soldiers violently attempting to take over public space in real, physical ways. From the streets of Berkeley to Charlottesville to Gainesville to East Lansing, anti-fascists have turned back neo-Nazis and Klansmen and denied their leaders the possibility of claiming space—ideological and embodied—as theirs.

In over twenty years of various forms of teaching, I have always struggled to ensure classrooms are bastions of anti-racist refusal and active resistance to colonial, capitalist, patriarchal white supremacy. But never has that struggle been more visibly immediate and close, just a glance out the window. And so too has the classroom never seemed so important.

On February 16, 2018, I received an email threatening an Identity Evropa protest at the offices of my department unless I and other "subversives" were "investigated," largely for the assumed threat of teaching Marxism. The email concluded by saying: "Enough is enough . . . we will confront the students to make sure they are aware of the brainwashing and lies being forced on them by your institution."

Critics of academia would generally agree that American institutions of higher learning have become debt traps for students as tuition rises, especially at private schools, while the work of actually teaching falls increasingly on contingent or precarious labor—contract instructors or adjuncts, who compose 66.5 percent of the workforce, with nearly none, if any, of the protections afforded tenure-track faculty. Rather than being brainwashed by disciples of Karl Marx, it would seem that many people in the university classroom are being soaked by neoliberal

---

1   "Julian Carr's Speech at the Dedication of Silent Sam," June 2, 2013, accessed June 8, 2019, http://hgreen.people.ua.edu/transcription-carr-speech.html.

capitalism. Graduate students and adjuncts across the country are unionizing and striking. The capitalist exploitation of education and its labor is being confronted simultaneously with the exposure of universities colluding with white supremacy—from cowardly administrators giving "white identitarians"—Nazis—public venues to Chancellor Folt of UNC refusing to remove Silent Sam.

Within all the struggles over university space, it is important to recognize the spatial power of the classroom. It is within this small location where I ask my students—and myself—to undertake a reimagining of social relations, continuing the task of creating the world we desire and refusing to be constrained by coercive mechanisms of fear. It is in this room where debt is incurred and low wages eked out. But this is also the room where the world as it is can become unmoored and destabilized. The classroom is a singular location for facing down fascism. The classroom is the space where I articulate with my students the fears we share and begin to unravel them. It is this act of dismantling fear, that fuel of fascism, that makes the classroom such a dangerous place to the far right. I and other faculty are being targeted for our political positions and activism, particularly because of the volatility of the classroom itself. We are assumed to be putting society at risk by naming and challenging normalized power structures of white supremacy, war, exploitation, incarceration, and dehumanization. What are we saying that the students cannot already see with their own eyes? That the statue guarding the campus entrance is a soldier in a white supremacist army intent on killing to maintain a capitalist system of chattel slavery? They can see the nexus of fear standing in plain sight.

The email I received threatened that the Nazis would "confront" students. They imagined they could cause the classroom to be abandoned. They hoped to intimidate me to vacate the seminar table, to cancel the syllabus out of fear, and if I would not respond to fear, they wanted to mark me as a dangerous ideological subject, a threat in and of myself, and thus to have the university remove me. I am sure my job may still be precarious, but, honestly, it always was. I never imagined that joining others in direct confrontation with fascism would earn me job security—or any security at all. Silent Sam persists as an effect of white supremacy being all too secure. But not for long, never for long.

In the classroom we plot out new paths for ourselves, some alone, some together: through mutual recognition of the queer struggle, the refugee struggle, the Black struggle, the immigrant struggle, the femme struggle, the impoverished struggle, the depression struggle. The classroom is the redoubt of enacting the possible and sharing stories. I speak directly about what I am and what I am doing: my solidarity with comrades who pulled down the Confederate statue in Durham, my anarchist ethics, my appearances before the court to face charges for carrying a rifle against the KKK, my subsequent trial. I ask my students to help me to restructure the demands of the university into collectively created projects where autonomy of action is privileged and shared labor is prized. We begin to change things, to destabilize the order of the world, to reject the status quo, to build relations anew through experimentation and collaboration and trust; all in solidarity with one another and in deep belief of one another's struggles and experiences.

These last eight months have been the most intense of my life, and the classroom has been a consistent space where I have practiced my ethics and politics. Rather than becoming timid or uncertain, I inhabit the classroom as anti-fascist action itself, a zone of bold expression and unfettered intellectual provocations. As one student wrote, "the deconstructing can never be done." She points out what we all comprehend: even when the last Confederate statue is pulled down, the work persists, and the courage to continue it comes from among us, inside spaces we create, like classrooms saturated in radical love.

This time is fraught with failing institutions and distrust. It is exactly in the dangerous, perhaps frightening, fissures opening up that we can insist on playfulness and non-hierarchical games enjoyed in the shadow of faltering systems. Classrooms are our theaters and pageants for new ways of being, released from fear, shaped through intentional equality and justice.

It is a time for public courage. I endeavor to always renounce aloud the fear and complicity demanded by Silent Sam and the white supremacist system that keeps him there. We are all being transformed and revealed in this crucible of struggle, and I find myself more honest now when I walk through the door to face my students, more myself in ways I never imagined. For those of us who teach, it is a time of great responsibility to fight back, to liberate our classrooms, and to risk ourselves. It is a time to lose our fear completely. There is less of yesterday to cling to and, yet, more to give, more to be received. Nothing to lose.

>> Radical teachers know that a classroom is by no means a one-way information pipeline from teacher to student(s). Radical teachers know that truly resonant knowledge production and learning involves a complex, ever-shifting process of dialogue and mutual respect. Radical teachers are always learning from their students and understand that a student can very much be a teacher as well. One of the core tenets of truly student-centered teaching practice is to listen—not to be afraid to allow students to turn the lens of reflection on us (or our bosses/administrators) so we can start to break down the hierarchical structures and authoritarian tendencies of our profession. It is in the wake of radical actions like these that we can all learn to be better human beings together.

The next piece was written by **Kadijah Means**, who wrote the original draft in 2015 while a student at Berkeley High School, in California. In 2018, when she made a few revisions to the original piece, she was starting her senior year at University of California Santa Cruz. Back at Berkeley High, Kadijah was a student leader, heading up the Black Student Union and Amnesty International groups on campus, and she was regularly interviewed in local media—particularly with regard to her involvement in the ongoing civil rights struggle that is the Black Lives Matter movement.

Berkeley High has an international reputation as an enlightened, modern high school that has sometimes employed radical measures to address systemic educational inequities that are rooted in racism, class discrimination, gender/sexuality biases, and other problems that plague schools across the U.S. (and worldwide); it is generally considered a "model school" as far as social justice issues are concerned. Even in this relatively "enlightened" institution, however, society still exists so the same problems persist, and these problems often end up extra-magnified when they are not addressed well (or at all). In her essay, Kadijah highlights specific examples of major issues at Berkeley High to illustrate the repeated failures of the educational system in addressing racism, both within the school context and in the wider world. She also gives some concrete suggestions for ways that teachers, administrators, and school districts can work long-term to be more responsive and help combat the pervasive reality of race-based inequities and injustice.

How Schools Can Address Racism

by Kadijah Means

> We know now we want more
> Oh ah, oh ah
> A life worth fighting for
> Oh ah, oh ah
> So let them say we can't do better
> Lay out the rules that we can't break
> They wanna sit and watch you wither
> Their legacy's too hard to take
> —Santigold, "Disparate Youth"

The topic of racism is again at the forefront of the average American's mind. In response to non-indictments and injustice catching the eye of mainstream media, movements like Black Lives Matter have spread across the U.S. The U.S education system, specifically in "progressive" places like Berkeley, California (the college town often teasingly called as the Peoples' Republic of Berkeley), has found itself scrambling to write lessons and alter curricula to meet the needs of the systematically oppressed. The education system, which serves as a window into this "developed" country's priorities, was completely unprepared to address the idea of anti-Blackness on their campus, let alone the current itera-tion of systemic racism. The choice to ignore the needs of marginalized groups and children is a disappointing but regular occurrence in this historically white supremacist country. Unfortunately, the popularity of Dr. Derald Sue's term "microaggression" has helped us to define how many well-intentioned but still willfully ignorant residents of Berkeley (and abroad) forget about the frequent explicit forms of bias that impact students on a daily basis. Faculty is ill-prepared to manage any classroom conflict, not to mention explicit racially motivated ones.

There are two major issues colliding in Berkeley's education system:

(1) lack of transparency with regard to preventative and reactive measures to protect and defend marginalized students and faculty;

(2) the neglect of Black and Brown student needs, which prevents them from flourishing in the ways their white counterparts can.

When preparing young minds, building trust requires mutual respect. In order to convince students that what they're learning matters and isn't solely government propaganda, they should trust you. Black and Brown kids know the world doesn't like them, and we're usually right—more on that later.

In order to prove we should value what we're taught, communication must be made a priority. Students should feel included in decisions concerning them. At Berkeley High there are no processes in place to facilitate dialogue between administration, teachers, and students. Furthermore, when concerning events take place, there is no effort made to inform the teaching faculty or students, which results in fractured trust. Here's a solid example of dis bullshit.

On October 1, 2014, a BHS security officer discovered a noose hanging from a tree on campus. The school administration waited more than five days to announce the incident, even after pressure from the dean of students and the Black Student Union (BSU). When they released a statement via email, it was ineffective, as the majority of the student body remained ignorant of the incident. As president of the BSU and the Amnesty International club, I reached out to the Gay/Straight Alliance to put pressure on the administration to act decisively. We decided to force a response by releasing a statement to local news notifying them of the occurrence. In addition to organizing for news coverage, employing the tactics of guerrilla warfare, I read a statement over the school's public announcement system to inform all the students of what happened on our campus—not in the 1960s (an era people associate with the Civil Rights Movement, although it has not subsided) but in 2014.

There was no plan to tell the students about the noose. A student group (comprised of one Black girl and her faculty advisor Christina Mitchell, with the help of members of the GSA) had to bring this information directly to the student body. The administration planned to put paper hearts in the tree as their recognition of the incident. The hearts were placed in the tree prior to both announcements. Some students were mildly curious about the paper hearts placed in a seemingly arbitrary tree, but most of the 3,200 students didn't think to inspect it, especially considering how they were never directly informed about the noose in the first place. Instead of allowing us to feel shitty about this despicable event that occurred on our campus, the administration rushed into a band-aid solution. As presumptuous as this may be, I imagine the administration felt the classic "this *couldn't* have happened at our school" or the also classic "not in *we like Black people here* Berkeley."

After all, Berkeley High has a reputation for being a picturesque high school, boasting double-digit varsity sports teams, a small learning community program, Advanced Placement and International Baccalaureate class offerings, and the only high school African American studies department in the nation. Their reputation as a *good* school in a *good* place sometimes abstracts the fact that Berkeley High is a microcosm of the world around it, a world that does not like Black people, or at best is ambivalent about them. We cannot expect an administration conditioned to feel apathy toward Black and Brown students to prioritize consoling the students affected.

The noose was a reality check for many—much like the recent events in Ferguson, Missouri, Charleston, South Carolina, and so many other places. We are not post-racial. Putting hearts in a tree without telling the student body what happened was a rush to solve something that is not solvable in the short-term. This incident illustrates the disregard for Black student needs and racial tension stirring on campus. I felt the administration didn't want to face the fact that this malicious act had occurred in Berkeley and, therefore, attempted to cover it up. In the case of the noose, those affected by the triggering imagery were neglected. This is a prime example of how the burden to educate students and staff falls on the affected community. A racially charged incident took place, and people of color, namely Black girls like me, were expected to respond. Black and Brown students carry this burden, and it definitely impacts them in the classroom. In instances like this the marginalized continue to be actively disenfranchised, even when "it's not on purpose."

The administration downplayed what happened to make sure the minority in the school, the white students, were more comfortable than the student of color majority of 60 percent. Rather than confront the fact that anti-Blackness and prejudice still exist, the administration acted as if ignoring the noose made the problem disappear. I was concerned the situation was not being taken seriously. I felt the history of violence against Black and Brown folks (they lynched Mexicans too) was being minimized. We remember the Holocaust, but we constantly try to move past the hundreds of years of racist and violent history against Black people in this country. The discriminatory treatment of Black people is easily ignored today, because it is less tangible than at the height of lynchings in 1895 or the violence surrounding the 1960s Civil Rights Movement, but it is no less insidious. The silence of the Berkeley community around issues of race play out in a very dangerous way for Black and Brown students. Many experience discrimination, microaggressions, and outright bigotry and have nowhere to turn. Learning in this environment isn't impossible, but it is arduous, and that's what matters. Black and Brown students shouldn't be asked to be resilient no matter what. It is integral that we support students, so they feel able to express when inequities occur.

Toward the end of my time at Berkeley High, I was somewhat of an unpaid advisor on race relations. I felt a tremendous amount of pressure to help combat racism as the school had diagnosed it. Unfortunately, their conceptualization of racism centered Black boys and men as the victims of its atrocities. I felt a unique call to place my race before my gender at a time when I was still developing my thoughts about girlhood and its impact on my racial identity. My efforts at the time failed to highlight the reality of police violence against Black women (especially transwomen) because of my ignorance and the pressure to solely discuss race. It is imperative to consider how Black girls (especially transgirls) could feel alienated by initiatives that seldom acknowledged their plight.

Kimberlé Crenshaw's theory of intersectionality is especially salient in this regard. Crenshaw begs us to consider the new oppressions, discriminations, and prejudices created in the center of Blackness and womanhood. This means intersectionality isn't about layering identities on top of one another, but rather noticing the ways freedoms are limited when certain identities intersect. In light of this monumental work, I want to encourage educators to trouble any foundational desire to view anti-Blackness as a Black man's issue. As one of my favorite authors and researchers Monique Morris says, "I believe that the investment in

black boys, and other boys of color, is necessary. However, that investment should never be to the exclusion of black girls."[1] Morris's book,
Pushout: The Criminalization of Black Girls (New York: New Press, 2016),
addresses how discussions of anti-Blackness in schools often center
boys. Recognizing the Black woman and girls (especially transwomen
and transgirls) who don't fit the "racism is a Black man's issue" narrative is imperative and not difficult to include in discussions of racism.

At a place like Berkeley High, where the school is dramatically
divided by race, class, gender, and worldview, it is intimidating to teach
about race and racism (they are different conversations). I have found
that difficult topics like these are often avoided. Conversations about
racism, how it affects people of color and the community at large, are
essential to preparing critical humans. The bare minimum is encouraging creativity to help young people interrogate their world and problem
solve within it. The production of race cannot be explained as if it is
natural and, therefore, right. It should be taught as a production that
is meticulously maintained to produce specific negative outcomes for
anyone who is not in the dominant class. Racism's ever-changing tactics
should be monitored and dissected so that students see how white
supremacy is prioritized and implemented in their learning environments. This is not as daunting as it seems.

I love teachers. I don't want to complicate their job. They are
already playing so many roles (mentor, therapist, etc.) in the classroom.
I understand that the omission of certain topics is due to lack of training and a fear of discomfort. No one wants to be the racist teacher who
said something unintentionally offensive, so they'd rather just skip the
conversation completely. I get it, but we must acknowledge their role in
indoctrinating kids and help them challenge the sexist, racist, ableist,
and classist norms that are usually enforced in the classroom. Teachers
simply haven't been taught about systemic oppression, the state's role
in how the classroom functions, how to facilitate discussions about
these things, and how to resist them. The intent of omission is to avoid
hurting anyone's feelings, but the impact of omitting these realities is
damaging for all students. I believe that loving teachers must include

---

1   Melinda D. Anderson, "The Black Girl Pushout" (interview with Monique W. Morris),
     Atlantic, March 165, 2016, accessed June 8, 2019, https://www.theatlantic.com/
     education/archive/2016/03/the-criminalization-of-black-girls-in-schools/473718/.

holding them accountable for their role in indoctrinating kids. The one institution charged with preparing young minds for higher-order thinking employs a pedagogy that appeals to rich, able-bodied, neuro-typical, cisgendered, heterosexual, white male students, and even they are being robbed of the necessary tools to critique this world. We must reframe our approach.

SOLUTIONS

I am not an expert in education. I am a student who is keenly aware of the impact anti-Blackness and negligence has on students. My reflections would be valid whether they included solutions or not, but I have some suggestions to improve the system in any case.

1. Stop Buying Textbooks from Texas

Make a conscious note of the values and limits of all sources you bring into your classroom. If all that is available to you is white supremacist propaganda, then make an example out of their manipulative practices.

2. Cultural Competency Training

There are skilled educators who can explain the ideas of privilege and power, systemic racism, micro vs. macroaggressions, explicit vs. implicit bias, anti-Blackness, etc., and every school needs attention paid to these concepts. If a place like Berkeley (obsessed with their image of progressiveness) needs this training, then every city in the U.S. needs it. I would suggest integrating an inclusive curriculum that highlights the contributions of all people to the world, as opposed to a solely eurocentric curriculum. That means social studies, math, and science would need to acknowledge contributions from all cultures. This will take time. We have to be dedicated.

3. Diversifying Thought

When discussing the Black Lives Matter movement in class, someone said, "They couldn't support such a violent movement." In my experience at Berkeley High, I've had lots of students tell me that "nonviolence" is the only way to change things (their idea of violence is looting and property damage, which I do not believe is violence). If I respond, it is usually something like this: "I am not asking nicely for those oppressing me to stop. In fact, I am not asking at all. I am demanding the freedom and equity my people deserve. So maybe that means some windows will be broken, and some noise will be made after ten p.m.—so what?" Unfortunately, I can count the number of teachers who share these radical thoughts on my hand. We can't expect students to question the status quo if the people teaching them aren't willing to question it. We need minds stretching across the political spectrum (though there's a difference between tactical disagreements and advocating for oppression based on inherent characteristics, for example, denying transpeople their right to humanity and life—the latter should be shut down without question). Diversity of thought is what enriches the learning experience. It seems the entire reason educators advocate for ethnic diversity is to expose students to different walks of life. If everyone in the classroom looks different but has a parallel mindset, that is not enriching. Identity politics will never save us. We need to expose students to more radical ideas.

4. Building Trust

There should be clear processes to inform students and teachers of current events on campus, especially harmful events. Your students will become adults with a worldview impacted by what you teach them. Treat students as full humans who deserve to know what is going on in their school environment and in the world around them.

5. Sustained Focus on Critique

Read Joan Scott's "The Evidence of Experience."[2] The essay is a thoughtful critique of politics and knowledge production. Scott's writing can be applied to the concept of identity politics quite well. It explores the limits of how we come to know and view things as important, natural, and true. I think it is an excellent place for educators to begin pondering how they know and what shapes their beliefs.

I hope this limited reflection can spark the important introspective journey needed to teach your students and yourself to question what you consider natural.

---

2 Joan W. Scott, "The Evidence of Experience," *Critical Inquiry* 17, no. 4 (Summer 1991): 773–97, accessed June 8, 2019, https://lucian.uchicago.edu/blogs/ea-media-project/files/2018/02/Scott_TheEvidence_1991.pdf.

If you are a public school teacher in the United States, the likelihood is high that you will be working with at least a couple of students, and perhaps an entire classroom, who are dealing with some kind of trauma. These traumas often dovetail with and stem from poverty and other systemic oppressions (racism, misogyny, homophobia, etc.), as well as specific abuse on the individual level. The sad reality is that many (if not most) teachers are overwhelmed and freaked out by this, and unless some form of additional support is available for these students, they often run into problems and fall through the cracks in a crowded public school environment. In light of this, teachers and counselors who have personally survived trauma—including many punks—can be an invaluable resource for these students as they try to navigate an environment that is heavily weighted against them.

This essay's author, **Lindsay McLeary**, is the academic coordinator for the Upward Bound program for low-income and/or first-generation college students. Lindsay spent his formative years knee-deep in SoCal's survivor-heavy punk/hardcore scene and now has the peculiar distinction of being the most heavily tattooed person in University of California Berkeley's Department of Equity and Inclusion. He has worked in education and educational outreach for well over a decade, including stints as a lecturer at University of Southern California and Stanford and a classroom teacher in Oakland and Richmond, California, public schools.

The Legacy of Trauma

by Lindsay McLeary

> **How your body still remembers things you told it to forget.**
> **How those furious affections followed you.**
> —The Weakerthans, "Watermark"

My couples' therapist (the therapist that my wife and I go to for couples' counseling) has been getting a bit frustrated with me. Specifically, she's been getting frustrated with my complaints that I "don't feel safe in the room."

She tells me this: "I think that your wife and I have been very reassuring with you that you're safe here. I would like to reflect on the possibility that your feeling of being judged and threatened is something that you're projecting onto me and onto these sessions."

She's not wrong. But the reality of the situation is that I spent the first decade of my life living in fear of verbal and physical abuse by my parental authority figures, and then spent the following two decades getting into conflicts with every other authority figure in my life: cops, teachers, supervisors, landlords, movie ushers, crossing guards, and, yes, even therapists.

Between the ages of fourteen and thirty, I was either abusing substances or walking around as a bundle of tense muscles ready to defend my very existence. So, yeah, when I'm in a room with a very serious looking therapist and my wife, and they're both critiquing my behavior, it triggers something deep inside of me. Something that says that I'm not safe.

This voice that says that I'm not safe, it's not something I hear intellectually. It's something I feel in my shoulders and in my chest.

It manifests psychologically as an atmosphere in the room. I feel like I'm in an eighties horror movie, suddenly sitting alone in a big, scary, empty house, and the lights have just gone out. And there is a cello playing one long, deep note. Everything in my body screams: *Get the fuck out right now!*

I pause for a moment to think of the most diplomatic way to respond to my therapist.

I tell her this: "Y'know, I think there's some validity to that. And it's something I'm working on. But with all due respect, this is an issue that's embedded very deeply within me, and I don't think we're gonna resolve it in a handful of sessions. Please be patient with me."

That was the best I could muster at that particular moment. Twenty years ago, as a teenager (the same age as many of my students) struggling with trauma, I would have probably just yelled out, "Fuck this!" and left the room. Now, I can get my shit together at least enough to be diplomatic.

MY BACKGROUND AND A DISCLAIMER

For my entire adult life, I have been employed in education in one respect or another. I've taught in high school classrooms, lectured in universities, and mentored student teachers. I went into education for the same reason a lot of people go into education: I wanted to give young people the opportunities that I never had.

After I started in education—teaching in high school classrooms in Oakland and Richmond—I noticed that I had a specific talent for connecting with kids who had discipline issues. I connected with them, because, in certain respects, I was them. I had been where they were. And I knew that discipline issues don't come from nowhere. They often come from undiagnosed and untreated learning disabilities, emotional distress, and (in the worst cases) domestic and environmental trauma.

For over a decade, I helped administer academic services for the federally funded academic outreach program Upward Bound. I worked specifically with low-income high school students from "distressed" urban and rural communities throughout California and Nevada. The kids I worked with, who grew up in these communities (typically communities of color), tended to be exposed to some pretty traumatic stuff (gang shootings, drug addiction, overdose, police violence, domestic violence, etc.) early in life. Part of my job was listening to these kids and their stories.

My reason for writing this piece is simple. I think that most educators working with students in distressed communities will, at some point, find themselves needing to provide trauma-informed care for the children that they work with. I want school districts and administrators to know that they have the responsibility of providing trauma-informed training to these educators. Rather than merely citing statistics, I hope to make my point by focusing on the personal experiences I have had working with these students. My hope is that after reading this you will be moved to champion my cause and put pressure on school districts to provide these resources to educators.

Now, before we start, I want to offer a little disclaimer. Some of the stuff that I'm about to discuss is a bit rough. I want you to know it's okay (and expected) for you to feel a bit of emotional and even physical discomfort reading some of these stories—especially if you have had a history of trauma. If the tone or subject matter of the discussion makes you start to feel uncomfortable, please, please, stop reading and go take care of yourself. Taking care of yourself should be your first and top priority.

RECOGNIZING TRAUMA AND ACTIVATION

When you informally survey the kinds of people who enter into underpaid, service-oriented occupations that work with marginalized and traumatized communities, you often find that they are people who have been marginalized and/or traumatized themselves. I am no exception.

I grew up with two drug-addicted parents, one of whom was physically and emotionally abusive and both of whom were neglectful. As a teenager, I sought refuge in the Los Angeles punk rock scene, which was (ironically) rife with violence, drug abuse, homelessness, and trauma. For better or worse, heavily tattooed, drug-addicted, and alcoholic teenagers became my chosen family.

Besides the fact that I could relate to many of these alcoholic street punks, I think I was also attracted to the fact they seemed to have this ability to listen to difficult and painful stories and to turn toward them when most people would turn away. As I got older, I have tried not to lose this capacity to remain open to people who are sharing painful experiences. It turned out to be invaluable to me in my work.

One day a student (we will call her "Julia") leaves her group of friends, sits down next to me on a bench, and starts talking to me. She tells me about her birth family. Her biological father was African American, and she was born to a drug-addicted Asian woman. Since her mother was unable to care for her, she gave her up to her Asian family who hated Black people and, by extension, her. In their care, she was neglected and mistreated.

"I think they probably were hoping that I would die, so they could be rid of me. I wasn't wanted," Julia tells me, matter-of-factly. Stoically. There are no tears in her eyes. And there are no tears in mine either. This is common among people with a history of trauma. We have a kind of external numbness when discussing our own trauma and hearing other people discuss theirs.

One day, when Julia was an infant, she suffered burns to her body because they tossed her in a bath of hot water without testing it first. She was taken to a hospital and child protective services was called. She was taken away from her family and placed in foster care, at what is called "a group home."

"Things at the group home weren't much better," she comments and smiles at me, kind of sadly.

"I bet they weren't. Those places can be pretty fucked-up." I smile back.

At the time I had been reading *Evolution of a Cro-Mag,* the autobiography of the punk rock singer Jon Joseph, where he discusses what it was like growing up with a physically abusive and neglectful foster family. Although I had to stop reading it because the homophobia and misogyny were beginning to get to me, the stories he tells about his early life illustrate an important point: it's sometimes better to be homeless than to live with abuse.

"I have to tell you, Julia, I've heard a lot of stories of bad childhoods. But yours is . . . particularly shitty. Maybe one of the shittiest."

"I know," she says shyly, kind of laughing a bit.

"But I'm really grateful that you came to me and trusted me with your story. Thank you. Any time you want to talk, I'm here. Seriously."

She thanks me for listening and runs back to her group of friends. Pretty soon she's laughing again, and everything seems to have gone back to normal.

Nothing was "normal" with Julia's situation, however.

Often, heavily traumatized children play and socialize just like any other kids. Sometimes, as adults, we mistakenly praise their resilience without fully understanding the nature of their situations. The past still lives within them. It resides in their neurons and their nerves, which are so tightly tuned that their nervous systems are put into overdrive whenever they receive the slightest hint of a possible threat to their perceived safety.

Although Julia seemed to play and socialize like any other fourteen-year-old, she had endured massive amounts of trauma. When she was activated by a triggering situation, she would struggle with the same kind of PTSD symptoms you might see in a Syrian refugee or a Vietnam War veteran.

When I watched Julia become activated, her behavior no longer resembled that of a "normal" fourteen-year-old girl. Rather, she was more like a perturbed panther that has been forced into a cage. Her eyebrows dipped, her forehead wrinkled, her eyes narrowed, and she paced nervously. She was unable to stay still. Her hands became balled fists. She too was a bundle of nerves and muscles, ready to defend her existence. And what would trigger this? Her teacher asked her to stay after class so they could talk about her missing assignments.

Having worked closely with her, I knew that this was all it took: the slightest hint of a possible rebuke from one of her teachers, and she would become activated.

Julia and I are a lot alike. Her having to wait after class to talk to her teachers is a lot like me sitting in couples' therapy. At the slightest provocation, we can become frightened, caged creatures whose very existence seems to be at stake. Luckily, I am an adult, and I have learned the tools to cope in situations where I am activated. She, on the other hand, is a pubescent fourteen-year-old girl whose prefrontal cortex isn't fully developed enough to deploy strategic long-term decision-making. On top of that, she must cope with some of the worst trauma I've ever encountered.

These are the kinds of challenges we must face as educators working with traumatized students from distressed communities.

UNDERSTANDING OF TRAUMA IN AN URBAN SETTING

Before we go any further, I want to clarify what I mean when I talk about trauma, because I use this term a bit differently than how it is typically portrayed. Our initial understanding of trauma was informed by studies done regarding the social and emotional difficulties that veterans encountered when they reintegrated back into society—for example, initial post–World War I observations of soldiers who were "shell-shocked." The way we see trauma played out in the present day, however, encompasses a lot more than the narrow understanding we initially gleaned from observing combat veterans.

My understanding of this issue is more informed by the problems experienced by the population I have worked with. The trauma encountered by low-income children and families living in distressed urban areas typically involves either (1) a perception that one is in a dangerous situation or otherwise lacks safety or (2) the expectation that one's basic needs—housing, emotional support, food, sanitation—will not be met. Many of my students had families who struggled with housing insecurity. Their caregivers simply weren't able to provide stable housing. Even those who had temporarily secured an apartment or other housing might suddenly get evicted and end up living in hotels, with friends or extended family, or in cars.

The media focus typically makes it seem that a twenty-five-year-old soldier who watches his friend get blown up by an improvised explosive device probably fares worse on the scale of trauma than a twelve-year-old kid with an alcoholic father who has also been housing insecure for six months.

In my experience, that's often not the case.

Adults who have grown up in supportive, loving families have brains that are well adapted to cope with the intense stress reaction that accompanies a traumatic experience. Children don't. Especially if, since infancy, they have grown up in a family that is coping with constant distress. Also, it has to be mentioned that veterans generally have access to some form of psychiatric and therapeutic treatment, while low-income kids often lack access to these resources.

There's a kind of equation that I employ to think about who is most likely to experience trauma. The more vulnerable a population is, the more likely they are to have been exposed to really terrible situations that can leave permanent psychological scars. People of color are more vulnerable than white folks, low-income folks are more vulnerable than affluent people. Young people (especially women) are—quite obviously—more vulnerable than male adults: and so the majority of reported rapes involve girls under fifteen years old.

Low-income kids are in a very dire situation.

They are the demographic most likely to be exposed to unrelenting stress, lack of physical and emotional safety, and food and housing insecurity, and they are the most likely to be exposed to traumatic experiences, which change the way their brains work. Permanently.

Some statistics: trauma affects kids' ability to regulate their emotional reactions. Low-income kids who are exposed to traumatic situations often act impulsively and destructively, especially children under the age of ten. Far too often, psychiatrists respond to this by prescribing really heavy medications. Children in low-income families are four times more likely to receive antipsychotic medication. In 2008, twenty thousand low-income kids under the age of five were prescribed antipsychotics! These drugs (including Seroquel, Risperidal, and Abilify) carry warnings that recommend against their use by children because they can inhibit learning and development of important cognitive functioning.

With the exception of psychiatric interventions meant to calm the most out of control kids, low-income children who experience trauma generally don't have access to mental health professionals. Further, for many of these children, it is their communities, households, and parents that are the sources of their trauma and their emotional distress.

The reality of the situation is that, for most of these children, the only controlled and safe atmosphere they have is their schools. This presents us, as educators, with a unique opportunity: to use our classrooms as the setting in which they can begin the difficult work of learning to cope with and contain their trauma.

COPING, CONTAINING, CURING

When I say that classrooms and schools can be a setting where students learn to cope with and contain their trauma, there is a very specific reason why I say "cope with and contain," rather than "cure." In tackling my own issues with complex PTSD and trauma, I've learned that "curing" or "healing" from childhood trauma is a complicated and difficult endeavor. The two treatments I've heard about most often—Prolonged Exposure Therapy and Cognitive Processing Therapy—both take around ten or more weekly sessions, and (from what I've heard) each session can leave you pretty activated and edgy, sometimes for several days.

At the time of this writing, I'm thirty-seven years old. I've received neither of the treatments mentioned above. I keep on wanting to and saying to myself, "Someday." First, therapy is expensive. Second, both of the therapeutic treatments that are available to cure PTSD—rather than merely contain it—require one to confront and revisit the very experiences and events that made one traumatized in the first place. The thought of doing this really scares the crap out of me.

In the beginning of this piece, I noted that people who enter into underpaid, service-oriented occupations that work with marginalized and traumatized communities are often themselves people who have been marginalized and traumatized. I want to revisit this point, because there is little doubt in my mind that my own history of trauma has affected my work as an educator of low-income students.

I have worked with students who have witnessed very horrific acts of domestic violence. It isn't uncommon to see the domestic violence that has been perpetrated in their households reenacted by the students themselves, often in the form of extremely intense and aggressive shouting matches between female and male students. The sort of shouting matches that would attract police attention if the shouters in question were full-fledged adults rather than teenagers.

One particular afternoon, during a week I was particularly overworked and underslept, I had to break up a near fight between a young man (let's call him "James") and young woman (let's call her "Jasmin") who were around thirteen and sixteen years old, respectively. James had just told Jasmin to "suck his dick," and Jasmin (who was normally somewhat even-tempered) was crying and screaming at him at a volume, timbre, and pitch that made my ears ring and also made it very difficult to decipher what she was actually saying. It was my job to separate the two and disperse the very large crowd that had amassed around them, specifically by getting everyone not involved in the incident into their classrooms.

I was prompting one of James's friends to go to class, and he was resisting, insisting that he wanted to remain outside with James. At my wits end (and quite activated myself), I angrily told the student, "Get to class right now, or I'm getting you kicked out of this program."

His response surprised me. He looked at me up and down and said, "Why are your hands shaking? Are you afraid?"

That's when I looked down to confirm what he had just inquired about. My hands were, indeed, shaking quite violently. My whole body was shaking. Rather than answering him, I just walked away from the situation, sat down on a set of steps, and waited for the shaking to stop. When it did, I called my wife and told her that I was coming home for the day, that I'd had a rough day at work.

With the exception of audiences of afternoon talk shows, I am not aware of a lot of people who enjoy watching two people go at each other (verbally or otherwise) with the intention of doing the other person harm. It would upset most people with a modicum of empathy and emotional awareness. However, this incident didn't actually "upset" me in the typical sense of the word. Rather, it triggered me. Which is to say, I wasn't aware of any particular negative emotion that I was feeling. What I felt was more like a basic feeling of bodily danger. My body was betraying me by shaking uncontrollably. I was, quite honestly, physically unable to do my job.

At the time, I had not considered the possibility that I struggled with trauma-related issues, and I hadn't pursued treatment for my childhood trauma. Looking back now, my lack of awareness of my own trauma-related issues made me a liability. In my own defense, I can only say that until very recently, my organization hadn't been offered training in how to recognize the nuances and effects of trauma in ourselves, much less our students.

Blind to the realities and dynamics of trauma, educators put themselves and their students at risk.

TURNING LIABILITIES INTO ASSETS

Although having staff with a history of trauma can be a liability when they are sent in, uninformed and unprepared, to work with traumatized communities, they may also be an invaluable asset if trained the right way.

One evening, about six years ago, I sat with a girl (we'll call her "Anna"), a high school senior who was spending the summer away from home at a residential academic program at University of California Berkeley. She had just received a phone call from her family informing her that her aunt, who had been struggling with drug addiction, had died from an overdose. Her family did not have any money to fly her home or take the time off work to drive down and get her, so she had to remain in the program. She ended up missing her aunt's funeral.

There was no sobbing. Anna just stared into space while tears streamed slowly down her otherwise impassive face. This is something I've noticed about kids who have grown up in toxic, traumatic environments. They learn to cry in total silence.

"I'm so sorry," I said. "You're too young to have to deal with shit like this."

Anna looked up at me and smiled, but with pain in her eyes. "Do I really have a choice? I've been dealing with this shit my entire life." I could sense her frustration.

"I know. And it's just not fair."

I asked if it was okay to give her a hug. She said yes and reached out to hug me. And when I hugged her the silent tears transformed into vocalized grief, as she finally allowed herself to really cry.

Later that night, I sat and reflected on my own trauma. How my mother overdosed when I was eleven. How the paramedics came to the house. How the doctor came out into the waiting room and told me and my father that he was doing the best he could, but she might not make it through the night.

I realized that when I had expressed to Anna that she shouldn't have to deal with shit like overdoses, I was (to some extent) also talking to my younger self. I was too young. I shouldn't have had to deal with the consequences of my parents' drug addiction. It wasn't fucking fair. Not for me and not for Anna.

For the last two years, I have been getting up in front of audiences full of people who work in education and trying to convince them of one thing: we need more mental health professionals working in low-income neighborhoods and our underfunded, under-resourced public schools. The sad irony is that my students come from the population most in need of mental health care, but because they're low-income, they are least likely to get it.

All too often when I approach educators and say, "This kid has had really stressful traumatic shit going on his life. He's experienced some really heavy stuff," their response is, "That's terrible. But what can I do? I'm not a psychologist or a therapist. This isn't my wheelhouse."

I have something to say to these educators: most of these kids aren't gonna get professional help. They don't have their own psychiatrist or therapist. They have you. So you're going to have to learn how to help them as best you can.

CLIMBING OUT TOGETHER

It's not easy for anyone. Especially if you have a history of trauma yourself.

If you're an educator working with a traumatized population, you do have the capacity to help children and adolescents who have experienced trauma. You don't need a degree in psychology to sit with someone who is experiencing grief or to help them process their emotions. You don't need to be a licensed therapist to be able to deliver psychological first aid. You don't need to have gone to college or even graduated from high school. You can still learn to listen receptively to children who have a story to tell you.

By offering educators training in providing trauma-informed care to their students, we can transform educators into nonclinical practitioners. For the last several years, I have been on a mission to convince more educators to become trauma-informed nonclinical practitioners. I feel like all individuals working in education and community services need to embrace and learn trauma-informed care.

Let me briefly lay down the difference between a clinical practitioner and a nonclinical practitioner. A clinical practitioner is a psychiatrist, licensed therapist, or licensed social worker. They're people with degrees and expertise. A nonclinical practitioner can be anyone who is knowledgeable in practicing trauma-informed care. I work in education not mental health, but I am also trained in providing trauma-informed care, so I'm a nonclinical practitioner.

Here's an analogy I've been using, which I shamelessly stole from *The Punisher* TV series on Netflix.

Imagine that a child is stuck a deep hole in the ground, and they're injured. Some people are going to walk by that hole, look in and see someone stuck and quickly look away. It hurts them too much to see someone in that condition. Some people are going to go to the edge of the hole and shout words of sympathy or encouragement. "You'll get out of the hole someday! I believe in you!" This does no good at all. Some people are going to try and give the person tools to get out of the hole but not show the person who is stuck how to use them. Some people are going to throw down medical supplies, but the person's injuries need to be treated by a doctor.

Then one day a person jumps into the hole with the child. The child freaks out and says, "What are you doing?! I'm stuck in this hole. I have been for days. Now we're both stuck! Can you even help me? Can you treat my injuries? Are you a doctor?"

The person who jumped into the hole says, "No, I'm not a doctor. But I can help you. You see, I've been in this hole before, and I know the way out, so we're going to climb out of this hole together."

I think this is the most powerful thing that educators with a background of trauma have to offer: we come from a community where many of us have experienced and survived trauma and come out the other side as (relatively) healthy and functioning human beings. We have been to some scary places in our lives. These are the some of the same places that our students now find themselves. All we need to help them heal is the courage to go back to those scary places with these kids and help them find their way out.

> **Confess the faults you hide.**
> **Approach what seems repulsive.**
> **Teach those who seem unteachable.**
> **Give away what you are attached to.**
> **Go to the places that scare you.**
> —The Five Slogans of Machig Labdrön

>> Teachers, especially radical teachers, are faced with a problem. They are operating within a system circumscribed by state education policy, constrained by curriculum requirements and guidelines that often have little to do with actual education. In the Israeli occupied territories of Palestine, teachers face the same issue, only with the immense weight of the Israeli occupation hanging over everything. To understand how teachers in Palestine experience this situation I interviewed my friend **Murad Tamini**, a teacher from the village of Nabi Saleh in the West Bank. Murad is currently a teacher in the classroom after spending many years as an official in the General Union of Palestinian Teachers (GUPT). In addition to this experience, he was and remains an activist against the occupation, from the time of the First Intifada in 1987 to the nonviolent Popular Resistance movement initiated by the villagers of Nabi Saleh in 2009.

—**Mike Corr**

Resistance in the Palestinian Classroom

Mike Corr interviews Murad Tamini

نحنهو واحد,
واحد بي هل ارد ال سم
لاحلنا, رحنبكي
و معبعدنا, رحنبكي

هازا ال دونيا ال جديد

One on this ground of poison
Alone, we will cry
And together, we will cry
This is the new world
—Haram, "What Is This Life?"

Mike Corr: Education in the West Bank was run by the Israeli military from 1967 until 1994, right? What was that like?

Murad Tamini: First, the curriculum was written entirely by Israelis. You couldn't talk about Palestinian history or the Palestinian cause. Of course, the teachers in the schools were Palestinian, so they weren't totally tied to that curriculum, but they had to be careful. You could never talk about current events, like the struggle in Lebanon or anything. Also, the curriculum was terrible. There was no creativity, just memorizing everything.

Mike Corr: What were the conditions of life for teachers during that time?

Murad Tamini: In general, teachers had low salaries—900 shekels, about 250 dollars, a month—and if anybody tried to do anything political, to resist, they were fired, or at least moved to another school with no warning, so the teachers were always oppressed and humiliated by the military administration. But you can say the same for the whole Palestinian people. Teachers got involved in resistance, either underground military resistance or forming unions and doing different things. Some were arrested and suffered, others carried on and played a role in the revolutionary movement.

Mike Corr: How did things change after Oslo and the introduction of the Palestinian Authority?

Murad Tamini: After Oslo, let's say from 1994 to 2000, there was a big change. In the schools they started teaching about national issues, Palestine, the PLO, etc. But from the Second Intifada in 2000 until today, it has gone from bad to worse. At first, teachers felt like they had freedom of speech within something like their own state, but the Palestinian Authority (PA) kept paying the same terrible salaries, and the Education Ministry introduced its own curriculum, just like the old one with some superficial changes. Teachers still teach to the same exit exam—the *tawjihi*. The ministry talks a lot about critical thinking and holds workshops, but it's superficial. The teacher has to cover the book or the text, and it doesn't allow them to do any activities or anything like that. If the teacher misses some pages, then the students can't answer the questions. Teachers are handcuffed to the test.

Since 2000, the ministry also started to remove Arabic and religious studies material from the text books. They blame Hamas, but Hamas is just a symbol. These things are pillars of Palestinian identity and culture. Every two or three years, from 2000 until now, there have been three or four big curriculum changes. It has gone from bad to worse. You can ask any teacher and they'll say, "This is the worst curriculum I've ever taught."

The ministry is not a Palestinian institution! They manipulate the students' and parents' minds by superficial activities. They throw big celebrations and parties for graduation, and you see the officials in their black suits taking pictures for the internet, especially for the donors. In terms of education, I think it's worse than ever. In 2016, there was a big teachers' strike and a march in Ramallah. The PA repressed it using police checkpoints and everything. That was bad for the teachers, because they started to really feel that they are under occupation again and their freedom won't improve.

Mike Corr: What is the reasoning behind changes in the curriculum, especially less emphasis on Arabic and Islam?

Murad Tamini: The Education Ministry is doing a fishy thing. I think the Israelis have a big role in all this. They sent a message to teachers to tell students not to memorize verses from the Quran because it won't be in the final exam. This has never happened!!! I heard people at the ministry are talking about erasing the Quran verses, because it teaches students to be terrorists. I'm not defending fundamentalists and terrorists, but Islam and the Quran, you know, it's culture, it's a pillar of nationalism. Now, in history class they say if you want to teach history you have to teach the other side—the Israeli narrative. I think they're taking away the history of Palestine as a nation. Maybe we'll teach about Ramallah and Nablus, Mahmoud Darwish, etc., but that's it.

Mike Corr: Official public education isn't the only kind of education, right? Can you talk about the popular education during the First Intifada?

Murad Tamini: During the First Intifada, in 1987, we had popular education. From 1987 to 1990, the Israelis would close the schools for months. Students held class in the streets or in homes, and many activists started doing popular education. We had classes in social centers and sports clubs. Of course, we took the old curriculum to prepare students for the test, but the methods were different because the teachers were activists. They started talking about real issues. After Oslo, all the old ways came right back.

Mike Corr: As a teacher, how do you deal with the system?

Murad Tamini: The main problem we suffer is classroom management. The students feel they are going to prison and not school, and there is a big gap between teachers and students. The teachers have one main goal—control the class and cover the text. It's a sort of programming of the mind. They program teachers to be machines without stopping and thinking about what they're doing. They're just a machine going in the morning and leaving in the afternoon. You ask any teacher, "Do you have good results in class?" He'll say, "No, I'm just going there to spend time and take my salary."

As for me, I had a big fight with my supervisor. She came by my class at different times and saw that I tried to teach outside of the curriculum, telling stories and doing activities. She said, "You have to go back to the curriculum." I had a big fight with her, so I was suspended. Before that, they kept moving me from one school to the other. Which is a big problem—if you start telling students the truth, they move you. So you have to be a machine. The administration and the ministry staff go to these workshops and conferences all around the world, spending millions of dollars from private donors and international aid, supposedly for improving the teachers. What are they doing? Just talking about modern teaching, but there is no application. Who's the victim? The students. You can't change curriculum every fucking year, man. And it's not a strong curriculum! At school, everything is a mess. No manners, misbehaving, no respect, and even if the teacher tries to punish or suspend a student, the whole ministry comes and blames the teacher. Nowadays, you see drugs too, which you never saw in the past.

Mike Corr: How do you see working inside or outside of the education system in Palestine?

Murad Tamini: We can't go back to the same system with teachers as slaves and students as prisoners, and nobody feeling like they learn anything. This Education Ministry is leading us toward something, and it isn't good, so we need a big revolution against them. Fuck the donors, and fuck their money. Ask any Palestinian teacher, "What are you teaching? What are the students learning? Do they love the school?" Of course, they will say, "No!" This is what the occupation needs. You want to destroy a people, destroy their education. You ask any student what are they going to be after they graduation, they will say Palestinian Security. They are just recruiting soldiers, illiterate and brainwashed, to fight each other. We are in a 100 percent corrupted situation here, and the only ones who make decisions are the corrupted ones. The ones who speak loud and tell the truth are going to end up like me, suspended and fired.

The occupation is not just Israeli, it's in the mind. I lived in the U.S., and I saw some similarities, even if students and teachers have some freedom. Corruption is everywhere. Capitalism is everywhere. Business is business anywhere you go. Education is big business. They talk about investing in education, but they aren't investing in students. They are investing in education to make money. It's the same all over the world. Here in Palestine, and in the U.S. too, in a way, we're all under occupation. So I want to say if you want to be a teacher, the first thing is you have to be free.

POSTSCRIPT

Murad suggested that if people want to help in a small way, they can donate any amount of money to Al-Quds Bard College for Arts and Sciences, in Jerusalem, where thirteen Palestinian teachers are enrolled in the Masters of Arts in Teaching program. This program is one of the very few efforts to really help Palestinian teachers find ways to bring creativity and critical thinking into the classroom. For more information, please contact Rana Al-Surkhi, rsurakhi@staff.alquds.edu.

>> Pundits and trolls, Republicans and (American) Libertarians, moderate Democrats and so-called "classical liberals," "red pilled" adherents to the reactionary/neocolonialist/hypermisogynist/transphobic politics of the "intellectual dark web," and more traditional fascists/white supremacists, CNN, Fox News, MSNBC, Breitbart, NPR, and InfoWars alike—all of these devote lots of space to freakouts about the "PC culture" in schools, which they claim is generating a generation of "snowflakes," supposedly unable to handle the "real world." However, in the blur of hysterical mainstream media clickbait taglines/anecdotes and right-wing fragility toward anything that robustly challenges toxic structures like white supremacy (aka the "real world" they always refer to), a more essential question is lost: By what means can educators help fulfill their responsibility to protect students from needless harm while helping strengthen them to tackle the challenges they will face in an often unjust world?

This essay is by **Frankie Mastrangelo**, a Gender, Sexuality, and Women's Studies educator in Richmond, Virginia. She delves deeply into a powerful and nuanced discussion of the necessity, effectiveness, and practical reality of "safe(r) spaces" vs. "brave spaces"—the latter of which is distinguished, broadly, as environments in which uncomfortable, even harmful, ideas and expressions are not necessarily prohibited. Rather, they are named and openly acknowledged for what they are, in the express service of ultimately creating new, transformative conversations and deep mutual community support. As my confidant Megan March puts it, "There's more than one way to fight a cop."

Safe(r) Spaces and Future Cops

by Frankie Mastrangelo

> we live in a system, it shall always be a system
> we will get used to it cause we'll always be a part of it
> —Kebab, "System"

Space is central in teaching and creating. I think about what space can do, how it can be formed, and the ways that it can grow. I also think about what space can limit, how it can be threatened, and the ways it can undermine our goals and objectives. One of my favorite authors, adrienne maree brown, talks about space in ways that inspire my thinking around how i understand teaching and DIY culture. brown is a long-time social justice facilitator and author of *Emergent Strategy: Shaping Change, Changing Worlds*: a book that uses Octavia Butler's science fiction and an appreciation for permaculture to revisit and revise how we understand what it means to envision and create change. I was listening to adrienne maree brown speak recently about the concept of brave spaces. She says that brave spaces function to recognize and name harm, where folks can feel okay with saying "that hurt or offended me" and get back to the work of productive, transformative conversations, where we build critical connections, where it doesn't matter what your intentions are—what matters is what impact your words or behavior create.

brown made me think of how often the concept of safe(r) space comes up in the classroom and DIY communities. I think the concept of brave space distinguishes itself from notions of the safe(r) space in that a brave space prioritizes what a space *does* rather than what it *proposes to do*. Despite what the aims of a classroom or DIY space are, how that space functions and creates impact takes precedent to what it promises to accomplish. I question how we can really promise safety within a space when our perspectives and lives are shaped by our relationships to systems of privilege and oppression—we are not always aware of how those systems will show up in our interactions and cause harm or distress. How can we really ensure that a space will always be safe for everyone when folks may call the police for issues that can be sussed out with a simple conversation or when those who manage a space refrain from holding themselves accountable for causing harm? When students voice racist perspectives or misogynist views in a classroom, how can we say that this space remains understood as safe by those hurt and affected by shitty comments? Recognizing how oppressive systems show up for us requires constant reflection, an openness to critique, and commitment to shared growth among all those who move within a space. I think the notion of safety limits us at times in creating the radical spaces we want to see and take steps to maintain. The intention of ensuring safety is often eclipsed by the impact of words and behaviors that inflict harm.

I teach in a Gender, Sexuality, and Women's Studies program and think about what it means to cultivate a classroom that does the work of brown's brave space. How can I build connection and community among myself and students in ways that are defined by the experiences and lives of students? How do I work from a place of embracing how students' perspectives are a culmination of their relationships to systems, their histories, and their traumas? How do I facilitate conversations in which students lean into discomfort when called to confront their privileges? How do we collaborate on pinpointing where white supremacy or carceral thinking shows up in their lives? These questions guide how I go about teaching, because they're questions that I am consistently grappling with in my own life. I've come to realize that there is a power in modeling vulnerability in educational settings, so when I say, "Here's what I struggle with in engaging racist family members," "Here's what I fear in navigating street harassment," or "Here's where I see my whiteness affording me privilege and what it means to decenter myself in spaces where I should listen more than I speak"—those moments can be entry points for collaborating on navigating discomfort. I think those moments encourage us to identify what dominant systems make fragile, broken, or tense. Recognizing how dominant systems show up in each of our lives and how they shape our perspectives creates the potential for the types of conversations brown refers to—those discussions needed to transform our world and build critical connection.

I want to talk about a recent instance in my teaching that was uncomfortable and difficult but that, I think, represents striving for a brave and radical educational space.

One student I had not too long ago told me early on in the semester that he wanted to be a police officer. The Intro to Gender, Sexuality, and Women's Studies class I teach is considered a general education requirement, so I can get majors that range anywhere from studio art to biology. This particular student was pursuing a criminal justice major and expressed genuine interest in learning more about feminism, privilege, and systematized oppression. I'm an abolitionist and will talk with anyone about why police and prisons are antithetical to collective liberation. How I go about these conversations will usually shift based on who is engaging in this conversation with me. So how I talk about why police and prisons contradict liberatory social and political futures will obviously look different for an aspiring police officer than it will for a friend of mine that organizes books to prisoners initiatives. This student of mine began to speak up more and more over the course of the semester, and sometimes his questions were met with resistance, anger, and frustration from fellow classmates.

In a conversation about the importance of Black Lives Matter, he asked why people are so distrustful of the police and why the actions of a few cops should be seen as representative of the entire police force. Within that conversational space, other students looked at me with expressions of exasperated irritation, because they saw this person as just not "getting it."

In the event that questions like this arise, I would try and push the class to consider his questions and offer suggestions for responding. I think practicing coming up with rich answers to questions like this is a good exercise for anyone interested in social justice. Navigating conversations like this is a balancing act, though, because I don't want to promote a cultural taxation on those most marginalized by an issue being discussed to educate their classmates. In other words, the onus of responsibility for explaining police brutality against Black folks should not fall on Black students. I am constantly learning how to do a better job of handling these conversations in ways that push discussions forward without creating those forms of cultural taxation. Posing generative questions that refrain from positioning anyone as spokespersons for an identity group usually helps with this. For instance, asking the class what they think police exist to do or what their purpose is can lead to deeper understandings of how our relationships with police are informed by race relations.

Our conversation came around to identifying how experiences with the police differ based on identity and examining what the police force represents. While the discussion got off to a tense start, it ultimately felt productive. When the class ended, I remember the student who wanted to be a cop approaching me to talk. He was concerned that he made people upset with his questions and asked if his questions were stupid. I started off by thanking him for his questions and turned his attention to how he sparked a lively discussion. I think a little bit of validation through expressing appreciation for inquiry can go a long way in engaging people in difficult conversations, especially when they think they may be uninformed or at ideological odds with those around them. I also think there's a fine line between validating/appreciating and unnecessary/disingenuous ego stroking in these situations. I think we enter ego stroking territory when fears of upsetting someone's fragility guide communication, as opposed to using conversations for the sake of challenging that fragility. My student then went on to express how he believes in the good that can come from policing and wished that people didn't have such bad experiences with police. "Why do you think people have bad experiences with police?" I asked. He said that he knew racial profiling is an issue and part of this. I agreed and pointed out that he and I would have different experiences with police than a person of color, because we are white. I shared how I didn't always realize that my whiteness afforded me privilege with police, but that it led me to understand how policing in the United States is historically rooted in controlling communities of color. He continued to ask me questions related to understanding white privilege.

I think that this conversation continues to stick out in my mind as an example of how important it is for me as a white teacher who facilitates discussions on privilege and oppression to share vulnerability. Vulnerability takes the form of sharing with students times that I struggled to understand a concept, issue, or aspect of my experience and identities. I didn't always understand what was fucked-up about policing, and beginning to examine my white privilege was certainly a part of developing that understanding. Discussing elements of these personal experiences with students goes to show that examining and resisting dominant systems is an ongoing, dynamic process. It's not like you write a song about why cops suck or attend one racial bias training and are set in your politics for life. I'm wary of anyone who gives the impression that their politics are static or fine-tuned and that they have nothing to learn about and grow from. Humility and self-reflection go a long way in creating the spaces we want to see and communities worth cultivating.

As the semester went on, that student would often talk with me for a few minutes after class to kind of recap that day's discussions. It's hard to gauge as a teacher if conversations like this will have lasting influence. I'd often walk away from those conversations thinking about what could have gone differently or what could have been explained in greater depth. I try my best to channel those kind of thoughts into reflections for enhancing future discussions so anxiety doesn't get the best of me. I don't know if that student took what we talked about and laughed about it with future cop buddies. I don't know if that student took what we talked about and continued meaningfully discussing it with other white folks and men that could really benefit from those dialogues. I won't lie. I sometimes wonder if they still want to be a cop or if the class had any impact on their goals. Who knows. What I do know is that it's difficult to create and maintain the space(s) that led to making my conversations with this student possible. Yet, any space that does that work of valuing impact over intention is going to be a difficult exercise in challenging privilege and enacting resistance.

Prioritizing impact over intention also takes the form of holding ourselves accountable as teachers. I think about what genuine collaboration looks like a lot, and I know that it requires me to actively engage student feedback in my teaching. This sort of ongoing forum for critique means cocreating and co-facilitating threads of communication with students that can be messy and difficult. It is messy to keep up, gain interest in, and balance with other responsibilities. It is difficult to acknowledge and put to use. Yet I think when we open ourselves up as teachers to this critique, our egos become less important than collaborative visions for radical education and what those visions create. In the last few years of teaching, I've tried my best to make myself accessible to critique inside and outside the classroom. For me, this accessibility can take the form of just presenting specific opportunities for feedback and also of modeling vulnerability (sharing experiences, joking about mess ups, acknowledging fragility). Sometimes this critique led to big points of growth. Last semester, while teaching my first feminist media studies class, one student I would often talk to approached me with some feedback. She felt like the class could do a better job of centering transwomen of color in conversations about media and offered some great thoughts on how. My first instinct was to feel like I fucked up and should have done a better job with this from the get-go (that's my own imposter syndrome, anxiety, and fragility at work), but I realized that my student wouldn't have approached me and offered these thoughts if they didn't care about the class. Not only did they care about the class, they gave enough of a shit about it to promote its growth. Classrooms get stagnant and wind up reinforcing inequitable power dynamics when teachers get scared of criticism. There are enough tenured shit-heads out there who believe what they've been doing for twenty years is amazing and needs no improvement. A classroom that resists critique is like a one-sided conversation (that's probably wearing elbow patches). I'm always inspired by the teachers that are consistently brainstorming ways to "do better" in facilitating radical spaces. By really engaging with criticism, teachers subvert the forms of authority that traditional education offers us by default. Challenging authority and enacting accountability are ongoing processes that pushes us all to do better in confronting privilege, power, and oppression. I know I can always do better, and staying grounded by that realization makes teaching a space that feels radical and brave.

When turning a critical eye toward widespread media and broad cultural landscapes, it can be very revealing to note how and to what extent cracks in traditional facades have the effect of shifting the balance of power. It is worth examining whether the #MeToo movement has restructured power disparities and changed the conversation on consent and sexual violence at a deeper and broader level beyond the headlines and high-profile individual cases it has served to highlight. It is worth asking if any purported shift in power dynamics has been felt in communities where power is experienced differently, particularly by those who are marginalized. Is the epidemic of sexual violence being understood as symptomatic of a deeper set of structural inequities that have been built, in part, to facilitate and perpetuate this kind of abuse?

How does the conversation about sexual violence and consent need to change in the classroom? Anecdotally, if you asked any given group of teachers to name a topic that they are uncomfortable discussing with students, it has often been anything related to the ever-present issues of sex, sexual violence, and consent. Yet in a society—a world—where the dynamics and structures of power imbalance are so deeply intertwined with these issues, it is more important than ever to help students connect the dots and learn how to approach these issues critically. For educators, it is vital to have a strong game plan with regard to navigating these issues in an age where sexual violence and abuse of power are being brought to light at an ever-increasing rate, yet few perpetrators are truly held to account, with a sexual assaulter being appointed to the Supreme Court and another elected president. In a world like this, an eye needs to be turned toward resisting and dismantling the "systems" that make sexual violence and violations of consent so pervasive.

The next essay frankly reflects on doing the necessary (and difficult) task of helping students come to understand what consent means, details differences in pedagogy between widely divergent groups, and discusses how lessons are impacted and must be informed by the existence of very real structural and socioeconomic schisms in society. The author is **Sarah Orton**, a sexual violence prevention educator and advocate for victims/survivors in the Bay Area. Sarah can be emailed directly at specialagentmcnab@gmail.com.

The Dissent of Consent:
An Educator's Experience Teaching Sexual Violence Prevention

by Sarah Orton

> The role of the attacker and survivor become distorted
> So the majority of rapes are never reported
> The threat of rape is always there
> It's like a poison that saturates the air
> A society stricken by a cancerous disease
> Where men know they can do as they please
> —Aus-Rotten, "The Second Rape"

"Stanford Swimmer Rapes Unconscious Woman Passed Out Behind Dumpster"

I read the headline aloud to a class of eighth graders. Twenty pairs of blinking eyes stared back at me, questioning. A few studious listeners in the front row squinted and peered closer at the newspaper headline that I had projected onto the whiteboard. They were trying hard to understand.

"After everything we've discussed today about media portrayal," I started, "who can tell me what's wrong with this headline?"

I looked into a sea of blank stares. A kid in the back row sneezed loudly and everybody started.

"Okay, let's try thinking about this in a new way," I said. "We know from this piece of media that a woman was sexually assaulted, right?"

Students started to sit up in their seats; I saw sympathetic nods around the room.

"Okay, then. Well, who was responsible for that?" I asked, "Who is at fault in that situation?"

Their faces twisted in confusion and discomfort. Some looked at me with disdain, as if they suspected I was trying to trick them. The clock ticked audibly, and I knew we had minutes before the bell rang.

Finally, a student raised his hand, and I nodded at him enthusiastically.

"It's *her* fault," he said.

My shoulders slumped. I rolled my head, cracking my neck, and took a deep breath. I paused again to let everyone collect their thoughts, hoping for someone to burst out in protest.

"Okay, does anyone else think anything different?"

My eyes darted pleadingly from student to student, but their heads all shook "no" in unison.

"Help me understand, then—if *he* assaulted *her*, then how could it possibly be her fault?"

Another student raised his hand: "Well, because, she was at the party, and she got drunk and went off with that guy."

A girl at the same table chimed in: "Yeah, and she like, passed out in a dumpster or whatever," she snorted. "Who does that?"

Suddenly, I felt exhausted.

These students had proved and missed my point at the same time, and they didn't even realize it. The bell rang, notebooks slammed shut, and over the shuffle of everyone rushing out the door, I yelled after them that I'd see them next time.

As I packed up to leave, two female students approached me.

"I think they're all wrong," one said. "It wasn't her fault, it's his."

I asked why she thought so. She continued to explain that it shouldn't matter what someone is doing at the time of their assault, and that someone who is that intoxicated is incapable of consent.

"The news just wants to make him look good and make her look bad, because his parents are rich and he plays sports," she told me. "It's so stupid, that stuff shouldn't even matter."

Her voice cracked, and her eyes filled with tears. Her friend put a hand on her shoulder. She was speaking from experience. I told her that she was exactly right, that of course it shouldn't matter.

I wanted to tell her that it gets better, and that when she's older, it will be easier for people to understand, but I didn't want to lie to her. Instead, I referred her to the school counselor.

When I was in school, we didn't talk about rape, at least not in any educational context. We may have watched the news and overheard our parents talking about what that "poor girl" was wearing or how much she had to drink. Our parents wouldn't mention the perpetrator. They'd only express a vague sense of relief that their children would be taught how *not* to become victims rather than how not to become offenders.

Consent, as it applies to sex, wasn't a concept I was familiar with until my late teens, which was long after I had become sexually active. In childhood, I had learned to share and learned to ask if I wanted to borrow something that didn't belong to me but had little information to contextualize my body in this way. Rape, as far my peers and I knew, was something that happened to girls and women who didn't know how to protect themselves and was always perpetrated by a masked stranger lurking in the bushes near the schoolyard or offering poisoned candy to kids in the suburbs.

This notion was confusing, though, as no one I knew ever encountered this insidious stranger. When sexual assault happened in our friendship groups, it usually came from one of our peers. There weren't any strangers involved, and no one ever told horror stories about it. According to the Centers for Disease Control and Prevention, about 50 percent of American high school students are sexually active and one out of four will contract a sexually transmitted infection and/or be victimized by sexual assault. The latter statistic is based on sexual assaults that are reported, so it can be estimated to be dramatically higher. According to a statistic cited by the Rape, Abuse & Incest National Network, about 70 percent of sexual assaults are perpetrated by someone whom the victim knows.

When one of our friends was sexually violent, it was almost always met with the age-old idiom, "Boys will be boys." Of course, no one ever mentioned that boys were victimized too—contrary to common knowledge, one out of six boys before their eighteenth birthday. The absence of discussion regarding male sexual assault implicitly invalidated the boys who may have experienced sexual violence and prevented them from coming forward. This is particularly problematic because a lack of disclosure means a lack of support, which can cause children and teens to be sexually violent themselves.

Sexual assault, especially among younger folks, is drastically underreported, and the scope of its definition is narrow. Commonly cited statistics usually do not account for acts of sexual violence that include sexual harassment, revenge porn, coercive sexual activity, alcohol facilitated sex, and sex occurring between individuals with unequal power dynamics like teacher/student or minor/adult. Sexual violence exists on a continuum, but it seems that if we have the opportunity to potentially prevent most of it, shouldn't we give it a shot?

It is a common misconception that people who perpetrate sexual assault are sociopaths with faulty wiring and no moral compass. While this may be true of pedophiles and violent serial rapists who stalk and kidnap their victims, it is not true of most people who commit acts of sexual violence. Sexual violence is an umbrella term used to describe the various ways that consent might be violated during a sexual encounter. This can include rape, sexual assault, "consent violations," and "consent accidents."

A consent violation refers to a situation in which someone's consent is ignored or disregarded due to a lack of full understanding. This is common among young people who haven't received consent education and may believe that a partner saying "no" might be their partner "playing hard to get" or someone who exploits their position of power to get what they want sexually.

A consent accident occurs when someone violates consent without having all of the information. Consent accidents frequently occur when one partner doesn't realize how intoxicated the other is, or is unaware of a partner's trauma history and unknowingly re-traumatizes them through seemingly consensual sexual activity.

A person who is the victim of a consent violation or a consent accident will often experience the same trauma symptoms as someone who is a victim of a violent rape, and these experiences should never be discounted. Similarly, it is essential to always mirror the language that the victim uses to describe their experience. It is also important to acknowledge that someone who commits a consent accident is usually not someone who should be labeled a rapist.

But if someone commits a consent accident or violation, they're not off the hook. If I hit someone with my car—on purpose or by accident—it still hurts them tremendously, and I must attempt to make amends and vow to change my negligent behavior so it never happens again. If I continue to hit people with my car afterward, the punishment for my behavior should escalate. It is necessary to be aware of these nuances as an educator to effectively reach your target audience by using examples that are applicable to their experiences.

Standard sexual violence prevention education curricula usually include key issues such as consent (legal and personal), boundaries, sexual harassment, rape, drug facilitated sexual assault, and rape culture. I have developed and administered various versions of curricula exploring these topics with youth spanning a wide range of demographics. One of the most important factors about the teaching material is that it must be accessible in order to be effective. Common terms like "culturally competent" and "population specific" often translate to simply making our curriculum more inclusive.

Examples of inclusive terms are "people with a penis" or "people with a vagina" instead of gendered terms ("you guys") or assuming heteronormativity. This makes information more inclusive of LGBTQIA+ folks, as we know that not all people with penises identify as male, and not all people with vaginas identify as female. Another example of cultural inclusivity might be to make sure the educational materials are translated into a variety of languages, so a student can share materials with a caregiver or guardian who is not a native English speaker.

As educators with little or no funding and increasing demand, attempts at classroom inclusivity are usually the best we can do. However, if the intention is to develop a culture of nonviolent, sexually healthy adults, we must do more. It is imperative that sexual violence prevention education relates to the students' lived experiences.

I started work as a prevention and sex educator in a small county where there was a stark contrast between affluent residents and residents from low-income households. I alternated between teaching some of the most privileged Bay Area youth to those who were incarcerated, usually coming from economically disadvantaged homes. It quickly became clear to me that if I desired to reach both groups, twin approaches would be ineffective.

In addition to the disparity of financial and physical freedom, the students in wealthy, preparatory high schools were mostly white, and my students in Juvenile Hall were primarily Black and Latinx. Both of these perspectives must be considered and catered to, especially taking into account the institutionalized racism that makes the incarceration of people of color a trend nationwide. For this reason and many others, students' priorities tend to differ immensely.

Both privileged and disadvantaged people can lose empathy for sexual assault victims through environmental conditioning, but those environments are drastically different. The privileged person may have difficulty feeling empathy, because it's never been essential to their status as a "good" person—they were likely born into the world gifted with that assumption. The disadvantaged person may struggle, because they haven't felt as if anyone has been empathetic toward them. This isn't to say that privileged folks are never empathetic and that less advantaged folks are all callous, but these unique conditions often cultivate a similar result.

It is human nature to have our capacity to feel for others entangled with our own life experiences. Ultimately, one of the most effective tools for successfully delivering prevention education is conjuring empathy for others, but teaching empathy is a challenge. When considering education as a tool to prevent people from committing acts of sexual violence, one should ask: What is this group's motivation for refraining from a consent violation? Is it compassion for others? Fear of the law? Shame or fear of public ridicule?

As educators, we must be aware of the ways various communities are conditioned to accept sexual violence as the norm even if the outcomes are the same. If we recognize that the delivery of the poison is different, then we know that the antidote must be as well.

Tailoring curriculum in this way, however, can get us into some sticky territory. It's important to cater to students' sensibilities, while being careful not to assume their viewpoint based on their societal position. In regards to class, however, I've seen a key difference between fortunate and less fortunate youth.

Teens coming from extremely affluent families have a hard time accepting the fact that sexual assault is prevalent in their well-to-do communities. Conversely, their less privileged counterparts are well aware of the sexual assault in their communities, but they find it difficult to care about it, because they face many other problems that affect them more directly. Both communities, however, handle instances of sexual assault in strikingly similar ways, which is to ensure that if an assault occurs in that community, the knowledge of it never leaves that community.

Generally, well-off kids have an appreciation for the rules. Certainly, many in this position have the tendency to think that the rules don't apply to them as well, and that makes for a dichotomy that's hard to crack. But one can often make the assumption that a classroom full of upper-class teenagers fear and understand certain rules, although many have never experienced the consequences of breaking them.

Consequences can seem more severe to people who have never had to experience them. If I explain to a group of affluent teens the definition of legal consent, they are more apt to pay attention. If they think there will be legal ramifications if they break the law during a sexual encounter, they're more likely to obey that law. For example, I might tell them that the state says it's illegal to get a person drunk in order to coerce them into sexual activity. In my experience, this statement is usually followed by a line of questioning about how close one may walk up to that line without technically breaking the law.

Male students often ask, "Well what if we're both drunk?" or "What if I don't know she's drunk?" or, further, "What if she lies and says she was drunk, how can she prove it?"

These are reasonable questions for curious learners, but the questions that never surfaced were disconcerting, like questions about consent and pleasure for all parties involved or questions about ethics.

"Does it matter?" I would ask, pushing back. "Don't you want to know that your sexual partners are capable of consent and enjoying themselves too?"

Following this challenge, I often noticed female students nod with furrowed brows, and traditionally masculine students roll their eyes or avoid my gaze altogether.

It was after these classes that students would most often disclose to me that they had been assaulted by their classmates. They either hadn't known or didn't have the courage to come forward before then. The predominant make-up of these schools—white, affluent males—are the most dangerous group of potential predators. Caucasian males commit around 60 percent of sexual assaults and a variety of other races and ethnicities account for the remaining 40 percent. After they leave my class, those whom I might have reached are bombarded with information suggesting that what I've taught doesn't fully apply to them. Many will go to college and join fraternities that encourage the very behavior discussed in my lesson.

They will see the faces of Black men not their peers plastered all over the news, being punished for raping white women. Some of these students might feel guilt or fear afterward, but they will soon learn that because of what they were born into, the law is eternally on their side, regardless of what is written in it.

"Stanford Swimmer Rapes Unconscious Woman Passed Out Behind Dumpster."

After a day of giving these workshops in the suburbs of the North Bay Area, I would climb into my truck and begin the thirty-minute drive to the most rural part of the county. Inside an enormous concrete building encased in oak trees and razor wire, I would empty my pockets into the familiar grey bin and walk through the metal detector where a security guard waited to pat me down on the other side. The receptionist sitting behind bulletproof glass would take the contraband out of my bag—paperclips, stapled paper, ballpoint pens, hairpins—anything that could be used as a "weapon."

In the beginning, the staff eyed me suspiciously. "You the rape lady?" they would ask.

The residents in my Juvenile Hall groups were usually Black and Latino teenagers, with some white folks from low-income households. Groups were all male, and their offenses ranged from petty theft to murder. Unlike the preparatory middle and high schools, I led groups here once a week for ten weeks, rather than once or twice per school year. I thought I was prepared for the challenge of teaching these kids. I was under no assumption that any of them would be interested in my advice, so I didn't expect any miracles. But I still fumbled through my first few groups.

To them, I was just another white, female social worker telling them what *not* to do. Don't drink. Don't do drugs. Don't fight. Don't steal. Don't rape. Group after group flooded these kids with information that wasn't applicable to their lives and never offered any alternatives to all the "don'ts." Even if they had, many of them couldn't return home rehabilitated. It wasn't a safe option for them. A stint in Juvenile Hall paled in comparison to the reprimand they'd face at home if they didn't re-assimilate when they returned. Who was I to expect them to be accountable to me rather than the gangs they had grown up in?

I tried anyway.

I began these groups with an exercise I referred to as "moral dilemmas." I explained to the eight participants that this was a lesson in critical thinking and a practice in engaging in respectful discourse. During the activity, I read a controversial political statement aloud, such as "Women should have safe, legal access to abortion." Participants stood under a sign posted in the room that best represented their feelings on that particular issue. Signs ranged from "strongly agree" to "strongly disagree."

After each student chose their position, they would each have a turn to defend their point of view. One major rule in this activity was that certain arguments that didn't demonstrate critical thinking skills were off limits. These included God or the Bible, the opinions of parents, siblings, or gangs, opinions formed based on provably false information, and blanket morality statements such as "right or wrong" and "good or bad."

As the moderator, I asked students to hold each other accountable and determine if an argument acceptably demonstrated critical thinking based on the aforementioned criteria. Establishing this framework on the first day usually allowed for this dynamic to carry through to the subsequent group sessions as our topics became more focused.

"I don't always have to like your opinion," I would tell them, "but you need to be able to defend it."

One of the biggest challenges I faced is that these groups usually had egregiously rigid ideologies pertaining to gender roles, heteronormativity, and violence. Violence experienced in their own lives often left them numb in their desire to feel for others. But this could also be used as a tool to explore its relation to their lived experiences. I might ask a group, "What does it mean to have your power taken away?" or "How does it feel when someone else has control over you physically?"

Exploring these broader questions in a way that was indirectly related to rape and sexual assault helped them make important connections between consent and agency. In every session we would explore news articles on police brutality in the Black community, violence against trans people, or the incarceration rates of people of color or people living in poverty. Eventually, I saw my students zoom out from the microcosm of gang and life in "the hall" to make the connections that I was silently pleading with them to make. Often I was filled with pride and relief watching their synapses fire away as they debated among themselves and pored over current events.

"You're the smartest people I know," I often told them.

Our groups had another major rule: what's talked about in group, stays in group. They often mentioned crimes they had committed since they arrived at Juvenile Hall but had not been charged for. They had my word to keep their discussions confidential. This was risky, as it directly contradicted my contract agreement with Juvenile Hall, which mandated that I had to report if I had knowledge of crimes occurring within the facility. In return, my students kept quiet about the fact that I had completely gone off script from the curriculum I had initially proposed. In order to build trust, the playing field had to be leveled. I had been a runaway and sent to a couple of juvenile detention facilities in my teens, and I had always felt that the providers would have been more effective if they had allowed themselves to be vulnerable, to be on the same team.

The staff was already suspicious of me, because I was the only group facilitator who refused to allow a guard in the room during sessions. As I walked down the long, sterile corridor to the maximum security unit, I encountered staff members patrolling the halls. "The boys really enjoy your group" one might say to me, but it seldom felt like a compliment. Even the services that were meant to help the residents were supposed to feel like punishment.

We eventually had to get to the rape and sex stuff. Around week four, I'd bring in the lesson plan that I used in my high school classrooms. We'd discuss definitions for rape, consent, and the like, but at this point students were able to engage with the material at a level I hadn't seen in the shorter workshops. I still taught it, but I knew information about the law was not going to be relevant here. My group participants weren't afraid of the law and didn't have much use for it anyway. Most of them had already been victimized by racial profiling and stereotyping in the criminal justice system and were jaded and calloused to its effects.

Our discussions explored the conditions that allow sexual assault to flourish and the socialization of gender and sexuality. Students started to dismantle their own biases about gender and sexuality, realizing that the societal rules that they had learned only reinforced the status quo, which, in turn, reinforced their own oppression. Once they began to realize that conventional attitudes about gender, sexual orientation, and sexuality *are* the rule, they became much more interested in breaking it.

The last thing left to cover was *good* sex. What good, healthy sex looks like puzzles most American adults, not to mention youth. While I posed this question, it was often clear in their candor that many of them had not ever received any sort of sex education. Alarmed, I brought in all the diagrams I had on the subject. My students, several of them young fathers, stumbled through reproductive anatomy. I had to help most of them label appropriate anatomical terms on printouts of penises and vaginas. There were always several students who hadn't previously understood the function of the clitoris. Performing oral sex on vulvas had seemed confusing to them as they didn't understand the purpose, and it was not often featured in the porn that they were consuming.

Discussions regarding good sex are essential and, in my experience, work well with all demographics, at least those who are or intend to become sexually active.

Helpful, exploratory questions include: "What is good sex?" "How do I know if my partner is enjoying themselves?" "How do I know if I'm enjoying myself?"

These questions are usually helpful to tie into conversations regarding consent, and it can be beneficial for students to frame how they might check in with a partner whom they suspect isn't enjoying the experience. It can also be advantageous for a student to help map out how they might advocate for themselves if an encounter is not what they want. Questions about bad sex can also be pertinent: "What is bad sex?" "Is bad sex always sexual assault; how do we know?"

No matter the population, we must have solid foundational structure if we want young folks to grow up into sexually healthy adults. When talking to younger kids, it's important to use words like "safe" and "unsafe," rather than "good" and "bad," so as not to conflate sexuality with moralizing language early in sexual development. As kids mature and become sexually active, they begin to develop the skills to know the difference and also know that "safe" sex doesn't necessarily mean "good" sex. Boundaries should be taught to and modeled for children early and often.

When children are forced to hug or kiss a relative or wear clothing that they don't want to wear, they are implicitly being told that they don't have any bodily autonomy. Surely, children must be kept safe by their caregivers, and there are many times when a child's "no" must not be respected in order to do so, but people interacting with young children should be curious about what it might look like to oblige a child's "no" as often as possible. It becomes difficult to undo those messages as the child develops into an adolescent, and suddenly we expect them to understand that they must respect another's "no." It is my opinion that it is never too early to have age-appropriate conversations regarding sexual abuse and sexual health.

Another essential component of prevention work is assisting young folks in our classrooms with media literacy. White males commit a disproportionate number of sexual assaults (primarily against women of color), but that statistic is not one that is reflected by many news outlets, particularly broadcast news. These outlets/channels often hold up faces of Black men as the primary perpetrators of sex crimes, a trend not far enough removed from the post–Civil War era, where Black men were wrongfully accused and put to death for the alleged rape of white women.

Committing an act of rape is about power and control and so is the way it is portrayed in American culture. Power in societal positionality affects who we deem a victim and who we deem a perpetrator, and there is power in the way that message is communicated. Power dynamics are reflected in the rates of reporting and prosecution.

The United States was founded on the rape and pillaging of Native peoples, especially the brutalization of Native women. Today, Native American women are still sexually assaulted at the highest rate of any race or ethnicity. People generally appear surprised to hear this, as most people read the headlines not the research. Children who are born into privileged positions need to be made aware of the power that they hold and, later, held accountable for any abuse of that power.

Body rights and sexual/gender inclusivity are of the utmost importance in sexual violence prevention work. Conservative ideologies about same sex relationships and reproductive freedom signal to developing brains that others should have a choice about what happens to somebody else's body. There is an inextricable link between these attitudes and the normalization and acceptance of sexual violence.

Perhaps it seems far-reaching, but incorporating a holistic approach to violence prevention is essential to its efficacy. Youth who are raised to believe that only certain people should be able to make choices regarding their bodies and relationships can become confused about bodily autonomy, consent, and respecting the choices that others make about their own bodies. Coupled with the standard bones of the prevention curricula should be an additional three-prong approach, including umbrella topics such as sexual health, media messaging, and body rights/autonomy.

A caveat in my work as I've outlined it thus far is that I am one individual with only one lens. Like my students, I pull from my own lived experiences to make sense of and interact with the world around me. While I like to think I've learned a thing or two, there are volumes more that I will likely never fully comprehend. A more effective curriculum could be generated in a collaborative effort with fellow educators spanning a much wider range of backgrounds and experiences, and I encourage readers to continue to pull knowledge from as many sources as possible.

The strategies suggested here for implementation are based solely on my own experiences, and much of my evidence is anecdotal. Positive outcomes for this work are immeasurable, and it's difficult to know what the future entails once the class has adjourned. It would be naive to think that two hours or even ten group sessions with students will undo a lifetime of exposure to implicit messaging about the cultural acceptability of sexual violence. But I do know that apathy and complacency are twin pillars that uphold a system that condones and ignores sexual violence.

Education might be the best tool we have to dismantle that system.

Miriam Klein Stahl is the cofounder and lead teacher of Berkeley High's Arts and Humanities Academy (AHA), where she has taught since 1995. She is also an artist who specializes in printmaking, sculpture, paper cuts, and public art. Miriam is internationally known among activist and punk circles for her powerful, iconic portraits of political activists, misfits, radicals, and radical movements; some of her more well-known portraits include Phoolan Devi, Emma Goldman, James Baldwin, and Harry Hay. In 2011, she collaborated with her former student Gabby Miller to create original interactive artwork for the Occupy Oakland movement and, in 2017, designed original posters for the Women's March and for the mass demonstrations against fascism in Berkeley and Oakland. She also designed the cover for the book you are holding right now. As an educator, Miriam has dedicated her teaching practice to address equity through the lens of the arts, with a particular emphasis on dismantling structural racism, fighting for women's rights, and advocating fiercely for LGBTQIA+ students and staff.

Starting in 2015, Miriam Klein Stahl has illustrated a series of (all ages) children's books with author Kate Schatz called the *Rad Women* series, including *Rad American Women A–Z, Rad Women Worldwide, Rad Girls Can*, and *My Rad Life*. These bestselling books have become household and classroom staples, introducing thousands of kids and adults to profiles of twenty-six inspirational and deeply radical women in public life, including the likes of Angela Davis, Mary Shelly, Sophie Cruz, Yusra Mardini, Hatshepsut, Poly Styrene, Ella Baker, Billie Jean King, Patsy Mink, Nellie Bly, and many more. She has also done art and design work for punk bands including Jawbreaker, Interrobang, and Street Eaters. Miriam lives in Berkeley, California, with her wife, artist Lena Wolff, daughter Hazel, and their dog Lenny. She was interviewed by *Teaching Resistance* editor John Mink over two separate lunch periods in her classroom at Berkeley High, where students were buzzing around the whole time working on art projects and occasionally interjecting with comments of their own.

Interview with Miriam Klein Stahl

interviewed by John Mink

Try and try
That's the way you want it
If you know
That ain't the way it always goes
A little bit
A little bit more
What you makin', man
Takes time
—Minutemen, "Martin's Song"

John Mink: When did you start to be interested becoming an educator and why? How did your experience as an artist and activist and your overall personal identity impact this journey?

Miriam Klein Stahl: I moved to the Bay Area from Los Angeles in 1988 and went to San Francisco State and got my degree in printmaking and sculpture. In Los Angeles, I grew up next to an oil refinery, so I developed really bad asthma that didn't really flare up until I moved up here. I was in my late teens/early twenties, living in San Francisco, and I was going to the emergency room all the time with asthma, because it was new to me, and I didn't know what the deal was, and I was figuring it out, and I was getting huge medical bills. So I finished San Francisco State with a Bachelor's Degree in Art and had to figure out how to make money pretty quick, because there's only so many times you can give a fake name at a hospital. I was making stuff and screen printing, getting by.

At the time my rent was two hundred dollars a month for a room in a four-bedroom place in the Mission in San Francisco. I was scraping by, but I was having these bills, and I needed insurance, I needed a decent medical plan, I needed to figure out a job I could have that was real, decent. I'm a creature of habit. So teaching made sense to me in a lot of ways, having a schedule like that. I wanted to do something arts-related, and I wanted to do something that would make the world a better place in some way, somehow—something social justice–related. Art teaching just seemed like an obvious fit for me, just from experience I have had in the world. I really hated high school—it was very painful for me. So I went into it thinking I could make it a better place for the outliers and outcasts and the queer kids and the kids who didn't totally fit in, and that's kind of the lens I went into it with.

I really changed to an equity focus pretty quickly after I started working in a school like this that's so diverse—you know, where I did fill that role of providing a haven for the outcast. But I really saw the bigger picture of how the high school is kind of a micro version of our macro world, and all the inequities and injustices that exist in our outside world exist in a really intense way within the school, but there's also hope because [high school] is a small place where you can effect change. You have the prison industrial complex that we see as a whole in the macro world. It is daunting and overwhelming to me. So those are some of the reasons why I started. You know, it sounds shallow to say "the health plan," but the health plan was real to me at the time.

John Mink: It is real, yeah.

Miriam Klein Stahl: I really needed health insurance.

John Mink: It is one of the few middle-class amenities left in any job.

Miriam Klein Stahl: And it has been twenty years since then.

John Mink: Are you familiar with the Pedro Noguera book *City Schools and the American Dream*?

Miriam Klein Stahl: I have an essay in that book [laughs].

John Mink: Right, so obviously you're familiar with it [laughs]. [The book deals a lot with] what you are talking about with equity and what he saw as the differential issues.

Miriam Klein Stahl: Yeah, I should really talk about that. I was really lucky as a young teacher; I was twenty-two when I started here—really young. That year was the second year of a thing called the diversity project, where Pedro was the principal investigator, the primary on that.

It was a project as teachers, students, parents, and grad students—PhD students—at University of California. The whole purpose was to hold a mirror up to the high school and say this is what you look like, because there was lots of anecdotal stuff.

So I was this young teacher, and I felt really lucky that I got to work with this group of people who were totally like-minded, because it was like an instant community for me. Otherwise, this place can feel really huge and daunting, and at the time it was just one big school—there weren't any small schools. So it gave me a community of teachers who were also trying to make this place better and had an eye on equity. We'd present the research to the larger staff, and it was very eye-opening for me, because we would present how the school is serving one group of students who have a lot of privilege and resources really well, and kids who didn't have a lot of privilege and resources were just being duped, were not being served well, were totally failing and having a lot of trauma.

John Mink: It almost feels like kids were being dumped into a university where they were being asked to select their whole program, and that's really difficult because of how large the school is.

Miriam Klein Stahl: It was really disturbing but eye-opening for me, as a really young teacher, that there would be veteran staff here who were like, "We know this exists. We know that we are failing with these kids. You're not telling us anything new." And as a young person, I was like, wow! I'm working with all these people who know that there is this huge problem, and that there is this is this huge gap between white and Asian students and Black and Latino students in achievement, yet some of the teachers would say the most horrendous things in those workshops we would do as the diversity project.

So out of that project grew a couple of things that have become part of our school now. One was the Parent Resource Center, which still exists. A lot of parents that we interviewed for the project felt like they would only come to the school in a pissed-off mode. They were coming to school because their kid was suspended or their kid was accused of something. They were never coming to celebrate their kids' achievements. So there is this. . . just pissed off faction of parents, largely parents of color, who were like, "Don't make me come to that school!"

John Mink: They're only invited when there is a problem.

Miriam Klein Stahl: That was a great thing that happened out of the project, a welcoming place for parents to be treated well and invited.

John Mink: Do you feel there has been an effective effort toward outreach with that, actually bringing parents who might not come otherwise?

Miriam Klein Stahl: Yeah. Another thing that was started was PCAD— Parents of Children of African Descent—and that group was very powerful and effective in making change happen at school. Another thing that we got out of [the diversity project] was the small school movement. Our high schools were set up to train people who work in factories, and it feels very much like that. When you hear the bell ring, you get up and you move to another class, you sit down and do your work, you get up and move to another class—it is very much a factory model. There was research about creating schools around themes where you can try to do school in a different way, block time differently, get out of bells and cells, get out into the world. That sounded great to me.

John Mink: How do you feel in the present, a couple of decades into the small school experiment? How do you feel in terms of Berkeley High and the context here and how [small schools] have panned out as far as increasing equity and social justice?

Miriam Klein Stahl: Well, sadly. . . Obviously I am one of the founders of AHA [Berkeley High's Arts and Humanities Academy, a "small school" program of a few hundred students among Berkeley High's more than three thousand students], our small school, and I adore our kids, and I think that we have made huge jumps in achievement. We've had kids come in, freshman class, at 19 percent proficient in English and math and end up graduating with 85 percent of them CSU eligible.

John Mink: That's major.

Miriam Klein Stahl: It's huge. So I feel really good about our student population and what we are able to do with them, and I also like to try to create systems of being in school in a different way; of doing interdisciplinary projects where teachers collaborate. As you know, we just got back from bringing our senior class to overnight retreat, and we bring our juniors on an overnight retreat. A lot of students' experience in schools is that they are not seen, and teenagers want to be seen and heard, and we are taking them out of the school and giving them a chance to say whatever they need to say in a safe environment. This is the kind of thing they need to remember and the thing a lot of them need; the kind of social and emotional support that you can't really do in the classroom.

John Mink: What are some of the ways that teachers at AHA coordinate to create spaces like that and the opportunity for students to have spaces like that, pull together curriculum, and just try to core things in a more integrated way so that [teachers and students] are really working together? What are some of the methods?

Miriam Klein Stahl: There's some big institutional support that's really helpful in the common preps, during which teachers have time to really plan their day, so it's not just free labor after school—that's really key. Being in each other's classrooms. . . a lot of teachers close the door and have their private realm.

John Mink: That's the traditional mode, right?

Miriam Klein Stahl: Yeah, while all of our teachers are in and out of each other's classrooms all the time, and we do month-long projects where we all study the same thing. So our ninth grade students do a project on immigration, tenth graders do a project on respiratory health linked to geography or location—basically environmental racism—and our juniors do radiation, and then our seniors do an investigative journalism project on a topic of their choice.

John Mink: Tying radical [classroom] themes to broader social justice themes—not just within the school community but in terms of their overall communities.

Miriam Klein Stahl: Yeah, and they are in there working on all that in science, history, English, and art, and it culminates in a big exhibition that's on display in downtown Berkeley right now.

Bella (student): I am Isabella DeVito Brown, I am a senior at AHA, and I've been here all four years. So the thing about AHA is that we're a huge community, and we are definitely taught to look at the world in different ways and look past barriers—that's really important. Something that makes us different from the other schools is this interdisciplinary project that Ms. Stahl is talking about, and it's really good because a lot of schools separate this stuff around and between classes, and with the IDP [Interdisciplinary Project] we are blending together all of these important aspects of school and creating this project that might help us look at the world in a different way.

It's really fun, actually. It's one of my favorite things about AHA, because most other students have finals, and I'm like, yeah—I'm making this really awesome book, and I'm learning all this stuff, and it's not just learning about math or science. It's learning about how all these different things mix together to create something different.

John Mink: Kind of makes it all make more sense.

Bella: Yeah, I think every school should do that—an IDP project. It really brings together the whole. . .

Miriam Klein Stahl: . . .interconnectedness.

Bella: Yeah, it really does. It shows you how the world is not just black-and-white, it is really this whole mess of stuff, and that's one of the greatest things about AHA—that's what they show us, that's what they teach us.

John Mink: It shows the point of all these different disciplines too, right? To show how they can actually work together to effect some kind of change.

Bella: You are writing about English. You are writing about history and using all of this English you have learned in school, creating art to help emotion, and to help exemplify what is happening in the world, and it's a lot more powerful than just writing an essay about it.

John Mink: Thank you for that, and it's really nice to hear how effective these programs are. I just did my student teaching last semester here in the International Baccalaureate program, which is way more exam focused for sure.

Bella: Of course the people see that [the exam-heavy curriculum] and go, "Oh, those students are so prepared for the world," but really it is sort of a micro vision of things. Like, "I know exactly what happened in history," but you can't connect that to everything else—which is what is great about [AHA's IDP project]. I think every school should do an IDP project.

John Mink: I think a lot of the other schools may be emulating that model, but maybe not to the extent that this particular program has. So, Miriam, in terms of one really good question here that you got from one of the students in your classes last week—she was asking about when it is okay to be biased when teaching about our culture or social inequalities in our culture, especially when you disapprove of these inequalities. If so, how can you still allow teens to be open-minded/have different perspectives?

Bella: We have a teacher who is sort of biased about stuff.

John Mink: Well, everybody's got some bias, right? I mean, we all have our beliefs.

Bella: Well, the interesting thing is that she's biased on history, so her whole thing is that she shows us all the minorities that were disregarded in history class, so you come out knowing so much more about the Harlem Renaissance, and I could talk about, say, African Americans in this situation, whereas everyone else gets a sort of whitewashed history.

John Mink: Miriam, how do you feel about this question?

Miriam Klein Stahl: Well, I think that question is speaking to the Berkeley Bubble, right?

John Mink: Sure. I mean, it could be applied in converse in Texas, right?

Miriam Klein Stahl: Yeah. I am clearly part of the Berkeley Bubble [laughs]. I am biased.

John Mink: [laughs] Yeah, and transparent about it, right? That's the key.

Miriam Klein Stahl: Totally. [pauses] So I don't know totally how to answer that question.

John Mink: Which is okay. I guess the question, which is from a student, is if you feel it is okay to be "biased," and is there anybody who really isn't biased—I guess that's the issue with the question, right?

Miriam Klein Stahl: I don't think so. I think effective teachers aren't scared to bring in their life experience and who they are and aren't afraid to be vulnerable in that way and be honest about how the world sees you. The students see us. They see a white woman who dresses like a boy, and I'm not going to pretend to be something that I'm not. I'm not going to hide that I'm living in the world in this very queer way, *and* that I have white skin privilege. And I think that you need to be honest about those things to be honest to students, to be real with students and present whatever it is you are presenting. Obviously, it's not relevant for everything you are doing, but I think it's bullshit when these teachers get up in front of a class and think that students don't see anything other than what they are delivering as the content.

John Mink: The context is so important.

Miriam Klein Stahl: Right, so we all have a bias or a perspective we are coming from, and I don't think there's anything wrong with that. Hopefully in a student's day they are getting a diversity of perspectives, anyway, because we all have our view on the world.

John Mink: Right, and of course if you are just teaching the "standard view"—that's a bias as well.

Miriam Klein Stahl: Sure.

John Mink: But I guess these are the questions that students think about, and when we step outside of our bubble, other questions arise. A mutual acquaintance of ours has had struggles in [a nearby district] with regard to [their] identity as openly queer, and that created a lot of problems for [them]. So I guess the context counts too—where we are.

Miriam Klein Stahl: Right, and in a lot of ways I am in a privileged place where I have not experienced homophobia in the classroom.

John Mink: Not openly, anyway.

Miriam Klein Stahl: Yeah.

John Mink: So another student question here: When you teach kids to express themselves through art, is there ever a line not to cross in terms of offending people?

Miriam Klein Stahl: There's always a line to cross. I think that line does get crossed in my classes, and it's always a good conversation to have. I think the thing they butt up against more is creating something and having an idea of how they want it to be seen and having people see it in a way that was not intended, so there's that thing that every artist struggles with. Say you use a swastika in an art piece, and you mean your piece to be anti-racist, is it going to come off as being racist or anti-racist? I think students straddle that line when they choose to make work that can have an emotional resonance with the audience. So that's always a good conversation to have!

The other thing we have conversations about. What was that conversation we were having about the news, intent vs. . . . .

Passing Student: Impact.

Miriam Klein Stahl: . . .intent vs. impact. So even if you choose to put a naked woman in an art piece—which many people do, it's part of the art canon—what is the intent vs. the impact? Is that piece gonna come off as totally sexist—or not?

John Mink: I guess this is an environment where kids can learn about how that goes, which also leads into another excellent student question—I am leaning toward the student questions, because they are better than mine. Leading into how people develop their own styles and their own ways of expression that make the most sense to them, the question was: How do you motivate a teen to create art with their own style, and how do you help a teen discover their style? I would add, how do you make it so they can express themselves in a way that they can be happy or comfortable with?

Miriam Klein Stahl: We started AHA with an eye toward equity—the only reason we started this small school was to address the equity gap—and so, for me, it is really important that students have really strong skills.

In freshman/sophomore/junior year, I focus 90 percent on building technique and skill—because I know that my students need to be better than most people, because they are judged a little harsher because of who they are in the world. So I want them to have really strong skills and technique.

Then, in senior year I focus more on conceptual work and developing ideas and style, and I don't think you can jump into that before you have skill and technique, or it is just frustrating. The senior Advanced Placement class is 100 percent student-focused, where they are developing their skill and technique with their concept and their own personal style. It's a balance of keeping everyone on the same page, hammering in skills and technique, and then knowing when—as a teacher—to back off and let them develop their style and their concepts.

John Mink: And if they always wanted to express it more rawly, they could always stop in at 924 Gilman for the weekend.

Miriam Klein Stahl: [laughs] Sure. [To group of students] So what do you all think makes AHA different from other schools?

Student 1: Teachers care.

Student 2: The teachers are much more. . . people who like each other. [AHA] is not just school; it is about how you build relationships and how you think about the world, not just "do some problems," academics, etc. It is about social skills. I think teenagers need a platform to figure it out. AHA has teachers who are not just teachers, they are friends, and they care about you.

John Mink: You coauthored (illustrated) an awesome looking new book with Kate Schatz coming out this year [2015] titled *Rad American Women A–Z*.[1] How did collaborating with Kate Schatz come about, and what was the process by which the book was completed? How long did it take to create?

Miriam Klein Stahl: Kate is an author and a teacher at the Oakland School of the Arts; she teaches creative writing. I had submitted some images for a previous book project she had done called *Encyclopedia*, a collaboration between her and two other authors. They went out and talked to a bunch of other artists and writers to make a project [where]

---

1   Kate Schatz and Miriam Klein Stahl, *Rad American Women A–Z* (San Francisco: City Lights Books, 2015).

they did a series of encyclopedias and then had authors and artists choose the word they wanted to illustrate or write about.

I did that project, and she liked the work that I did for that. Kate and I are both mothers of young kids. I have a seven-year-old, and she has a five-year-old and a one-and-a-half-year-old. So when she had her daughter, who's five, she had an idea to do a children's book, and there's so few. There's a need right now for diverse children's books. There's a hashtag you may be aware of called #weneeddiversebooks. She had an idea, like, "I want to make a book for my daughter that has rad women in it"—strong, powerful, feminist women. So she thought of doing an A to Z book.

[Kate is] part of this group called "Binders" on Facebook. It's all these women writers. The name came out of that thing from when Mitt Romney was running for president, where he said, "I have binders of women." She kind of put the call out onto there, "Hey, if I did a women A to Z book, what women should be included?" It kind of started there, and she sat with the idea for two years, and then called me, and we had coffee and talked about collaborating on it. So she asked, "Do you want to do this book?" And I tend to say yes, so I said yes. And I had already made paper cuts of five of the women that were on her initial list.

John Mink: What were some of the specific ones that really grabbed you, that you were super stoked on?

Miriam Klein Stahl: Well, she had an initial list, and then we worked on that list together, and that's where our collaboration started. We were in pretty much agreement about most everything besides one—she wanted Sonia Sotomayor for S, and I wanted Sister Karita, this radical nun.

John Mink: When was Sister Karita active? I think my parents were really big fans of hers.

Miriam Klein Stahl: The sixties and seventies, Vietnam War. Yeah, she was awesome [laughs]. So that was our only disagreement. I was mad at Sonia Sotomayor, it was during that Hobby Lobby stuff last summer, and she wasn't saying anything [about it]. I also wanted to kick Patti Smith out at one point, when she decided to play the pope's Christmas party.

John Mink: At least Patti hasn't gone full Exene Cervenka yet.

Miriam Klein Stahl: [laughs] Aw, man. So [Kate and I] met for coffee, and I just started making paper cuts for the people on the list, and I tend to work really fast, so I think I made about twenty of them in a week. It was summer [laughs]. We got A thru E together in a week, and she did the writing for those. I had known Michelle Tea for a really long time, who does Sister Spit and Radar Productions, so I emailed Michelle A through E with the images and some of the writing, and I was like, "Hey! Wanna put out a children's book?" Kate and I were busy and didn't have time to do a kickstarter thing, and I'm not really interested in doing that. I see the value of those projects, but my ideal was to work with a local publisher with a feminist perspective. But Sister Spit is known more for queer debauchery and not children's books [laughs], so I wasn't quite sure—though I knew at the time she was pregnant, so maybe she would be interested. I didn't hear back from her for a couple weeks, then all of a sudden I got an email from her, which was like, "I just saw your email and yes I wanna do the book!" Right after that we had a meeting with City Lights, and they said, "Yeah, we wanna do your book," and I had all the images, so I brought them in a portfolio and they totally loved them. Then Kate wrote the book over the summer.

John Mink: That came together fast!

Miriam Klein Stahl: Yeah, it was really, really quick.

John Mink: [The book] almost seems like it could be a shelf reference or even assigned for classes.

Miriam Klein Stahl: Well, we are both teachers, so we have reached out to teachers to write lesson plans for it in trade for a free book. Wanna make one? I'll give you a book and some posters.

John Mink: I'd love to!

Miriam Klein Stahl: Yeah, we don't have much for middle school or high school lesson plans yet. My kid's at Malcolm X Elementary School in the second grade, and her teacher's doing a whole project with it for International Women's Month. So for the month her class is researching their own rad women and doing drawings and are gonna make their own book, which is really great.

John Mink: Are you going to have the lesson plans online?

Miriam Klein Stahl: We have radamericanwomen.com, and that's meant to be a resource; there will be lesson plans, etc. online there. The book will be available at many independent bookstores, and I always tell people to order direct from City Lights and avoid Amazon.

John Mink: So it was designed as a children's book *and* an educational tool.

Miriam Klein Stahl: It's a really fun kid's book. Me and my daughter, the seven-year old, have been picking one a night—she'll pick a letter and we will read it. She's going to read at some of the local readings. She likes X.

John Mink: Who's X?

Miriam Klein Stahl: X is the unknown woman. The woman who made you dinner. All the women who do things and don't get acknowledged. [Bell sounds, everybody scrambles.]

>> While most of the teachers in this book work in public/state educational systems, the importance of autonomous, independent, collectivist, and explicitly anti-capitalist educational projects across the world cannot be understated. Yet as anyone who has collaborated on such justice-oriented projects knows, collectives and counterinstitutional projects face daunting obstacles in almost every case: internal, external, and experiential. In hindsight, we can learn much from these internecine struggles, but the work must always be evolving and ongoing in order to avoid small-scale reproductions of oppressive systems from the macroworld.

Of the countless physical spaces where semi-autonomous zones and collectivist educational projects have taken root, one of the most well-studied are the postwar squats of Europe. As of 2018, there are now fifty-plus years of academic ruminations on the modern history, practice, and societal reaction to cultural and/or political radicals squatting and transforming abandoned buildings in both Western and Eastern Europe. Belgrade, Serbia, has had a long history with squats dating back to the early twentieth century, and the war-torn, often economically distressed era that followed the breakup of Yugoslavia (1991–1992) has been no exception.

Belgrade's InexFilm was a large, multi-sectional building that was originally built as a production studio for the burgeoning Yugoslav film industry of the mid-twentieth century, before its abandonment and subsequent squatting by a group of artists and radicals in 2011. Koko Lepo, an autonomous, collectively run free school, operated in the InexFilm squat from 2013 until the squat was evicted in 2015. Shortly before the squat was evicted, Koko Lepo was described for September 2015's "Teaching Resistance" column by **Frederick Schulze**, an anarchist, anti-fascist, and teacher who has lived in Central and Eastern Europe for a decade and is an active member of the Koko Lepo youth solidarity program. His scholarly work concerns racism, the state, and political economy in Belgrade. Before he received his doctorate in anthropology on these themes, Freddie worked a lot of odd service and education jobs in Texas, where he developed his anti-capitalist and anti-etatist politics. In this 2018 update of Freddie's original column, he tells the story of Koko Lepo, starting with its inception, and does not shy away from describing the kinds of difficult, real-life internal and external struggles such collectives often face. Freddie has been in Belgrade for over five years and he plans to stay there as long as "they" let him.

Koko Lepo: Kindergarten and the Struggle in Belgrade, Serbia

by Frederick Schulze

> You must learn; spreading fire won't help to light the way.
> —Replica, "Pitchforks and Torches"

In the Summer of 2013, a young woman named Tanja thought of a way to make an impact in Belgrade's only squat, InexFilm. A small group of Serbian anarchists had made themselves a little infoshop there amid the ateliers of rabidly apolitical artists, and Tanja took advantage of the developing social politics of the space to propose a free kindergarten for Roma children. She was no radical herself; in an interview, Tanja admitted that her primary motivation was to ingratiate herself to an avantgarde space that was rapidly picking up steam in Belgrade's alternative scene. This is not to say that she was uninterested in social activism, quite the contrary. She quickly reached out to her friend's NGO, but they did not manage to accommodate the children of nearby Mali Leskovac for long, as the bureaucratic and monetary strictures that define nongovernmental work did not look kindly on the wild informality that defines squat work. Guja was a member of her fresh new collective, a crusty ex-heroin addict from Skopje who sold himself to the general assembly of the squat as an anarchist. He suggested they instead reach out to the nearby Deponija slum which was walking distance away from the squat. Tanja and Guja, along with anarchist feminists Sonja and Maria, went out to meet with Ibn, the patriarch/slum-lord of the fifty-year old "gypsy" settlement, and pitch their idea. Ibn gave them his children and their cousins to participate. Sonja, a member of the nascent infoshop collective, brought this new *vrtić* (kindergarten) into her own collective's space. It was around this time that I caught wind of their project and asked to join.

Back in Texas, I was the "lead kindergarten teacher" of a private after-school and summer program with around thirty kids under my sole care. In my tenure there, I freely experimented with autonomous forms of organizing, super advanced subject matter, and restorative and voluntary systems of justice and redress. I also tried to organize my coworkers into a wildcat union, and my failures and successes there drove me to Eastern Europe in the first place. It goes without saying that the idea of an "anarchist kindergarten" in a squatted warehouse for Roma children from a shantytown hit all my activist buttons, and I was even flattered and intimidated that I could be trusted to join what looked so much like my dream come true. As it turned out, it was not an anarchist kindergarten at all, and my own vestigial liberal tendencies toward "cultural diversity" and the "marketplace of ideas" (as well as reflexive anti-imperialist guilt) culminated into a kind of political paralysis under the patriarchal shadow of the manipulative Guja.

Sure, there were anarchists among us in the beginning, but the bulk of the collective was made up of apolitical young women at whom Guja obsessively leered. You have to understand, he came from what he sold to us as a similarly radical collective in Shutka, the only predominantly Roma municipality in former Yugoslavia. He spoke a Roma dialect conversationally, and it was his familiarity with what I then believed to be Roma culture, coupled by my total unfamiliarity with Belgrade culture and counterculture, that cemented his position in my mind as our unofficial leader. Sure, our collective acknowledged no formal structure beyond consensus and claimed to be autonomous, but Guja was a master at getting what he wanted. He combined his purported expertise with the charisma of someone who had obviously suffered and, in his own words, "loved too much" to push his vision of the kindergarten into our own. He formed strong relationships with the men and women of Deponija, and his presence is still felt today long after his exile, which we'll get to in a moment.

Deponija is Belgrade's largest surviving "gypsy" slum. Between five and eight hundred people live in one of two distinct hemispheres that we refer to as the *mahala* and the *naselje*. The mahala, an old Turkish word meaning "neighborhood" but used in Serbia today mostly for Roma-inhabited areas of a city, is significantly older than the naselje, dating back to the mid-1970s. Residents here are noticeably better-off and more integrated than those in the neighboring section, and their children attend school more regularly. Families here are commonly employed in the city cleaning services and have strong ties to the city itself, their very presence made possible through agreements with formerly state-run firms that stretched back decades, though today their continued existence there is in question. The naselje's residents are mostly refugees from Kosovo, from which upwards of twenty-eight thousand of the province's Roma/gypsy population were expelled due to retaliatory violence from returning Albanian and Serb populations immediately after the war in 1999. These families are primarily occupied as informal waste pickers, and existing literature argues that their existence in the naselje presents an unwelcome competition to recyclers in the mahala, marginalizing them in an already marginalized urban wasteland. The vrtić was almost entirely made up of children from the naselje. Here, garbage is everywhere and running water is a precious luxury, while efforts to mix the two neighborhoods have been generally unsuccessful and remain so today.

Guja's vrtić was didactically authoritarian; it resembled what Paulo Friere used to call the "banking concept of education," just shoving data into well-behaved little minds. Classes were held five days a week in the early morning and each was formally subdivided into rigid parts: introduction, calendar lesson, lecture, songs, meal, and closing games. Despite recognizing the unmistakably repressive basis of Guja's "Little Friends" kindergarten, named after his former group back in Macedonia, his charismatic hold over us was blinding, and we all loved the way we felt, each good intention another paving stone toward what had to get better eventually—right? We enjoyed showing off our grand work to visitors, and Guja himself became the subject of at least one student documentary at Belgrade University. He assured us that gypsy children responded to this sort of thing, and the fact was that our new little friends did listen to Guja. Meanwhile, we found ourselves exhausted and panicked as we herded the kids here and there, always dangling at the edges of our own ropes. Guja seemed to have the little ones wrapped around his finger; he spoke, we listened. "Gypsy kids respond to force," he would claim, "Gypsy kids respond to consistent management," "Gypsy kids only understand punishment," etc. Tough love was the order of the day, its edges softened by "cultural sensitivity."

As it turns out, all that shit really was just as racist, authoritarian, and backwards as it surely looks to you now.

We anarchists slowly began to raise concerns about these tactics when we finally began to feel some collective ownership over our little project. Guja would respond indignantly and act hurt that we had not accounted for his vast expertise in such matters. Our youngest apolitical, Anja, was the first to raise Guja's gendered prejudice in the collective, though by this time he was already becoming a persona non grata for similar reasons in the infoshop that hosted our kindergarten (then called "Little Friends"). He was, Anja claimed, dismissing female voices in our collective meetings and generally throwing his weight around. This was an uncomfortable truth for a lot of us, and having it out in the air was electrifying. I remember this meeting well. We met in his room in the squat (he was the only person to live there at the time) and shortly after Anja's criticism, he told us he had written down the names of every member in the collective, ostensibly for the sake of records, and showed us the paper. Neither of the men in the collective were on this list, and the names were obviously written in order of whom he found most attractive judging by the attention he gave to each woman listed. We stared at him incredulously.

Despite all of this, we anarchists in the group had yet to turn against him. We made him a victim even as he victimized others. He was a recovering addict, we reasoned, and poorly acculturated to a radical political environment. As the weeks wore on, however, his arrested development could go unmentioned no longer, and I was selected to confront him on his increasingly obvious sexism and predatory behavior. I invited him into our brand-new unfinished classroom near the entrance to the squat, a room that finally freed the infoshop from the dirty little burden we had become on the space. The meeting did not go well. I spent the next hour in tears, wondering if I had done the right thing. My comrades assured me that I had, and I ended the night feeling the solidarity of those with whom I would continue the struggle for years to come. From that moment, we were determined to excise Guja from our collective body. By this time, the collective had shrunken to about seven or eight of us: Guja and three to four of his apolitical young female defenders on one side and myself and my two anarchist feminist colleagues on the other. Since our naive commitment to consensus prevented us from ousting him from the vrtić—now, after some internal campaigning, called "Koko

Lepo"—we decided to stick closely by him so as to ensure that neither he nor his supporters would be alone with the kids or parents.

As Guja's spell was broken, at least for us anarchists in the squat and in Koko Lepo, so was his hegemonic hold over the structure of the project. We began approaching the weekly meetings strategically, proposing and achieving fundamental changes to our approach to the kids. Sonja took a Montessori class to introduce us to new tactics, and I began to both believe in and express the value of my own experiences and experiments in Texas. We increased our repertoire of songs, including a number of originals, and started phasing out punishment while making the children more responsible for each other's education by having them lead the calendar lessons and creating multiple simultaneous activities for them to choose from. Perhaps it was this weakening of Guja's grip over us that prompted him to assault little Elena's mother Ela.

Guja went over to Elena's family home in Deponija one rainy day with a trash bag full of clothing from the squat's utterly disorganized "free shop." She let him in out of the rain despite her reservations about having a non-family male adult in the house while she was alone. She told us she trusted him. He said the bags were for her children, and then moved on her, trying to kiss and grab her. Ela resisted, pushing him away and telling him to leave. He continued to press until she shouted out, at which point he fled into muddy slum. Ela told her sister-in-law who then called Sonja. She, Maria, and Guja's closest comrade and staunch defender Una went to visit Ela, who told them the story. Ela said that Guja told her that he was in love with her, that he couldn't stop thinking about her, and that he had to have her. Una knew these words well and heard Guja's voice clearly in Ela's report. She was convinced and became the fulcrum that allowed us to force him out. We asked his other victims to come and speak to their own experiences now that they had an unmistakable context among others and a promise of action— finally. Guja's reign of terror was over. He was banned forever from the squat and, if we have anything to do with it, from Belgrade entirely.

With Guja finally gone, anarchy enveloped our little collective. If you'll forgive a little mashing together of our developmental timeline, I would proudly describe to you the day-to-day of our newly liberated vrtić. We reduced our working days to three to keep from burning out but continued to pick each student up at their homes individually at the start of each morning. Our influence spread rapidly in Deponija, and we soon had "students" joining us from areas previously inaccessible to us. I put scare quotes around "students, because we cycled both that word and concept out of our working lexicon. We would no longer be teachers, just older folks who helped these young'uns figure out what *they* wanted to do with their day. We kept the calendar lesson, but it became optional, the burden moving to us to keep it interesting enough to hold them. Often, we didn't have to lecture at all, as the children who had begun the program with us would take over, particularly a young boy called "Friday," his younger brother "Smiley," and little sister Nora, who lived on the absolute margins of Deponija, both spatially and socially. We abolished all forms of punishment and no longer explained to parents why we had to take some kids home when they posed a danger to others, keeping our business our own and protecting our more violent students from further violence from their family; solidarity means trust. We made sure that the children could expect a hot vegetarian meal every day, a task shared with the children, who often helped us chop, stir, and wash in the squat's dirty little kitchen. Cooking was often done by guests to the squat, some of whom became regular supporters of the project and even minor celebrities among our little comrades.

Reforms were somewhat slowed, however, due to the continued influence of Tanja, the founding mother of the old program, and Mara, close friend of the deposed king, who maintained many of Guja's authoritarian and racist sentiments. Both argued that corporal punishment was a culturally dictated necessity despite our ardent demands that all forms of punishment be abolished outright. Tanja would eventually be reprimanded harshly both for these positions and for apparently betraying the trust of Koko Lepo's radicals in a series of messy events in the squat, and she slowly disassociated herself from us. Mara, on the other hand, would be crudely shouted out of the collective in a dramatic collective meeting about Koko Lepo's uncertain future by yours truly. More radical members would join up, and apolitical members would leave, until finally the politics of Koko Lepo became so well-defined that we were able to collectively author a shared text spelling out our shared values. Our collective would henceforth be founded on three immutable principles: autonomy, equality, and solidarity.

Autonomy meant both autonomy from the state and capital as much as was possible and relying on each other to handle conflicts and reproduce collective responsibility among ourselves, between the children, and in the way the two mixed. Our sense of equality utterly rejected liberal notions of equality of rule and stricture. Instead we sought to attack the foundations of inequality by rejecting authoritarian methods of organizing, undoing the iniquitous norms of gender that were beginning to grow in our young comrades' minds just as they were slowly unraveling in our own, and aggressively addressing racism where and when it developed in our collective, our squat, and our city. Finally, as alluded to above, solidarity meant creating a condition of trust among ourselves in the collective and with the children but also with our supporters in the anarchist and antiauthoritarian scene worldwide. Solidarity with our kids in the naselje and the mahala also meant solidarity against the forces that brought them there and keep them there today. We enshrined these principles in a collectively authored document for future members, inviting all existing members to examine themselves and decide then and there if this was still the collective for them.

The real impetus of this text was the loss of our squat in the autumn of 2015. The property's owner, the ultra-wealthy owner of Jasmin perfumes, met us with a small contingent of private security and offered us a carrot or a stick. We took the carrot after a lot of soul-searching and hard questions to ourselves and each other, keeping as much of our stuff in the squat as necessary until we found a new space, and began phasing ourselves out of the building. Three more attempts at a social squat were made over the years, before we finally gave in and began renting the building now known as AKAB Okretnica on the border of the Deponija mahala. As the squat vanished, so did the kindergarten. Koko Lepo continued in a new form as a youth program, focusing primarily on field trips in the city and encouraging the self-organization of Deponija's young boys and girls, many of them brothers and sisters of our former kindergarteners. We did our best to keep ties with our youngest comrades, but, sadly, as time wore on, our attentions shifted to older participants, finding ourselves with upwards of fifty teens and preteens sometimes joining us. We saw our youngest comrades less and less as the months wore on. With our new space, though, another kindergarten seems inevitable, and there is every reason to expect that we will be made whole once again in due time, one way or another.

The last time I wrote a text about Koko Lepo for "Teaching Resistance" [September 2015], I had blood in my eyes. We were on the cusp of eviction, and my soul was armored with callouses after fending off attacks from "fucking artists," neo-hippies, and gutless libs for what seemed like a lifetime. Now, InexFilm seems like a lifetime ago, and all the fire in my stomach has cooled. The struggle is still painful, and I find myself lashing out at my dearest comrades in AKAB Okretnica when something stokes the embers of old battles now and then. I'm still angry at the world, as all decent teachers must be, but I am also patient with the world, as all decent teachers must be. In contradiction to the bluster with which I began my article for *Maximumrocknroll*'s original column ("a battle may have already occurred," I wrote), I must now admit that I'm not entirely sure where the Koko Lepo collective will be this time next year; perhaps it will not be at all. I can say, however, that if it goes, something better will rise in its place, and if it stays, it will take on new and exciting experimental forms that only a fool would dare to predict. I love Koko Lepo, because I believe in Koko Lepo. I hold dear both what we achieved and what we could not achieve, as well as all the lessons yet to come. Teaching resistance is teaching love, anger, and the courage to acknowledge that a better world is necessary—and knowing that our path there is paved not by our good intentions but by difficult choices, heartbreaking failures, and the support of our comrades struggling alongside us.

>> Miles of ink have been spilled debating and dissecting the fabled school-to-prison pipeline, a problem endemic to the U.S. education system that almost exclusively affects its most socioeconomically disadvantaged students. For these students, realistic options for survival, success, or resistance are always slim and high-risk due to the overwhelming structural obstacles built directly onto their path. Less commonly discussed, however, is the question of what options exist for these students' educational attainment following incarceration at the hands of the state—and what options for survival and resistance remain for them in this most restrictive of mental, physical, and spiritual environments. The next chapter features some powerful reflections from **Lena Tahmassian**, who has taught inmates at San Quentin State Prison, is an assistant professor at a major university in the Southeast, and is a regular contributor to *Maximumrocknroll* magazine. Her column focuses on the importance of not-for-profit prison higher education and solidarity in this post-truth, reactionary era.

What Prison Teaching Can Teach Us

by Lena Tahmassian

> I was brilliant at school but not in exams
> My teachers they could not understand
> How five years work went to the wall
> And then I got into trouble 'cause I got in the way
> When things went wrong, well I got the blame
> I was idle through no fault of my own
> None of my own
> —Newtown Neurotics, "The Mess"

On February 1, 2017, inmates took over a wing of the Vaughn prison in Delaware, protesting Trump and demanding better conditions and "remedies conducive to reform and rehabilitation," with access to education topping the list. A guard who was taken hostage died, and a civil rights coalition began asking for a transparent federal investigation. Little more than that information was made known to the public at the time. While most prisons are public institutions, there is not much knowledge about what goes on in them. This action was highly symbolic: members of the most marginalized and disenfranchised group in society protesting an administration that more than ever will value private profit over basic human rights, an administration making explicit that various—disproportionately nonwhite—sectors of the population are essentially disposable.

Returning to the prisoners' demands, this column is in defense of not-for-profit higher education in prisons and of what this can teach us—not only because my teaching philosophy is underpinned by a fundamental belief that people are not disposable, but also because I believe that teaching and learning go both ways. Teaching in the accredited college program at San Quentin State Prison is an experience that has both shaped my teaching practice and informed my understanding of the prison system. I did prison teaching with a team of co-teachers during the last year and a half that it took to wrap up my PhD dissertation, juggling it with grad student teaching. Since graduating, I have done a stint teaching at a small prestigious liberal arts college and am now in a tenure-track position at a big state school in the South.

Back in California, I got involved in prison teaching through a direct email recruitment from the program director, because there was a shortage of humanities/foreign language instructors. I had been wanting to participate for a while but could never find the moment in which I was not already totally overwhelmed with work and life. I finally just jumped in and found that dedicating an afternoon a week to the cause actually gave me a lot of purpose and helped to structure my time. Happy to have a break doing something less solitary and seemingly individualistic than getting a PhD, I was also hoping to become more comfortable in my teaching skin. I wanted to raise the stakes in what my teaching could accomplish, and I was up for the challenge of teaching people whose experiences would mostly be very different from my own.

Some background about the institution reveals that San Quentin's notoriety can be attributed mostly to its famous visitors (from Johnny Cash to Mark Zuckerberg), housing high-profile inmates and California's only death row, and the institution's proximity to San Francisco and Silicon Valley. Among the California Department of Corrections and Rehabilitation (CDCR) men's prisons, San Quentin is perhaps best known for its many programs including the on-site university where students can earn an associate's degree free of cost, so many people end up there through requesting a transfer. Being in a Level 2 institution that is relatively resource-rich, the average general population inmate spends most of the day outside of the cell, working (for wages so low that it has been considered a form of slavery) and participating in various programs, activities, and groups.

For volunteers, getting into the compound is a regimented but streamlined process. The route from the parking lot to the classroom includes passing through two security checkpoints and traversing the prison yard. The yard is a curious scene where all kinds of daily activities take place together out in the open—exercise, guitar, grooming, laundry, use of urinals, etc. We intruders are typically well received, especially by students of the program who walk and chat with us (as we're not allowed to stop in the yard), while other guys are indifferent, and a few of them stare you down a bit. The geese pecking away at the dried grass on the track is a reminder that beyond the enclosure, just barely walled out from view, is the idyllic bay. After signing in, I grab my box of supplies and get to the classroom where the early students greet me and ask me to chime into their debate on current events.

Fundamentally, prison teaching is not *that* different from teaching more conventional college students, but with some logistical limitations and nuances specific to interacting with incarcerated adults. Prison students have little to no access to technology, and instructors cannot use any technology in the classroom. This imposes obvious limitations, but the success of prison education also raises the question of the extent to which perpetual classroom "innovation" is a creation of false needs. Awareness of classroom dynamics and building a healthy rapport is important in all teaching, and this is accentuated in the prison classroom, because the stakes are higher. For example, what the prison administrators refer to as "overfamiliarity" with the students is forbidden for various reasons, mostly safety related. Perhaps most importantly, though, even if it's really the instructor's fault for becoming too friendly, overfamiliarity can result in disciplinary action taken against the student, which can interfere directly with their daily life, parole prospects, etc. Also, it is always good to keep an eye on class participation and to try to distribute the space taken up by each student as evenly as possible. Again, this is part of a methodology that I apply to my everyday teaching, but which can carry weightier consequences teaching in prison. Incarcerated students are, in general, deprived of interaction, and many view taking classes as an opportunity to express themselves verbally as well as creatively. Letting one or a few students take up a disproportionate amount of space can generate resentment among students as well as toward the instructor.

On that note, when the student's everyday reality is characterized by literal confinement, the classroom acquires a new, liberating dimension. I think this is particularly true of humanities education because studying other cultures and in other languages is a form of traveling and reexamining one's place in the world, especially if one lacks the right to physical movement. Students are eager to speak and share their experiences, and the classroom is, unlike their cellblocks, racially integrated. The notion that education can transform your life seems epitomized in this highly restrictive environment.

For us, as instructors, being a volunteer in a free program is liberating, provided you have the free time to give. This dynamic does seem to partially inform the students' attitudes, which shift more toward "Thanks for teaching us!" than the "Hey, I'm paying for this!" vibe of the increasingly neoliberal academy. I suppose that in defense of the "student as consumer" mindset from a student perspective, the astronomical cost of higher education, and the fact that many students will be indebted into the foreseeable future, places increasing pressure on them to see learning as a serious financial investment on which they must see a return (more on this later).

Incarcerated students tend to ask: "Is this how they do things at (Stanford, Berkeley, etc.)?" They want to know that they are being challenged and not patronized. It is also a good practice for me to always question and reflect on my methods by having to explain why we assess learning a certain way. I've come to believe strongly, however, that it's not just about importing and adapting methodologies from the elite academy to those who in many cases were never afforded the opportunity of higher education, but that prisoners also have a lot to teach us. The average student age is over forty, and bringing all of their diverse life experiences to the table opens up new possibilities for discussion.

Living on the outside permits one to slide through life avoiding problems, burying traumas, repeating mistakes, and never facing insecurities head on. For those seeking rehabilitation, on the other hand, self-reflection is unavoidable and can be a matter of life or existential death. Continuous reflection on the circumstances and choices in one's life that resulted in incarceration is often bound up with understanding and identifying a twisted (and all too widespread) conception of masculinity and fundamentally changing these patterns of thought and self-identification. I've observed that the various programs offered, including college education, help develop self-awareness, discipline, resolve, and an intense spirit of cooperation. Those who go through the rehabilitation process have accomplished the very difficult task of confronting their issues head on and facing those whose lives they may have damaged. To survive and thrive within the walls for the time being, one must be able to imagine something better beyond them. Perhaps this is something we can all learn from. While I've taught in very different learning environments, my basic objectives are fundamentally the same: to teach students to create meaning out of texts and to critically think and rethink the basis of knowledge production.

Yes, there are some truly damaged people who may be incapable of, or unwilling to, change. What seems to ring true for any type of rehabilitation is that you have to genuinely want (or at least begin by wanting to want) to change yourself. It has been my impression that completely intransigent inmates constitute a minority of the prison population, and they, in turn, are the prisoners who are amplified through media representations of criminals and criminality. My classes were composed of a sample of the general population, from those with a reasonable expectation of getting out of prison to lifers with no possibility of parole. The general population excludes those in protective custody who are likely to be targets (i.e., sex offenders, active gang members, former cops) and those on death row—referred to as the "condemned"—who are deemed by the institution to be unworthy of resources and rehabilitation programs altogether.

By advocating for prison higher education, I know that ethically I may be mostly preaching to the choir here. But when the empathy bridge fails—for the naysayers at your next family function or before smashing the "unfriend" button on someone—it helps to explain that educating the incarcerated also makes a lot of sense from a practical standpoint. Even though most of us don't have much of a clue nor think about what goes on in prisons, we nevertheless fund them through our taxes. Like it or not, most prisoners are eventually released, and access to education while incarcerated dramatically decreases the rate of recidivism. Higher education in prison is a common good, and those who initiated the Vaughn prison uprising surely also believed that. But the new status quo of corporate fascism—or to be more precise, authoritarian capitalism—is indeed a double whammy, as it seeks to designate enemies of the state *and* profit off of their subjugation, which can take the form of public prison labor and private prison contracts, border walls, armaments, immigrant detention centers, etc.

The college program at San Quentin in its current form, funded entirely by private donors (like many of the programs across the country), emerged in 1994 as a solution to the revocation of Pell Grants (federal higher education funding) for prisoners. The Violent Crime Bill—written by the then senator Joe Biden and signed by Bill Clinton—defunded all prison higher education. Barack Obama reintroduced funding for prison education before leaving office, but its future is unclear. Opposition to federally funded prison education seems to be rooted in a sense of morality or a warped conception of fairness—i.e., "Why should a murderer get a free education when I did everything I was supposed to and yet I am drowning in student debt?" I would suggest reframing the question: Why is it that you either have to end up in prison or be shackled—so to speak—by debt in order to access higher education? Shouldn't we demand better? The fact that the prison population has nearly doubled since 1994, and that state expenditure on prisons has increased by even more than that—to the point where many states now spend more on prisons than on education—raises serious concerns about American society's values.

Meanwhile, slashing taxes has constituted an enticing political platform in America precisely because we apparently get so little in return—education, housing, and health care have become increasingly commodified and unattainable. In the meantime, public funds are poured into waging wars, the prison system, and securing the border—in other words, exercising the sovereign right to exclude. Ultimately, the double whammy is that those who come to power on the platform of the privatization of everything (in other words, the separation of "my" money, goods, and services from that of *those other* [less deserving] people) are those who ultimately benefit most from inequality and exclusion, both materially and politically.

A bigger picture begins to emerge illustrating how designating a sector of the population as existentially "bad" people seems to generate valuable political currency (read: "We need prisons in place so that society can function; we need borders so that we can be a country"). Considering prisons as a sort of border space and recognizing the tendency to demarcate the space between the "we" and the—often racialized—other shines a light on the political value of conflating crime with nonwhiteness. To make matters worse, many of the hundreds of thousands who are processed through the prison system remain disenfranchised (lose their voting rights) for life.

How does one combat this self-fulfilling prophecy of retreating to private individualism, either as an adherent to consensus politics, or as a left-wing defensive position in avoidance of this reality? If there is to be any hope of changing course, we have to avoid the ideological trap of pursuing an agenda of political purity over meaningful engagement. My hope is that promoting critical thinking and cultural competency helps to build the understanding and respect for people's humanity that is lacking in the increasingly dominant political discourse and the worldview it represents and shapes. These days, people seem to be asking a variation of the difficult question: "What is our responsibility to people we disagree with?" This debate has manifested itself in response to highly mediatized issues, such as the cultural phenomenon of the viral punching Richard Spencer meme in 2017, the return of neo-Nazi visibility in its various forms, and the antifa responses, liberals defending free speech over all else, debating the right to defend or destroy confederate statues, etc.

There may be a simple formula for tackling this quandary: if your worldview is defined by exclusion and denying people's humanity, then you're actually the one shutting down the possibility for discussion. But how do we get this point across? Do we have a better shot at trying to convince liberals or those who have adopted the most troubling views? Should we try to change people's minds? Is there a tool to measure when it's no longer worth our breath? I don't purport to have the answers, but if and when it's not too late for discussion, I have come to believe that more than ever it is important to default first to openness rather than exclusion, to try to judge people less. A prevalent attitude I've observed on the left, especially among those who identify with a marginal identity or have endured a lot of hardship, is something to the effect of "It's not my job to school you, to do the emotional or mental labor, just because *you* don't get it." Fair enough, sometimes there are legitimate reasons for adopting this attitude, but it can also be a symptom of a larger problem of refusing to engage with political power as it stands, which imposes some serious limitations on what we are able to accomplish.

For some, it literally is our job to school people and help expand their horizons. The demands of the teaching profession dictate, rightfully, that you must in principle give everyone a fair shot at learning, whether that entails engaging with someone who took another's life for no good reason or a student who is truly offended by Black athletes kneeling for the national anthem. I think that because of this, teachers are in a privileged position to promote dialogue, expand minds, question existing bases for judgment, and also to build empathy bridges in the classroom and way beyond. While a lot of my students, both in the prison classroom and on college campuses, share my worldviews, many do not; and in light of the current reality in which the failures of liberal democracy are being effectively converted into political currency for the far right, I'm all for increasing the possibility of encounters with people you would probably otherwise never engage with. Sometimes I feel like our social media echo chambers will truly be the death of us. However, on a positive note, there is a whole new generation of resistance cropping up who are questioning what they have been told about who the "bad guys" are in the first place. The consensus has fallen out. Let's hope that sliding back to the former status quo is not the best we can do.

On a final note, I do not intend here to present incarcerated students as a uniform group. Rather, I have both reflected on my anecdotal experiences and called on empirical evidence to highlight some trends—both the hopeful and the troubling. I encourage grad students, graduate degree holders, and higher education faculty to get involved with prison teaching in your area. There are also organizations that take book donations to send to incarcerated people—I've met students who have accessed interesting and surprising literature this way! You will likely talk to many interesting people, learn about the prison system, and subsequently become a prison abolitionist or at least an advocate for the humanity of those who deserve a second chance, or even an actual first chance, at a decent life. Compounded by the fact that American reality is now producing marginality at a rapid rate, it has been reassuring to hear the marginal voices growing louder and more plentiful in the last months. We must continue to defend the basic rights of those who have no voice at all.

>> The reactionary, even neofascist, character of how political power is exercised in the present (circa 2019) seems unrelenting. Its unapologetic (almost gleeful) brutality and hyper-oppressive rhetoric toward marginalized people are almost enough to make liberals and some progressives pine for theoretically "simpler" times, such as 2015 (when the following essay was originally written), when ostensible "political centrists" controlled the levers of power in much of the industrialized world and political rhetoric was not quite so openly racist, misogynist, and xenophobic. And it is true, for example, that there was no serious consideration of objectively ludicrous ideas, such as arming teachers, and political rhetoric could, theoretically, very well shift back to a purportedly more "civil" tone in the years ahead.

The current hypercharged tone and wackadoo ideas of those in power aside, however, the mechanisms and manner of deployment of power and violence by the state has changed little over the last few decades (or centuries). When we look at the example of policing in the United States, which has consistently and relentlessly brutalized Black and Brown people regardless of the tone of political rhetoric, it becomes apparent that any real change in how we approach discipline as teachers will, necessarily, not include cops in the equation. As noted above, I wrote the following essay in 2015 and have watched as militarization and the armed police presence in schools has steadily increased, with the bipartisan political support of both major parties in local and national government. Nascent restorative justice programs have been eliminated (as recently happened in Oakland), active shooter drills have been ramped up, and cops make the rounds constantly. Meanwhile, radical teachers fight on the ground to try to keep these cops as far away from students as possible—it is a matter of life or death.

Cops Out of Our Schools!

by John Mink

> They already built the fences
> Clipped your feathers, built your tethers
> —Poison Girls, "Fear of Freedom"

Cops and teachers: both have been the subject of shit-talking by punk bands since the first day some zitty kid from nowhere decided to pick up an instrument they didn't know how to play and immediately sing songs about how and why things suck, especially things they have to personally deal with. Both teachers and cops were and are worthy targets of hatred—cops always, teachers frequently. Both serve as instruments of coercive authority that is often institutionally supported, and both can act as lethal agents of oppression in that capacity (often in tandem). Both tend to treat their "charges" in very different ways, depending on the levels of structural privilege said "charges" have from their individual circumstances and specific context, with highly dissimilar personal outcomes based on race, gender, sexuality, class, and other factors being the norm. In their modern form, both policing and teaching sprang from colonialism, slavery, and capitalism, and both professions are subject to overwhelming, relentless top-down pressure from those who explicitly support those toxic practices/philosophies from which the modern professions sprung.

The difference between teachers and cops, however, lies in their basic functions on the social and individual level and in the methods by which they work. Philosophically, the difference is simple and stark: teachers are (at least on paper) expected to nurture, support, and protect their students as human beings, while the function of police is to protect private property and enforce law by capturing and punishing those who they suspect of breaking it. On the surface of it, these professions should not share any common ground. In practice, in the modern world these professions often dovetail into interconnected mechanisms of social control that explicitly and implicitly (quietly) maintain established hierarchies of structural inequality and injustice. We ignore the history of these institutions at our peril, and the history of both policing and modern state-directed teaching practice are full of stark disparities that forcefully (and often lethally) marginalize many, while others benefit from levels of structural privilege carefully calibrated to maintain the status quo.

Punks are (and have been) right to go after both teachers and cops, as both have long track records of serving as agents of oppression. Yet we need to keep in mind that the basic function of these professions is different at the core. There is no way that policing can be utilized in a liberatory fashion for marginalized people who necessarily come into contact with police, and it almost always ends up as purely toxic to those people who are being "policed." In contrast, it has been shown time and time again that teachers who are genuinely dedicated to the core (non-institutional) philosophies of their profession can, through radically innovative practices and active subversion of the institutional aspects of their jobs, play a major role in helping empower their students to take greater control over their own lives and potentially become catalysts for effecting real structural/social change.

This difference is why there are punks who are teachers, but there are no cops who are punks, at least not by any definition of "punk" that makes any sense at all.

Back in the fall of 2015, just about everyone in the U.S. (and probably much of the world) saw the video of a Black girl student in a South Carolina high school being beaten in class, dragged violently from her seat by a white male cop who worked at the school. The reason offered for this abuse of the student's civil rights was that she was being "disruptive" by refusing to relinquish her cell phone to the teacher, and then refusing an order to leave class with the cop—while she never once acted violently toward the teacher or the cop.

The defiant student's removal by force, with the cop flipping her out of her seat and dragging her across the classroom, was initially welcomed and approved of by the teacher and school administration. The student was arrested, as was another student (also a Black girl) who was filming the incident and verbally confronted the cop. Both students faced charges under a notorious South Carolina law that prohibits "disturbing schools" (there are similar laws in twenty states), with penalties up to one thousand dollars in fines and ninety days in jail. After the video was posted, amid a massive national outcry and some protests, the charges against the girls were (eventually) dropped, and the cop was fired, though he was not charged with any misconduct or violation.

While this individual case was thoroughly and obviously fucked on about ten thousand levels, it is far from isolated. Undocumented versions of incidents like this happen to young Black and Brown students on a daily basis in public schools across the United States. In the aftermath of such incidents, the law is weaponized against Black and Brown students via statutes like the "disturbing schools" law (partially amended in South Carolina in 2018), under which Black students were four times more likely than their white counterparts to be charged and sent into the juvenile justice system. The core problem, of course, is racism, where teenagers being teenagers are not all subjected to the same structures and consequences for similar actions. Even beyond extreme examples of draconian laws like the "disturbing schools" statutes, there are specific structures of racist/white supremacist oppression embedded deep in modern public school disciplinary procedures across the United States. These structures guarantee these situations will endlessly repeat unless things fundamentally change, from the institutional level to one-on-one communications in the classroom.

Let's go ahead and state what should be obvious: cops do not belong in schools, period. In fact, as radical educators (particularly in schools with high proportions of socioeconomically disadvantaged students of color), we should be doing everything in our power to insulate and protect our students from contact with police and the punitive, oppressive institutions they represent. Just about any contact with police inevitably becomes toxic for these students, beginning a downward cycle into the modern slavery of incarceration; the long-term result often being fatal. If we do nothing, the school-to-prison pipeline will only widen and suck more young Black and Brown people into its hungry maw.

Obviously, structural racism has been a constant in our institutions (including the schools), but how did we get to the specific, hyper-punitive point we are at? When did schools become an extension of the police state? Cops are only posted to active duty in urban (and low-income suburban) schools because of a lingering Faustian "law and order" bargain made between mainstream liberals and conservatives back in the 1980s and early 1990s. This was a time when the drug war and middle-class hysteria about teenage gang violence were at a fever pitch. Highly punitive, often racist legal approaches—mandatory minimum sentencing, increased criminalization of drug addicts, disparate law enforcement/sentencing for crack vs. powder cocaine, heightened profiling and mass round-ups of Black and Brown "gang members," privatization of prisons, etc.—created a hostile new legal environment with dozens of nasty traps set primarily to ensnare young people of color.

During the peak of this hysteria, teens were widely tried in court as adults for the first time, setting the stage for lifetimes of total marginalization and prison labor exploitation that bears an uncomfortable resemblance to indentured servitude at best and slavery at worst. Schools filled their halls with cops, metal detectors, and "zero tolerance" policies that resulted in countless arrests over minor (primarily drug-based) infractions—despite the fact that the vast majority of serious violence between students, particularly involving weapons, occurred off campus and away from the purview of these campus cops. Meanwhile, the gangs, which often provided the most potent social cohesion and sense of empowerment that many poor students of color had, eventually came to a state of relative peace with each other and ceased open warfare in most major U.S. regions (with a few notable exceptions).

This slowdown in organized gang violence dovetailed with grass-roots community building efforts, macroeconomic changes, and other factors that together drastically reduced street violence in impacted communities. The decrease in overall violence was either ignored by policymakers or erroneously credited to an increasingly militarized police presence and "zero tolerance" policies (including longer-term incarceration of young teens), which served mainly to increase tensions and make things markedly worse in many ways. Experts on the subject tend to agree that the constant presence of cops in urban and low-income suburban schools had little or no positive effect on those particular environments, and the involvement of law enforcement in many nonserious on-campus infractions has, in fact, had a very distinct negative impact that is reflected in a vast increase in the lifelong criminalization of young Black and Brown people. We now must wrangle with the multigenerational fallout from this unprecedented widening of the school-to-prison pipeline.

Meanwhile, highly publicized mass school shootings in rural areas and exurbs (well-off, predominantly white outer suburbs) like Columbine, Colorado, and Parkland, Florida, have contributed to lingering public acceptance for continuing and even increasing the armed police presence in urban (and low-income suburban) public schools. This is despite the fact that these heinous mass shootings have been almost exclusively perpetrated by young white males and generally take place in schools with predominantly white populations—schools that rarely have a substantial, consistent police presence on campus.

Fear and racial prejudice continue to drive support for punitive approaches in schools today, from parents, administrators, politicians, and others. Sadly, these approaches are also supported by many teachers, who have bought into white supremacist narratives, have been bamboozled by harsh "discipline" policies that just make us into cops ourselves, or are simply overwhelmed and poorly trained in de-escalation, empathetic communication, and restorative justice techniques. With countless resources available for these nonpunitive techniques online, in print, and through direct training seminars, teachers and counselors should not only familiarize themselves thoroughly with them but be ready to openly agitate and fight for their implementation and full support at the district level and higher.

As teachers, *we* need to push for a paradigm shift in schools. We need to leave behind the lazy, oppressive option of violence that we perpetrate by pushing the big, shiny red panic button and calling police in to handle problems that could be handled in a better way. We need to get rid of the cops in our classrooms *and* in our heads. We need to fight to change the entire system from a punitive model to a healing/restorative model, and we need to say *cops out* of our schools!

>> Radicals know better than to make assumptions that any nation-state, particularly one based around a capitalist system, will have a government that will meaningfully provide for all its residents, work consistently to increase universal equitability, and have a system that promotes restorative social justice. At best, even the most seemingly benign of governments must be relentlessly pressed upon, and often actively resisted, to ensure that it maintains basic respect for and accountability to its people.

However, living in the United States, particularly in openly neofascist times such as these, it is easy for me (and many other people) to indulge "grass is greener" fantasies about what life must be like living under the robust social welfare systems of other countries. In particular, we are intellectually tempted to idealize governments in Northern and Central Europe, though we are aware that the prosperity and relative social equity found in these countries is often the direct result of colonialist genocides, exploitation, and centuries of theft. We warily watch but still underplay the rise of formerly fringe parties on the neofascist far right across the continent on platforms of racial exclusion and resentment. And while it is true that quality of life for most people is overall better in, say, Germany, if one scratches the surface it can become evident that the brutality of capitalism, exploitation, racism, and intense political oppression of radicals still lies very close to the seductive surface.

The following chapter is written by **E. Schmuse**, a political radical and teacher in the German state of Bavaria. E. Schmuse is a pseudonym used by the author due to the harsh Bavarian state policies about the personal political ideologies (to say nothing of actual activism) of teachers.

Becoming a Teacher in Bavaria: Making Up and Finding Leeway within Structural Conservatism

by E. Schmuse

> Democracy is a con job they got you fooled
> if you step out of line they'll have you pulled.
> You can't go against them it ain't allowed
> so watch yourself, hide in the crowd.
> —DIRT, "Object Refuse Reject Abuse"

I hesitate before I tell people that I work as a teacher: the ties between the profession itself and the systemic conservatism in Bavaria just seem indefensibly strong. To give people a rough idea of Bavaria beyond Lederhosen and Oktoberfest, some use the tongue-in-cheek comparison: "It's the Texas of Germany." Drawing on stereotypes, the implied notion is that of a southern, very traditional, religious, and conservative federal state that sports a strong sense of identity and historical uniqueness. By and large, that is true. Although its history is indeed fascinating and at times quite ambivalent in its political currents, it is more than fair to write that Bavaria is one of the most conservative states in Germany: tough law enforcement, mostly exclusionary and monolithic concepts of identity and language, adherence to the Roman Catholic Church, and the list goes on.

Bavaria is the largest federal state in land area and the second most populous state in Germany and has been governed by the Christian Democratic and conservative CSU (Christian Social Union) without coalition partners since 1962. It is important to note that the responsibility for the educational system in Germany lies with the federal states. Bavaria's three-tiered school system has a reputation for being rather conservative but also for providing a fairly high standard of education compared to other federal states. That is partly ascribed to the extensive training you have to go through to get a teaching degree here. For the highest level of secondary education at a Gymnasium (sometimes compared to British grammar schools or to prep schools in the United States), aspiring teachers complete about five years of studies at a university and sit for final state exams in at least two majors, which amounts to something like a master's degree in both subjects—in my case, English and history, with social studies as a third.

After university, the practical part of teacher training takes another two years, followed by a second state exam—the preparatory service, or *Referendariat*. This is when the political reality of Bavaria hits the student teachers. Structural conservatism is deeply ingrained in the Bavarian civil service, and it becomes palpable during the preparatory period. To apply and register for the training program, you have to sign that you have never—financially or ideologically—supported any of the organizations and parties named in a very extensive list. It includes a variety of religious sects and fundamentalists, extreme leftist and right-wing groups, and terrorist organizations—in short, groups that do not uphold the values of the German constitution. While much of this makes sense (and not only from a state's perspective), two items on that list should be pointed out here, because they epitomize the general political climate in Bavaria. The first is the democratic socialist party Die Linke (The Left), which is one of the parties represented in the German parliament, the Bundestag. Without question, when it was founded Die Linke showed very problematic continuities from the Socialist Unity Party (SED) that ruled the GDR, but it is now no longer generally considered extreme left or a threat to the democratic and constitutional order in Germany by the Federal Office for the Protection of the Constitution (Verfassungsschutz). This deviation from federal policy is not unusual for Bavaria. In practical terms, you cannot become a teacher in Bavaria if you are a member or supporter of Die Linke. Such caution does not seem to be exercised at the other end of the political spectrum. The right-wing to far-right party Alternative für Deutschland (AfD, Alternative for Germany) won 12.6 percent of the vote in the German federal election of 2017. However, membership in this German nationalist and populist party is not an exclusion criterion for teaching in Bavaria.

The second remarkable item listed is "anti-fascist action coalitions." Although the Ministry of the Interior claims that in this case the individual circumstances are decisive, the broadness of the phrasing is deliberate and dangerous. It leaves every teacher with anti-fascist and leftist stances in a relative state of insecurity at a time when populist, exclusionary, and even anti-democratic views are becoming part of the political landscape. To give a few examples: the ruling party in Bavaria, the CSU, led by Markus Söder, the president of Bavaria since March 2018, and Horst Seehofer, the leader of the CSU since 2008 and minister of the interior, building and community since 2018, has enforced a series of decrees and laws to toughen their law-and-order policies. Fearmongering and soundbite rhetoric against migrants and asylum seekers (Söder: "asylum tourism") translates into harsh border security and so-called "transit centers" to prevent people from (legally) entering Germany and to facilitate deportations. In May 2018, the Bavarian state parliament (Landtag) drastically extended the powers of Bavarian law enforcement at the expense of civil rights and liberties. As of June 2018, Christian crosses are mandatory in all state government buildings in Bavaria to "uphold its cultural traditions."

This set of anti-immigration practices, an identitarian and monolithic assertion of culture, and the strict security policies are being fuelled by the rise of the right-wing AfD and the sharp decline of voter support for the CSU. On his birthday in June 2018, Horst Seehofer joked that the number of deportations that day coincided with his age (sixty-nine). As air-sea rescue is being criminalized, and the external borders of the EU are being fortified, the recorded number of migrant deaths in the Mediterranean for 2018 has reached almost 1,500. Looking north, the by and large peaceful protests against the G20 summit in Hamburg were portrayed as civil war–like events by the tabloids. Former German minister of the interior Thomas de Maizière announced on August 25, 2017 that Indymedia Linksunten, a German Indymedia site, would be raided and shut down. In June 2018, Bavarian activists of the "Chaos Computer Club" (Europe's largest association and NGO of hackers for governmental transparency and freedom of information) were subject to searches and confiscations under flimsy legal pretexts. Populist demands for tougher stances and prevention programs against the "far left" are not only voiced by the AfD. Right-wing violence reached a frightening peak, with over 3,500 attacks on asylum seekers and shelters in 2016 alone. Meanwhile, refugee centres continue to "suffer near daily attacks," and the trial of the extreme-right terrorist organization the National Socialist Underground (2013–2018) has provided crushing evidence of institutionalized racism within the German security services.

During my brief time as a teacher, conservative, right-wing, and discriminatory views have sometimes surfaced quite openly. I have seen this in the racist or anti-Semitic jokes that are casually told by one fellow history teacher in training, recurring varieties of chauvinist and sexist behaviour in the staff room, and a member of the school administration who openly reads literature from a publishing house known for producing books overflowing with conspiracy theories, esoteric Nazism, right-wing populism, pseudoscience, and far-right politics. These examples provide a glimpse of the level of political normalization that far-right ideologies have apparently achieved, which continues to go unchallenged. Maintaining a political stance in the workplace may seem complicated, but if the very documents you signed to work as a teacher leave deliberate room for interpretation of what is "too extreme" on the left, this adds yet another layer of concern.

Needless to say, it is essential to speak out and uphold emancipatory and anti-fascist views in times like these. But questions arise: Could you be removed from your position as a teacher if you attend a talk or discussion in your spare time that is organized by a local group that might be considered "antifa"? What if you use leftist symbols at concerts you organize, perform at, or attend to introduce emancipatory and inclusionary aspirations into that particular event or space? What if you take part in a demonstration against fascist groups? Could that be considered an unacceptable enough form of an "anti-fascist action coalitions"? Is it necessary to use a pseudonym when you write about a political issue?

These questions are not simply hypothetical, because the system of preparatory service does not encourage critical thinking and individuality—it suppresses them. While the Bavarian constitution states, "Schools shall not only impart knowledge and skills but also develop the nobleness of the heart and the character," the opposite is required to complete the two years of teacher training. The reasons are systemic. A short digression might be necessary to understand the various converging layers of pressure here: depending on the federal state, shortsighted hiring policies make the recruitment situation for teachers rather bleak, despite a proven shortage of teachers; teachers in training are used to fill this shortage in Bavaria, and thus are systematically overworked and underpaid. To become a fully qualified and pursue a career as a teacher, it is necessary to complete the preparatory service with outstandingly high marks. Given the fact that each seminar instructor for the respective subjects not only coaches but also evaluates and marks the aspiring teacher, their didactical and pedagogical views develop a dogmatic quality.

To put it plainly, teacher training means to fall in line with your instructors without question, discussion, or critical thought. Of course, this description of the overall structural dependency and subordination should not obscure the fact that there are, in fact, instructors who deviate from this pattern—there are always exceptions to the rule. Yet the unchecked power structures ensure that sympathy and antipathy turn into favouritism and bias on a systematic basis. Supervision and evaluation of the instructors, as well as confidential complaint management, are scarce.

The scope of what the instructors are subjected to varies from the pedestrian to the devastating. It is the 3:00 a.m. email that is relevant for the next workday, the sexist remark about the outfits of female coworkers, and, in some cases, degradation and verbal abuse of teachers in training. Double standards regarding professionalism, quality of teaching, organization, and pedagogic reliability are daily fare. Moreover, developing a personal teaching style is hindered when meticulously copying the instructors' views is a prerequisite for success—the graded demonstrations of your teaching skills become showcases of imitation. In short, highly educated, confident adults are systematically turned into yes-people, because they cannot afford to risk their grades. Sooner or later, every colleague has admitted to anxiety, depression, and/or frustration because of the working conditions. The seminar instructors, who should be didactically sound trainers of aspiring teachers, often do little more than point out mistakes. This systemic failure of pedagogy is worsened by the aforementioned political issues. In this context, every "let's agree to disagree" uttered by instructors has proven to be not an acknowledgement of intellectual diversity as part of an academic professional discourse but a euphemism for a lowered grade. Ironically, one instructor lamented that he had to view his trainees as "neuters," because the political climate did not allow controversial debate anymore. The very same instructor ranted about "multiculti ideology," slandered gender equality, and recommended pseudoscientific literature by climate sceptics. Teachers in training are worn out by the struggle between personal convictions and structural constraints, compounded by the unfortunate necessity to sell one's labour.

This might be the time to explain the subtitle of this essay: "Making Up and Finding Leeway within Structural Conservatism." "Making up leeway" is why I decided to become a teacher despite the structural conservatism of the work environment, despite these problems and concerns. Structural change in the Bavarian education system might seem frustratingly slow and maybe even unobtainable. Hence, it is more than understandable why many socially and politically conscious or active people might eschew a profession within the constraints of the education system. However, in practice, I strongly believe that it does make a difference what kind of teacher stands in front of or amid a class of young people. Conservatism is left unchallenged if key positions that might enable us to question and shape society are left to the conservative, or even the reactionary. "Finding leeway" is, therefore, identifying and using the corridors for action in the curriculum to emphasize critical approaches to the educational content.

It is fortunate that the Bavarian curriculum, in fact, provides that option: exploring the ambivalence of nationalism in the nineteenth century, teaching about the importance of the Lutheran Reformation, while also challenging Luther's anti-Semitism, giving pupils the opportunity to learn about European voyages across the globe in the Early Modern Age, but also mentioning that "discovery" in this context is far from being a neutral or appropriate term. Not only history lessons but English classes also offer the possibility to discuss current events and highlight progressive perspectives. Some textbooks might still use the word "Indian," but at least they cover the discrimination against Native Americans in the film industry. It is up to the teacher to provide learning opportunities that question exclusionary concepts of society, reveal the political ideologies in phrases and words, and show that some of the text, images, and videos are not just learning materials for defining relative clauses or introducing new vocabulary and are more than just as an occasion to speak English. Given the right approach, they have the potential to inform, to challenge, and to spark critical thinking. Idealistic? Of course—but not impossible. For me, it was uplifting and sometimes crucial to see that some members of the resident staff shared these views.

Despite the forces of conformity within the education system, teaching has the power to encourage "what Brazilian Educator Paulo Freire . . . expressed as the very essence of being human—the ability to act in and (re-)create reality through culture, and to be in the world not just as a participant of history but as creators of history. In this light, revolution and societal transformation is not just an inevitable result of history but an objective reality organized by people conscious of their own consciousness and drawing on their creative abilities mediated by particular historical, objective material conditions."[1]

---

1   Curry Malott and Milagros Peña, *Punk Rockers' Revolution: A Pedagogy of Race, Class, and Gender* (New York: Peter Lang Publishing, 2004), 16.

>> "Critical Thinking" is one of the most overused and poorly understood tropes in education. Students, a hell of a lot of parents, and some teachers often mistakenly conflate critical thinking and analysis skills with contrarianism—the tendency to dismiss any broadly accepted and/or well-researched information or analysis as patently false simply due to its common acceptance. In contrast, genuine critical thinking can (and should) involve healthy scepticism with regard to what are considered established "facts" ("By whom?" is a good question), but it shouldn't hinge on simply taking the opposite position to every such assertion.

For many people—rebellious teens, lots of punks (particularly those for whom being "anti-PC" is a primary motivator), Republicans, fascists, your shitty Alex Jones–loving uncle/former bandmate, politically sketchy member(s) of the Sex Pistols/Velvet Underground/X/Gism, etc.—this amounts to replying to every argument or statement that hits uncomfortably close to home by spouting off the intellectual equivalent to "I know you are but what am I??" maybe backed up by some memes or YouTube links to other contrarians. While being a reactionary for the sake of it can seem damn exciting and often gets a rise out of one's target (along with whatever satisfaction one gets from wasting their time), it pales compared to the long-term danger to the status quo one can represent when you know how to genuinely, thoroughly research an argument or topic and carefully evaluate the sources used to back assertions up.

This chapter details a lesson plan for helping students evaluate their sources and think critically for real. It is by the amazing **Jessica Mills.** Jessica is a punk lifer who has played sax and bass for quite a few bands since the early nineties. She is a former *Maximumrocknroll* columnist and author of the punk parenting memoir/guide *My Mother Wears Combat Boots: A Parenting Guide for the Rest of Us* (Oakland: AK Press, 2007), current MRR book reviewer, assistant editor for this volume, and English instructor at Central New Mexico Community College in Albuquerque. Jessica can be reached at yardwideyarns@hotmail.com.

Personal Pedagogy

How I revised a major essay assignment since the 2016 presidential election to reflect more critical thinking and evaluation of news media

by Jessica Mills

> The do
> The how
> The why
> The where
> The when
> The what
> Can these words refine that truth?
> —Minutemen, "The World According to Nouns"

I love a good, clichéd punk rock joke as much as the next punk, yet the *Well, at least punk music is gonna be as awesome as it was under Reagan and Thatcher* sentiment that I heard too many times soon after Trump was elected fell upon my ears as flat as a deflated nihilist. Maybe it's the middle-aged, wise punk speaking, or maybe it's the community college writing instructor in me, but my gut told me to reevaluate and revise how I teach evaluative writing—one unit of study in the College Writing curriculum (of course, this was in addition to starting a new band and protesting the daily shitstorm).

For College Writing (think Freshman English 101), our faculty-developed curriculum includes a unit each of personal narrative/life as text (to engage), evaluation (to persuade), and multisource research report (to inform). For the evaluation unit that I taught prior to 2016, I introduced my students to the genre of evaluation (using certain criteria, make a judgment of your subject that is supported with reasons and evidence). Students read and analyzed sample evaluations in class and worked toward writing an evaluation (review) of a local restaurant, a book, or a new technology. Students gained practice in crafting specific thesis statements, making claims that support the thesis, and supporting claims with reasoned evidence. Moreover, students learned to create criteria that met their given audience, purpose, and writing situation.

After the election, however, several of us faculty got together to expand our vision of what this unit could and should be. What follows is a summary narrative of my revised unit plan, followed by an outline of a rough, collectively brainstormed sequence that can span seven class meetings.

Instead of asking students to analyze different local restaurant reviews found in the local, free newsweekly, go out to eat at a local restaurant, and write an evaluation of it, I introduced basic information literacy concepts that included analyzing the credibility of sources. Actively engaging in teaching critical thinking while teaching rhetoric and composition brought back my first-year teacher excitement twenty-two years later!

I started my students off with a reading, "Wikipedia as a Site of Knowledge Production" by Danah Boyd to provide them an example of what an evaluation essay might look like and to introduce the idea of actually questioning the validity of easily accessible information. We spent an entire class meeting discussing the reading, and I revealed the myriad reasons why they were learning about evaluating sources. We chatted about the fake news crisis and how it's been around forever, but due to the heavy trafficking of misleading information via social media of late, it is in the spotlight in a way it hasn't been since the "golden" days of yellow journalism.

I then sent my students off with additional articles to read, some of which are found in the outline that follows, and with instructions for them to take a short quiz from the BBC to see if they could tell real from fake news.

In teacher-speak this is called "scaffolding," as these articles and the quiz would serve as the basis for the next class activity—using predetermined criteria checklists to investigate different popular news websites. For this next activity, I compiled a list of thirty news websites that included actual news, propaganda, hoax, and conspiracy theories. Students used the CRAAP (Currency, Relevance, Authority, Accuracy, and Purpose) checklist that I provided them, which I had created from the articles they had read as homework and the widely used CRAAP test, to take notes on each website. At the next class period, students compared notes, and perhaps the most engaging, lively discussion of the entire semester unfolded before my eyes. I knew I'd struck the proverbial teacher gold, the teachable moment.

With the foundation set, I then assigned my students to write a formal evaluation of one of the websites on the "Website Evaluation Assignment" handout. In addition to an overview of their task, content requirements, organization tips, formatting guidelines, due dates, and grading criteria, the assignment included the following instructions:

- The evaluation will include your opinion, but opinions should relate to specifically defined criteria, rather than saying what you "like" or "dislike" about the website.
- Ultimately, you are making a judgment of the information found on the website and of the website overall.
- The following content should be included in the introduction of your evaluation essay: a brief description of the website, a description of the criteria you are using to evaluate the website, and a judgment (thesis statement) of the website according to these criteria.
- Remember that evaluation judgments make a claim along these lines: fakeassnews.com is (not) a "good" news website because it (fails to) meet criteria A, B, C [criteria you use to evaluate topic].
- Make sure that you support your judgment with specific evidence. If you are judging that the fakeassnews website provides credible news, because it is unbiased and includes news beyond this city, then you need to support these statements with specific examples from articles found on the website.

At the end of the semester, when I asked my students for feedback on the course, I heard from many of them that they initially wished I had assigned the easier local restaurant evaluation assignment instead of the website evaluation assignment. At first, they didn't want a more difficult challenge that included critical thinking, but they did wind up admitting that their "minds were blown," and that they had never before thought to analyze and question news sources, let alone know *how* to do so.

I felt my mission was accomplished. Sure, the learning objectives for the course were met, and I could then check the appropriate boxes on my institution's end of semester assessment report, but more importantly, to me anyway, my students would be building upon the skills they learned in the evaluation unit, and, going forward, they will have a lot of evaluating to do.

OUTLINE OF THE ROUGH, COLLECTIVELY BRAINSTORMED SEQUENCE TO SPAN SEVEN CLASS MEETINGS

Part I. Introduction to Unit 2: Evaluation genre

1. Textbook Chapter 16, Evaluations and Chapter 32, Evaluating Sources—Instructor can create reading guides for students to use as a homework reading assignment.
2. Donut Day! This experiential in-class donut evaluation activity focuses on making a fair and balanced judgment based on criteria, resulting in low-stakes homework paragraph writing assignment.
3. In-class freewriting to access prior knowledge and aid class discussion:
   a. Where do you get your news?
   b. What do you already know about these sources?
   c. If you share or read shared news posts on social media, (how) do you verify if the information is accurate or credible?
   d. What current event or news topics do you care about?
   e. Which of those topics would upset you to be misinformed about?
4. Assign "Wikipedia as a Site of Knowledge Production" by Danah Boyd—an evaluation essay sample for students to read for homework and to answer questions to prepare for class discussion.

Part II. Introduction to Information Literacy, the topic of Evaluation essay

1. Handout—"Breaking News: The News Is Broken"
   a. A brief history of yellow journalism—https://en.wikipedia.org/wiki/Yellow_journalism
   b. Fake or Real? Take this BBC quiz—http://www.bbc.com/news/magazine-38005844
   c. Professor Zimdars's guide: False, Misleading, Clickbait-y, and Satirical "News" Sources—https://en.wikipedia.org/wiki/Wikipedia:Zimdars%27_fake_news_list

2. NPR article reading homework: "Fake or Real? How to Self-Check the News and Get the Facts" by Wynne Davis—https://www.npr.org/sections/alltechconsidered/2016/12/05/503581220/fake-or-real-how-to-self-check-the-news-and-get-the-facts

3. YouTube videos—Here are just a few; there are many more!
    a. Fake or Real How to Self Check the News and Get the Facts—https://www.youtube.com/watch?v=B1LatoVQ3tg
    b. From "True" to "Pants on Fire": Google Launches Fake news fact check—https://www.youtube.com/watch?v=LjW6ESB-X9c
    c. 4 Ways to Spot a Fake News Story | What the Stuff?!—https://www.youtube.com/watch?v=g5ON3u5rrmI
    d. Helping Students Identify Fake News with the Five C's of Critical Consuming—https://www.youtube.com/watch?v=xf8mjbVRqao
    e. How Real Is Fake News? | Sharyl Attkisson | TEDxUniversityof Nevada—https://www.youtube.com/watch?v=UQcCIzjz9_s

4. Students color code and review The Media Bias Chart created by Vanessa Otero. The mission of Ad Fontes Media is "making news consumers smarter and news media better"—https://www.adfontesmedia.com/

5. Activity—Examine the same article through three different lenses

Part III. Computer Lab activity using an instructor-created CRAAP checklist to explore three different news websites. (The CRAAP test is a test developed by Sarah Blakeslee and her team of librarians at California State University, Chico [CSU Chico] to check the reliability of sources across academic disciplines.) Students can use information gathered here as prewriting for essay #2—https://www.csuchico.edu/lins/handouts/eval_websites.pdf

Part IV. Assign essay

Part V. Planning and organizing

Part VI. Drafting

Part VII. Peer reviewing

ADDITIONAL ONLINE RESOURCES

- The Information Literacy User's Guide: An Open, Online Textbook—
- https://textbooks.opensuny.org/the-information-literacy-users-guide-an-open-online-textbook/
- Can You Spot the Deceptive Facebook Post?—https://www.nytimes.com/interactive/2018/09/04/technology/facebook-influence-campaigns-quiz.html
- How to Evaluate a Wikipedia Article—https://upload.wikimedia.org/wikipedia/commons/1/16/How_to_evaluate_a_Wikipedia_article.pdf
- Media Bias/Fact Check website—https://mediabiasfactcheck.com
- Free learning tools on media literacy and First Amendment freedoms—https://NewseumED.org
- Snopes' Field Guide to Fake News Sites and Hoax Purveyors—
- https://www.snopes.com/news/2016/01/14/fake-news-sites/
- Archived page of a professionally curated list of online sources, includes an excellent list of source analysis methods—https://web.archive.org/web/20190209115423/http://www.opensources.co/
- Associate Professor at Merrimack College, Massachusetts, Melissa Zimdars's list of fake news websites—https://en.wikipedia.org/wiki/Wikipedia:Zimdars%27_fake_news_list

RELATED ARTICLES

"The Fact Checker's Guide for Detecting Fake News" by Glenn Kessler

"Fake or Real? How to Self-Check the News and Get the Facts" by Wynne Davis

"When to Trust a Story That Uses Unnamed Sources" by Perry Bacon Jr.

"Which Anonymous Sources Are Worth Paying Attention To?" by Perry Bacon Jr.

"10 Journalism Brands Where You Find Real Facts Rather Than Alternative Facts" by the Berlin School of Creative Leadership

"To Test Your Fake News Judgment, Play This Game" by Tennessee Watson

"Why Fake News Works" by Edward Burmila

"How Fake News Goes Viral: A Case Study" by Sapna Maheshwari

"We Have a Bad News Problem, Not a Fake News Problem" by David Mikkelson

In the United States, college is expensive. The cost of tuition at four-year universities, especially state/public colleges, has skyrocketed in recent decades, a reflection of administrative bloat, poor fiscal management, increasing privatization, and declining revenue from taxes, after decades of devastation to the public sector thanks to supply-side economic policies. Oligarchs like Betsy DeVos have taken control of education policy at the federal level, not only refusing to offer students relief from their current dire conditions but actively trying to make things worse via policies doing away with student loan forgiveness, a refusal to investigate malfeasance by for-profit colleges, the slashing of regulations and limits on interest rates for student loans, etc. Untenable debt burdens are exploited by unscrupulous, profiteering student loan issuers, who are enjoying record profits and fueling a speculative bubble trading in derivatives built from these loans—evoking echoes of the home equity credit bubble in 2006, which led to the Great Recession.

Meanwhile, as the number of jobs paying a living wage has dwindled for people without college degrees, the pressure on high school students from many parents and institutions has ratcheted up, pushing them to get a college degree as quickly as possible, preferably in the STEM fields (science, technology, engineering, and mathematics) where good jobs are (often erroneously) considered easier to come by. The most basic social democratic reforms, such as free or very cheap college tuition at public universities, are derided as "free stuff for freeloaders" by reactionary conservatives and dismissed as "impossible, unrealistic dreams" by (neo)liberal centrists. These are not radical ideas, and despite mountains of evidence proving the social and economic value these policies provide for the vast majority of top-tier economies in the world, many of which spend far less revenue per capita than the United States does, they are presently considered to be outlier policies on the American political landscape.

Until there is a political sea change, however, there is an accessible alternative for students who have collegiate aspirations but want to blunt the immense fiscal impacts of spending four years at a university. The next essay is a primer on the importance of an institution that many of us have found essential in our lives yet we often take for granted—community college. It is from the razor-sharp mind and keyboard of **Michelle Cruz Gonzales**, a language arts professor at Las Positas College, an open-access community college where nobody has to take a standardized placement test and where anyone can now take transfer-level English and transfer-level math during their first semester. She is also a punk scene veteran who drummed and wrote lyrics for legendary Bay Area bands such as Spitboy, Bitch Fight, and Instant Girl. Michelle's most recent book, *The Spitboy Rule: Tales of a Xicana in a Female Punk Band* (Oakland: PM Press, 2016), is essential reading.

Community College Is Totally Punk Rock

by Michelle Cruz Gonzales

> Oh, bondage up yours.
> Oh, bondage, no more.
> —X-Ray Spex, "Oh Bondage! Up Yours!"

Community college is the punk rock of higher education. It's true. Both are filled with so-called social misfits who don't quite fit in anywhere else, people with ideas, creativity, and energy, all in need of direction. Community college is like your first punk band—you didn't need to know how to play your instrument to start one. And like your first punk band, you don't need to be good at English or math or even have any student skills to go to community college, because community colleges are open-access institutions.

What does that mean? It turns out that not quite understanding what it means to be open-access or the true mission of community college has a lot to do with American elitism, classism, and, I would even argue, anti-intellectualism. All are to blame for the rampant jokes, assumptions, and stereotypes that exist about the community college system.

"Community college: there are worser ways to disappoint your parents."

You can buy this on a tee shirt from redbubble.com.

Students at the community college where I teach have been known to call Las Positas College, Las Po, short for lost potential, or the university behind Costco. Many believe that those who don't go straight to a four-year school have failed, that a community college is somehow inferior, of lower quality, cheaper, and, therefore, not a real education.

Being a product of community college and tenured community college English instructor, I'm of course going to say none of this is true, but what I won't do is let you believe that community colleges are utopias either. Both community college and punk rock are, in fact, imperfect in many of the same ways. They are both institutions whose rules and culture have been created by the larger dominant culture in America in a way that can be alienating for people of color and/or other marginalized groups.

Still, both punk rock, the subculture, and community colleges attract young people and are open-access institutions, meaning anyone can join. It doesn't matter if you totally fucked up in high school, or English is your second language, or you spent time in prison, or had parents who were drug addicts, or you were an addict, or you spent much of your childhood hospitalized, or one of your parents was deported, or you were born in Afghanistan and then fled to Iran and then Germany, and now you're here in America, or you're transgender, or you were a teen parent, or had a break down, or used to be anorexic, or you were born with no fingers on one hand, or you're the first person in your family to go to college, or even the first who graduated high school, or you had an Individualized Education Program, (IEP) and you're dyslexic. Community colleges will take anyone who wants an education, and if you're low-income, some of your fees might be waived, and if you need extra time on tests, you can get that too. In fact, as of January 1, 2018, in California, you can, as a first-time community college student, do your whole first year for free—if you don't count the cost of books. Perhaps one of the reasons elitist Americans believe that community college is inferior is the very fact that community colleges allow anyone to enroll, resulting in a student body that looks very different from a student body at a four-year college.

I went to community college straight out of high school. I had a vague idea that I'd like teaching, but I also wanted to be in a band. It didn't have to be a famous one, but the idea of being known for doing something creative, something groundbreaking, appealed to me. No one in high school ever really encouraged me to go to college. I got the feeling no one thought I was college material, and when I scored in the zero percentile on PSATs in math, I felt those suspicions were confirmed. I don't even know what I scored in English, but it didn't matter. My mom was on welfare, a drug addict, and we couldn't afford higher education anyway, but I still wanted one. Bitch Fight's bass player Nicole Lopez's mom reminded us about community college and told us we could afford that. When we moved from Tuolumne to San Francisco, we enrolled in San Francisco Community College (everyone called it Silly Knowledge), but we dropped out during the first semester, not quite feeling grounded or capable of navigating the huge campus or really having any idea of what classes we should take or where it was all leading to. We also had shows to play and beer to drink.

Anyone can enroll, but not anyone, as I learned when I went back, can take "college level" classes straight away. Community colleges are two-year colleges, and the majority of the courses offered are general education courses that make up the freshman and sophomore year of any four-year institution. However, most students take more than two-years to finish and transfer to a four-year, when that is their goal. There are a few reasons for this, and most have to do with the fact that community colleges have been underplacing students (an overwhelming number of whom are poor and/or people of color) for years and years using standardized testing placement methods.

- Standardized placement testing: community college students can enter their coursework in two ways. They can choose to start at the lowest level math and English or they can take a standardized placement test that places them into "the appropriate level." The problem here is that standardized tests are totally biased (culturally, economically), *and they don't* predict success in college level math and English courses and should not be relied on as a sole measure of placement—using only one measure to place students in English and math is a violation of California's education code rules, but the majority of colleges have almost completely ignored this law until recently. See California bill AB705 for more on a more equitable development.

- Prerequisite courses: another reason that it might take students longer than two years to finish at a two-year college is that freshman composition is a prerequisite course for some general education courses, so students must pass freshman composition before taking those classes. If students started one or more levels below freshman English, they will have to wait until they complete these classes, and then freshman composition, before being allowed to take courses in which reading and writing at a college level are required.

- Remediation: many students (but not as many as we used to think) do need at least one semester of basic skills English or math before being ready for college level courses (and some need more than one). We used to call these "remedial" courses. Now we call them basic skills courses. When students are placed into these courses whether using standardized testing or some variety of placement measure, as required by law (something like overall high school GPA), these courses must first be completed before beginning college level courses, the courses that are transferrable and will be applied to your bachelor's degree.

Community colleges are like punk rock in another way too. Just like people often say that punk isn't real music, many like to say that CCs aren't real colleges with real professors. People think that the level of education is inferior, that what you'd learn in a community college is a watered down or simplified version of what you'd learn at a four-year school. While teachers can vary widely in degree of difficulty (true in any school), be assured that CC courses are required to align with four-year courses, and there are a variety of ways that individual colleges meet this mandate. But like punk, the radical thing about CCs, aside from its open-access policy, is the fact that they provide a much less elite and less expensive education, with instructors who know and expect as much (more in many cases) as a professor at a four-year institution. In fact, the primary focus of a community college instructor (it is not the standard to call ourselves professors) is to *teach*, not research, publish, or travel around the country, leaving the teaching and grading to teaching assistants. While it has happened, it's also much less common for community college instructors to sleep with or get busted for harassing their students. It might have something to do with the fact that CC instructors, whose main job is the practice of teaching, are more likely to see their students as actual people and not objects. Just in the past two years there have been sexual harassment cases against professors at Columbia University's School of Arts, University of Texas, Central Washington University, Columbia College of Chicago, University of California Santa Cruz, and University of California Berkeley, to name *just* a few.

Because community college teachers are focused on teaching and see their students as people and not just faces in a crowd, many people who went to community college speak very highly of their experiences there (many who transfer from CCs to four-years also do better academically). Susy Riot, vocalist for Las Sangronas y El Cabron had this to say about her community college experience: "CC tends to get a bad rep in higher education, but it's a space that fosters opportunities for many marginalized folks as a site of possibility for activism, creativity, pedagogy, and critical thinking and scholarship. I would not be where I am at today without CC and the teachers and peers I met throughout my experiences there."

Like Susy Riot, 1990s East Bay/Gilman punk Dr. Kate Bean, American Indian Studies scholar and history professor, found her way to her life's work through her community college education: "I left high school at fifteen and started at Laney and Vista (now Berkeley City). Eventually received an Associate in Arts from a community college in Minneapolis and transferred to University of Minnesota for a bachelor's followed by a PhD. Now I work in public history and teach American Indian Studies/history at the community college where I received my Associate in Arts."

Many, like Shawna Kenney, journalist, DC punk, and author of *Live at the Safari Club*,[1] who attend community college, do so because they did not quite have the grades in high school to go straight to a four-year, and because it is affordable: "I started at a community college, then night school at University of Maryland while working as a nanny, before transferring to American University for my last two years (while working as a dominatrix), because my grades were not good enough from high school, and I had no guidance or financial support from my family. I got a Master's in Fine Arts ten years after that, then taught at several community colleges. I always told my students that's a great way to start—don't take out loans or waste your parents' money until you know what you want to do."Portside singer and East Bay punk Pawsi Brittney said, "I started at Delta CC in Stockton and on to a four-year college from there (University of the Pacific), where I graduated with a BA in Sociology. Wouldn't have been able to do it without CC! It helped

---

1   Shawna Kenney and Rich Dolinger, *Live at the Safari Club: A People's History of HarDCore* (Los Angeles: Rare Bird Books, 2017).

give me time to figure out what I wanted to truly pursue without the high cost of a four-year."

And because community colleges are open-access and affordable, they also are responsible for educating the majority of students of color in higher education in the U.S. Yes, the majority of people of color who hold bachelor's degrees, master's degrees, and PhDs transferred from a community college, Black and Latino students in particular. Have you heard people call community college "ghetto?" This is why, but, for many of us, these so-called "ghettos" provided access to knowledge, job skills, exploration, music theory classes, photography dark rooms, art studios, journalism courses, affordable general education, critical thinking skills, and self-actualization.

Sadly, though, getting a college degree and all the purported promises have become synonymous with the myth of the American Dream. Simply going to college doesn't guarantee you anything, and it's grown far too expensive for so many, but it remains a potent illustration of pulling oneself up by one's bootstraps (of course, so is starting a successful business that doesn't pay workers a living wage and getting rich off their sweat and labor.) Higher education has saddled many with extraordinary debt and not delivered on its promise. Remember this next time you or someone else talks shit about community college, which is affordable and a bridge to so many things for so many people.

Alice Bag: Alice Bag, The Bags, Castration Squad
East LA Community College, Cal State LA, USC
singer, author *Violence Girl* and *Pipe Bomb for the Soul,* taught elementary school
David O. Jones: Alice Bag and the Sissy Bears
BA in World Arts and Culture UCLA, Santa Monica CC, and in that order, L.A. College of Music
professional bassist, realtor
Sharif Dumani: Alice Bag and the Sissy Bears, Future Shoxxx
Pasadena CC, BA from CSUN, MLIS from UCLA
guitar, synthesizer, vocals
Stacy Russo: author of *We Were Going to Change the World*
Cypress CC, UCB, San Jose State, Chapman University, professor and librarian at Santa Ana CC (was Candace PK Hanson's teacher!)

Kamala Parks: Kamala and the Karnivores: Cringer, The Gr'ups, Hers Never Existed
> Diablo Valley CC, BA in math, Mills College, MS in Civil Engineering UCB
> drummer, transportation planner

Susy Riot: Las Sangronas y El Cabron
> Glendale CC, UCSC, University of Arizona, Women and Gender Studies
> vocals, tambourine, PhD student

Dr. Kate Bean: Gilman Street East Bay Punk
> Laney and Berkeley City College, BA and PhD in American Indian Studies UMN
> CC history professor, public historian, museum professional
> State of Minnesota Historical Society

Camylle Reynolds: Midnite Snaxxx, Bad Daddies
> Modesto JCC, UCB, MA in Education from Humphreys College
> bassist, vocals, middle school teacher, fitness instructor

Matt Reynolds: Bad Daddies, Twerps, Masturbation
> Santa Rosa CC, BA UCB, JD UCLA
> bad daddy, professor of law/administrator at Humphreys University

Vega Darling: Riot Grrl documentarian
> various CC's in SoCal, Kneesaw U, Florida State, BAs in Psychology and Social Behavior and Film UC Irvine
> filmmaker, community organizer, manager at Atlanta Pride Committee

Mari Campos: Sarchasm
> Berkeley City College, SF State
> guitar, vocals, sound engineer

Mike Freidberg: Kontaminat
> Oakton CC, Northeastern Illinois University
> middle school science teacher

Owen Peery: Good Grief, Jolt, Both Hands Broken
> Laney College CC, BA UCB, Teaching Credential Holy Names College
> computer science teacher, San Francisco School Unified District

Jessica Mills: sax in Less Than Jake, Citizen Fish, Against Me, Glave, and grp.txt; bass in Reina Aveja, former MRR Columnist and book reviewer, editor of *Yard Wide Yarns* zine
> Dayton Beach CC, University of Florida
> writer, instructor of English at Central New Mexico CC

Brendan Stephens: Perfect Future, More Pleasant Adventures, Symbiosis, god L, nobodies
> AA Garett College, BS Forstburg State U, MFA U of Central Florida
> writer, teacher, PhD student

Traci-lin Burgess Buntz: Get Out Productions
> Delta CC, BA UOP, MFA Humboldt State
> event planner, talent buyer/promotions

Rob Buntz: Last Communion
> Delta College, BS and MS in Natural Resources Planning UOP
> GIS program manager

Mason McGeorge: Stay Out
> Las Positas College
> vocals, guitar

Chlesea Starr: Vegex, Candyhead, Bed of Eyes
> Santa Monica CC, UCLA, PhD from UC Irvine
> assistant professor of sociology at Eastern New Mexico University

Candace Hansen: Alice Bag and the Sissy Bears, Yaawn
> Santa Ana CC, UCLA
> drummer, journalist, organizer

Daniela Sea: The Grups, Cypher in the Snow, The L Word
> Laney College

Dr. Donna Manion, Clitfest Organizer
> Mohawk Valley CC, Virginia Commonwealth University, University of Buffalo,
> PhD, sociology professor at SUNY Poly

Anna Marie Armstrong: drove Billie Joe Armstrong to Gilman and bought him his first record
> Contra Costa CC, Marin CC, BA English with Creative Writing emphasis Dominican University
> freelance writer, personal assistant

Billie Joe Armstrong: Green Day, Pinhead Gunpowder, The Long Shot
> Contra Costa Community College

Jimmy Alvarado: Plain Agony, The Looters, Butt Acne, Our Band Sucks, Ollin, La Tuya
> East LA Community College, CSUN
> musician, writer, filmmaker, zinester, historian, union worker

Paula Rubin: Punx with Lunch (meals to homeless folks in Oakland, CA)
> College of Marin, SF State, University of Maryland

Steve Rogers: Surrogate Brains
> Delta CC, CSULB
> small business owner, cybersecurity consultant

Jeff Ott: Crimpshrine, Fifteen
> Yuba CC, Sonoma State University
> RN, PHN, FNP-BC

Cruz Fernando: Cruz Radical, Bumpklatt, Run for Your Fucking Life, Sleepwalkers RIP
> San Diego CC, San Diego State University
> collections manager

Shawna Kenney: author of *I Was a Teenage Dominatrix* and *Live at the Safari Club*
> Montgomery CC, Northern VA CC, UNCW
> writer, journalist, creative writing teacher

Tonya Pearson: curator of Women of Rock Oral History Project
> Cape Cod CC, Smith College, UMass Amherst

Kelli Callis: *That Girl* zine
> College of the Canyon, BA SFSU, National University M.Ed., UCLA, Vanguard University
> high school English teacher

Nicole Thomas: Fire Party, Hard Left
> UDC (a public university), BA Mills College, JD UCB
> elementary school teacher

Jesse Michaels: Operation Ivy, Big Rig
> BCC, UCLA
> singer, artist, filmmaker

Miriam Klein Stahl: Epicenter Collective, Queers Together in Punkness Gig Series (QTIP)
> El Camino CC, Laney College, BA/Teaching Credential SFSU
> illustrator of NYT Best Selling *Rad Women* book series, educator, activist

Joel Steven Kuszai: Crucifucks
    assistant English professor at Queensborough Community
    College

**Dr. Sara Sutler-Cohen: 924 Gilman Volunteer, booked first metal show
and first academic conference at Gilman**
    Laney College, AA BCC, BA Mills College, MA Humboldt State,
    PhD in Sociology UCSC
    sociology instructor at Bellevue College, lead faculty at Colorado
    State-Global

Shawn Ford: Shred of Dignity
    assistant professor of languages, linguistics and literature at
    Kaipiolani CC

**John No (Mink): Street Eaters, Fleshies, Difficult, Harbinger, Triclops!,
former Gilman and Geekfest booker, Nervous Intent Records
co-founder, MRR columnist, editor of *Teaching Resistance***
    Diablo Valley College, Berkeley City College, San Francisco City
    College, Laney College
    social studies teacher for adult education

**Michelle Cruz Gonzales: Bitch Fight, Kamala and the Karnivores,
Spitboy, Instant-Girl**
    SFCC, Laney College, Merritt College, Diablo Valley College, Mills
    College
    writer, instructor of English and creative writing

In schools in the United States and Europe (especially primary and secondary schools), many current historical narratives contend that the enormously destructive era of Western colonialism officially "ended" with the national independence movements of the nineteenth and twentieth centuries in the Americas, Africa, the Middle East, and Asia. This oversimplified assertion, in turn, gives those with reasons to ignore the legacy of colonialism a cover for their insistence that the world should simply "move on" from over five centuries of blatant oppression, sans reparations or further reflection.

While this stance is most blatant in reactionary politics, such as the neofascist sect the Proud Boys' self-proclaimed "Western chauvinism" and "refusal to apologise," the Western world's tendency to ignore the fallout from its colonialist malfeasance can also manifest itself in social expressions as diffuse as language/dialect policing in schools and culture production. In the latter, there are an increasing number of reductive narratives (often produced by liberals) that further fuel the distortion that we live in a world no longer impacted by colonialism. In the critically acclaimed 2015 film *Beasts of No Nation*, the brutality of current Black-on-Black civil conflict in Sub-Saharan Africa is presented with no historic context as to how conditions in the region got so bad in the first place. This example in culture, however, is simply an indicator of the broader myopia found in every level of power structures. Colonialism is everywhere in the world, in the present. It is embedded in our languages, in our institutions, in our religions, in our beliefs and ideas about "common sense," in our distribution of wealth and health, and in our education, in our knowledge production.

In response, simply acknowledging the total and ongoing impact of colonialism is not enough. The following chapter deals with the educational imperative of *decolonization*, what it means, and how we can facilitate this process as teachers in a world where literally no one is exempt from the structures and processes that have kept colonialism and oppression intact. It is by **Natalie Avalos**, an ethnographer of religion whose research and teaching focus on Native American and Indigenous religions in diaspora, healing historical trauma, decolonization, and social justice. She is currently a visiting assistant professor at Connecticut College. She was born and raised in the Bay Area and cut her radical consciousness teeth in its underground music scene.

Insurgent Pedagogies: Decolonization Is for All of Us

by Natalie Avalos

> Don't look ahead, there's stormy weather
> Another roadblock in our way
> But if we go, we go together
> Our hands are tied here if we stay
> Oh, we said our dreams will carry us
> And if don't fly we will run
> Now we push right past to find out
> Or either win what they have lost"
> —Santigold, "Disparate Youth"

We hear the word decolonization often in resistance circles, but what does it mean? Some of you may dismiss decolonization as irrelevant to your life, thinking "I'm not a person of color, I haven't been affected or constrained by colonialism." Sorry to break it to you, buddy, but we are *all* reconfigured by colonialism's effects, not just in the U.S. but around the globe. The parallel logics of modern colonialism can be seen readily in twentieth-century U.S. interventionism, such as in El Salvador or Vietnam, but its contemporary expression, contingent on racial hierarchies (where civility or whiteness sits atop as the ideal locus of humanity), religious persecution, and "economic development" have been replicated in places like Tibet, in that instance by China. The strains of empire that transformed the Americas hundreds of years ago have morphed into a global, multinational system of neocolonial players that subjugate less powerful nations through economic bullying. We are still in the throes of colonization in the U.S.

Whiteness does not preclude you from decolonizing projects. If you are descended from European settlers, the social and economic privileges of whiteness contribute to your individual social capital. My constraint and dispossession have directly supported your access to wealth and prosperity. We are deeply linked through these overlapping histories and so share their legacy. Although they shape and constrain us in different ways, the ideological and material structures (racialization, patriarchy, heteronormativity, neoliberalism, the objectification of the earth) produced in their wake act as the foundation of our social life. And, thus, we have a collective responsibility to undo them—*together*.

We can think of decolonization most simply as the undoing of colonialism, not only its structures (see above) but also the amelioration of its effects, like historical trauma and internalized colonialism. In a material context, it can mean deconstructing settler states and redistributing lands back to Indigenous peoples, or even organizing against racist policies. In an affective context, it can mean personal empowerment, healing, and cultural regeneration. These two contexts are contingent—one necessitates and supports the other. Decolonization is the driving theme for many of my classes, meaning my primary pedagogical objective is for students to not only understand specific histories of colonialism, whether in the Americas, Oceania, or Asia, and their correlating structures but also to learn about the many paths of resistance, material (boots on the ground organizing) and immaterial (developing a radical consciousness).

As a religious studies scholar, I emphasize that we cannot decouple the material and immaterial dimensions of life, because they shape one another. Ideas, ethics, and beliefs are a major component of this resistance. We cannot transform our material conditions without deconstructing the ideologies and affective drives that have forged them. We cannot transform our material conditions without naming the multiple forms of our dispossession and claiming our existential rights to live in our full humanity. We are whole beings who have been subjected to ideological/structural violence for generations. Even those of us who have benefitted the most from these injustices are still affected and disfigured by their horror. It will take time and effort to undo this doing. First, we have to understand what we're resisting, why we are resisting it, and what forms of resistance have been effective and why.

My approach to teaching decolonization projects, since they are multiple and diverse, is exploring how at heart they are about transforming our relationships to power. Revolutionary theorist Frantz Fanon noted that colonization estranges the colonized from their own metaphysical worlds—their cosmologies, knowledges, and ways of being. Multiple forces of power (institutional, epistemological, religious) collude over time to produce this estrangement. Decolonial scholar Nelson Maldonado-Torres describes coloniality as a matrix of knowledge, power, and being. Naturally, a decoloniality that addresses these three dimensions of human experience is necessary. I agree with Fanon and Maldonado-Torres that understanding the nature of coloniality is critical to intervention. However, we can't stop there. We need to consider (and celebrate) real and existing solutions. The exploration of power is a generative starting place for understanding *how* to decolonize, because it is often a catalyst for resistance.

Although colonial dispossession of power (material and immaterial) has appeared totalizing, the dispossessed have found creative entry points to take back power. For example, individuals and communities may begin to take back their power by regenerating their ways of being through revitalized religious traditions and other forms of traditional lifeways or by researching their own institutional histories and forming a new locus of governance. The simple but powerful refusal to be complicit in racism or homophobia is a tacit way to take back power. Thinking through these possibilities denaturalizes hierarchies of power, forcing us to consider what more lateral forms of power look like. A framework of decolonization also forces us to see social life as deeply interconnected. When a constellation of social change in line with decolonization is taking place, whether through movements for Native sovereignty or Black Lives Matter, our web of relations is forced to continually shift and accommodate these new rules for living and being. We are forced to consider our relationship to unjust expressions of power and respond in kind. You may think, "Well, that's cool, but how do we negotiate decolonization in our everyday lives?"

Many of us in the underground music scene were intuitively resistant to normative social structures and expressions. For me, and likely many of you, I remember feeling distrustful of social norms that appeared to be rooted in unjust relations of power, whether this was traditional gender roles, racial hierarchies, or even normative beauty standards. I found myself reveling in social critique. It was a way for me to take back power. This critique motivated me to learn more about these structures of oppression and eventually understand them as complex expressions of empire. But after a while (years) of criticizing these structures, I found myself longing to believe in something, for a kind of social analysis that could both deconstruct and construct and maybe even instruct. I was drawn to working as a scholar because it provided me with unique opportunities to be critical but also generative.

As an educator, I am invested in helping students develop their critical voices, which is fundamental, but also to explore solutions to social problems. Why is this important? Because we need direction. Colonization has stripped many of us of our ethical and political systems and left us with a hollowed out social world that has exchanged consumerism for ethics and meaning. We need alternative visions for living and being. And we need to remind ourselves it is possible to live in a different kind of world. To remind ourselves that we have so much more power than we realize. To remind ourselves of the possibilities beyond all those oppressive structures shaping our lives, such as misogyny and racism, when they seem totalizing. To recognize that we have internalized these structures in ways that may take us a lifetime to unravel and to be gentle with ourselves when we feel defeated by our own shortcomings (not being "aware enough," not having "the right analysis," etc.). To recognize that needing community (and direction) doesn't make us flawed, it makes us human.

Yes, I love me some good social critique. Here, here, y'all woke boo boos around the world that can break down the problematic power relations in any given situation. We need these critiques. But we can get stuck there. Our love of critique may be rooted in our natural inclination to scratch beneath the surface, to act as dialecticians, seeking the antithesis of the thesis. But we often struggle with synthesizing our new insights into a coherent worldview that allows us to step into a better future. In other words, we *need* to understand what is wrong in order to fix it, but what is right? One of the problems we face teaching radical forms of resistance is that we can never come up with perfectly objective solutions. One community's decolonization is going to look different than another's. An individual's relationship to power, depending on their social position, will determine how they *decolonize*. We often have to feel our way through particular scenarios of injustice in order to understand our options for resolution. This is highly contextual and a lot of work. But teaching students to both critique and be generative allows us to see that this is not only possible but that the macro structures constraining our lives are replicated in the micro relations of our everyday lives.

We may not be able to eliminate racism as a structure in our everyday, *but* we can recognize and challenge our internalized assumptions about others—and ourselves—enabling us to build stronger, happier communities. We may not able to eliminate the settler state overnight, *but* we can work toward building functional communities from the bottom up. The fact that we intuitively seek to improve our social world is a sign that we want to live better, more equitable lives. We *want* to live in peace and harmony across difference, akin to what Mohawk scholar Taiaiake Alfred refers to in a context of Native sovereignty as peaceful coexistence. It just feels better. Many of us in this struggle are idealists who envision the big picture of a better world. But sometimes we lose track of the trees for the forest. We forget that when we transform the micro relations in our everyday lives—relationships with our families, coworkers, friends, partners, etc.—we are actively transforming our social world.

DECOLONIAL PEDAGOGIES: SETTLER COLONIALISM, KNOWLEDGE PRODUCTION, AND ANTIRACISM

As scholars and educators, it is critical for us to explore the racialized perceptions of non-Western peoples, as well as trace how these peoples continue to be structurally dispossessed as a result. As a Chicana of Apache descent, I feel obligated to use decolonial approaches to pedagogy. A decolonial approach understands world politics through the lens of its overlapping colonial histories. It recognizes that power and resources in a contemporary moment have been thoroughly shaped by ongoing colonial projects around the world. In addition, it makes legible the racial hierarchies that we continue to be constrained by and the correlated hierarchies of knowledge systems/worldviews.

In my classes, I provide a basic literacy of Native American and Indigenous religious traditions that simultaneously evaluates the lenses we use to understand them. These knowledge systems were, until fairly recently, perceived by anthropologists and scholars of religion as failed epistemology, the primitive musings of less complex societies.

Categorized as "animism," their views were framed as childish, superstitious, and clear evidence they lacked the rationality to govern themselves or lay legitimate claims to their own lands. Indigenous peoples in the Americas were understood to be not only without reason but also, according to Nelson Maldonado-Torres, without true religion, which became the central reason their full humanity was suspect. Did they know the Christian God? Did they even have souls? Settler colonial projects relied upon these ideologies to justify Indigenous enslavement, genocide, and dispossession. These ideologies produced legal structures like the Doctrine of Discovery, a series of papal bulls that declared lands not inhabited by Christians open to seizure by right of "discovery" (theft), which became one of the most enduring tools of Indigenous dispossession. By acquainting students with a genealogy of settler rationale, they are better able to understand how the mysterious sleight of hand of seizure was largely ideological but also squarely religious.

One of the reasons I pursued academia was to develop the social capital and expertise to teach others about how racism and Indigenous dispossession operate around the world. Given the rise in white nationalism in recent years, I am hyperaware of how dangerous teaching about white supremacy can be not only to my career but also, as a woman of color, to my personal safety. However, as a light-skinned Chicana, my Native features are less threatening to students/faculty, so I am sometimes (not always) perceived more favorably. As a junior scholar, I use this modicum of power and privilege to center Indigenous epistemologies in order to counter the legacy of Indigenous erasure and gross misunderstanding in the academy. Keeping this in mind, I take a two-pronged approach in the classroom. First, introduce the religious tradition, allow students to dismiss it as a curiosity (not all will but some might), and then provide them with the intellectual framework to understand why the Western world systematically dismissed Indigenous knowledge—in other words, unpack the politics of this perception as a strategy of settler colonial power; one that has become so naturalized, it is assumed by most in the U.S.

Some Native peoples in the Americas refer to this land base as Turtle Island, remarking that it rests on the back of a turtle; as others have said elsewhere, it is turtles all the way down. We can think of a decolonial pedagogy as denaturalizing all the way down. Critical pedagogies explain how power works as a diffuse network of ideologies and institutions. Power is not just brute force or coercion. Reframing critical and antiracist analytics with a settler colonial lens helps us understand how coloniality operates all around us; how power is rooted in perceptions of the world, in "natural laws" and the social hierarchies they produce. Part of the goal is to denaturalize assumptions embedded in Western epistemology that position Indigenous knowledge—and by proxy Indigenous peoples' claims to land—as illegitimate. In the process, students begin to recognize how the institutions we take for granted as inevitable, such as the U.S. and Mexican states, are socially constructed. They are also better able to see how racialization and power continue to shape the politics between them. Once students understand that the misreadings of non-Western religious traditions and peoples operated as a strategy for dispossession, they begin to question their own biases. They may even be eager to explore the possibility that these traditions have something legitimate to tell us not just about inner life but also about the complex nature of reality.

THE DECOLONIAL CLASSROOM: MAKING POWER VISIBLE

The goal of many of my courses on Native American and Indigenous religious traditions is to understand contemporary Indigenous life in relation to colonial histories. I employ both decolonial and Indigenist approaches to these ends. As noted above, a decolonial approach makes the mechanisms of colonial power visible. It denaturalizes our assumptions about Indigenous peoples and their religious traditions. For example, in my course Global Indigeneities: Religion and Resistance, we explore contemporary Indigenous movements for sovereignty and environmental stewardship in the Americas, Oceania, and Asia. Initial readings provide a broad theoretical framework for understanding the unique but often parallel strategies of settler colonialism, the religious traditions of the Indigenous communities dispossessed, followed by regional examples of resistance movements. Since there is so little popular media on these movements and peoples, students are often surprised to learn about their histories and continued resistance but also about how these peoples are often struggling to protect precious resources in order to feed and sustain their communities amid violent overdevelopment. Once students have the basic theoretical tools to understand racialization, missionization, scientism, natural law, and criminalization of Indigenous peoples/religion as mechanisms of settler colonialism, they are better prepared to understand Indigenous stewardship movements as a profound expression of sovereignty.

An Indigenist approach to pedagogy means deferring to Native peoples as the foremost experts of their own experience and knowledge systems. It can be implemented by using critical readings by Native scholars or those that center the voices and views of Indigenous peoples. Native-centered narratives often provide a more nuanced and tribally specific framework to understand sacred and interdependent relationships with land and spiritual power. Teaching these ideas is a layered and cumulative process. Students are sometimes reluctant to take the religious views of Indigenous peoples seriously. For instance, when Indigenous peoples frame plants, particularly medicinal plants, not only as persons but also teachers and relatives that provide the people with moral instructions, students are sceptical. Westerners have been trained to view the land as inert matter. This assumed materialism prevents us from seeing the natural relationships that exist all around us. Native-centered readings provide grounded examples that resist overly mystical interpretations of these relationships. For instance, Lakota scholar Vine Deloria Jr. often discussed the Three Sisters—corn, beans, and squash—who are recognized by many tribes within U.S. borders to have a familial relationship that necessitates these sister plants be grown together. Empirical study has confirmed that their co-planting produces a natural nitrogen cycle that fertilizes the soil, preventing depletion. As students consider the ethical instructions provided by these three sisters, they better conceptualize what Indigenous peoples mean when they say they live in an interdependent relationship to the land and one another. Students' curiosity to consider realities that differ from their own compels discussion, even if they remain sceptical.

We then use regional examples to explore how overlapping histories of settler colonialism produce environmental crises. By posing questions like "What is Indigenous stewardship? What might earth justice look like?" early on, we can later ask, "What does it mean to understand the land—and its inhabitants—as sovereign?" Here, the objective is to understand how Indigenous philosophies of land/living serve as the political foundation for challenging settler dispossession. When Indigenous peoples continue to assert the land's sentience, they are critiquing the dominant assumptions that it is inert, a position that has historically been used to justify its exploitation. I structure regional examples to include readings on the specific social-political history of the people, their religious worldviews, and their movements for sovereignty. For instance, a unit on Native North America may focus on Lakota water protectors at Standing Rock. The first class reading will explore Lakota/Dakota religion/political history with the U.S., while the second reading will include a short ethnographic vignette and/or collection of news stories on the #NoDAPL movement at Standing Rock. The aim of class discussions is to understand both these unique religious lifeways and how they ethically inform Indigenous fights for survival.

I generally reserve five to fifteen minutes of class time for short documentaries, YouTube clips, and other forms of media about these environmental struggles in order to make the voices of those involved salient. If you're interested in doing any critical, decolonial pedagogy, centering the voices of those you're discussing and learning about is key. For instance, I might show a clip of *Mni Wiconi: The Stand at Standing Rock*, a short documentary made by Divided Films that interviews Standing Rock Sioux Tribal Chairman David Archambault II and other members of the Standing Rock Sioux tribe on the fight for #NoDAPL.[1] Presenting clips in class humanizes discussions that threaten to become too abstract by providing additional context for their human stakes. It is often the first time a student has actually seen and heard a Native person, which can be powerfully instructive. Students often remark in their writing or in person that they are most affected by these first-person testimonies, often expressing disgust, shock, or even outrage that Indigenous dispossession continues so egregiously within the U.S. and beyond.

EMBRACING ETHICS AND POSITIONALITY

At heart, my courses are about ethics, understanding Indigenous ethics—right relationships to land and community. When we take the time to think about the ethics of Others, it provides us with a space to consider our own—what kinds of responsibilities do we have to the land and one another? What kind of collective values do we need to assert right now? I've remarked to students (and colleagues) that we can learn

---

1   *Mni Wiconi: The Stand at Standing Rock* (New York: Divided Films, 2016), accessed June 10, 2019, https://standwithstandingrock.net/mni-wiconi/.

so much from the moral breakdown of our political landscape. We can see it as an opportunity to see through the political performances, witness the most depraved human activity. Take stock. Then, collectively, choose to do something totally different. Lift our voices. Express dissent. Discontent. Our classrooms are the incubators for these discussions. I provide an intellectual framework that is part philosophy and part anthropological survey, with decolonial critiques constituting their creamy center. Religious studies as a discipline has the flexibility to take an interdisciplinary approach to questions of meaning, the sacred, and ultimate concern. As we learn to use new antiracist analytics, we can better consider how religious lifeworlds intersect with material horrors in the present in positive and negative ways. My particular goal for the course described above is for students to learn enough about Indigenous stewardship that they better understand the overarching relationship between contemporary expressions of neocolonialism/ neoliberalism and environmental destruction. When they do, they may begin to advocate for intersectional forms of justice that center the well-being of the land, as they see how their own health and well-being are dependent on it.

One of my overarching goals as an educator is to seriously disrupt the stigma around Indigenous knowledge as "primitive" and irrational. I've noticed that when I'm teaching about Buddhism, students are often enamored by its reference to interdependence, an idea rooted in dependent arising, a philosophical framework that describes all phenomena as interconnected. My guess is that racialization works differently here. Our Orientalist conditioning allows us to consume the worldviews of the East as "exotic" and enchanting, while still viable. Students are sometimes more dismissive of similar concepts rooted in Native America and other Indigenous communities, because the stigma of their views as failed epistemology is more pronounced. If we want students to understand racism as structural, we have to make these epistemological assumptions legible. We have to illuminate how these perceptions structure the very way we think about the world and the Other. When students can deeply conceptualize how Others have become so deeply ontologically and structurally dispossessed through these assumptions, they can change the way they relate to the greater world.

An important exercise in making power visible is to teach about power from your own position. Complicate your positionality and relation to power to your students. This will model both how they can think about their own positionality and why it matters to do so. I will occasionally assign a short paper that asks them to think about their own relationship to power, access to resources, upward mobility, etc. by asking them to think deeply about the place(s) they've lived. When we think about the layers of the places we know and take for granted as "ours," we are confronted with not only each place's history of Indigenous dispossession but also its degree of violence. That violence still reverberates in the minds and hearts of the communities that exist at its margins. This assignment is called a "Decolonial Autobiography." I've adapted it from multiple sources, and it essentially asks students to answer the following questions in six hundred words:

> Think about the land that you were born into. Imagine the land itself has many layers. What is its history? Who were its first inhabitants or peoples? Or even the many inhabitants that coexisted there? What is its colonial history? What is your position in relation to this colonial history? How do you and your family fit in this picture? When did they arrive to this land (if known)? From where? Where do you live know? What is this place's history? What is your relationship to the colonial relations of power in this land?

While teaching about settler colonialism and white supremacy is dangerous in these times, I find that many students, at least the many I recently taught at an elite small liberal arts college in the Northeast, are hungry for this contextualization, for these analytics. They are bearing witness to a chaotic and violent world and want to know why and how it came to be this way. Many are quite relieved to receive the tools to better understand it. When they do, they are better equipped to reenvision it entirely.

BEING GENERATIVE: REENVISIONING A BETTER WORLD

My *ultimate* goal in the classroom is to cultivate a space where students learn how power operates but also about how marginalized peoples take their power back, how they empower themselves through their ethics and religious lifeways. In the process, students may reflect on their own relationships to and possibilities for power. College students, even in their first couple of years, can easily become disillusioned and overwhelmed by the injustice they witness around them. They often feel powerless in the face of structural violence. They think that it is inevitable and will continue to eat and destroy everything in its path. They, like many in the U.S., feel powerless to affect change. Most of us have become estranged from the many processes of social change and equity making. Students don't see just how much power they actually have. Part of my job is to help them see their own power. To disrupt. To deconstruct. To reconstruct our social world. Teaching about relations of power can and should be linked to how we as individuals have power to effect change. The "on the ground" narratives that make up a good portion of class material instruct on multiple levels. They provide examples of effective organizing, resistance, and, sometimes, remarkable change. They challenge the illusion that these structures are totalizing and inevitable by revealing that they're actually teetering, waiting to fall.

We are at the precipice of deep change. Our relationships to one another, to gender, to the land, to power are all changing. We are recognizing that we cannot remain stagnant. That we are not static. We are changeable and emergent. When I say emergent, I mean that our potential for new ways of being is far beyond what we currently know. We as a collective people, human and other than human, are shifting in dynamic ways. The we that we were is no longer. We are currently being revealed to ourselves, but in often unorthodox ways. You may ask: How do you teach being emergent or fluid ways of being? By teaching students that we can *know* through our bodies as well as our minds. We can feel who we are as much as we can know who we are. Learning about non-Western Others and Indigenous and even Eastern epistemologies provides us with a space to reconsider our relationship to knowing itself. To peace and conflict. It provides us with new roadmaps to think about our own internal processes of violence and struggle. To contend with our own hatred and envy. When we deepen our relationship to our own minds and hearts, when we listen to what our bodies tell us about what we really feel. Our fear. Our loneliness. Our shame. We gain an opportunity to accept ourselves in all our human frailty on a very deep level. Radical acceptance. This is the entry point to a better world. To resolving the zero-sum violence among us.

Part of what we are learning is how to be in the world in a nonviolent way. How do we share power? How do we share resources? How do we live ethically? The irony of living in a secular, religiously plural society is that religion becomes interiorized. It has become part of the personal and private sphere. We can believe whatever we wish in the privacy of our own homes. We can choose to attend any number of religious institutions or events. But we no longer have a common set of ethics. We have no coherent moral center. Our most vocal voices on the religious front most often veil the most hateful racist and sexist bigotry, so we've become disillusioned about religion, we've lost hope that we can act morally, that we can act with integrity. *But* when we are seriously faced with the worst expressions of inhumanity on our political stage, as we are now, we are forced to make a decision. Will we be cynical and believe that we really are the Hobbesian beasts that would live brutishly to protect our own interests, or will we see the "helpers," those that choose to work together to solve problems? Who will I be in this arena of chaos? Who will I choose to align myself with? What will I choose to do in the face of injustice? What are the stakes of standing up to hate and bigotry? How does it make you feel in your body to work for goodness in the world, to work toward bettering yourself and your community? How does it feel in your body when you choose to dedicate your life or set an intention to live with honesty and integrity? These questions are part of a radical pedagogy, because we need to radically rethink how we live. We need to evaluate the very core of our relationship to life and living. When we do, we will, collectively, manifest a better world.

>> "Special education" is an umbrella term used in United States public schools to refer to programs and services that support students who fall under a range of categories outside what the state and administration consider the "mainstream" of the student population. In practice, this primarily means students with institutionally recognized physical and/or mental disabilities, diagnosed learning challenges such as ADHD and/or autism spectrum conditions, and other non-neurotypical students who cope with a variety of behavioral and emotional disorders—with the latter category of students coming disproportionately from backgrounds of poverty and systemic, often racial, oppression.

As anyone who grew up attending public schools knows, "special ed" has long been used as a bigoted insult/ableist joke among students not in these programs, as well as a slur that can be directed toward students who fall under that official classification. Part of this is due to the near total separation that "mainstream" and "special education" students used to have in typical public school settings, including physically separate classrooms and counseling facilities. In very recent years, one thing that has improved this situation and helped students to see each other as equal human beings has been the implementation of fairly radical new policies of integrating special education students into the broader school population. These policies are sometimes referred to as "mainstreaming"—an assimilationist term radical teachers tend to not care for much at all—or "special education inclusion," which is much closer to the policies' goals and recognizant of the importance and existence of diversity within the "mainstream" student body.

This chapter is by **Stephen Raser**, a special education teacher who is deeply invested in the radical, proud inclusion of his students into the greater student body. It was originally written in December 2017 and updated in August 2018. It now includes a detailed description of Stephen's professional practice at the day-to-day level, particularly in the beginning of the school year, bringing transparency to a still developing process in the education system that has proven absolutely vital to myriad marginalized people.

Radical Inclusion and Special Education

by Stephen Raser

> Twist away, now twist and shout
> The earth it moves too slow
> But the earth is all we know
> We pay to play the human way
> Twist away the gates of steel
> —Devo, "Gates of Steel"

Author's note: *This article uses the terms "disabled" and "disability." Efforts have been made to use person-first language (e.g., "person with disability" instead of "disabled person"). Some disability rights advocates prefer to use "differently abled" as it is less ableist and less deficit based. I (the author) do not intend to promote any exclusively ableist language in this article* [nor do I in the introduction—ed.] *and am very open-minded to suggestions about how to improve the language, especially from people who identify as falling on the spectrums described in this article.*

It feels a bit out of touch to write anything positive about the public education system these days. I imagine that it comes as no surprise to readers that the current administration's agenda is having immediate and widespread implications for public school systems, their teachers, and their students. Things seem to be going from bad to worse on a large scale in public school districts across the country. With Betsy DeVos at the helm, the minimal formal support of public education that existed before the Trump administration emerged is declining and doing so rapidly. Ms. DeVos, the secretary of the Department of

Education, is interested in diminishing the public school model as we know it, while promoting a charter school model, among other confused policy persuasions. Underfunded public schools are hanging on despite a system that is actively rigged against their functionality. They have to—there are a lot of children out there, and they deserve an equitable education. Yet we all know that there is an empirical achievement gap between students across class/race lines. Specific numbers aside, it seems uncontroversial to say that affluent children have more access than their peers to post-graduation opportunities. This is, in large part, related to their education during those twelve-ish years that the state is supposed to pay for schools to educate them for free. It would be easy to fill an entire article with the problems with this model, with the ways that it perpetuates poverty, and with possible suggestions to make it better. Instead, all of this considered, I would like to point toward something positive in the midst of this crisis. I believe that "special education inclusion" is an emerging practice in public education that is fundamentally positive. I would like to briefly describe the history of inclusive practices for disabled people in the education system, discuss my role and philosophy as a special education teacher, and touch upon how I set up my program and what I have learned in trying to do so.

I am a special education teacher at a public high school in a large urban school district in California. I have been supporting people with disabilities for the last ten years and have been formally teaching in this school district for five years. I do not identify as having a disability. This is salient, because I don't want to position myself as a spokesperson for the differently abled. Rather, I would like to draw upon my experiences as a special education teacher to discuss what is working and suggest ways that I feel it could improve. However, I do not want to overlook the fact that the students with disabilities who travel through these systems are the real experts when it comes to suggestions for reform or best practices in supporting them.

I currently support ten students aged fourteen to eighteen in an "Inclusion Program." What this means is that I spend all of my work hours (and the occasional Sunday) trying to facilitate the inclusion of these students in the general education school environment. I have a degree that allows me to support students with "moderate to severe disabilities," so I am cleared to work with students who are more impacted by their disabilities—students on the autism spectrum, students with

Down syndrome, students with significant physical impairments, and many other less frequently experienced conditions. The program that I run is unique, and I believe that Inclusion Programs, though admittedly flawed and developing, represent an important and powerful paradigm shift in attitudes toward students with disabilities.

In California public schools, there are a variety of different settings and classrooms that students with disabilities participate in, depending on a variety of factors. Ideally, a student is identified as having a disability early on in their education, many times in preschool or before. Their "primary disability" is defined by their physician, the school psychologist, or a combination thereof, and this "qualifies" them for an Individual Education Plan (IEP). In short, the IEP is a set of documents that comes as a product of a yearly meeting among the student's IEP team (family, support agencies, school district, specialists, etc.), and this represents the intended model of support that the student will receive for the next year. I like to think of this document as being the foundation of the student's school program.

The IEP defines the modifications and accommodations that the student will receive, the "minutes" of support that different programs and/or specialists will provide them, goals that they will work on throughout the year, their possible exemptions from state testing, and, most importantly, the setting of their education. There exists a spectrum of educational settings among people with disabilities, and, to use the formal language, these settings range from "least restrictive" to "most restrictive." The "least restrictive environment" (LRE) is the general education classroom, for example, your average Algebra 1/U.S. History/English classroom. The neurotypical student without support from special education is educated in the "least restrictive environment." The "restriction" levels go something like this—General Education Classroom, General Education Classroom with resource support, Mild/Moderate Classroom, Inclusion Programs, and then Special Day Classes. The Special Day Class (SDC) is what I imagine many people that have travelled through the California public education system have experienced—the students with disabilities (a loose and indefinite/problematic label) are put into the same classroom, because it is imagined that they all are far enough away from the typical student's ability and academic achievement that they ought to be put in their own classroom all day, or at least most of it. There are educated arguments that support the SDC classroom model, but I would like to suggest that movement toward inclusion, done well, is almost always the correct path to take.

People with disabilities have been excluded from the education system in this country since its formation. Up until very recently, if you experienced a disability you were thought of as not relevant to the offerings of public education. Before fifty years ago, millions of children were denied access to public schools because of their disabilities. Things slowly started to change: the Education for All Handicapped Children Act (1973) and the passage of Americans with Disabilities Act, or ADA, (1990) started to formalize the support for students with disabilities, but these had limited implications in terms of inclusion. In 1997, the Individuals with Disabilities Education Act was passed, and it mandated the inclusion of students with disabilities in public school, but much work still remained to be done as to what this would look like. In short, this act mandated that students with disabilities ought to be afforded free and appropriate education in the least restrictive environment possible. The trouble that I have seen in the interpretation of this law is how "appropriate" is defined. The different stakeholders on different sides of this discussion have divergent definitions of "appropriate." For instance, a school district may define the appropriate setting for a student with a disability to be a Special Day Class. The student and their family may feel that the appropriate setting is an Inclusion Program. The purpose of the IEP process is in part to resolve these frequently encountered differences in definitions.

In an ideal world, a student with an IEP is included and offered all of the courses that the neurotypical student is offered. If the student has a processing delay, they are given extra time to complete assignments. If the student experiences a mobility impairment, they are allowed to be late to class. If the student is nonverbal, they are allowed to communicate through an assistive communication device. If the student has autism, they are allowed to take sensory breaks when the classroom environment is overstimulating. If the student experiences Down syndrome, they are given an alternate assignment that mirrors the assignment of their peers and is formatted to their current abilities. The list goes on and on, and it ought to.

We do not live in an ideal world, and as such, these ideas about proper inclusion are often not manifested. However, many special education teachers, families, and students are actively trying to realize the possibility of full inclusion. We imagine and work toward a new model of public education in which competence is presumed and differences are recognized as important and crucial.

The issue with the Special Day Class model is that neurotypical students are not exposed to students with a variety of different abilities, and, in much the same way, the nontypical students are not exposed to the daily goings-on of the general education school environment. I am sure that many people who were educated in public schools in the USA experienced this model. You might have seen kids with disabilities at lunch or in your physical education classes, but they were likely not in your English class or your biology class—the content in those classes was reserved for the "typical" students and denied to everyone on the margins. In most cases, the marginalization of students with disabilities is manifested not just socially but physically. Most special education classrooms are pushed into a literal corner of a school campus.

This trend is changing, and while there is not ample space to explain and consider all of the reasons for this, it does represent a sort of social/philosophical progress in an otherwise grim state of affairs. School districts across the country are implementing inclusive practices for people with disabilities. Typical kids are sitting next to, talking to, and getting to know kids that up until very recently were cast out of public schools or grouped together by falsely perceived "ability" levels in separate classrooms.

It seems obvious to me that a public education system ought to provide equitable access to classrooms, teachers, and curricula, regardless of a pupil's perceived abilities. Of course, it is not only the students with disabilities that benefit from this exchange. If you go to your math class and sit next to a student with cerebral palsy who has limited motor function, no verbal speech, and uses a tablet to communicate, I've got to imagine that you are more likely to grow up respecting the humanity and defending the rights of people who present like this person. Maybe you will start to understand that "typical" is an operative social construct. Maybe you will see that your preconceived ideas about intelligence are ableist. Maybe you will see that we have been filtered into made-up categories that preserve the status quo. This is where I think the revolutionary seed exists. I feel fortunate to have watched many typical students come to this realization due to the inclusion of students with disabilities in their classes. I have to imagine that everyone is better off for it.

I would like to briefly discuss the way that I set up my Inclusion Program, in hopes that other educators reading can take away from it. In the beginning of the school year, I am given a list of the students that will be in my program. I also am given access to their IEPs, which, if they have been managed well, will contain the entire formal record of their special education career—their scores on assessments, their past goals, the minutes of support they have received, notes from all of the meetings in the past, and much more. In an ideal situation, I will also be given the students' work samples and will have contact with their teacher(s) from previous years. I will then attempt to arrange an informal meeting with their family. It is best if this is in person but over the phone works as well (bear in mind that many of these conversations will require language translation, and to have a designated site translator is a luxury not offered in many school sites).

After I have all of this information, I work with the school counselor to schedule the student in their general education classes. Their schedule almost always includes one period of the day when they are in my room/office, and it is during this period that we try to work on all of the social/life skill practices that they may not be getting in their general education classes. It should be noted though that full inclusion does wonders for the development of appropriate social conduct for students with disabilities. It is much more natural to mirror the behaviors of others than it is to be told by some teacher how to act and behave. Those who believe that the SDC class is the best model will often point to the fact that the students with disabilities do not have instruction in life skills if they are included in only general education classes. This argument is debunked with my one period a day of just this.

The next step after scheduling is to meet with all of the general education teachers that will have my students in their classes. This is, surprisingly enough, one of the most challenging aspects of the process. Many teachers are resistant to having students with significant disabilities in their classes. I think this is mostly due to the fact that they believe that it will mean that they will have more work to do. I assure them that I will do most of that work, we come up with a plan of support, and I hope that they follow through on their portion of said plan. I have only had a few teachers straight-up refuse to have the students in their class, and although this is technically illegal, I try to place the students elsewhere, because there are only so many battles one can fight (plus, I don't want to have to work with these types of teachers for an entire year). Most teachers are excited by the possibility or have already had students with disabilities in their classes. The most important thing about meeting with the general education teachers is coming up with a plan as to how they will report the upcoming assignments to me so that I can be prepared with modifications and accommodations for the students that I support. Most years, I will work with over thirty teachers all over the campus, so communication and my availability are crucial elements to running an effective program.

After the meetings and the scheduling, I will come up with staff support schedules for at least the first week of school. These are often subject to change as everything settles into place after the first month or so. I have three staff members that work in the program, and the four of us work together to support all of our students in their classes throughout the day. The initial formation of these schedules is a puzzling nightmare, and there will be some challenging August evenings where I will be in my room stressing out over how to put together all of the pieces of the puzzle. It would definitely be easier if all of my students were just in an SDC class together, but I didn't get into this work because I thought it would be easy. And I already told you why that model is outdated, right?

At this point, I am as close as possible to being ready for the first day. I don't believe any teacher is really ready, but I am at least semi-prepared for the chaos to ensue—and, believe me, it is chaotic at first. Someone gets lost on the way to their first class, someone has a tantrum because of the change in their routine, two busses are late, and no one can get in touch with them. The district arbitrarily and at the last minute removed one of the staff members from my class. I could go on forever. Hopefully, everyone gets to the end of the first day without too many tears and tantrums, and we brace ourselves for day two.

On a perfect day, of which there are maybe five in a school year, everything works out. General education teachers have given me the classwork ahead of time so that I can modify it for my students. Everyone comes to work and does so on time. Lunchtime finds my students socializing with a whole range of other students and doing so appropriately. My students are happy, they are learning, they are included, and no parents call my cell phone with impossible requests. Of course, one of the above often goes not so well, and we figure it out. There are a lot of moving parts to a successful Inclusion Program, and I am absolutely still developing my approach. I will say, though, that it feels good to be tired after a long day doing something that I feel is for the betterment of these students, rather than being well rested and complacent.

I would be lying if I suggested that the introduction of Inclusion Programs has somehow fixed all of the inequities that are upheld and promoted by the public education system. There are a disproportionate number of middle/upper-class white students in Inclusion Programs. Oftentimes, the only way to argue for your child's inclusion in the general education schedule is by hiring an attorney. The mere act of "hiring an attorney" is a privilege afforded to very few families. In addition, there are limited resources to make inclusive practices successful. The school districts have impossibly tight budgets, the turnover rate of special education teachers is obscenely high, etc., etc. Yet despite all of this, the integration of Inclusion Programs as a way of supporting students with disabilities does promote the possibility of a better future. And in times like this, it feels like any way that the paradigm shifts from "bad" to "better" is a small triumph worth celebrating.

The modern international DIY punk scene is complicated. We interact in a sub-subculture that can be aggressive and insular, with some degree of ignorance toward oppression and abuse, often difficult interpersonal behaviors stemming from non-neurotypical mental states, and ethical contradictions that don't jibe well with the ideological stridency projected by the subculture at large. Modern punks can also, however, be highly focused on the necessity of personal, individual, and community growth, the effective leveraging of essential criticisms (which may involve callouts and call-ins as appropriate), and pushing for positive radical change at all levels. Likewise, as with punks and teachers, our students are a complicated and often non-homogenous bunch. All of these elements of modern punk can provide valuable lessons and practice in the interpersonal communications and self-critique that are absolutely necessary for teachers, especially those who really want to connect with pupils and individualize their teaching for students who are well outside the fabled (mythical?) "mainstream."

The next chapter is by **Ash Tray**, who teaches children with autism in England. It was originally written in 2016 and has a follow-up reflection from 2018—the latter containing a powerful self- and community critique that shows how personal growth and change can be painful and sometimes forces one to make difficult decisions about the communities, relationships and practices one is immersed in on the path to figuring out what is truly important. Ash played in Frau and Good Throb, among London's best punk bands in the 2000s, and spent a lot of time and energy to help make some pretty amazing things happen in the London and UK punk scene.

Neurotypicals and the Rest of Us

by Ash Tray

> While you're getting kicked to death in a London pedestrian
>   subway
> Don't think passers-by will help, they just look the other way.
> They've seen too much, they don't wanna know, they don't wanna
>   know,
> Violence grows, violence grows, violence grows, violence grows.
> Everybody keeps it shut cos everybody knows
> Violence grows, violence grows, violence grows, violence grows.
> —Fatal Microbes, "Violence Grows"

JUNE 2016

I teach year one children with severe autism spectrum disorder (ASD) in an inner London school. I have seven students who are all killer people. Their learning happens at a painstakingly slow pace sometimes, and that's fine. There are benchmarks that neurotypical children will reach before the age of two that some of my students are still working toward, and that's fine. It's all fine, because at school, at least, we don't exist in the neurotypical world, we exist in the realm of the spectrum. And that's great. Because fuck integration politics, ASD is something that clearly (to me) demands that we change ourselves, our environments, and our teaching methods to be personalised to each individual child.

Going backwards from that list, let's look at teaching methods—change the learning experience so it becomes visual, kinaesthetic, and relevant to that child's needs—once you know the child, that's easy enough. We do this in punk too, right? We encourage new bands to be experimental, we celebrate the addition of a hammer against a bell, because when that thing hits we feel like, "Fuck, I see." Experiences are vital to our understanding, otherwise it's just something that looks questionable on paper. I could say I saw Asesinato del Poder play one of the toughest gigs I've ever seen in a basement in France, but unless you were there, you won't know what it felt like to stand in that room with your fists balled into the side of your ribs so hard you thought you'd puncture a lung and possibly die happy and angry all at once, screaming "*Infierno*." Second—change the environment—my class is a low-stimulus room (and we have a playroom, and a separate workroom, and two outdoor pods—but who's bragging—did I mention this is a state funded school? Who loves ya, Hackney), and that's exactly what each child needs—then they are way more able to focus on me and my teaching, ergo, themselves and their learning. In punk, we make our environments as open and safe as possible, right? Right? Right?

Now, the first thing I mentioned is what I mostly want to talk about in this article. This is the big one. Changing myself is something I've been learning to do slowly and begrudgingly over a long period now. Punk shows us that you either stick with something that's already there (oh, hey, your band sounds like Discharge, cool) or you steer off course and make something new (oh, your band is a gothy, plus sized, Greek woman singing about nightmares, hello dream lover—Efialtis is my girlfriend). Either way, changing ourselves is something that we have to struggle with if we are to do it actively, to be reflective enough to say, "I don't know what I'm talking about here" or "Maybe if I tried to be less A, I wouldn't suffer so much B"—whatever the thing that you don't really want to admit about yourself, be assured that to be truly reflective that stuff is gonna come up, and you'd better be prepared to look at it if you want to handle your shit and change yourself. To look at yourself under a glaring light of "How do I make me better?" isn't anything new—women have been taught to be self-critical from birth, so in a way, perhaps, we have an advantage with this—but it's important to remember that there is a history to your thought patterns, your responses and reactions, the way you organise yourself, and the lifestyle you have chosen. The point is to have an objective—you can't reshape all of that history, but you might be able to understand how it has left you and choose which specific parts of that might need tweaking, fiddling with, or just straight carving the fuck out.

Things like misogyny, for instance. You might not know that it's there until you're faced with someone saying that you did a fucked-up thing. You might not have even seen your actions as harmful at the time, or even a few months down the line. You still might not really understand what all the fuss is about when people stop wanting to hang out or won't really look you in the eye at shows anymore, all because one time this one girl said that one thing about this total nonevent that you didn't even think twice about. That's something you might want to get the carving knife out on—I give you permission to bleed over this one. Just till you think it's all gone, then I'm gonna need you to go for regular checkups in the mirror with a hefty dose of "What am I bringing to the world and why?"

What about validation? We all seek validation in a myriad of interesting ways. Do you ever stop to ask why? You ever stop to question if it's meaningful—or purposeful, or harmful—and how? And again, *why*? You ever just stop?

At work, I have to be reflective; anything less is a disservice to the community I work in. I guess my question is: Why isn't this more of the norm in punk? And I don't mean sitting around discussing intersectionality (though, *hi*, that's always good). I mean looking deeply into yourself, the words you say, the body you control, the actions you choose, and the cultures within cultures that you promote. You feel okay with them all? A good teacher is always reflecting; I reckon a decent punk will be too.

UPDATE AND REFLECTION, SEPTEMBER 2018

When I wrote this article, I was struggling with what felt like two halves of myself. I wanted to stand up for what I believed in, even when it felt like a complex mission striding directly against people who were dear to me. I had many taut and exhaustive conversations about the wrongs I believed existed in punk and that had been acted out upon me. I capitulated somewhere, at some point, and tried to just "be cool" and accept that maybe these things that ate me up inside were a problem I should lay to rest quietly on my own, so no one else (certainly almost none of my male friends, at the very least, who to me seemed to dominate the attitude of the London punk scene) should have to hear about or see my pain. So I became complicit. I involved myself in time-consuming, reckless relationships with people I convinced myself "heard" me when I whispered about these things. I worked harder than ever, practiced with my bands when I could scrape myself out of school and relationship exhaustion, saw my friends less and the phone screen more. It was dizzying, and eventually the spiral of both running away from and trying to chase some sense of myself broke me down, utterly.

I rendered myself useless to the world. I left London. I quit my job, walked away from those kids I loved. It took me a year, but at this point I feel punk to be a distant relation. Someone I might see if I have to at Christmas, perhaps.

I now work in a different city with different children. These guys are the youngest class in a social, emotional, mental health school. There are five of them. They are immensely unique, hilarious, shocking, and oppositional. They're sad and so very vulnerable. It's easy to throw myself into this work, to recap and grow on all the ways I worked with my previous class (a side note regarding my labelling of those pupils as having autism or ASD: as language around autism evolves, so must we; I would now refer to those pupils simply as "autistic"). This time, those things I implemented at school and was simultaneously seeking in punk, I feel like I might be able to find somewhere within myself. I think I managed to sidestep punk being the middleman.

So my environment is somewhere between a homely living room and an early years classroom. If you need to process your early childhood trauma through role-play and play therapy, then you'd better be provided the opportunity to do so as fully as possible. I needed to process nearly every relationship I had within punk. My own therapy came with a woman named Sarah, who made me berry tea every time I arrived and plonked myself down on her sofa. Together we sorted through a plethora of fears, bruises, and wounds, and at some point I found myself highly accountable for the choices I'd made to stay in places I didn't belong.

My differentiation now goes far beyond learning. My pupils and I spend chunks of our time together considering how best to de-escalate that oncoming crisis. For some, it's needing to run up and down the corridor sixty times if their pencil needs sharpening. For others, it's needing a head massage or a foot rub, the opportunity to pound a football against a wall or play with some Legos for five minutes if another kid looks at them the wrong way. These tactics are some of the ways we can work together to keep these guys feeling steady enough not to blow. For these children, full crisis is permanently moments away. I cannot claim to know what a lifetime of fight or flight feels like, but I can at least now recognise that punk held me somewhere between my own versions of those modes. My de-escalation was to walk away. I'm still friends with punks, of course. I play board games and go for dinners and coffees or, sometimes, holidays with them now instead of to shows and fests. We don't really talk about "the scene."

Finally, reflection: it's an ongoing process. For the most part, to be the best I can be with these kids, the best reflection I can do is to give myself a break. I recognise if I pushed too hard too soon, if a de-escalation tactic didn't work for a certain reason, if I needed to frame a question in a different way. If, actually, they needed me to take control of them sooner, because that's the reality of their mental health, they can't always stop themselves. Control is a concept I have meticulously watched play out in as many scenarios as I could throughout my entire life. In any given room at any given time, I always believed that someone had to be in control. I thought my role was to be in control of all aspects of my life, of myself, as much as possible. My reflections on control are muddy, and I still have occasional vicious thoughts about situations I found myself in where someone else tried to exert control over me. I don't know. I think the only way I found I could control what sent me spinning into oblivion in punk was to leave it behind. I don't have any malicious thoughts on it. It's an incredible beast spread across the world, and it gave me so much power to express myself at times that I became lightheaded. I suspect I will dip back into it at points. I suspect it still lurks behind my eyes when I stand in front of the mirror. But for now, exploring the myriad of different ways of being a human interested in music and art, mental health, and apple and pear tea, I think I'm okay with crooning to my records at home. Having dance parties in the car with the other disaffected punk in my life.

I remember getting into punk as a teen and meeting a bunch of older kids who were all playing in bands. They were all nurses or support workers to adults with learning difficulties. Those guys resonated with me so much because they were about being kind human beings providing dignity to those that need it, and at the time that felt so incredibly radical. I still think it's punk as fuck to be in any kind of profession that supports people in vulnerable positions, and I think I'm just at a point where teaching is the main way I want to punk. For now, at least.

>> To punks and teachers of the smart, socially conscious persuasion, **Alice Bag** (sometimes known as Alicia Velasquez) is about as dynamic an icon as you will find. A first-generation Chicana from Los Angeles, Alice began writing and performing music at the age of eight in English and Spanish; this need for wild expression eventually developed into her work as singer for the legendary, innovative punk band The Bags (1977–1981). In the mid-80s, Alice's political activism and desire to enact positive change in her community eventually led her down the path toward teaching; a career she pursued for decades. All the while, she has remained an active punk musician (in Cholita!, Stay at Home Bomb, Alice Bag Band, and other projects), became a mother, and has written the acclaimed books *Violence Girl: East L.A. Rage to Hollywood Stage—A Chicana Punk Story* (Port Townsend, WA: Feral House, 2011) and *Pipe Bomb for the Soul* (self-published, 2015).

In this interview, Alice talks about a wide range of topics—the intersections between punk and teaching, being a radical in the early SoCal punk scene, getting into teaching as a radical Latinx woman, immigration, xenophobia, and "assimilation," the intersections of punk and teaching, taking time off to write, her work with Chicas Rockeras, and the experiences she had doing volunteer work for the Sandinista educational system in revolutionary Nicaragua in the mid-eighties. Alice Bag is a national treasure, and we are lucky to have her.

Interview with Alice Bag

interviewed by John Mink

> Don't need no false reasons for why I'm out of place.
> I don't goose-step for the master race.
> I don't scream and twist just for the fun of it.
> I've poisoned blood when I'm pissed!
> Here I go
> Babylonian gorgon.
> I'm gonna babble babble on.
> So when you're near me don't be fake—Its gonna be your last
>   mistake.
> —The Bags, "Babylonian Gorgon"

John Mink: In your recent book, *Pipe Bomb for the Soul*, you talk about falling in love with teaching while working part-time as a teacher's aide in college—even though your original vision was to become a lawyer. Where and who did you want to teach? Did the ideals and culture of punk, which you helped to create as an openly radical woman of color, influence your decision to become a teacher? Or was it more from other factors in your life, such as your upbringing as the child of immigrants? Or is it a mix of all of the above?

Alice Bag: I thought I would be a good lawyer, because I wanted to make positive change in my community, and because I enjoy the art of argument. Not the destructive, name-calling type of arguments but honest and thoughtful discussion. As I was pondering which law school to attend, I landed a part-time job as a teacher's aide, and I was put in charge of working with the non–English speaking students. It was such a gift to be able to teach kids who were in a situation similar to the one

I'd been in (starting school without knowing the language of instruction). I felt a lot of personal satisfaction in being able to provide them with the type of learning experience that I wished I'd had. Teaching was like a salve over a wound that hadn't fully healed.

John Mink: When did you get your own classroom?

Alice Bag: I started teaching in 1984. I was hired while I was finishing up my student teaching through University of Southern California.

John Mink: When you started teaching, were you still active in the Los Angeles punk and radical art community? If so, how did those worlds interact and collide, and how did they influence each other?

Alice Bag: I was still playing music, but when I started teaching I wasn't living in the thick of it—I wasn't completely immersed in the scene the way I had been when I was younger. By the time I became a teacher, I was working full-time, putting myself through college, usually attending band rehearsals midweek, and playing concerts on weekends.

John Mink: Were you open about being a teacher to other punks in the scene and/or open about being a musician/radical/punk to other teachers/administrators/students at your work? If so, how did other musicians and artists during this period of punk react to your status as a teacher, and other teachers/students/administrators react to you being a radical punk artist?

Alice Bag: I was open about being a teacher to my musician friends, and they were all supportive, but I did not share my musical alter ego with the PTA. I really wanted to keep my two lives separate, and I sometimes worried that my appearance would scare or intimidate the parents of my students, so I had a sort of teacher costume; I dressed up like what I thought a teacher should look like. I enjoyed playing dress up, and I think my professional presentation helped parents feel like their children were in good hands. The punk side of me can be a little scary. There were hints that I wasn't completely normal. I used to wear a button on my jacket with the slogan "Question Authority," and sometimes there were streaks of Manic Panic or Crazy Colour in my hair, but I never wore spikes, ripped fishnets, or black leather at school, so my appearance in the classroom wasn't punk but my attitude always was.

John Mink: In your book *Violence Girl*, you are very frank about a lot of the political dynamics, divergences of opinion, and sometimes reactionary or racist/sexist attitudes from some people within the early

SoCal punk scene. Do you see punk as an implicitly radical subculture? How so or why not? Has it changed over time in this regard?

Alice Bag: I guess it depends on how we define the word "radical." I think punk is meant to challenge the status quo. It's about rebellion, but it's not about dichotomies or divisions or working within traditional political constructs. Punk is about expressing ideas, finding communities that can engage in dialogue, and working together toward making positive change. In other words, punk is about empowerment and autonomy, rather than left- or right-wing ideologies, and the punks that I know are fiercely independent in their ways of thinking. Sometimes they drop sparkling words of wisdom, and other times it's pure crap.

John Mink: You've written a few songs about teaching in your recent projects, i.e., the song "Programmed," yes? Tell us about some of those. Also, Paolo Freire's *Pedagogy of the Oppressed* has been profoundly influential to many teachers. Tell us how it affected you and what circumstances in your life, context, and personal experiences created greater resonance and connection with this foundationally radical work.

Alice Bag: "Programmed" was inspired by Paolo Freire's *Pedagogy of the Oppressed* and by my time volunteering in postrevolutionary Nicaragua, just a few years after the Sandinistas took power. When I first started teaching, I was working with an emergency credential, which meant that I still had to take a few classes beyond my BA. In one of those classes, I was assigned *Pedagogy of the Oppressed*. The author, Paulo Freire, describes a type of education that I recognized, the type that I had experienced as a child. Freire called it the "banking method": it regards children as empty vessels to be filled. When the "banking method" is used, students are treated as receptacles for the values of the dominant class. The practice dehumanizes and disempowers children, whose culture, experience, language, and ideas are subjugated in order to indoctrinate the students with the ideology of those in power. It fails to teach critical thinking skills, and it does not teach the value of dialogue. I used to think that Freire referred to it as the "banking method" solely because teachers were expected to make deposits of information into their students, but I think I might have missed another way in which this sort of teaching resembles banking. The practice creates a culture of apathy, ignorance, and compliance, further enriching those in power and reinforcing the status quo.

John Mink: In *Pipe Bomb for the Soul,* something very interesting that you described was how in the classrooms in rural Nicaragua where you worked—Escuela NICA being one, I believe—there were a lot of dynamics at play that might be unfamiliar to teachers in wealthy industrialized states. In the Escuela NICA classroom, small children, adult farmers, women with babies, and more all learned the same lessons together in a very discussion-oriented learning environment. Were the small groups and discussion partners mixed in age, gender, profession, etc.? How did these dynamics play out in the small groups, partners, and class discussions? How did the teacher monitor these discussions?

Alice Bag: The literacy classes were not run by the NICA school. The NICA school focused on helping to find volunteering opportunities for internationalists. The NICA school was also used as a community meeting space. I volunteered in literacy classes and elementary school, and the literacy classes were different from the regular elementary or secondary school classes, they were held at different times of day or night and sometimes on weekends. The Sandinistas hoped to eradicate illiteracy, and they consulted Freire in developing their literacy campaigns. In the literacy classes, the students varied in age, occupation, gender, background. It's interesting that you ask me this question about the class discussions, because it was an area that really required people to reeducate themselves and adhere to respectful guidelines for constructive dialogue. Sometimes there were disagreements, but people actually worked on being attentive and respectful. It definitely took effort, and it was evident that people considered this type of personal growth as an extension of the revolution. The teacher took on the role of facilitator, offering guidance if a discussion became heated. The goal was not consensus, but rather a respectful exchange of ideas.

John Mink: Who came to the classroom with different life experiences?

Alice Bag: The differences I observed were mostly between the people who worked in the small towns and those who were from more remote areas in the countryside. Their way of life, their connection to the earth, their knowledge of business, access to medicine, to books, to plumbing; all of these created a distinction between, say, a farmer and a store clerk. The cool thing about the literacy campaigns is that they would enlist the help of teen brigadistas who would volunteer to go teach literacy to the campesinos who lived in more secluded or distant places. So the goal was not just to address the problem of illiteracy but to unite

Nicaraguans from different backgrounds and include those who might have otherwise been politically disenfranchised, the farmers, who were traditionally voiceless in government. It also illustrates how teenage students became teacher/students and how the campesinos became students who were also teaching the teacher about their culture. This reminds me so much of punk rock, where the lines between audience and performers blur, where everyone is involved in creating a mutually satisfying, enriching experience—but I digress.

John Mink: Not a digression at all! A good deal of *Pipe Bomb for the Soul* has to do with reassessment and questioning your own internal biases and assumptions. For example, when you were processing your perception of Sandinista Commandante Gladys Baez, you had to reconcile her powerful, Indigenous, womanly identity with your subconscious perception that the role of military commander is intrinsically masculine/male. After gaining a greater understanding of the huge role played by women in the Sandinista revolution by talking with her military comrade (and your host) Francie, you bring it around to a powerful (and dark and funny) imagining of Gladys' torture at the hands of the right-wing Somoza regime, where she is interrupted mid-questioning by her husband and children who are complaining about their cold tortillas—to which Gladys replies, "Heat your own damn tortillas! Can't you see I'm busy?!" This sort of honest accounting of your reflections and personal assessments, for which you also developed an icon system in the beginning of the book, provides a really useful modeling tool for teachers reading the book as far as methods for their own practice. How did you come to decide on this method for the book, and what are some other ways you see the book as a teaching tool for teachers or, really, anyone who wishes to engage in self-critique?

Alice Bag: Ha, ha, ha! When I decided to share my journal with the public, I knew that I wanted to leave my original voice, which is young, innocent, privileged, and quite naive, but I also wanted to be able to add historical details, as well as commentary with the benefit of hindsight, offering a more mature assessment of my experiences. Naturally, these were missing from the original journal, so I modeled *Pipe Bomb for the Soul* after the *For Dummies* series, which allows for lots of little side notes that don't interrupt the narrative but expand or enhance it.

John Mink: Was this approach to the book and the way you keep the language accessible influenced by the methods of the school? Was it influenced by the way that you approach and perceive punk culture/ music/art? If so, in what ways? How are these things similar, and how are they different?

Alice Bag: Some of my methods were influenced by my experiences in Nicaragua, but before I started teaching I was a philosophy major in college, and I'm sure I was influenced by the Socratic method. I suppose punk also had some influence in my methods, as punk is all about questioning and challenging authority. I think it worked the other way around too—teaching influenced my punk. Teaching is a very performative profession, you have to be engaging to be a successful teacher—you have to know how to adapt to the needs of your students. You need to build a safe space where people feel like they can be themselves. I think engaging the audience, creating a safe community, and being able to adapt to different situations is also important in punk.

John Mink: Tying into resistance culture and adaptation here, another interesting topic/subcurrent in the book has to do with the incongruities between revolutionary ideals and the development of new institutions following a revolutionary seizure of power (even if conflict is ongoing) and how education plays a strong and complex role in literally teaching resistance and revolutionary history. Prime examples were the sample topic sentence that was posted on the first day you were in the classroom, "*La reforma agraria la recupera la producción de la tierra para el pueblo*" (Agrarain reform recovers the land for the use of the people), the fact that the institutional revolutionary party, the FSLN, was almost exclusively mentioned in textbooks when discussing political parties, and how prisoners were given greater levels of autonomy upon achieving literacy goals yet were fearful of criticizing the Sandinista government. Looking back at your reflections in the book today (most of it is from diary entries in 1986) and the convoluted history of Nicaragua since then, what are your current thoughts and feelings with regard to the crosscurrents within this complex grey area of resistance, education, institutional revolution, and elements of authoritarianism?

Alice Bag: What is institutional revolution? It doesn't make sense to me. Can there be benevolent authoritarianism or a benevolent dictator? I don't think so. Any institution that finds its way around the autonomous will of the people can be neither revolutionary nor benevolent. It makes me sad to know that the spirit of revolution, reinvention, and autonomy that I witnessed in 1986 is now withering in Nicaragua.

John Mink: And while the situation in Nicaragua is dire, it is even worse in countries around it like Honduras, El Salvador, and Guatemala, where oppressive U.S.-backed right-wing regimes clung to power; and now thousands and thousands of displaced refugees from these countries are having to migrate north just to stay alive. How did you talk to your own students about immigration? Did you often talk about being the child of immigrants?

Alice Bag: I worked to create a classroom where children felt safe and supported, not just by me but by each other. We spoke about their experiences if they were comfortable speaking about them. I also reached out to the school psychologist for help with students who had been traumatized by either the war in their country of origin, the immigration experience, or by any other experience. I spoke often about my immigrant parents and about learning English in school, just like them. I wanted my students to know that we had a lot in common.

John Mink: What are some ways teachers can validate their students and celebrate their languages and cultures and push back against the homogenizing assimilationist agenda that American society so often demands?

Alice Bag: I firmly believe that developing a child's primary language will produce better results than truncating that development. We can build on a sturdy foundation of rich language much quicker and more successfully than building on fragmented language. As for ways in which teachers can validate their students' language and culture, of course they can do it by including it in everyday use, but oral language is just one form of communication. A lot can be expressed through patience and kindness. We also understand each other through our actions and expressions. A teacher who does not understand the language of the student can convey approval or disapproval through nonverbal cues.

John Mink: What are some ways that teachers can help nonimmigrant students to push back against the ugly racism of much of the U.S.'s attitudes toward immigrants, particularly immigrants from Latin America, and confront their own prejudices? What are some of the ways in which this can become complicated, in your classroom experience, for example, when the students expressing xenophobia are from other marginalized classes, such as other people of color?

Alice Bag: I honestly believe that the more dialogue there is in the classroom, the more safe and inclusive it can be. Students need to be able to process statements and points of view that they've heard at home or in their communities without being judged. They need to have the opportunity to practice critical thinking skills, and all skills need to be practiced to stay sharp. Xenophobia is not a topic that can simply be suppressed or swept under the rug—we need to shine a spotlight on it, because it cannot stand up to scrutiny. Also, it's important to note that xenophobia is expressed in mainstream as well as marginalized groups. Sometimes, the oppressed learn to be the oppressor. The teacher needs to create an environment where questioning is productive and helps students to reach rational conclusions. We also need to allow for divergent points of view. Teaching kids to have respectful dialogue is very empowering and a valuable life lesson.

John Mink: How can a teacher help students to be more empathetic and positive, to find greater solidarity between students who have systemically oppressed, marginalized identities—people of color, queers, immigrants, etc.—and draw greater empathy from those who are not marginalized?

Alice Bag: I don't know, maybe have them play on a team together or play music together. Learning to depend on others is a trust building exercise. I don't play sports, but the people I have played in bands with usually become like extended family to me. I trust them onstage and off.

John Mink: What were key differences between teaching in California and teaching in Arizona?

Alice Bag: UTLA [United Teachers of Los Angeles]—having a strong teachers union made a very big difference. I enjoyed working in both states, but I felt much more supported in California. I had a teacher assistant, I made more money, I had better access to classroom materials, science and art supplies, and I believe all those perks came from having a strong union. However, both states have a very long way to go before they do right by teachers, students, and parents. We need smaller classes, more support in the classroom, materials beyond textbooks, access to professional growth opportunities, music and art classes, and teachers need to be paid like they're the guardians of our most precious resource—because they are!

John Mink: What are the greatest lessons your students taught *you*?

Alice Bag: My students made me a better person. I was very impatient before becoming a teacher, quick to judge and not very tactful when communicating displeasure. Working with children made me take responsibility for how I interact with others, regardless of their actions. Children are innocent, they make honest mistakes, and I always felt it was up to me to step up and be patient—to be clear about my expectations, to be consistent in providing structure and discipline, to help them understand that mistakes are okay. It's easy to feel that way about children, but the thing is that after a few years I learned I could be more patient with adults as well. Not completely patient, I'm not there yet, but I'm not as snappy as I used to be.

John Mink: Do you know a lot of punk teachers? Are there any punk teachers who have been inspirational for you or helped inspire you in your own teaching?

Alice Bag: I don't know a lot of teachers who are into punk music. I do know a good number of college professors who are very punk. One person who inspires me is Marin Joshua Vee, the founder of Chicas Rockeras SELA, a girls' rock camp in Southeast Los Angeles. She and her *comadres* created a mentorship program where young girls can learn to own their power, where they can feel the strength and support of other women, where they can learn how to have dialogue and work with other young girls. On top of that, they get to form a band, write a song, and perform in front of wildly enthusiastic fans. I am very inspired by what Marin has created; she sets the tone for camp every year, and every year it floors me.

John Mink: You were a teacher for over twenty years, until 2011, the year *Violence Girl* was released. What brought about this major change in your life? How have things changed for you since then?

Alice Bag: When *Violence Girl* came out, I made the decision to take time off from teaching. I did this for the sake of the students. I knew that I wanted to tour and support my book, but I didn't want to take time off from the classroom and leave my students with substitutes. Students need to have consistency and a book tour would impede that, so I decided to take a year off from teaching. I fully planned to return to it, but something unexpected happened: professors began assigning my book to their students. I discovered that by visiting classrooms in colleges and universities across the country, I was still engaging with students. It was a different age group but every bit as satisfying, so I decided to keep doing it.

John Mink: Tell us some details about Chicas Rockeras, how you (a very experienced teacher) help to facilitate a powerful education experience through the Girls Rock Camp model in a camp oriented toward young Latinx kids. What's the difference between teaching at Chicas Rockeras and teaching in a classroom?

Alice Bag: Chicas Rockeras doesn't really have a music-centered curriculum; the curriculum is about female empowerment. I wish all classes were more about the whole child instead of inputting information. I probably focus more on teaching music and performance than some of the other volunteers, because I'm used to a lot of structure, but I'm learning to ease up and not worry so much about whether they can play; it's more important that the girls figure out what they want to express and that they know someone will listen.

Joh Mink: You have talked about having "teacher damage"—the compulsion to educate, well outside the classroom. What do you hope to be able to accomplish, education-wise, today and in the future?

Alice Bag: Ha, ha, ha! I do have teacher damage! I want to challenge people to think, to question, to foster dialogue with others who don't share their point of view, to find common ground, create change, shape their world and speak up for those who cannot speak up for themselves, and to save our planet for future generations.

Anti-intellectualism and reactionary, deeply conservative thought run very deeply in the dominant cultural and political systems in the United States, a problem long recognized but first dissected at length by historian Richard Hofstadter in his book *Anti-Intellectualism in American Life* (New York: Vintage Books, 1963). As of late 2019, the most blunt and brutal of these tendencies continue to be politically prominent via neofascist/faux populist backlash movements, such as Trumpism, religious (particularly Christian) fundamentalism, and the viral, "rebellious" appeal of conspiracy-minded, hard-right contrarian ideologues such as Alex Jones from Infowars, whose bizarre conceptualizations of knowledge sometimes read like a broken funhouse mirror version of postmodernism (sans any meaningful structural or social critique).

One of the favored targets for these reactionary anti-intellectuals has long been the hallowed institution of the university, where the fabled "Ivory Tower" of academia is believed (by reactionaries and those mindlessly parroting their rhetoric) to insulate students and faculty from the so-called "real world" of capitalism, colonialism, patriarchy, and inequality outside the confines of the school. This belief has led to numerous and increasing right-wing attempts to force professors and university departments to cease centering the views of marginalized voices, to end criticism of U.S. and European imperialist/colonialist actions, and to insert a greater number of reactionary voices against social and economic justice into the curriculum—regardless of their intellectual merit—in order to promote greater ideological "balance." These attempts at forcing academics and intellectuals to adopt what is essentially an anti-intellectual, anti-critical, pro–status quo stance have been organized by powerful right-wing organizations and promoted on the ground level by a small but driven number of students who see their mission as being against what they perceive as total control by radicals in academia.

Though the sciences are not immune (particularly from religious fundamentalists), the humanities departments have borne the brunt of these right-wing attacks as of late in the wake of five decades of radical scholarship that deeply critiques and challenges long-held academic assumptions and biases—especially those supporting white male supremacy. Ironically, of course, the kind of reactionary pushback to these critiques described in the preceding paragraph serves to effectively insulate the most privileged students—those who directly benefit from white male supremacy—from the very complex "real world" that is best understood through rigorous, critical scholarship, promotion of social equity, and the centering of voices that have been marginalized for so long by dominance and oppression.

The next chapter is from punk lifer (and frequent contributor/shitworker at *Maximumrocknroll* magazine) **Mimi Thi Nguyen**, who is an author, public speaker, and professor of Gender and Women's Studies at the University of Illinois. Her writing for this book focuses on what questions of justice, intersectionality, and radicalism actually mean at college campuses today, for students, their teachers, and society at large—aka "the real world." Mimi can be emailed directly at mimi@mimithinguyen.com.

Our Students Are Radical *Because* They Live in the Real World

by Mimi Thi Nguyen

> What are your big problems?
> I'm sorry for your problems
> Didn't you just say
> You wanna be the boss?
> You wanna taste the grit
> Well you can die die die die die
> —In School, "Cement Fucker"

In a conversation between our faculty and a prospective candidate (one I opposed), one of my colleagues said, "The students we get in Gender and Women's Studies are so radical, so activist, but they don't understand the real world. How do you think your scholarship could teach them about the real world?" The candidate happily agreed that radical students are impractical "heads in clouds" dreamers and bubbled on about statistics and samples as useful instruments for familiarizing students with the truths of the so-called real world. This was despite the fact that she admitted that her own samples in her studies of gendered expectations in the workplace did not disaggregate according to race, occupation, or economic status, while referring to Black women—and I suppose the rest of us—as "subgroups" and trans persons as "statistically non-impactful."

Because a candidate interview is not the time or place, I said nothing, as I sat stiffly, staring down at my notes—which the offending colleague kept trying to read over my shoulder—or Vaguebooking my outrage (my only outlet during the meeting). It is true that our students in Gender and Women's Studies are among the more vocal campus activists. In the past few years, our students successfully fought for trans-inclusive health care in the student insurance plan—a perhaps "statistically non-impactful" but tremendously significant concession to the necessity of more expansive practices of health and caregiving. They walked the picket line with our graduate student instructors and other non–tenure track faculty whose contracts (teaching each course for a few thousand dollars, far below minimum wage for all their hours) are held in suspension by the administration, year after year. Furthermore, our students often work multiple jobs on top of their course loads, which tend to be heavy, because most of them come to Gender and Women's Studies after they've declared other, more traditional majors—majors they are told will prepare them for the so-called real world, defined narrowly as "employment"—and also complete our requirements for love and rage. Many of them are women of color or queer or gender nonconforming youth who've either witnessed their friends and peers being policed by adults—administrators, cops, teachers, and other authority figures—or experienced these encounters themselves, for years. Because a substantial number of our students hail from Chicago, where the Chicago Police Department has committed racial terror for decades, I have met more than a handful whose family, friends, or neighbors have been beaten or shot in so-called "police-involved shootings." For all these reasons I wrote on Facebook, in the heat of the meeting, "Our students are radical *because* they live in the real world."

This is a side step, of course. So many people (young and old, students and professors) live in the so-called real world and are not radical at all. But it was important to me to refuse the condescension implicit in that declaration—*our radical students don't live in the real world*—aimed at both our students and those of us who hope to encourage our students to *fuck this shit*.

I went to graduate school on a whim, back when it was more economically viable to do so "on a whim," to think through my concerns about politics and activism, with no particular desire to become a professor—that decision came later. When it did, I imagined, naively, admittedly, that "being a professor" (whatever I thought that meant) would allow me some autonomy, flexibility, and creativity, and I strongly identified with an idyllic view of the work—writing, teaching—and its nonmaterial rewards. We know now that these same qualities are pitched to us as pluses to ameliorate the troubles with uncompensated or undercompensated labor, as attributes of an ideally flexible worker of the neoliberal economy—increasingly subject to insecure employment, semi-secured in temporary networks. I remember saying, as a young punk, that it was not my "job" to educate others, whether about race or gender or empire. *I'm not getting paid to teach you!* was and is a familiar refrain about such uncompensated labor, one we all learned from Audre Lorde. And yet teaching others about race or gender or empire is totally (part of) my job now. It is how I access an income, health care, and retirement, and, because I am in that increasing minority of tenured faculty, I do that with higher status (however limited); so I hope to do this job thoughtfully and with intention.

That the neoliberal academy treats students as consumers is a frequent target of criticism; universities build state-of-the-art recreational facilities and stadiums for students and alumni, while decreasing the number of tenure-track faculty positions in favor of exploitative contingent labor, including graduate students. We should not treat our students as consumers; it's a shitty way to teach and to learn. Every faculty member, especially those of us who are women, gender nonconforming, queer, or of color, has a story or two about students who complain that they do not pay tuition for a B+ or who fill evaluations with loaded microaggressions about our accents, clothes, and characters. Yet neither do I believe that we need to return to an older model of apprentice-master, and that is what galled me about the encounter with my colleague—the condescension implicit in imagining that young persons are the ones caught in an impassable tower, and that we professors are conduits to the "real world." The reverse is also not true—I come from the real world too, not a tower.

With that in mind, I try to bring a DIY politics to my classroom. I teach from a position that knowledge is not neutral and that both knowledge and its history—how we know what we know—bear upon all our social arrangements, even those that might seem minor or trivial. I argue for a refusal of the alienation and divisions of activities or skills—which is to say that theory is not distinct from practice, and all practice is informed by theory—as well as for a *sliding under* institutional or state overpresence. No state, as the anarchists say, can give you freedom. Or, as French historian Michel Foucault wrote, freedom is nothing more than the relation between the governors and the governed. At the same time, because I know now how much I did not know as a nineteen-year-old (without presuming that these nineteen-year-olds in front of me also don't know what I didn't know), I aim to approach the work of teaching with generosity and compassion, with regard to students' foundational and critical knowledge—whether about the world or about the categories we use, sometimes to our detriment, to make sense of our places in it. I also do my best to recognize the histories that have put them there in those seats, saying those things, because it has never occurred to them that other possibilities, other worlds, are sayable, let alone thinkable. I teach with this insight from Gayatri Chakravorty Spivak in mind: "Why not develop a certain degree of rage against the history that has written such an abject script for you that you are silenced?"[1] Toward that end, I also disagree with my colleagues that to engage in seemingly impossible dreaming is somehow childish, foolish, or shortsighted, and that the path to "useful" knowledge must take the familiar forms of institutional or state appeals—such as policy or law, none which have protected us yet from the violence of their evaluation and implementation. As someone who has a critique of reform-minded, ameliorative campaigns and yet also recognizes that what I do in the classroom might be understood as such, and as someone who has been inspired by revolutionary movements and yet also knows that these can foster authoritarianism and political arrogance, I hate prescriptions and imperatives. *This is the right way! We have to do that!* We hear all the time that our moment of ongoing crisis requires practical action, straightforward prose, clear reasoning, hard facts, common sense, and so forth, and we hear this from both reformist and revolutionary comers. I am not against these things, but I am against arguments that these things are the only forms through which we define "activism" or politics now. Our imaginative leaps and wild theorizing are what make it possible for us not to succumb to the already known directives and demands—*be practical, be straightforward*—that haven't yet gotten us out of this mess.

---

1   Gayarti Chakravorty Spivak, *The Postcolonial Critic: Interviews, Strategies, Dialogues* (London: Routledge, 1990), 62.

>> What does intersectionality look like? Where are the openings, the physical/emotional/political cracks in the facade, the patches of untilled ground from which solidarity can grow between people who have experienced marginalization in such a myriad of different ways in modern societies that are rife with systemic oppression? How do we, as educators, help to reconcile our classroom environments and our own life experiences, to foster and facilitate student growth with regard to inter-student solidarity, mutual respect, and, hopefully, coordinated resistance to these oppressive systems? To start with, teachers need to be willing to openly discuss and develop creative ways to confront and undermine the pervasiveness of racism in modern societies, and our classrooms are very much part of the given society they exist within.

The next piece was written in two sections, the first published in "Teaching Resistance" in July 2015, the second being written in July 2018 as a follow-up reflection and a sample teaching unit. In his writing, author **Ian McDeath** deals with the often uncomfortable, inevitable complexities of communicating about systemic racism—particularly anti-Black racism—in the U.S. with students who are primarily from immigrant backgrounds, many of whom experience racism and other threats themselves. Ian grew up in Philly, where he is an indispensable shitworker and super-busy musician (in excellent bands like Ronnie Vega) in the DIY punk scene. Like your editor, Ian teaches at an adult school for older teens and adults working toward goals that include learning English, getting equivalency diplomas, making up lost high school credits, passing GED tests, fulfilling requirements for advancement in their jobs, and for a variety of other reasons.

Talking to ESL Students about Anti-Black Racism

by Ian McDeath

> We are not isolated by distance
> But by greed and our racist history
> Just a wall's width away
> Still impossible to see across
> This space in front on me. . .
> It's we who write this history
> We who guard the money-tree
> We support the companies
> We stole the colonies
> —Chumbawamba, "Invasion"

I sort of started teaching ESL (English as a second language) as a work-study job while in college in New Brunswick, New Jersey. I say "sort of," because my actual job there was assistant to the teacher of the bilingual kindergarten class, and I basically just read weird stories and did cool art shit with five-year-olds. I got the job because I qualified for financial aid, and because I had taken an extra year of Spanish in high school. I imagine there was probably a person who needed the job more and spoke Spanish better than I did. A few years later, I began working at an ESL school for adults of many different language backgrounds, also in New Jersey, and then at a similar school in Philadelphia.

I like teaching and see it as a radical act, because, as a friend once pointed out, it's a form of authority that inherently undermines itself. I try to apply my politics to my classroom in fundamental ways. For example, every cycle, the class works together to create agreements (rather than rules) for themselves and for me. I try to empower them to teach each other. A lot of my lessons involve teaching students how use free and widely available resources to learn things on their own, so that they don't feel like they have to rely on some gatekeeper of knowledge.

I also try to talk openly about racism in my classroom. I do this when I hear or see something that strikes me as racist, and I encourage my students to do the same. Generally speaking, these incidents aren't directed at anyone in the classroom, and I haven't heard a lot of students say that they have felt personally hurt by racism from fellow students. What I more commonly find myself stopping class to talk about are anti-Black (specifically in reference to American Black people) comments reflecting people's personal experiences, which range from feeling uncomfortable on the subway for absolutely no reason to being victims of mugging and assault. I am white (and straight and cis male and college-educated), so I am familiar with people saying racist (and other types of fucked-up) shit to me and thinking that I'm going to agree with them.

In my initial years of teaching adults, I made the mistake of treating these comments from students as if they were coming from someone in the political punk scene. That is to say, I got angry (sincerely so) or tried to embarrass the person who made the comment with the objective of pushing them to reflect on what they had said, understand why it was fucked-up, and never say it again. I've come to realize how misguided and uncool it was to take that approach with someone who hasn't had the same opportunity that I've had to unlearn a lot of shit. It's especially troubling when you consider that these were students who trusted me to help them.

Once I realized that my approach to anti-Black racism from my students was not helping them and mostly just making them uncomfortable talking to me about their feelings and experiences, I tried to simply avoid the topic. I told myself that I was there to teach a language and anything else that they needed to know, they would learn one way or another. If someone told me that their child's teacher was lazy and thought it necessary to mention that the teacher was Black, I would simply omit that detail in my head and carry on the conversation as if the person hadn't mentioned it. If a young student said that they had trouble understanding Black people when they talked (followed by a ridiculous, caricatured imitation of Black American English), I would just say, "I don't know what to tell you." Taking this approach made me feel just as bad about myself as my previous approach.

The comment that caused me to reevaluate my response to my students' anti-Black racism came from a then student, a few years younger than me, who I have always liked and respected as a person, about a coworker of mine who I deeply admire as a teacher and as a friend. Purely in the interest of illustrating the complexity of the situation, I will say that the both the student and the teacher in question are Muslim and that the comment centered on criticism of Black American Islam because of its connection to prisons. The comment also rang hollow of conviction, like the student was repeating something they had heard said with confidence but that they didn't necessarily believe. I didn't know what to say, but I felt like the longer I let the comment linger in the air, the deeper the frustration set in. I wanted to go off for hours about history and capitalism and the media and capitalism and the police and capitalism, but I didn't even know where to start, and I could feel myself getting more frustrated, so instead I just asked "Have you ever read *The Autobiography of Malcolm X*?"

"No, teacher. I don't like to read. Only what you give me for homework."

"It's also a movie. I'll find you a copy, if you promise you'll watch it."

"Of course, teacher. I love movies."

We ended up watching it together after class and talked about a lot of the themes and messages in the movie, as well as the important historical background and how that history has morphed into the current landscape of anti-Black racism in the United States. We talked about how that gets exported via mainstream television and movies to people in other countries.

I'm not sure if all of that was the right way for me to go about addressing the student's comment. On the one hand, it kind of feels like it was just a white person (me) lecturing a nonwhite person about racism, but I think it was also a lesson on the historically and culturally specific way that anti-Blackness exists in the United States. There are also a few things that I learned are important about discussing American racism with recently arrived adults from other countries:

1. Most places in the world have their own forms of anti-Blackness. In some places, it's similar to the United States, where Black people

continue to be the victims of poverty and violence at disproportionate rates as a result of the trans-Atlantic slave trade and the racist
institutions that it morphed into. In other places, Black people are
immigrants, seen by the population as an invasive Other, taking
jobs, contributing to crime, and tainting the cultural (read: racial)
purity. In some places, anti-Blackness is the process of occupation
and colonialism by foreign armies and companies that deplete
countries of resources and pit people against each other for survival.
In some places, anti-Blackness is simply racist American media
imported and internalized, which brings me to my next point.

2. Racist American media is consumed worldwide, and, just like
    it does here, it influences beliefs and feelings toward American
    Black people. American television and movies tend to portray
    Black people as violent and prone to criminality, and this becomes
    internalized in some of my students (some of whom would be con-
    sidered Black by most Americans) even before they arrive in this
    country. I'm often asked which parts of the city are fun/beautiful/
    safe to go to with the expressed or implied understanding that
    Black neighborhoods are none of these things.

3. For someone who has not been raised and educated in our spe-
    cific and complicated formula of coded racism, it can seem pretty
    absurd. They see a world where most Americans hate and fear Black
    people but never say it directly. The cultural ideal they are pre-
    sented of an American is a middle-class, white, college-educated
    person. They see these Americans afraid to go to Black neighbor-
    hoods or uncomfortable around young Black people, but then have
    to learn a new set of culturally specific words and phrases to avoid
    saying that, which is a lot for someone who is already adapting to
    a new language.

4. Most non–Black American people, including ESL teachers, need
    to address their own anti-Black racism before they can really talk
    to their students about the topic. It's important for a teacher (or
    anyone, really) to understand how they themselves are affected by
    anti-Black racism. A teacher's anti-Black racism can present itself
    in the topics that the teacher chooses to talk about in class and
    how they choose to talk about them. It can also appear in how the
    teachers talk about the places they live, their friends and coworkers,
    and current social and political events. If they are afraid of or less

comfortable around Black people or in Black neighborhoods, then for that teacher to tell students not to make anti-Black comments just seems ridiculous to them (and it kind of is). Additionally to this point, ESL teachers (and everyone) need to educate themselves on the history of U.S. racism and the current legal and economic policies that perpetuate racism. Otherwise, it can seem like all this anti-Blackness just came out of nowhere or that Black people are themselves responsible for the situation they're in.

5. Students coming to the United States for the first time see a racially segregated society where most Americans tend to interact with people who come from similar racial, economic, and language backgrounds, where Black people are disproportionately victims of violence and poverty and most non-Black people don't do anything to change that. It is easy for students to look at non-Black people in society and believe that they are racist (which a lot of them are). Unless a non-Black teacher makes a point to address racism in their class, it is possible, and not totally crazy, for students to think the teacher might dislike Black people. All non-Black people have the responsibility to fight anti-Black racism. For ESL teachers, this means having meaningful conversations with your students about American anti-Black racism.

GENERAL GUIDELINES FOR A TEACHING UNIT, JULY 2018

In the three years or so since I had the conversation with John Mink that led to the article that I wrote for "Teaching Resistance," I have continued to have difficult conversations with my students on the topic of race and racism. These conversations are often described by my students as being an interesting and energizing part of the class, but for a while I struggled with how to make them more participatory. They often happened spontaneously when I didn't have a lesson prepared, so I usually ended up talking more than I would like. Because ESL classes really need to be centered around the students' use of the language, because the conversation felt important to have, and because I had come to feel confident in my ability to facilitate that conversation in a useful, ethical way, I decided to develop a unit about anti-Black racism and how to fight it. This is intended for intermediate to advanced ESL students, and I have grammar and vocabulary components to go with it. I have also included some information about the materials that I use for the discussion/critical thinking part of the class. I assume most ESL teachers know what they need to about teaching grammar and vocabulary, so I don't get too deep into that, but if you have any questions about that stuff, I am down to share those materials as well.

Two notes to add:

1. I have laid this out less like a typical lesson plan, which is intended to be picked up and used by anyone, and more like a personal account of what I do and have found to work for me, a cisgender, white, college-educated man. I imagine that teachers with different identities will want and need to approach the topic differently. This information is not meant to be a prescriptive lesson plan in any way. I do hope, however, that it might find some use outside of the ESL classroom, either in native English-speaking classes or with anyone trying to educate their friends and families about racism.

2. Teachers must consider their own identities as well as the identities of their students when deciding how to have these conversations. We need to be considerate of who this might impact and how. What are your students' own experiences with racism? What kind of racism are your students carrying with them? These kinds of questions should inform how you structure this discussion in both big and small ways. We need to able to create an environment where people can safely talk about difficult shit, and we need to be confident in our ability to do that. The lesson that I teach grew little by little over several years, starting with very simple, one-on-one conversations with both students and non-students, allowing me to practice, learn, ask questions, and make mistakes. With all political education, it is necessary to point out the problems but just as important to offer solutions. Otherwise, you are not helping anyone. I suggest that you take your time feeling comfortable with this topic before committing to lead your students into it.

This unit is divided into five lessons, because that's how the school where I work is structured.

The first lesson is based around the history of racism in the United States. I find it useful to go as far back as the Middle Ages to give the topic some context: sugar cane, originally from Southeast Asia, was brought to the Middle East and Europe by Muslim traders. Demand for the product grew, which necessitated land and labor, prompting both the colonization of the Americas and the advent of the transatlantic slave trade. A particularly important point for students to take away from this is that anti-Black racism in America stems from our laws and economic system rather than from a sense of tribalism that is inherent in humans. Religious and pseudo-scientific components of white supremacy developed later as a way of justifying the institutional barbarity. The PBS miniseries called *Africans in America* has a useful video about the development of legal racism in the English-speaking colonies. The language is accessible to higher level ESL students. I have curated some texts about the history of the enslavement of African people and discussion questions to go with *Africans in America* [see lesson plans at the end of this chapter—ed.].

I spend most of the first lesson on this notion of racism as an economic and legal institution, because, conceptually, that is the hardest leap for students to make. Most people, regardless of where they are from, tend to view racism as something natural to groups of people, which can make the problem feel unsolvable. However, if we understand racism as an institutional phenomenon, we can solve the problem by reimagining and restructuring our institutions.

The second lesson deals with the brutality of slavery and the psychology of white supremacy. Here, I try to use primary texts, such as documents outlining the laws that controlled Black people throughout slavery and Jim Crow. The Southern Poverty Law Center has a website called "Teaching Tolerance" that offers hundreds of texts intended for teachers of American-born middle and high school students. With some modification and accompanying grammar and vocabulary lessons, I have been able to use a number of them for my ESL class. My goal with these texts is to compassionately illustrate the extent to which slavery and white supremacy damaged and dehumanized Black people. As with any difficult but important topic, there are a lot of points to consider when deciding how to go about this, especially if you have students who have experienced violence and/or racism. Another point to make here is that the n-word, which foreign students often have questions about, comes from this period of extreme and violent dehumanization. I explain that it is still used in a similar way by racists of many colors today, so when a non-Black person uses it, it can be traumatic regardless of that person's race or intentions. The next time I teach this lesson, I would like to find a video or audio source in which Black American people explain their experience with the n-word instead of lecturing on it myself.

Another important part of this second lesson is understanding how these racist institutions affected (and continue to affect) both white and Black people in America. I ask my students to imagine that they were alive in this time and to think about how they would react and respond to the violence around them. I ask them to think about what could make white people, even white people with no economic or insti-tutional investment in white supremacy, defend it and participate in it. There is an essay that I have used, but the most effective thing that I've found has been a video about the "blue eye/brown eye experiment." Following the assassination of Martin Luther King Jr., Jane Elliot, a white kindergarten teacher from the Midwest conducted a simple social experiment with her all-white students. She divided the class into those with brown eyes and those with blue eyes and explained that the stu-dents with blue eyes were better in every way, using specific blue-eyed students as examples. The brown-eyed students, she said, were lazy, derelict, and dirty. Over the rest of the day, she observed the blue-eyed students become both more confident and energetic in their learning but also more abusive and cruel to their brown-eyed classmates. The following day she explained that she had been mistaken and that it was actually the brown-eyed students who were inherently gifted and the blue-eyed students who were repugnant. Within an hour, the effects were reserved; the brown-eyed students began excelling at their studies, while the blue-eyed students sank into a debilitating lack of confidence. After showing them the video that is available on YouTube, I ask them to draw on the video to imagine the ways in which a national policy of white supremacist segregation lasting hundreds of years might affect both Black and white American people. The video is fairly simple and the language is not difficult for mid- to high level English learners, but because the recording is old, it helps to find a version with subtitles.

The third lesson focuses on media representation of Black people and the effects that it has on both white and Black Americans. This part seems to feel more relevant to a lot of my students, possibly because it takes the discussion from the past to the present. Usually, the day before this lesson, I ask students to watch any movie or episode of a TV show that takes place in an identifiable American city, meaning the city can't be made-up or a generic metropolis. They should count the number of Black and white characters in the movie or show and make notes on what kind of roles they play (doctor, cop, poor person, rich person, etc.). When they come to class, we look at demographic information about each city that was presented and see if the racial make-up of each city reflects what it is being shown on the screen. It very rarely does, and I ask students to reflect on why that might be. In their discussions, they usually come to the assumption that either this is purely unconscious, or it happens for economic reasons (i.e., a movie or show will be more successful or popular if it has white protagonists). I use an article titled "Hollywood's White Summer: Where's the Diversity?" written in 2010 for the website The Wrap, to confirm the latter. It explains that movie and TV producers consciously choose white actors over Black actors because of the proven economic outcomes. I then show students the famous study in which Black and white children are asked to choose the "better" and "more beautiful" of two dolls, one Black and one white. The original study was done in the 1950s, and it was repeated as recently as 2006 with the same results: most children of both races tend to choose the white doll (the most recent versions of the test suggest that Black children today have less anti-Black bias than in the past, while white children remain just as likely to describe the Black doll as bad). The next time I teach the lesson, I plan to include a listening activity on the effect of *Black Panther* and other recent films starring Black actors.

In this section, I also ask the students to read an article from the Economist website (https://www.economist.com/democracy-in-america/2018/02/20/black-americans-are-over-represented-in-media-portrayals-of-poverty) that shows how Black Americans are overrepresented in news media's depictions of poverty and how this affects people's beliefs about race, economics, and government. The original article is hard for English-learners, so I use a version that I have modified for grammar and vocabulary. Again, I would love to share it with anyone who would like a copy (feel free to email me for it).

The fourth lesson reflects on racist laws and policies that have led to the disproportionate impoverishment and incarceration of Black people in the U.S. I use passages from "The Case for Reparations" by Ta-Nehisi Coates and *The New Jim Crow* by Michelle Alexander, both of which I have adapted for ESL students. With these texts, I hope to illustrate for students the way that past racist laws morph into modern "color-blind" laws that solidify distributions of justice and wealth along racial lines. This often feels like a spot where some of my students hit a bump in the road, so to speak. At this point, I am asking them to think critically about not just race but about class and current laws. I push them to think of possible solutions to the problem. Because it can be extremely difficult to shift one's understanding of racism from the idea of individual bigotry to an institutional system of power, I generally don't expect them to suggest that the U.S. government pay reparations, but I try to encourage abstract and critical thought here.

Something to add to this lesson that I have thought about more recently but have not yet tried is a discussion on the viral videos of white people calling the police on Black people for doing completely normal, nonthreatening things. There are several articles and videos that I think provide a good analysis of these incidents and would be worth including, but in order to ask students to think critically, they need to be given a question to answer. I am considering something along the lines of "How should the police respond to a white person who calls them to report Black people doing nonthreatening things?" I can't know for certain if the question will provoke critical thinking or be met with a blank stare. I can provide an update once I try it out.

The fifth and final lesson is centered around steps that everyone can take to fight racism on a both a personal and societal level. I ask them to read another adapted passage from "The Case for Reparations," in which Coates lays out his main thesis: there may be no way to undo the damage done by white supremacy without compensating Black people for what has been taken from them throughout the course of American history. The students can either agree with the argument and explain why or outline an alternative solution and why they think it would be more effective at correcting the problem of racism. I also ask students to think about what they would say to a friend or family member that said something racist about Black American people. I give them time to brainstorm ideas independently and then together as a class. After that, I ask them to role-play with a partner. It's really powerful to see how good people feel when they begin to see a problem as solvable rather than unsolvable, even if the steps to take are small.

In writing this, I revisited some of the articles and videos that I mention here. There is an interesting piece on The Root about the doll experiment that was used to illustrate the effect of internalized anti-Blackness. To briefly quote psychiatrist Dr. Welansa Arsat:

> Society's anti-black bias can be effectively counteracted with a pro-black bias. In psychiatry, we talk about risk factors for particular disorders. However, there are also protective factors that can minimize or diminish the impact of the risk factors. Exposure to anti-black bias is a risk for internalized racism and low self-esteem. However, a pro-black identity can protect against that risk.[1]

I would love to find a longer reading that develops this argument further. I'm not sure exactly how I would ask my students to use it or respond to it, but it might be useful to either of the two activities that I do in this lesson. If anyone has any thoughts on this or really anything else mentioned here, feel free to share them with me.

I love teaching and I love justice, so I appreciate the opportunity to meld the two. I also love talking about teaching and justice, so I welcome anyone to contact me with their own thoughts, experiences, advice, or questions: igwinter@yahoo.com.

SAMPLE LESSON PLANS FOR ANTI-BLACK RACISM UNIT
Calibrated for intermediate to advanced ESL Students, this is a basic structure adaptable to your classroom purposes. Plans also available online at http://teachingresistancearchive.blogspot.com.

Part I: Africans in America (PBS) 2:55–27:37—https://www.youtube.com/watch?v=6UeLHl7Xo7w
- Describe the conflict between the white farmer and Black farmer in Virginia in 1645. What is surprising about the outcome of this conflict?

---

1   "The Doll Test for Racial Self-Hate: Did It Ever Make Sense?" The Root, May 17, 2014, accessed June 10, 2019, https://www.theroot.com/the-doll-test-for-racial-self-hate-did-it-ever-make-se-1790875716.

- Describe the goals and experiences of the first English colonists to Jamestown. What happened between the years of 1609 and 1610?
- When did the first Africans arrive to the Virginia colony? How did they end up there? What happened to them when they arrived?
- What was the major cash crop of Virginia? What was the original source of labor used in the colonies? What was the experience of these people in the colonies?
- Who is Anthony Johnson? What was his experience in Virginia? Why is it surprising? What larger message about race and racism does this story deliver?
- What two important events happened in 1640? What were the lasting effects of the second event?
- What was the first colony to recognize slavery as a legal institution? What did Virginia decide in 1662, and why was it significant?
- What factors led to the unrest in Virginia? What happened in 1676 to establish racial slavery as an attractive economic system?
- What was the Royal African Company? What were the effects of this company?
- What is the common misconception about the beginning of slavery in the American colonies?
- What happened to the plantation that belonged to Anthony Johnson's grandson?
- What are your impressions about the information presented? What information did you find new, interesting, or surprising? What feelings did you have about the information?

Part II: The History of African Slavery in Europe
Sources:
1. SPLC's Teaching Tolerance website https://www.splcenter.org/teaching-tolerance.
2. PBS, *Africans in America*, 1998 https://web.archive.org/web/20180719203349/https://www.pbs.org/wgbh/aia/tvandbeyond/tvbeyond descr.html
The history of the European seaborne slave trade with Africa goes back fifty years prior to Columbus's initial voyage to the Americas. It began with the Portuguese, who went to West Africa in search of gold. The first Europeans to come to Africa's West Coast to trade were funded by Prince Henry, the famous Portuguese patron, who hoped to bring

riches to Portugal. The purpose of the exploration: to expand European geographic knowledge, to find the source of prized African gold, and to locate a possible sea route to valuable Asian spices. In 1441, for the first time, Portuguese sailors obtained gold dust from traders on the western coast of Africa. The following year, Portuguese explorers returned from Africa with more gold dust and another cargo: ten Africans.

Forty years after that first human cargo traveled to Portugal, Portuguese sailors gained permission from a local African leader to build a trading outpost and storehouse on Africa's Guinea coast. It was near a region that had been mined for gold for many years and was called Elmina, which means "the mine" in Portuguese. Although originally built for trade in gold and ivory and other resources, Elmina was the first of many trading posts built by Europeans along Africa's western coast that would also come to export slaves.

The well-armed fort provided a secure harbor for Portuguese (and later Dutch and English) ships. Africans were either captured in warring raids or kidnapped and taken to the port by African slave traders. There they were exchanged for iron, guns, gunpowder, mirrors, knives, cloth, and beads brought by boat from Europe.

When Europeans arrived along the West African coast, slavery already existed on the continent. However, in his book *The African Slave Trade*, Basil Davidson points out that slavery in Africa and the brutal form of slavery that would develop in the Americas were vastly different.[2] African slavery was more akin to European serfdom—the condition of most Europeans in the fifteenth century. In the Ashanti Kingdom of West Africa, for example, slaves could marry, own property, and even own slaves. And slavery ended after a certain number of years of servitude. Most importantly, African slavery was never passed from one generation to another, and it lacked the racist notion that whites were masters and Blacks were slaves. By the start of the sixteenth century, almost two hundred thousand Africans had been transported to Europe and islands in the Atlantic. But after the voyages of Columbus, slave traders found another market for slaves: New World plantations. In Spanish Caribbean islands and Portuguese Brazil by the mid-1500s, colonists had turned to the quick and highly profitable cultivation of sugar, a crop that required constant attention and exhausting labor.

---

2   Basil Davidson, *The African Slave Trade* (Boston: Little, Brown and Company, 1980).

They tried to recruit Native Americans, but many died from diseases brought by Europeans, such as smallpox, diphtheria, and tuberculosis. And the Indians who survived wanted no part of the work, often fleeing to the countryside they knew so well. European colonists found an answer to their pressing labor shortage by importing enslaved workers from Africa.

By 1619, more than a century and a half after the Portuguese first traded slaves on the African coast, European ships had brought a million Africans to colonies and plantations in the Americas and forced them to labor as slaves. Trade through the West African forts continued for nearly three hundred years. The Europeans made more than fifty-four thousand voyages to trade in human beings and sent at least ten to twelve million Africans to the Americas.

Part III: "The Case for Reparations" by Ta-Nehisi Coates
https://www.theatlantic.com/magazine/archive/2014/06/the-case-for-reparations/361631/
(print it or, if you have laptops, let students read it online for the multi-media aspects)
After reading Section I, have students answer and discuss the following questions:

1. What are your impressions of the situation that Clyde Ross experienced? How did you feel reading it? What words, sentences, or paragraphs did you not understand?
2. Do you agree that the Clyde and the Contract Buyers League deserve reparations from the people who sold them the contracts?

After reading Section II, have students answer and discuss the following questions:

1. What are your thoughts and feelings about this section of the reading? What questions do you have? What words, sentences, or paragraphs did you not understand?
2. Why do you think that Robert J. Sampson says the difference between poor Black people and poor white people is a "difference of kind not degree"?

After reading Section III, have students answer and discuss the following questions:

1. What does the author mean when he says: "It is like we have a credit card bill and, deciding to charge no more, remain confused that

the balance does not disappear. The effects of that balance, interest accruing daily, are all around us."

2.   What does he mean when he says: "If we conclude that the conditions in North Lawndale and Black America are not inexplicable but are instead precisely what you'd expect of a community that for centuries has suffered racism, then what should we think of the world's oldest democracy?"

After reading Section IV, have students answer and discuss the following questions:

1.   What are your impressions after reading this section? What do you think and feel about what you read?

2.   According to the author, why was the United States able to become a large, prosperous, and democratic country?

After reading Section V, have students answer and discuss the following questions:

1.   What are your impressions after reading this section? What do you think and feel about what you read?

2.   According to the author, when did the suburbs of American cities develop? How were so many people able to buy homes at that time, and how were Black people excluded?

After reading Section VI, have students answer and discuss the following questions:

1.   What are your impressions after reading this section? What do you think and feel about what you read?

2.   What different strategies did white people in Chicago use to prevent Black people from moving there? What did they do when those strategies failed? Why might a nonracist white person decide that they didn't want Black people to move into their neighborhood?

After reading Section VII, have students answer and discuss the following questions:

1.   What are your impressions of this section of the essay? What are your thoughts and feelings about what you just read?

2.   Why did people like Clyde Ross and Ethel Weatherspoon buy houses even though they knew the contracts were exploitative?

3.   Why does the author mention Barack and Michelle Obama?

After reading Section VIII, have students answer and discuss the following questions:

1.   Why did President Johnson say, "Negro poverty is not white poverty?

2. Why do you think gang violence has become a problem in North Lawndale?

After reading Section IX, have students answer and discuss the following question:

1. Do you agree with the author that a conversation about reparations may be necessary for healing of the American mind? Why or why not?

After reading Section X, have students answer and discuss the following question:

1. After reading the full essay? What are your thoughts and impressions? What surprised you, and what was not surprising?

Part IV: "Hollywood's White Summer: Where's the Diversity?" by Brent Lang

https://www.thewrap.com/hollywoods-white-summer-wheres-diversity-17558/

(print it or, if you have laptops, let students read it online for the multimedia aspects)

1. What is the main point that the article makes about race and movies?
2. What is the controversy over *Prince of Persia* and *The Last Airbender*? Why were people upset about those movies?
3. Who are Samuel L. Jackson, Don Cheadle, Chris Rock, Eddie Murphy, and Ken Watanabe? What do they have in common and why does the author mention them?
4. According to Chris Hartigan, why do directors tend to choose white actors for their movies?
5. Why do you think audiences care about the race of the actors in the movies? How might this issue affect people?

Martin Sorrondeguy is a queer, Latinx punk. He is the singer for well-loved, influential punk and hardcore bands such as Limp Wrist, Los Crudos, and Needles. He runs the record label Lenga Armada, is a longtime shitworker for *Maximumrocknroll*, directed the 1999 punk classic film *Beyond the Screams: A U.S. Latino Hardcore Punk Documentary* (Chicago: Lengua Armada, 1999), and is a top-notch photographer who has authored three books of amazing photos he shot of bands from all over the world. Martin also happens to be a dedicated teacher who has been involved in radical education for decades and puts as much passion into his classroom work as he is known for in punk.

The following piece is an extended, wide-ranging interview with Martin conducted in fall 2018 for this book. Martin was one of the original inspirations for *Teaching Resistance*, and I am very grateful that he was willing to share part of his story as a teacher, a radical, and a punk—in all of its complicated, intersectional, interwoven, and inspirational glory.

Interview with Martin Sorrondeguy

interviewed by John Mink

Facades will crumble.
It's all crumbling.
Makeovers won't change you.
Ignorance is at your core.
We'll watch your facade come down.
—Limp Wrist, "Facades"

Martin Sorrondeguy: My first experience with teaching began when I got involved in activism with the American Indian Treaty Rights Committee here in the Midwest, and I started to go to certain events that they were holding and talks and all this stuff. I ended up finding out from somebody from the community, who told me, "Martin, there's kids who need help with homework at the center." It's called the American Indian Center, here in Chicago.

John Mink: What year was this?

Martin Sorrondeguy: Maybe 1990? Maybe 1989.

John Mink: Wow, you were really young.

Martin Sorrondeguy: It was probably 1988–1989. I ended up releasing a record to benefit the American Indian Treaty Rights Committee, and that came out in 1989. I had just finished my studies at Columbia College, and I was just going to punk shows and stuff. When somebody told me about this, when this person from the community said, "You know, there's kids who need help with homework," I was like, "Fuck it, I'm going." I started to show up, and I met some people and just started tutoring kids and helping after school, so that sort of played out for some time. Down the line about a year or two, I ended up getting a job at a Montessori school here in Chicago.

John Mink: What was your job there?

Martin Sorrondeguy: I was a Spanish teacher, and I worked primarily with six- to nine-year-olds.

John Mink: So you would have been in your early twenties?

Martin Sorrondeguy: Yes. I'm fifty now, so I've been working in education for some time in various capacities. After I did that, I was there for a couple years, and then kind of clueless, and everything [with music] was really sort of kicking off and everything. Then I left that [job] and kind of jumped into the nonprofit world for a while, working with a lot of youth in different capacities, like after school arts programs, doing that for a while. I worked with an agency on the north side, which now is a completely gentrified neighborhood, but at the time it was still a Latino/Puerto Rican neighborhood. I was working there for a while, and we did some really amazing stuff. I remember this one summer program where we did an exchange with other communities, and we ended up coming to the Chinese part of town here, doing an exchange with them. Through my connections, I actually took students to the Lac De Flambeau Reservation in northern Wisconsin for a long weekend, and it was amazing for the kids from the inner city to be out there on this Ojibway reservation. The exchange was, I think, probably unforgettable for most of them; it was amazing.

John Mink: Absolutely.

Martin Sorrondeguy: So I kept on the trail of jumping job to job, doing different kinds of teaching.

John Mink: You were also touring [with Los Crudos] at the time—you were doing a lot.

Martin Sorrondeguy: I would stop [teaching], and then I'd leave for tour, then I'd get hooked up into another job, and that went on for a while. What ended up happening is I moved to California, and I started working again at an elementary school doing after school arts. I did that for about two years, and then they basically dropped us. This was the problem that I faced being in the nonprofit sector—when the funding ran out, you lost your job.

John Mink: Yeah, I've worked in that sector too; it's terrible.

Martin Sorrondeguy: It's terrible. I was like—"Oh, my god, I can't believe this," and for some reason there was something in me that just said,

"You know what, I'm going to step away from teaching for a little while." And so I did, until I was offered a really unique opportunity in teaching. I was invited to an infant art program, and it was one-, two-, three-year-olds; it was in a center that worked with children with disabilities, and I got hired on to do arts with them. That was really interesting, and it reignited my belief in education and teaching because it went to the real core of discovery.

John Mink: What kind of pedagogy would you use with kids that age? I mean that's very pre-pre-pre-kindergarten.

Martin Sorrondeguy: I'll give you a prime example of a moment for me that I'll never forget. There was a little girl, and she was blind, and there was always one parent with the child. We were working on a lot of tactile stuff, like a lot of stuff with texture and touching and gluing. I remember the mom pouring glue on the girl's hand and whispering, and you could tell the girl was squeezing her hands together and was kind of confused by the substance in her hand, and the mom was whispering in her ear going, "That's glue, Mija, that's glue." It was this moment that hit me, something so fucking basic to us—that's glue—that we wouldn't think that there would be this moment that it would be such. . . it was something so impactful that I was moved completely, and it kind of rejuvenated my interest in education.

John Mink: What year was this?

Martin Sorrondeguy: This was about 2004. What ended up happening was I was in Southern California, Santa Ana, and I ended up moving to the Bay, and I went and worked at *Maximumrocknroll.*

John Mink: Where you were the distro coordinator.

Martin Sorrondeguy: Yeah, but I told myself, "You know what, I am going to get my teaching credential—I'm tired of getting screwed over."

John Mink: Where'd you go for that?

Martin Sorrondeguy: I went to San Francisco State. It was funny, because there was a punk girl, this woman I used to see at shows, and she was really into education and stuff. When we started talking, I was like, "You know what, I want to go get my teaching credential." And she goes, "Oh yeah, San Francisco State has a good program," and she started talking to me about it. And I said, "I'm going to go do it." She said, "Well, it's a lot of steps; you have to get a lot of stuff in order and in line to do it." And I'm like, "Oh yeah, cool. I'm going to go do that." I think she kind of looked at me like I was crazy or weird, but I kid you not, I walked into the director of the Programs Office and said, "I want to be a part of the teaching credential program," and he was so thrown off-guard, like "What?" So I asked, "What do I need to do?" And he goes, "Well, there's all these steps." So I go, "I'll do them." And he said, "Let me go get the list." I kid you not, within a couple months, maybe two or three, I was in.

John Mink: Well, with a resume like yours, that would make you a dream candidate.

Martin Sorrondeguy: Yeah, it was bizarre. But I ended up seeing her, that girl from the show, after that, and she's like, "What have you been up to?" I hadn't seen her in like six or seven months, eight months, and I said, "I'm in the program at San Francisco State." And she was like, "What?" And I was like, "Yeah, I'm in the program at San Francisco State; I told you I was going to do it," And she couldn't fucking believe it. As a matter of fact, she even ended up showing up at the school I worked at with some friends and their child, when they were looking at schools that they wanted to put the kid in. She walked into my classroom and her eyes nearly fell out of her head. She was like, "Oh, my god, I can't believe I'm in your fucking classroom."

John Mink: So after getting that classroom, what were your first experiences like when you started? You got your first state-credential teaching job in 2008, right?

Martin Sorrondeguy: Yep, that was in Oakland Unified.

John Mink: Secondary right? As in high school?

Martin Sorrondeguy: Yeah, high school; and it was really bizarre, because right out of my program I was recommended for a job there. That was because my teacher was Julia Marshall, and she was this really great art and art education person, and she recommended me for a job, because one of her former students worked there. I ended up working under this person; he was the head of the arts department at the school—Michael Radus—he was amazing. But let me back up a little bit, because when I did my teaching credential program, when I did my student teaching, I did it under Miriam Stahl.

John Mink: Oh, you did your student teaching with Miriam!

Martin Sorrondeguy: Yeah! When you sent me your interview with Miriam, I'm like, "I love Miriam"—she was sort of my lead teacher. I did my student teaching at Berkeley High. Unfortunately, I wasn't able to get [a job at] Berkeley High, which is what I really wanted; it didn't work out. Miriam, I think, was really kind of looking out trying to get me in there. She was always saying, "I really want you in the school," and it just never panned out, but I ended up working in Oakland Unified. I was the digital photography teacher, and I did heavy graphic design as well.

I worked at a high school in Oakland for four years. It was a rough start for me, like it is for any teacher. Just things that they hired me with, like this promise that I was going to have a computer lab. I was going to have computers, because I'm teaching digital photography and Photoshop, right? And for the first four months of my first year, there were no computers in my room. It was horrendous, and there was all this drama in order to get what I had to get. I had to run the class like a beginning art class for the longest time. It took time to build it up, but by the third year my class was the first to fill up in the entire school. All the art classes generally fill up, but they told me, "Your class and the ceramics class fill up first."

John Mink: I remember reading an interview [with Alan O'Connor] about how you planned to infuse your teaching with punk ideas and media, at the point when you were just planning your initial stuff—having kids make their own zines, talking about the significance of subcultures, stuff like that. Did that work out largely as planned, and did students engage with it?[1]

Martin Sorrondeguy: I'm glad you brought that up, because I missed a really important thing. Before I went back to San Francisco State, and when I was working at *Maximumrocknroll*, I worked at an alternative high school in the East Bay. That was my teaching job where I was doing really cool stuff, and a lot of my students were punks and rockers and weirdo kids, freaks and awesome kids that I loved, and that's where I had a lot of liberty. I actually did a history class, and it was the history of subcultures in the United States from the 1930s forward. It started out with the Zoot suits, like the pachuco movement out of L.A., coming out of the jazz scene, and went into Beatniks and all the way to punk and hip hop, and so on and so forth.

So that was a really awesome and important job for me as well, because I really got to work with kids who. . . keep in mind, I still wasn't sure. I loved that job, and then I did my teaching credential, and there

---

1   Alan O'Connor, "Apendix A: Interview with Lengua Armada," in *Punk Record Labels and the Struggle for Autonomy: The Emergence of DIY* (Lanham, MD: Lexington Books, 2008), 93–118.

was a period I was going to walk away from education, but I kept getting sucked into it somehow. I totally spaced on mentioning that job, but you mentioned the Alan O'Connor interview, and that's exactly what I did at that school.

John Mink: Wow. So you did kind of have a dream curriculum, where you were able to structure things, almost to tie them to the other side of your life that maybe you weren't so frank about in the classroom.

Martin Sorrondeguy: In terms of my "alternative life," they knew everything about me. I ended up one day with one of my bosses saying, "Martin, can you go to the computer lab and change the screen savers?"—because the students had put all the Limp Wrist lyrics for "Fags Hate God" on all the screen savers! I was like "Oh, my god, I'm so sorry," and I just told the kids, "You guys, don't do that!" [laughter]. But it was a really amazing place to be—it was wild. I could go on forever, stories and weird stuff, and I don't want to do that.

John Mink: It's fascinating that you were able to share with those particular students your "other life," which has been tied in since the beginning.

Martin Sorrondeguy: Yeah, they knew it though. I had kids who were in my class with Limp Wrist shirts on, so they knew who I was. I mean, two of the students, these two young girls, these punk girls, they jumped on a greyhound all the way to Austin, Texas, to see Limp Wrist. I remember their parents called me—"Martin, can you. . ." and I was like, "I will fly there, and as soon as I'm there I will find them, and they will stay with me. I will basically take care of them. Wherever I stay, they stay."

John Mink: Field trip!

Martin Sorrondeguy: [laughter] Yeah, field trip!

John Mink: Just give me a permission slip, and we'll get all this stuff organized. No problem.

Martin Sorrondeguy: [laughter] So let me just move forward into going into a more state-run school.

John Mink: Yes, let's go back to the school in Oakland. What was the difference in terms of how you were able to interact at that school with the people in charge of the school, the administration, the parents, the student population; and how did you reconcile those relationships with your own personal identities within punk, activism, and queer culture?

Martin Sorrondeguy: Right, so this is how it worked—it really did not work. Let me rephrase that—it would not *have* worked, so what I did was go to the courts and legally change my name.

John Mink: Wow, okay.

Martin Sorrondeguy: That's what I did. It was to protect myself and to protect the job I was going to do, because I know I'm a good teacher. I knew I could really bring something to the classroom, into these kids' lives, that has nothing to do with my music, with what I do, with my art—nothing. I can teach these kids skills, and I can teach them a lot of stuff about just life, and in order to protect that, there was no way I could walk into a classroom as "Martin Sorrondeguy" successfully without it blowing up in my face. It came really close on numerous occasions to blowing up in my face. My students would be like, "We Googled you; we didn't find anything on you." And I'm like, "It's because I'm a really boring person. I don't do anything; I just work and go home."

That was the sort of identity I had at the school. A lot of the students, they didn't know. Only one teacher once said, "Hey, Mr. Rock Star!" And I'm like, "What?" She was a teacher across the hall from me. It was at lunchtime and all these kids were in the hall, and they all look at me, and I go, "What do you mean?" And she's like, "Hey, Mr. Rock Star, I heard you're in like a rock and roll band." I just looked at her, and I go, "I'm not in a rock and roll band," and I felt bad. I denied it, and she felt really dumb, and all the kids laughed at her. But later I pulled her aside, and I told her, "Hey, you know what? I'm sorry I did that to you. Yes, I'm in a band, but I don't want the kids to know about that. That's a part of my life that I don't like sharing and making public."

She was really apologetic and said "I'm so sorry." I said, "No, no, it's fine." She asked why it would be an issue, and I knew she was an open lesbian teacher, and I said, "Look, I'm super openly queer. It's not for kids." Then she's like, "I'm sorry, I get it." I asked how she found out, and she said that someone down at a district meeting—who had huge plugs and was a punker—told her, "You have a famous punk rocker working at your school." They actually revealed it; they disclosed that. And I was just like, "Oh, my god, I can't believe this person did that!"—I mean, what happened to "What we do is secret. . .," right? Jesus!

John Mink: Right. You really would have to maintain a double life.

Martin Sorrondeguy: I think that's where my story gets really unique. In order to do what I wanted to do and to be effective, I felt that I needed to go and legally change my name.

John Mink: That is a difficult action you had to take, but it seems like that's a way that you were able to. . . I mean, you have this super strong, radical DIY punk ethos. It drove you in creating and expanding a vital and important space within punk, to elevate your ideas and to elevate those who you felt direct solidarity with—people who you help to platform, like Latinx and queer punks, in so many powerful ways. But you can apply those DIY radical ideas [in teaching] without necessarily having to get into the nitty-gritty of everything you do. And like you said, "What we do is secret. . .," right?

Martin Sorrondeguy: I think things have changed so much in terms of private versus public and who we are. In the past, there were old punk teachers who were punks way back in the early eighties, and nobody would ever figure it out, or they had some weird punk name—but I was always Martin Sorrondeguy, Martin of Los Crudos, Martin from Limp Wrist, Martin from whatever—and to try to kind of cover that up was really difficult. The only way that I could see it happening successfully was by doing what I did. I'm glad I did it—because within days kids [in your class] are googling you. They want to find out who you are. They want details, you know? I'm glad I did what I did, and I think it was one of the smartest things I've ever done. I was able to do the four years that I put into that school in the best possible way—and that was awesome.

John Mink: Did it end up okay? Was there anything in the end that you'd feel comfortable talking about?

Martin Sorrondeguy: You know what, everything ended up fine. I think there was something in me that felt like there needed to be a change, and it really was because I was focusing on my photography again. I was kind of unhappy with the school in general. You have to understand, at the school I worked in, in the four years I was there, there were five principals.

John Mink: Yeah, that's Oakland Unified.

Martin Sorrondeguy: Talk about unstable. It was really rough. When I spoke to other teachers, and their experiences, I was jealous; like: What the fuck am I doing? Where am I, you know? What am I dealing with? It was really unfortunate, because I got along, I kid you not, with I'd say 98 percent of my students—even kids who I thought hated me and hated my classes. One boy came in a year after he had been gone, and he said to me, "I really miss your class, because this was my favorite class." That shocked me because the kid did zero in my class, and I think it was the way I ran the class. The kids enjoyed being there. I had kids in my class for who every other fucking teacher they had was down their fucking necks constantly and giving them shit and trying to get them expelled—trying to get them fucking kicked out, like everything, you know? Trying to expel these kids from school or get them suspended.

I went to this meeting with this young African American girl, she didn't even live in a straight-up home—she lived in a group home. Every teacher was there, and I just remember all of them going around and saying all this really negative shit about her, and I was like, "I have no problems with her in my class. She comes in tardy, but that's the bulk of it; I have not had issues with her my classes." She leaned over and told her guardian, "This is the teacher I like" [laughs]. It was because I created an environment in my class that kids legitimately felt that they could be in and not get fucked with.

John Mink: Tell me how you did that; tell me some techniques.

Martin Sorrondeguy: It was a struggle at first. [Teaching in this school] wasn't something I went into it and was like, "Oh, I got this down"—it wasn't like that. It took time, and it took a lot of figuring out, but I was very stern—I wasn't this loose teacher. I mean, I don't think I cracked a fucking smile till Christmastime. So I learned that you have to really maintain—there was something about that *structure* that a lot of the kids like, but the thing is I knew my shit—you know what I mean? There would be some clown that would do something really weird on the computer and would think that I wouldn't know how to fix it, and I would hit a couple keys and get out of that mess, so they realized, "This guy really knows what he's doing." There's something to be said about when you really know your stuff, and you're killing that subject—there's a level of respect that comes with that. But I was also very attentive to the students. I remember I had a lot of inner-city Oakland kids. I remember one girl coming in one morning just crying; she came in late, and I had one of those electric kettles in my class. I would have water going, and I remember just making her tea and just setting it right in front of her. You know, just keeping going with my lesson, and you could just see on her face like, "Oh, my god." They sense when you care about them. I think there's a thing that some teachers, maybe they don't care enough, or maybe they do and don't know how to care. Or they don't know how to go, "Oh, my god, there's something really weird happening with the student right now. What can I do to let them know that I notice and that I care about them?" I'm really like, "Something's wrong here. What can I do to make them feel a little more at ease?"

So stuff like that—I have bottles of water—it's just really basic stuff, but the way I put their artwork up on the on the walls, just displaying their work, making them realize that what they had to say or create has value—that was huge for them. They would walk into the classroom and run up to the walls like little kids, just so proud of seeing their piece on the wall. I also did projects where there was relevancy, as I did to help this poster project where they had to research a health issue that was going on in their community.

They had to do legitimate research, and what we created using photography and Photoshop was a health poster, an awareness poster. So whether it was "I think smoking is terrible, it causes cancer" or whatever it was, every student would address a health issue in their poster. The last year that I was there, a few of the student posters got picked up [by the city of Oakland] and were running on buses around town, which is really awesome.

The other thing, though, is that I'm not going to paint a cute picture of [the school], because there were situations that were really messed up and not good and not cool and not positive. The really difficult situations every teacher has.

John Mink: That's teaching.

Martin Sorrondeguy: Yeah, that is teaching. You're dealing with adolescents—well I was, at least—and that comes with a lot of baggage. There's a lot to think about and unpack when you're dealing with adolescents.

John Mink: Absolutely. With punks too. To a certain extent, so much of the punk ideology and approach is not letting go of certain aspects of adolescence in some ways, right? You don't forget what it was like to be a teenager. I think that is one of the things that actually makes punks such good teachers a lot of the time.

Martin Sorrondeguy: I think so. There were definitely situations, and depending on who it was and what students. . . There was a little gang of lesbian girls in my one of my third period classes, and they were obsessed with me. They were always fishing and fishing and trying to find out if I was gay. I would say, "Oh, I'm going out of town," and they would ask a question like, "Oh, who are you going out of town with?" "A friend." "Uh huh. What kind of friend?" "A friend." Trying to get it out of me, you know? I remember finally, toward the end of the year, I told them. "Uh, since you're fishing, it's my boyfriend," because they were doing this all the time—and the look on their faces, they were just glowing. They realized, "Oh, my god!"

John Mink: Oh, you made their year!

Martin Sorrondeguy: Oh, and then they were like, "Can you be our chaperone at Pride?"—"Hell, no!" It was funny [laughter].

John Mink: "Nope! I have my own plans, thanks very much!"

Martin Sorrondeguy: Yeah, no, no, no, no, not happening. And there were other experiences I had that were so great. Teaching is extremely challenging. Being an art teacher, people think it's a blow off class, that it's easy—it's not. It is really challenging, and there's a whole lot of motivating and buy-in that you need to get from your students to get them to begin to work on something. It was rough, and there was a lot that I learned in that class. I sometimes think back at it and go, "Wow, I can't believe that I survived that shit." Year one was horrific, because on top of everything I was doing, and it being my first year, I was basically told, "You need to do the yearbook."

John Mink: Oh, wow. They dropped that in your lap.

Martin Sorrondeguy: Oh yeah, they did. It was crazy. I ended up leaving after four years, and then it went really sour for me, because the school didn't pay its yearbook debt. Then, all of a sudden, the yearbook company came after me and tried to sue me for thirty thousand dollars. So I felt really burned. I actually had to speak to a lawyer friend—luckily, I had this friend of mine who was a lawyer and attorney, and she ended up really helping me out getting things all sort of squared away, but I felt so betrayed by that school and system in general that I was like, "I can't believe that fucking happened."

John Mink: It's so awful realizing that with the broken system of financing and charters and poor administration in a lot of these districts, districts that are having so many problems, that the teachers can get so much unloaded on to them. They can end up being on the receiving end of so much of this terrible stuff. My dad taught in Oakland Unified School District for thirty-five years. He loved the kids, but I remember feeling like he was on strike for half of my childhood.

Martin Sorrondeguy: Yeah, it's really crazy, and I felt so betrayed, because some of us at that school were more than just the teacher. We were the teacher who monitored the hall, walked around and talked to students, who broke up fights when a fight broke out and nobody was around to stop it but maybe me, and maybe another person, you know what I mean? It was like you really put yourself out there. I could jump in and stop fights, and it would end somehow.

But there were teachers. . . There was a teacher who got jumped in the bathroom at that school. I wasn't one of those teachers that was going to get shot, you know what I mean? So, in a way, I just felt so betrayed. But enough of that, because I don't want it to seem like it was all negative. It ended negatively for me, and at that point I really thought I would never work in a school again. Now I'm back working in education, but it's a very different scenario. I've worked with age groups that range from infants on up, and I'm now in adult literacy.

John Mink: Oh, you're doing adult ed!

Martin Sorrondeguy: Yes.

John Mink: I did that too, for a few years. I loved it. It's a wonderful job.

Martin Sorrondeguy: Yeah, I got hired by the University of Illinois Chicago, and I got worked in by an old punk friend of mine. She's also in education, and she said, "Martin, you should really come see our program." And I'm like, "Yes!" We used to have these really cool conversations about education and theories we had and about activism and being a teacher and this and that, and she kept insisting, just kind of fishing and trying to get me to come in. Finally, I was like, "Okay, let me go see what you all are doing." And before I know it, I'm being interviewed, and next thing you know I get this job.

It's a great job. We don't work on campus; we work in the communities. I work in a neighborhood called "Back of the Yards" on the south side of Chicago, and I work in another community not far off from there. I work primarily with migrant moms doing digital literacy and helping a bunch of them do their high school equivalency, so I focus on language arts and social studies, and it's all in Spanish. So that's what I'm doing.

John Mink: That's incredible. So when you're teaching these classes now, and in the past, how do you talk to your students about immigration? Do you often talk about your own experiences as an immigrant?

Martin Sorrondeguy: Well, what is really interesting there is that it just depends on how it comes up. There weren't necessarily a lot of things being talked about in terms of immigration at the time when I was at the high school in Oakland, but with who I'm working with now? Is that the question?

John Mink: Yeah, or any of your experiences on this in general.

Martin Sorrondeguy: I think since the new [presidential] administration, it's gotten very heated, and there's been a lot happening, so it's not even like we have to try to talk about this; it's just a reality. I know there were times last year when all of a sudden the community would kind of work together—there'd be a call that come in, and it would say, "ICE is down the street doing a raid." We would keep our students [inside]; we would let them all know and keep them in school until the coast was clear.

John Mink: We had a lockdown for the same reasons at the adult school where I was teaching.

Martin Sorrondeguy: There would be communication between people who were outside of the school and people inside school to kind of make sure shit was cool before people left.

John Mink: Yeah, that's good, because it's an example of what I was going to ask next. Are there ways that a teacher can use their position to empower and protect migrant students of color from hostile forces of white supremacy?

Martin Sorrondeguy: Oh, hell, yeah. Oh, hell, yeah.

John Mink: That's obviously a really direct example, right? So what are some other ones? What are some other ways that teachers can help use their position to help empower and protect migrant students of color?

Martin Sorrondeguy: Since I've been teaching social studies and doing the constitution, we get into talking about their rights and talking about current topics and things that are happening in the news. This stuff just surfaces, and there's some students who have a permit, their green card or whatever, and there's some students who definitely don't. So we'll start having these conversations, like what is "we the people" really all about? What does this all mean? What does the constitution mean? Who's protected? We start talking about the history of this country and who's claiming ownership over what and who was here and what is the makeup of this nation. What is the West Coast? What *was* the West Coast? It wasn't pilgrims who landed on the West Coast—that's not what fucking happened. We just talk about all these histories, and there are just so many entry points where you can really get into a lot of issues. So it organically happens. When you're working with this population, these concerns will surface.

We also, as instructors, take time out of our classes and have somebody from one of the community organizations come in and talk to our students. We would talk about free legal help. These are things that we were bringing awareness of to our students, like, "Hey, there's ways to inform yourself around this. There are ways to get information, and there's a lot of misinformation that starts flying around, so here are some places that you can get some really good, accurate information."

John Mink: That is powerful. My class at the adult school I worked at did a research project, where we helped people do research, and then did a skillshare with each other about what advocacy resources they could pull up for community self-defense [see "Lesson Plans for Community Self-Defense" in this book]. It was really useful, because people also had the experience of discovering stuff on their own, or at least the satisfaction of like, "Hey, I found this, and I'm gonna be able to share this, and we're all going to share these useful and important things."

Martin Sorrondeguy: I think we got worried about that, like in the last year it was a little problematic, because sometimes you didn't know where that information was coming from or the organization that put it out there. And that was something we had to really address—"Be careful"—because there was shit going on out there that were actually setups.

John Mink: Right.

Martin Sorrondeguy: So it's like, "That's a trap!"

John Mink: That's so complicated and fucked.

Martin Sorrondeguy: It's complicated and fucked, and that is something we're always extremely vigilant about. "Hey, what is this? What are we looking at? What are we reading here? Who is this? Where did you get it? Let's look up who this group is." We're tied to so many activists in the community in Chicago, so somebody we know has to know if this is legit.

John Mink: You can assess it?

Martin Sorrondeguy: Oh, yeah, we'll find it out.

John Mink: It really requires a community to be able to suss out and aid in understanding when sorting through this kind of information, for this kind of advocacy—it's so important.

Also with regard to these issues around immigration and racism, I was looking back to one of the earliest interviews that Crudos did in *Maximumrocknroll* in like 1992. You were actually talking a lot about racism, assimilation, and resisting it, and how when you toured it was a shock to you that so many kids you met from Latinx families, usually second or third generation, didn't speak any Spanish. You were really specific in your personal comments; talking about how this was obviously still not shielding them from having to deal with racism. In the same article, you talked about your experiences all the way back in grammar school, where you were an immigrant kid from a family that didn't really speak English at home. And you had the experience of having your Spanish taken away from you, stolen from you by teachers who said, "You're in the United States, you don't speak Spanish here— you aren't in Mexico now." Of course, this was fucked in general and was also ignorantly not acknowledging that your family is from Uruguay.

How did these early experiences influence the ways in which you do the practice of punk and how you do the practice of teaching? Are punk and teaching similar to you as vehicles to address and push back against this kind of thinking, and in what ways?

Martin Sorrondeguy: Absolutely. I think that there are so many ways that could be answered, but punk and activism and teaching, they really do go hand in hand. If you're a teacher who is not doing this sort of rote system of teaching where everything is just a kind of repetition, if you're really talking about learning and critical thinking and assessing something and analyzing and getting into the deeper questions—that to me is punk. That to me is activism. Like, why is this? What is happening? How did I get here? And where am I in this crazy fucking place? Those experiences I had as a kid, what I saw happening in my community here, absolutely played a huge role in how I took on punk. The punk scene was doing what the punk scene was doing, and the way that we as Crudos kind of came into it really went against the norm of what was expected from punk, if that makes sense.

John Mink: Yes, it definitely does.

Martin Sorrondeguy: Those experiences are what really made Crudos what it was. It's crazy, but there were other things too. I mean, my mom was extremely influential in how I thought about that. My mom is highly educated.

John Mink: Almost a doctor, right?

Martin Sorrondeguy: Yes, she was in medical school, she didn't finish it, and she decided to walk away from it to just be a mom. But she was in medical school, she was really smart, she spoke numerous languages. She studied French, spoke Spanish, Italian, came here and learned English—she is this very smart woman. When I came up with something that was worthy of questioning, she'd fucking grill me, man, like, "What is punk? What is this?" She'd be like, "Yeah, but why?" and she's grilling me to really think about what is it that I'm doing, "What do you want to do with this?" I got questioned way harder by her than any punk ever in my life.

John Mink: I bet, and at the time she was working with Mujeres Latinas en Acción, right?

Martin Sorrondeguy: Oh, my god, you did your homework—yes! How did you know that?

John Mink: Well, I research like a teacher too, I guess [laughter]. But, yeah, she was going around to high schools, right? Doing outreach to get girls to protect themselves, to hold prenatal classes for young mothers in the Latinx community, and she's asking you this stuff, right? It seemed like the questioning connected in this sense, how she almost got this medical degree and then was like, "I'm just going to go out and actually do work in the community."

Martin Sorrondeguy: And that's what she did when she came here. She worked at Mujeres Latinas en Acción. She was one of the "old schoolers" at that agency, because now they're a massive organization, but when she was working there in the seventies and early eighties, it was super grassroots. So, yes, she was a prenatal classes instructor, and she worked for a program called Dar La Luz, meaning "To Give Light," and it was about giving prenatal class instruction to a lot of teenage girls and young women in the community so they could help themselves. She also had this really strong politic that dated back to Uruguay, so she raised us with a certain consciousness. I wasn't Joe American punk kid going, "Oh, I just discovered the Dead Kennedys, I like punk rock." No, I was coming in from some other fucking crazy fucked-up shit, in a good way fucked-up, you know? It was another level of consciousness. It wasn't about "I hate mom and dad." It was like, "No, I hate Ronald Reagan, and I don't like the CIA, because they are really fucked-up, I hate the FBI. . ." It was like a whole other level of consciousness as a young person coming into it.

I didn't trust governments, I didn't trust. . . We were coming from a place that literally experienced and went through a military dictatorship, so the last person you're going to trust if you believe in free thought and everything is the government? So I was coming into punk rock on a very different level, I think. I wasn't introduced to politics via punk. It was like, I learned about vegetarianism and shit like that, and

Crass did a really interesting job at laying out some stuff, and so did Conflict and bands like that. But my root in politics predates all that.

John Mink: It definitely seems like you didn't have to deal with assimilationist pressure within the home. It seemed like your parents weren't pushing that, and your community wasn't pushing it either.

Martin Sorrondeguy: The thing is that we were impressionable. We were like any other kids; we were young, we were in this neighborhood, and it got us all to thinking how we moved here in 1968–1969, and the neighborhood was not an all-Latino neighborhood at the time. We were struggling with our identity and hanging on to our language and all that. It wasn't until later that the community shifted and changed and became a Latino neighborhood. We were definitely pressured into feeling differently, but my mom made it really clear that in this house, this is how we do things—and that always stuck with us.

John Mink: So what can teachers do to push back against assimilationist dogma in the classroom, like the kind that teacher tried to force on you, and make students feel validated about who they are and where they come from?

Martin Sorrondeguy: Well, kids reveal a lot about themselves. They share a lot, and you need to be really alert to a lot of the comments they make, to what they're saying, because you will hear shame come out of their mouths about their ethnicity or who they are. And it's a very fragile situation, because you don't know what the root of it is or who it's coming from. Sometimes, it's coming from home. So there may be Latino kids or kids you know who are just like, "Yeah, I don't want to speak Spanish," or they were taught they shouldn't by their own parents, or their parents wouldn't teach them, because they think it's going to be easier for them in this society.

I mean it's such a tricky one. My partner, he's Mexican, and he looks very Mexican, but his family on his mom's side have been here predating the United States. But because Sam's this big dark man, people look at him and go "Mexican." They don't say, "This is an old school American, whose been here before this was fucking recognized as the United States," right? No. People don't think that way, they just look at him and go, "Mexican. What part of Mexico you from?" He's like, "Actually I'm from New Mexico, California"—that's where he's from.

My point about the kids is that stuff comes at them, and with the language thing, parents can forcefully change it—but the reality is that skin speaks way louder than what you actually say, because people look at you, and we're living in this society and then this nation that has to put you in some place, right? You can have the most perfect English and speak it so smoothly, just like an "American," but the way things fucking roll is like, no, man; somewhere someone is going to come up with some bullshit and everybody knows that. I mean, you don't even need to look at the Latino community, look at the African American community, the Black community—people who have been here forever and still get treated like garbage. That's just the fabric of this fucking nation.

John Mink: Yeah, white supremacy sucks.

Martin Sorrondeguy: As a teacher you know, there were things that you could do, just like the little littlest of things—like highlight how cool something is about them; it can be a detail, "Oh wow, that's really amazing," or, "I love this." Things like that, I think they really need to build themselves up, and it doesn't even have to do with race, ethnicity, nothing. It's just like, "You are a thinker, you can create. You are valuable to this classroom and not only this classroom." I think that sense of worth that you can instill in the students can go a really long way.

And I'll tell you something, this fact that I was Latino—I remember Latino kids, and a lot of Black kids in my class too, their jaws would drop when I started speaking Spanish. They would be like, "What? You speak Spanish?" and I'm like, "Yeah, I speak Spanish." They were like, "You're Latino?" I'm like, "Yeah!" Oh, my god, I don't think some of them had ever had a Latino male teacher ever. You know what I mean. It was like, "What?!" So I think they would sit there and just think, "Wow, okay." It kind of changed something a little bit. Even if you're not Latino, if you're not from that community, there's so many ways that you can instill that sort of positivity, and the fact that you're so positive can make them feel like they are going to look at you and examine you and who you are and maybe rethink stuff—you know what I mean?

When I taught my students, I had students come back and be like, "Oh, my god, I am so glad I had your class because of blah, blah, blah, blah, blah, blah, blah," but whatever. The thing is I wasn't a teacher that they would *not* come back and tell something to, per se. I was a teacher that they *would* come back and talk to, and they would remember. "Oh that's Mr. Blah Blah, he's a badass in Photoshop, he's Latino, he speaks Spanish. You know, he's fucking gay." There are just so many things that can change the way somebody may think, change the way they think about things. So you might have come in, year one, having all these sorts of walls, and as time goes on and you experience things in this world and in this life, you realize it—"You know what? I heard somebody say something really fucked-up about this kind of person, but I had really awesome teacher who was that kind of person; and they weren't a shitty person, and I don't agree with that fucked-up thing someone else said"—so it's a lot of that.

John Mink: It's huge, it's vital, and when you have the interplay of different identities with people who are powerful role models—it's invaluable. You want to be the kind of teacher who can live this thing that students can want to be.

Thinking about also your queer identity—you came out as gay during the Los Crudos years in the mid-nineties, and that was an intense and culturally transformative time in hardcore and punk; it was really powerful for a lot of people when you came out. For instance, I was a kid from the lower working-class suburbs of the East Bay, from El Sobrante, and I was a closeted but queer-positive bisexual kid. I knew the scene in the Bay Area had plenty of openly gay punk icons, but they weren't usually in the heaviest modern style fast hardcore bands, which is a lot of stuff that I liked. So you coming out as a singer of a very popular and intense fast hardcore band when I was in high school was huge for me. You became well-known as such, and I think it helped open the door for a lot of queer kids who are into more extreme music to come out, you know? I mean, the Bay is a bubble, obviously, and my perspective is pretty specific. But how was your coming out received in the wider hardcore scene and your local scene at home in punk and with your family and old friends?

Martin Sorrondeguy: Well, I think I had to deal with [coming out] like a lot of young queer people did—I came out a little older, but I still had to deal with stuff. It wasn't the most positive sort of thing in terms of family. I got pushback, and there were issues that really led me to kind of leave the house; to go move out on my own and just experience life for a while, you know? I needed to have my own space and figure my stuff out but also give space to my family so they could figure stuff out—I had my bumps, you know what I mean? And I think when I came out with Crudos, it was really weird, because we had gone on a tour, and I was coming out in every city we were in. It was the drive-by come out. I'd drive into the city, come out to our show, say something about being gay, and then we'd leave [laughter]. And that seemed safer to me than coming out at home. I hadn't come out at a show in Chicago until I came back home from that tour. Then, I finally did, and it was a really wild response, like a bunch of kids jumped up on stage and hugged me; it was really amazing and wild, like, "Whoa, I wasn't expecting that."

There was some pushback there too, because machismo is machismo. There's going to be people who have issues with [homosexuality] in the hardcore scene; there's gonna be guys who don't like it. And it was expressed to me that there were people who felt that something had changed, something was different. It wasn't just that something changed—something changed that they were not comfortable with. It was always there, they just didn't know about it—but knowing is what created the discomfort.

So it was it was really bizarre, but I stuck to my guns, like I'm not gonna run away from this, and I still don't to this day. I just had a photo show in Mexico City, and I did one wall that was all flyers and posters that I've made over the years, and I purposely and intentionally mixed up Crudos and Limp Wrist and all this other stuff. I didn't separate it, because I knew that if I just did all the Crudos stuff on one end, there would be a bunch of dudes staring at the Crudos stuff and ignoring the Limp Wrist shit. So I purposely put all of these fliers that are super homoerotic next to this super politicized Los Crudos stuff, and some guy had a problem with it. He said something to me about it—it was his view about an erect penis that was mind-boggling. He equated an erection to somebody Sieg Heiling and Nazism. And I just said, "Do you mean to tell me that every morning you wake up and you have a woody, so you think of Nazis? I think there's something wrong!"

John Mink: I think he might be going to some Death in June shows.

Martin Sorrondeguy: I don't know what the hell that was about, but I was just like, "No, no, no" [laughter].

John Mink: [laughter] "Nice try but no."

Martin Sorrondeguy: It's hilarious! I was like, "That's what you think of when that happens to you? That's a little weird."

John Mink: It's like, "So here's this thing, it's called the pink triangle—do you know where that came from?"

Martin Sorrondeguy: It was bizarre. This guy called himself an anarchist, and it was just really bizarre to me. I was like, "Wow, that's a rough anarchism to be in, because you're struggling with some really deep-rooted stuff if that's what you're thinking about, you know what I mean? Sexuality clearly bothers you." So it was weird.

John Mink: I also read that you did a queer history class in the alternative high school around 2009, right?

Martin Sorrondeguy: I did do a queer history class, and that was the beauty of that school—I could really create my own classes and bring in books and readings and documentaries. And it was amazing. So I did do that as a class, yes.

John Mink: How did you structure the curriculum? What was the general approach?

Martin Sorrondeguy: I had to really be specific—it wasn't just titled "queer history," because that's so vast. I was trying to focus, and I don't remember at this point exactly how I honed it down to a certain era, but I'd say it was more contemporary queer culture—it wasn't going way back in the history. We read books, I showed a documentary on Leigh Bowery, who was awesome—we talked about people like Boy George and performance artists, how they were really influenced by Leigh Bowery. We read David Sedaris books. I can't remember everything we did. I wish I could look back at my little syllabus and notes and figure that out. But I don't remember it all.

John Mink: Sounds like a good approach, though, in terms of like sticking to something of an era and a focus. It seems like that would be an easier way to do it than to just try to do the whole thing.

Martin Sorrondeguy: If you try to go super deep in the history. . . I found that with the subcultures class it was cooler to go way back, because it really made the students realize that young people from way back were always trying to do something different. I think that was a really cool point that they could connect with. It wasn't just "Yeah, we're doing this because we like this music." Those Zoot Suit Riots that happened—that was linked to a political situation, it was linked to race, it was linked to class, and it was linked to a lot of things. I know we read out of the book titled *Murder at the Sleepy Lagoon*.[2] But it was fucking great, and it was really about how subcultures, a lot of times, were linked to a lot of political stuff and activism. These Zoot Suiters were attacked in a time when there was rationing of material, of fabric, and they were into jazz,

---

2   Eduardo Obregón Pagán, *Murder at Sleepy Lagoon* (Chapel Hill: University of North Carolina Press, 2004).

and they were rebelling by wearing the big fucking baggy pants. People were just so outraged, they were saying it was over the clothes—but it was because they were Brown people, that was the heart of what people were irritated with. It was like, "How dare you do this?"

John Mink: How dare they flaunt those norms!

Martin Sorrondeguy: Yes, well they were saying "fuck you," but they were also Brown people doing that.

John Mink: Exactly.

Martin Sorrondeguy: It was like, "Oh, no!," so a lot of white soldiers and other people went out and fucking literally were tearing off their clothes and beating people up. We talked about other things, about the sixties and about punk; we got into everything, and it was good. And you can't talk about that stuff without really touching on the "whys" and what was going on, what was happening socially, what was happening politically during that time and place. What was going on? What was the landscape like? You really start to think about that stuff. And, you know, if a student says, "Well, these Mexican people. . .," that would bring up this whole thing, like, "Oh, wait, did you say they came over here? Well, let's talk about that. Did they come over here? Or were they already here?" It's interesting. Even when I was in the Bay, I was on BART [Bay Area Rapid Transit] headed toward the airport, and there was a man, he was travelling and we were chatting, and he was from. . . I can't remember now, somewhere in the Middle East, and we were talking, and he says, "Why are all these street names in Spanish?"

I said, "Well, the States of California, Arizona, New Mexico, Colorado, Texas, they all belonged to Mexico at one point, and the Spaniards were here too before this was the United States." This man's face was fucking shocked. And I was like, "People don't usually talk about that part of the history. But this was not the United States before." Nobody ever told him that, and he couldn't fuckin' believe it, but that's why it is like that, that's what the history is.

John Mink: And before that it was all Indigenous people. And so you teach somebody even on BART [laughs].

Martin Sorrondeguy: You gotta share yourself, you gotta share your knowledge, and I do that in punk too; I've done that with my bands. I have a lot of experience. I've dealt with a lot of shit, and that's what I'm sharing. That's another sort of level of. . . I don't want to call it teaching, but why not? Because I think it is.

John Mink: Yeah, it is like teaching.

Martin Sorrondeguy: You could just play a show and think about how the bands were really good that night, that you remember liking it, but when you do what I like to do or what I just do . . . it's not that I even like it, it's just that I do it. It's just the way I've handled things. There's something about leaving that impression, that mark, something about what I say to the audience sometimes that really resonates with people. But I'll be honest with you, there's things I don't even remember talking about—a lot, maybe the majority of it. And you know who reminds me? The people that heard it.

I don't want to go off topic, but I think this relates to education and to the impact that you leave on people. I remember when I had to move to Santa Ana, and Crudos was done, Limp Wrist was going, and I kind of really walked away to a certain degree. I was kind of feeling that "Crudos is behind me, Crudos is no more, Crudos is not going to happen again." I walked away from Crudos. I felt that the songs we did were no longer our songs, my songs. I felt like those songs became a part of the people, the community. That was my take on what we did with Crudos. I was moving on to other stuff in my life, and it had probably been four or five years down the line when I came across a video. I think it was online, and we were playing, and I don't know where it was—it might have been in Philly. But I was listening to myself, and I started tearing up, because I didn't even remember ever talking about what I was talking about. And I was just like, what the fuck? It was almost like reencountering something about yourself that you had forgotten about or that you kind of hid away, and it was really important for me to have seen that again, to witness that and experience it. Even though it was through a monitor, something about it really hit me.

I think that's how I think of education in general. It can really make that impact on somebody. My friends in Southern California used to talk about *huellas*; leaving fingerprints. We leave fingerprints everywhere. It's like when people talk about a ripple effect. You're leaving a mark, and you may walk away and go on in life, and you don't even realize the fucking impact you made. You don't see it; we don't stick around. It's impossible to stick around to really see what it is that you did and what is left behind, you know?

John Mink: You put it out there, and then you let it go to the ages.

Martin Sorrondeguy: Yeah, absolutely, absolutely.

John Mink: That's not at all off topic; it is very much a connected insight.

So the last couple things I want to ask you: you obviously know a few punk teachers. Are there any punk teachers who've been particularly inspirational for you or helped inspire you to teach?

Martin Sorrondeguy: Of course, Miriam [Stahl], because I worked with her directly. Miriam was huge, because she had a really unique sort of history, and I love what she was doing at Berkeley High. She's super inspirational, and she still manages to create her own work even though she's totally wrapped up with what's happening at her school and everything, and that's huge for me. She's created this really amazing balance of somehow figuring out having a family, doing her teaching, and still creating her own work.

I think a lot of teachers I know, especially the punk ones, are fucking workaholics like us. We don't get lazy. We're always thinking about what we do next—especially people with art in their blood. You've got to always find a way to make things happen. It's super inspirational.

John Mink: I was thinking about Alice Bag too.

Martin Sorrondeguy: Alice was just here last week with me! I love Alice, and she's a person who worked in the classroom, but now she's teaching on so many levels in so many different ways. She's still doing it, and she's highly inspirational. If you see her live, it'll fucking blow your mind. It's insane.

John Mink: Oh, I love [seeing Alice live]!

Martin Sorrondeguy: She's huge, and I'm really good friends with her. I didn't think about it really. It's one of those questions, and you're catching me off guard [laughing], and she's somebody I hang out with and talk to regularly, and I just didn't even think about it, you know?

John Mink: Well, that makes sense to a certain extent, because for the punk teachers we know everything is kind of a continuation of work in a lot of ways; it almost seems like a naturalized thing. So all the punk teachers are workaholics, doing this, this, this, this, and this. And it's just part of a long list of incredible things that a lot of these people are doing and have done. So it's sometimes hard to pull up that particular part of the resume, because there's so much other stuff going on.

Martin Sorrondeguy: Right, right.

John Mink: Sorry, I didn't mean to put you on the spot [both laughing].

Well, what else do you hope to accomplish as a teacher coming up? What do what do you see in the near—and a little further down the line—future?

Martin Sorrondeguy: That's a really good question. I don't know. I just think as a human being I get challenged. I'm always facing new challenges as an educator and also as a punk, because with everything, there's going to be challenges. In terms of education, in terms of our program, the State of Illinois Community College Board just approved the adult high school where adults will no longer have to take these high-stakes tests in order to obtain a diploma. The idea of the adult high school is coming into being, it's going to be a reality—they approved it, it got passed, it's a thing now. So our program is sort of at the forefront of trying to develop what that looks like.

John Mink: An adult ed curriculum?

Martin Sorrondeguy: Yes, yes, project-based learning with adults. We're doing the whole digital badging stuff; there are a lot of things going on right now that I think are going to be beneficial to our students and our population. So I'm really excited about that and excited to be a part of that.

John Mink: That sounds really exciting. As another adult ed teacher, it's neat to hear about some new ideas outside of the standard GED/equivalency diploma kind of paradigms that are usually used.

Martin Sorrondeguy: It is a huge deal. It's a tremendous amount of work to get that going and develop it, but it's happening, so I'm really excited about that.

John Mink: Well, Martin, really nice talking to you. Thanks so much for your time and your heart.

Martin Sorrondeguy: No, thank you; I'm glad we got to do it. Thanks for including me in the book, if I made the cut. I don't know. . .

John Mink: Yeah, I think you made the cut [both laugh]. Good night, Martin.

》》 In August 2017, a far-right coalition staged a series of nationwide rallies that culminated in the massive, openly neofascist "Unite the Right" rally in Charlottesville, Virginia. In Charlottesville, over a thousand torch-wielding white nationalists physically threatened Black churchgoers and marched while chanting "Jews Will Not Replace Us" and "Blood and Soil," the latter refrain lifted directly from the Nazi catalog (see dwayne dixon's account in this book for further details on this incident). In a further spasm of violence, anti-fascist and social justice activist Heather Heyer was killed and dozens of others injured by right-wing extremists and their enablers (very much including the police).

Immediately following Heyer's murder, U.S. President Donald Trump made a speech in which he declared the violence to be the fault of "both sides" and that there were "fine people" among the assembled white supremacists. These events, and the unpopularity of Trump, led to an unusual surge in overall public support and sympathy for anti-fascist direct action. In typical fashion, this support dissipated quickly under the weight of distorted narratives from media, police, (neo)liberals, and politicians from the center and right-wing that reiterated the old false equivalency narrative—echoing Trump's speech.

The following piece was written in July 2017, in the aftermath of a series of far-right rallies in early 2017 in Berkeley, California. These rallies represented the genesis of highly publicized mass mobilizations of both the far right and those who showed up to oppose them—the latter generally, though not always, in far greater numbers, and in Berkeley this included many students and staff from Berkeley High School, right across the street. As many of the players are the same and variations on this pattern have been repeated several times since then, with the results not terribly dissimilar, it seems instructive and appropriate to present this essay largely as it was written at the time.

False Equivalencies and the Resurgent Far Right in a Messy, Violent World

by John Mink

> Fascist scum
> Expected a parade
> Your welcoming committee
> Was an antifa brigade
> —G.L.O.S.S., "Fight"

On April 15, 2017, a group of around two hundred antifa, black bloc, BAMN (By Any Means Necessary), Bay Waters, and other assorted radicals came to Provo Park in Berkeley, California—right across the street from Berkeley High School, with its more than four thousand students from all over Berkeley and Oakland. The radicals, who were also mostly from Oakland, Berkeley, and other surrounding towns in the Bay Area, showed up to confront a "Trump Rally" attended by between two and three hundred people from all over the country, organized by a constellation of neofascist groups (the so-called "alt-right"). These groups included Identity Evropa (white nationalists inspired by similar identitarian groups in Europe), the Oath Keepers (a far-right paramilitary/militia made up of Islamophobic veterans of the post-9/11 wars), DIY Division/Rise Above Movement (ultraviolent neo-Nazis inspired by "Fight Club" who wear skull bandanas and work out way too much), 2 Million Bikers (notorious for the Altamont-style "security" they provided at the Trump inauguration in DC, where they viciously attacked protestors), Proud Boys (*Vice* magazine founder Gavin McInnes's "Western Chauvinist" gang/club, where to become a "fourth degree" member—the highest possible status—you have to have "endured a major conflict related to the cause"), the III% (a libertarian/separatist anti-immigrant militia group), and others.

United in their love for Trump and emboldened by his particularly American brand of neofascism, the rally organizers and attendees had recently been given a big boost by their orange daddy himself. In January 2017, Trump tweeted out threats to cut Berkeley's public university funding—citing Berkeley's supposed disrespect for "Free Speech"—in the wake of a decisive rebuke of far-right provocateur and former Breitbart editor Milo Yiannoupoulis on campus. In that incident, a scheduled appearance by Yiannoupoulis at University of California Berkeley—during which he planned to publicly doxx dozens of transgender and undocumented students—was shut down by a massive grassroots protest of thousands of people using a diversity of tactics, including "peaceful" protest, civil disobedience, and direct action. Unfortunately, in part due to the aforementioned direct threats from the president of the United States, and in part due to mainstream media manipulation of the optics surrounding direct action tactics (aka "burning garbage can porn"), typical liberal skittishness and radical shaming kicked in. In the time between the Milo shutdown and the April rallies, many liberals stopped showing up to confront these ever-growing and increasingly violent public displays by the far right. The mass response to fascist provocation dissipated, as liberals resorted to old tropes, including "ignore them and they will go away" (obviously didn't work too well so far), "let's just have a civil conversation" (about whether genocide, slavery, and exclusion based on gender identity are okay?), and a common misapplication of horseshoe theory by saying "anti-fascists and fascists are just extremists, all the same" (no comment necessary).

Partially as a result of this liberal retreat, things grew markedly worse on the ground for those who were left holding the bag confronting the growing wave of fascism. During subsequent neofascist rallies held in Berkeley—most notably on April 15, 2017—roughly similar numbers of fascist and anti-fascist protesters lost any semblance of conflict equilibrium due to direct neofascist collaboration with police. Antifa were disarmed by the police at the cordoned off entrance to the park, while many neofascists were permitted to keep their weapons (particularly the paramilitary, combat trained veterans from Oath Keepers). Verbal goading resulted in multiple assaults, and witness accounts plus a wealth of publicly available video footage show quite clearly that nearly all of these assaults were initiated by neofascist forces—particularly members of the DIY Division, 2 Million Bikers, Proud Boys, and Identity Evropa. However, there was only one charge filed against a neofascist participant (Kyle "Based Stickman" Chapman), while numerous anti-fascist radicals who engaged in self-defense from fascist attacks were charged with assault. In at least one instance, the police have used pho-toshopped "evidence" provided by anonymous 4chan message board trolls to arrest and charge a professor from a local community college.

In the end, this asymmetrical warfare (and make no mistake, this was a real fight) was so tilted toward neofascists and their state enablers in the police force that radicals had to make a full retreat from the park, following which neofascists poured into downtown Berkeley to terrorize people of color, queers, and women, shoot out windows with Black Lives Matter displays, and serve as a powerful message of hate to the liberals who were previously walking around eating ice cream and ignoring the open battle happening a scant few blocks away. During the entire protest, 4chan trolls, Infowars reporters, and related tech-savvy fascists were openly filming the entire rally, with a particular focus on capturing images of radicals whose faces were not covered—images they then put through facial recognition software and posted online along with what they could find out about the identities/addresses/etc. of the people they were doxxing.

Some of these doxxed images were of kids from Berkeley High, which, as mentioned earlier, is right across the street from Provo Park. Berkeley High is made up of several thousand teens from very diverse backgrounds who are furious about a bunch of white supremacist neo-fascists coming right into their neighborhood and screaming in their faces about how they plan to dehumanize and crush them under a Trumpist state sanctioned bootheel. However, many of these students are inclined to not wear masks, because they view this (rightfully) as *their* space and are not always aware of the gravity and potential danger of the situation (for themselves and their families) when they are doxxed on the internet. When one of their teachers (who may or may not be someone I am very familiar with) pops off their own mask for a second and tells them it might be a good idea to mask up for safety, we are defi-nitely crossing into the kind of scenario that right-wing propagandists salivate over as they spin tales of radical leftist teachers indoctrinating kids. Naturally, of course, these kids need no indoctrination—they are generally more capable of seeing fascism for what it is than their typically liberal parents and are less inclined toward false equivalencies such as "fascism and antifascism are exactly the same!"

Still, situations such as this are just one aspect of a giant, thorny question as to how teachers—radical and otherwise—contend with the steadily increasing rise of neofascism and the far right, as manifested on the streets by paramilitaries and bolstered by the state (now more explicitly in the U.S. than ever before). This is not just an American problem, of course, as Europe, Asia, and the Middle East see some of their flawed, corrupt democracies falter under manipulative, authoritarian pressure from many of the same people gaming those systems for individual advantage to begin with.

In their book *Trouble on the Far Right: Contemporary Right-Wing Strategies and Practices in Europe*, Laura Lalorie and Maik Fielitz define the far right as "a political space whose actors base their ideology and action on the notion of *in*equality among human beings, combining the supremacy of a particular nation, 'race,' or 'civilization' with ambitions for an authoritarian transformation of values and styles of government."[1] How do teachers reconcile the need to provide a safe, open space for *all* student inquiry, intellectual exploration/constructiveness, and critical assessment of information when such toxic and implicitly destructive political philosophy is ascendant? It is now a given that the current wave of far-right/neofascist sentiment has become part of the system or even taken overt power in many countries, including the United States. So how do teachers (especially radicals/activists) contend with the conversations and power disparities that inevitably result in our classrooms, with parents, with administrators, and deal with potential conflicts with internet trolls and/or even governmental authorities over content, outside class political activities, or other factors? How can we deal with the inevitable demands for a "conversation" giving equal time and a lack of "bias" when talking about neofascist ideologies that are rapidly becoming normalized, when one actor (student, parent, teacher, cop, whoever) openly advocates for things that would—and

1 Maik Fielitz and Laura Lotte Lalorie, "Trouble on the Far Right: Introductory Remarks," in *Trouble on the Far Right: Contemporary Right-Wing Strategies and Practices in Europe*, ed. Maik Fielitz and Laura Lotte Lalorie (Bielefeld, DE: transcript Verlag, 2016).

often already do—actively oppress other students in the same classroom, or maybe another classroom or another school or another city? How does a teacher in Iowa, in a class full of rural white kids, make it clear to a student that Richard Spencer (aka the Nazi who got punched on the internet) isn't just offering "another opinion" when he publishes a piece advocating for "peaceful genocide" of Black Americans—particularly when that student doesn't have to look any Black students in the eye or answer their questions when the "opinion" is asserted and when the student can back up Spencer's purported validity by his repeated appearances on mainstream media such as CNN/Fox/MSNBC/ etc. (in the name of "balanced coverage")?

What happens in a class discussion at an adult school, when an undocumented Salvadoran refugee and self-declared communist comes out as a Trump supporter, because he sees Trump as the only person who can supposedly crush neoliberalism and the corrupt political class, which pretty much everyone in the class agrees is a problem (though the rest of them hate Trump)? And what happens when he cites the basis for his support as a bunch of sketchy YouTube channels that peddle conspiracy theories and white supremacist hate—the same channels and sources that Trump himself cites? What happens when a teacher gets fired for allowing a student to elaborate on a chain of thought where the student was comparing Trump to Hitler in some respects; meanwhile another student fumes in the corner and quietly goes home to complain to his Trumpist parents, who then complain to the administration? The latter happened, by the way, not in Iowa or rural Ohio but in Mountain View, California—the home of Google, aka the ad- and profit-driven replacement for defunded libraries worldwide.

We find ourselves in an increasingly dark and dangerous world, where education will be redefined and weaponized in a million different ways that we can't even imagine as of yet. If you are a teacher or otherwise deeply invested in education, please consider the questions I just posed as just a few potential starting points for helping other teachers to understand the way *you* are dealing with these changing dynamics in the classroom and beyond. Don't forget to keep up the good fight.

>> The next section, "Guide for Youth Protestors," contains a printable graphic foldout, description, and lesson plans by **Jessalyn Aaland**, an interdisciplinary artist based in the San Francisco Bay Area, whose work integrates social practice, painting, and sculpture to explore how the K-12 (kindergarten through twelfth grade) education system functions both as a site for conformity and resistance. Through her project Class Set, Jessalyn has provided over four thousand Risograph printed, artist designed posters featuring social justice quotes to schools, libraries, and nonprofits nation-wide. A former public high school English teacher, Aaland has been an artist in residence at SÍM in Reykjavik, Iceland, and Facebook's Menlo Park Headquarters, and is a 2018–2019 Political Power fellow at Yerba Buena Center for the Arts. More information can be found, and the guide/materials directly downloaded, at the online links included at the end of the "Resources" section of this chapter, and also online at teachingresistancearchive.blogspot.com.

Guide for Youth Protestors

by Jessalyn Aaland

We fear for the thing we no see
We fear for the air around us
We fear to fight for freedom
We fear to fight for liberty
We fear to fight for justice
We fear to fight for happiness
We always get reason to fear.
—Fela Kuti, "Sorrow, Tears and Blood"

Systems just aren't made of bricks they're mostly made of
    people. . .
Silence is a virtue, use it for your own protection
They'll try to make you play their game, refuse to show your face
If you don't want to be beaten down, refuse to join their race.
—Crass, "Big A Little A"

OVERVIEW

Guide for Youth Protestors is a hand-drawn, two-sided, 8.5" by 11" quarter-fold sheet designed to help youth keep themselves safe while protesting, using humorous, food-related illustrations. It features such topics as basic info on police tactics (kettling, Long Range Acoustic Devices, or LARDs, tear gas/pepper spray), the ways cops might try to get you to talk to them, and your rights as a student.

The guide was created in response to a high school teacher friend (and former colleague) who was concerned about not being able to accompany students during the J20 walkouts in 2017 due to contractual obligations. She asked me to keep an eye out for students if I was in downtown San Francisco, but since I was staying in Oakland that day I wondered how else I might be of service to this population. I spent two days compiling information from various resources, laying out the guide, and drawing the illustrations. The first copies were Risograph printed at the Berkeley Art Museum and distributed at the San Francisco Women's March on January 21, 2018 (and some of the first young people to receive copies happened to be former high school students of mine, now in college, who were participating in the protest!).

Since then, thousands of printed copies have been distributed in libraries, bookstores, and at protests nationwide. *Guide for Youth Protestors* was featured as part of "100 Days Action," a calendar of activist and artistic strategy for the first hundred days of Trump's presidency, and the Arte Útil archive as part of the exhibition *Tania Bruguera: Talking to Power/Hablándole al Poder* at Yerba Buena Center for the Arts. The guide is available online [see link in intro to this section—ed.] as a free pdf for anyone to download, print, and distribute, and I continue to provide free Risograph printed copies for teachers, librarians, and youth workers.

For me, as a former high school English teacher, one of the most inspiring and hopeful responses to the election of Trump has been vocal student resistance. I strongly believe in the power of youth, and for many high school students, this might be among their first experiences in protesting. I wanted to provide information in a concise way that would also be engaging to youth, so the guide contains key points which address specific aspects of student protest (i.e., rights detailed in the California Education Code) and information that youth new to protesting might not be aware of. Each idea features a food-related illustration, because everyone loves food. In addition to providing information, the guide has a secondary benefit of helping youth feel included in protest, because they've been given something made just for them. Empowering youth and helping them see their voice as equally important is critical in the struggle for justice.

GUIDE FOR YOUTH PROTESTORS

Here is a simple guide to help you protest safely...

SCHOOL INFO

jessalynaaland@gmail.com

If you are participating in a school WALK-OUT, teachers may be in solidarity with you, but may be unable to be seen with you. Know that you have adult allies though!

→ See ACLU NC.ORG/YOUTH for detailed info on your rights!

(info adapted from this)

Section 48907 of CA Ed Code

because If you are skipping school, you are technically truant. Know your district's truancy policy, but you can't be punished more harshly for protesting.

You have the right to EXPRESS YOUR VIEWS at school!
Including :
- wearing buttons, t-shirts, etc.
- posting/distributing flyers
- distributing petitions

Doing something that may BREAK THE LAW? Don't wear a t-shirt with your school name or related org!

→EXCEPT WHEN :
- it is legally "obscene"
- it is untrue + would hurt someone's reputation
- it would cause students to break school rules (i.e. a walkout)

TAKE CARE of yourself + others

'SUP BUDS!

USE THE BUDDY SYSTEM!
Go with a group + stay
together. Make sure people
you trust know where you
are (+vice versa!)

LAS FRUTAS UNIDAS, JAMÁS SERÁN VENCIDAS…

USE YOUR VOICE!
- Make signs to carry.
- Join a chant — or
  start your own!

NUTS!

TAKE CARE OF YOUR
~ BODY! ~

- Bring snacks + remember to
  eat them. Bonus: if you can,
  bring some to share!
- Bring water + STAY HYDRATED!

JUST IN
CASE…
Write the #
for the National
Lawyers Guild (NLG)
in your area on your
arm in permanent
marker.

In case you need legal help!

Take a break when
your body/mind
needs it!

z z z

Become familiar with

POLICE TACTICS

KETTLING

Police will often force protestors into a contained area, making it difficult to escape if arrests are being made.

THEREFORE

:...▶

Be on the lookout for possible exit paths—know where to go to get out!

see also: PEPPER SPRAY, a different chemical with similar effects

LRADS

are not rad, they are sound cannons used by the police to scare protestors + cause panic. Stay calm + don't run or panic!

TEAR GAS is a chemical that police use to disperse crowds. It causes your eyes to burn + water and difficulty breathing.

DON'T GET ARRESTED!

Being arrested may cause additional negative consequences.

SUCH AS...

CRIMINAL RECORD
Name: Bananas
CONVICTION: Going too bananas

-if you have a prior record

where are your papers?!

-if you are undocumented

JOB APPLICATION DENIAL

COLLEGE APPLICATION DENIAL

-if you are convicted, it can affect your applications to schools/jobs

(not to mention the general hostility of police to youth, POC, + gender non-conforming individuals)

~ or if you have illegal items

BUT ↗

If you do get arrested, DON'T TALK TO THE POLICE!*

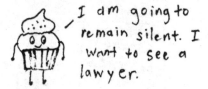

I am going to remain silent. I want to see a lawyer.

You must give your name + address, but have the right to remain silent. Anything you say can + will be used against you + your friends.

HOWEVER, cops will try to get you to talk to them anyway, often accidentally:

– by being a "friendly" officer of the same race/gender as you

– by making small talk about things like sports

If you help me, I'll put in a good word for you!

– by acting like they will "help" you if you talk

– being silent when someone is talking to you feels awkward

– I love the Giants!

– by saying they agree with you

this is ...weird

BUT, once you start talking, it's hard to stop!

Blah, blah, blah,

– I also hate Trump!

*adapted from disruptj20.org

MORE POLICE TIPS...

RECORD THE POLICE using the ACLU's Mobile Justice app, which immediately uploads footage (you have the right to film!)

DON'T RECORD PROTESTORS + don't post about illegal activity on social media - this can become evidence!

IF AN OFFICER STOPS YOU, you don't have to talk to them unless being formally detained. Just say the magic words!

If stopped, RESIST THE URGE to be rude to the officer. It will only make things worse.

OTHER INFO...

I declare this to be an unlawful assembly. You must immediately disperse...

ovie!   no fun!

※ → from medic. wikiq.com

If the police issue an order to disperse, it's a good time to leave. Not only may they begin arresting people, they will likely begin to use LRADS + tear gas

LAST...

Know that you are part of a long tradition in HISTORY of taking a stand against injustice. Be PROUD of yourself for making your voice heard! ☺

WHAT TO DO IF YOU GET TEAR GASSED:

- STAY CALM. Panicking makes it worse
- Move away from the area
- Blow your nose, rinse your mouth, spit. Don't swallow.
- Remove contacts + throw away
- DO NOT RUB IT IN!
- Flush your eyes first with water/saline, then 50% liquid antacid + 50% water

I mist me!   MAALOX 1/2   +   1/2   PEPTO BISMO

EDUCATIONAL RESOURCES DESCRIPTION

The two following graphic organizers were created for the workshop "In Print/Imprint: Designing Political Print Pieces with Users in Mind," which took place as part of the symposium *Does Art Have Users?* at the San Francisco Museum of Modern Art on September 30, 2017. My goal was for participants to conceptualize a politically oriented print piece that addresses an issue of concern to a particular user group, integrating the user's needs and interests into the design. These tools can be used to help students and others explore the *Guide for Youth Protestors* as a model, discussing its features, before ultimately planning and creating their own political print pieces for social action.

MORE INFO AND ONLINE VERSIONS OF LESSON PLANS

https://www.sfmoma.org/event/does-art-have-users-day-four
http://www.arte-util.org/projects/guide-for-youth-protestors/
https://100daysaction.net/actions/guide-youth-protestors/

BRAINSTORM: POLITICAL PRINT PIECE

Describe your user and the issue being faced by this community.

How do you know this issue is an important one for this user group?

What do you know about your user? Consider what needs, interests, likes, dislikes they have.	How do you know this information is accurate— what experience do you have with this user group?

Where and how will this object be distributed? What format (i.e., quarter-fold, z-fold, posters, etc.) will you use to support this object's use?

What elements will you include in the design to engage your user's interests? How will you address your user's needs?

DISCUSSION: *GUIDE FOR YOUTH PROTESTORS*

What is this object's purpose? What **use** does it serve?	What can you tell about the intended **user**? How do you know this (include evidence)?
In what ways does the design attempt to engage the user's **interests**?	How does the design enhance the **usability**? Consider the format, content, layout, etc.

In June 2016, two neo-Nazi groups with records of violence and advocacy for violent oppression against marginalized people, the Golden State Skins and the Traditionalist Worker Party (TWP), were granted state permits to organize a rally on the steps of California's state capitol in Sacramento. Both groups, the latter of which also had a strong presence at the Charlottesville, Virginia, "Unite the Right" rally in 2017, showed up armed with knives, sharpened flagpoles, and other weapons. Counterprotesters, including direct action–oriented civil rights groups such as BAMN (By Any Means Necessary) and Black Lives Matter (BLM) were also present in significant numbers. Tensions were high, and a series of assaults occurred, with all 133 California Highway Patrol (CHP) and Sacramento Police officers present standing by and doing nothing to intervene. During the melee, at least nine counterprotestors were stabbed, along with dozens of other injuries (again, mostly to counterprotestors).

In a pattern that has become increasingly prevalent nationally, the CHP and neo-Nazis collaborated to frame anti-fascist activists as the sole instigators of the assaults. Purported video documentation of the assaults posted online by far-right sources and alleged to have been altered was used in court as evidence against three counterprotestors (including one who was stabbed) who were charged with a variety of offenses, including rioting and assault. Meanwhile, only one neo-Nazi was charged with any crime, and a wide-ranging official CHP investigation into the personal and political activities of dozens of counterprotestors (including Facebook profiles/messages, events, employment backgrounds, etc.) was launched. TWP member Doug McCormack, whose name was listed as an organizer for the rally, was privately assured by police that they would protect his identity from public disclosure, while no such assurances or rights were extended to the anti-fascists being investigated.

In the media and legal shitstorm surrounding this event, one person stood out as a symbol of uncompromising anti-fascist resistance: the author of this chapter, **Yvette Felarca**, a longtime activist with BAMN and a teacher at a junior high school in Berkeley. A flood of angry calls and threats demanding her ouster (and much worse) poured in at the district level and at her school, including a credible bomb threat against students. The district placed her on "indefinite administrative leave," so she sued to get her job back and prevailed. As uncompromising and strident as ever, and always keeping an eye on the bigger political picture that has produced such a rising tide of extremist right-wing hatred, Yvette leveraged her notoriety to get a guest spot on *Fox News* in February 2017. There, she was able to confront host Tucker Carlson and passionately advocate for the power of direct action and confrontation in shutting down far-right extremists like the Sacramento neo-Nazis and provocateur Milo Yiannopoulos, whose scheduled speech at University of California Berkeley—where he planned to openly disclose the personal information of transgender students, while rhetorically dehuman- izing them—had been shut down in the days prior by anti-fascist activists including BAMN. This *Fox News* appearance and her continued status as a public school teacher cemented Yvette's reputation as an unparalleled bogeyman for the wider right wing in the United States and beyond, all as she, with the other two anti-fascist defendants, continues to fight charges brought against her over the events in Sacramento in June 2016.

While not everyone will agree all of with Yvette's tactics, no one can deny they are effective in making sure a harsh, critical spotlight continually shines on right-wing extremists, and her unabashed identity as an openly radical teacher in and out of the classroom (where she does not, as her detractors claim, "indoctrinate" her students) provides a case study in per- sonal courage. As one of the most high-profile activist educators in the world, Yvette is a lightning rod for controversy and an influential individual who continues to be on the frontline of direct action for social justice, while staying dedicated to her students and profession. In the following essay, she gives her perspective on the events in Sacramento and their aftermath, as well as levying an impassioned plea for the kind of real grassroots movement building that will be required to sustain lasting change.

Building the Movement to Stop Trump: Lessons from an Anti-Fascist Civil Rights Educator in Berkeley

by Yvette Felarca

> victory
> 'til the storm is gone
> and the temperature's high
> and delight is dining
> at my table
> —PJ Harvey, "Victory"

> Set around election day
> Demagogues and admitted minority-haters
> should never be president
> —Marvin Gaye, "You're the Man" (alternate version 2)

THE URGENCY OF NOW: TRUMP'S ATTACKS ON DEMOCRACY ARE REAL AND IMMEDIATE

The resistance needs to understand clearly that Trump and his movement have an ideology and a real program of political action for the United States of America. This is true despite Trump's own evident stupidity and incompetence and the divisions and confusion in his movement. Its aim is to create an American government completely subservient to the interests of a section of America's giant corporations and wealthiest individuals, without any meaningful constitutional or democratic restraints on the use of governmental power to serve their purposes, both domestically and in international policy. The view of these interests is that the preservation of their gargantuan wealth and power requires the conversion of the American political system into a form of government much more like those of America's current rivals, Russia and China.

Domestically, this requires a suppression of traditional labor and workers' rights and civil rights generally. Internationally, this requires a government committed to a policy of aggressive trade war, especially against China, intensified militarism, recognizing that any trade war must be backed up by the threat of actual military conflict, and the restructuring of an American system of alliances to favor relations with other authoritarian and despotic regimes with similar "state-capitalist" and authoritarian structures—regardless of the immediate harm done to millions of American producers.

Over the course of the Trump presidential campaign, it became increasingly clear that Trump and his most conscious advisers and handlers were convinced that achieving the kind of regime his most fervent capitalist backers sought required, in a country like the United States, the creation of a mass movement supporting Trump, a movement that had somehow been convinced to support the suppression of its own democratic freedoms on behalf of a small number of capitalist corporations and plutocrats. Trump and his ideological entourage understood that, given American history, the way to do this is to appeal to racist and xenophobic paranoias.

In Trumpism, as with the European neofascist parties and movements, a domestic policy based on white racist and ultranationalist demagogy leads naturally, almost inevitably, to the international policy of an alliance with and support for the most important European power embodying an authoritarian and white nationalist outlook: Russia under Putin. However illogical, irrational, and inconsistent the policy may appear to be, all these far-right, ultranationalist, white racist parties and movements internationally (including Trump's GOP) share the aspiration for a racialized foreign policy centered on an alliance with Putin. With this policy comes an implied fantasy that only through such an alliance of white governments, based on white people's support, can the "white" nations of the world prevent the rise to global domination of nonwhite nations—specifically China.

Some of Trump's supporters call this domestic policy "anarcho-capitalism." Some view the creation of a racist and xenophobic mass movement as a secondary question, a necessity, even an unfortunate one, in order to achieve the central aim of an authoritarian government committed without limits to use all the means at its disposal to protect and enlarge capitalist wealth and power. Government by the people must be replaced with government for the rich and powerful, but to achieve this, a section of the people must be duped with racism into supporting an authoritarian regime. It is obvious that the great majority of Trump's supporters, the overwhelming majority of Trump's electoral base, are fanatically committed to him, not to his program of profoundly increasing the power of the rich and powerful, but to his sick, seductive promise of recreating an America in which white people rule and white-skin privilege defines American citizenship.

Whether this program is called "anarcho-capitalism," ultranationalism, white nationalism, anti-globalism, or any other of the more or less incomplete and misleading terms that are favored both by Trump's supporters and his liberal political, journalistic, and academic critics, this perspective, taken as a whole and placed in the context of the growing number of organizations and leaders committed to essentially similar perspectives in countries across Europe, is essentially the twenty-first century form of *fascism*. This perspective plays the same role in history, is structured with the same dangerous logic, and is aimed at achieving essentially the same ends as the doctrines of Mussolini and Hitler in the first half of the twentieth century.

RECOGNIZING THE HISTORIC CHALLENGE FACING US
To rise to its own historic challenge, the resistance needs to understand that its task is not merely to end the political career of one particularly gross and odious American politician. Its challenge is to block, with democratic, bold, and courageous methods, the confused but supremely arrogant, determined, and dangerous ambitions of a fascist movement from coming to power in the United States and across Europe.

As before, such a movement can only come to power and hold power over the dead body of democratic rights and the actual bodies of millions of people.

The question of whether Donald Trump should be called a fascist may still be open. The resistance needs to understand that this is not the important question. The historical process we are going through is most truthfully and profoundly understood as a process of fascist transformation. Blocking that process requires the decisive defeat and removal of Trump from the American presidency, by whatever means are necessary, because the survival of the democratic character of the country and the world are at stake. For the resistance, it is no time for denial, evasions, self-deception, timidity, cynicism, pettiness, or any form of "business as usual."

The people of America are facing a historic crisis, and they will have to rise to a historic challenge in order to resolve it. The mass resistance to Donald Trump is the means history has so far created to meet this challenge. To do so, this new movement first needs to recognize the character of the challenge, affirm its belief in its ability to meet that challenge, and then learn what that will mean in practice. Building the mass resistance movement, integrated and democratically run and free from the feeble electoral politics of the politicians, is the greatest and most urgent challenge of our times. Our new mass movement, by mobilizing everything that's best in us, can defeat Trump and his ugly mob.

LESSONS FROM BERKELEY, CALIFORNIA

I know this firsthand, because I won my own victory against Trump's Nazi and KKK backers; I'm now in a fight for my freedom against the Sacramento District Attorney and the California Highway Patrol (CHP), who are conspiring with the fascists to bring a witch hunt against me. My name is Yvette Felarca. I am a dedicated middle school teacher in Berkeley, California, a longtime civil rights and trade union activist, and a national organizer with the Coalition to Defend Affirmative Action, Integration, and Immigrant Rights and Fight for Equality By Any Means Necessary (BAMN). I have taught ESL (English as a second language) and humanities for twelve years. I have consistently received strong teaching evaluations and support from students, coworkers, and parents. As a teacher and a political activist, I believe in engaging young people in their education by encouraging them to connect their learning to their own lives and struggles for social justice. I have repeatedly come under attack from the Berkeley Unified School District (BUSD) administration for my work as a progressive teacher. I have a long-standing record of fighting the administration to oppose the introduction of charter schools in the district, defending desegregation programs, standing up for Black and other minority teachers and staff, and standing up for students' rights, including their right to protest. Most recently, I came under attack for my political activism against Donald Trump and his fascist supporters.

On June 26, 2016, during summer vacation, I protested self-identified neofascist Trump supporters who were members of the Traditionalist Worker Party and the Golden State Skinheads. They had scheduled a rally on the steps of the capitol building in Sacramento. Over the past two decades, I have protested fascists and neofascists countless times. This time, in Sacramento, was, however, entirely different. Emboldened by Trump's thoroughgoing, violent racism and the immigrant bashing at the heart of his presidential campaign, the fascists physically attacked and attempted to murder anti-fascist protesters using knives, homemade spears, wooden shields, and clubs. They stabbed and attempted to murder unarmed Black, Latina/o, Asian, Arab, and white anti-racist and anti-fascist counterprotesters. The 133 police who were present on the ground stood by and did nothing to protect the counterprotesters or to stop the Nazi assault on us. As a result of the Nazi attack, at least seven anti-racists were hospitalized with stab wounds, head injuries, and fractured bones, some requiring invasive surgery. Thanks to the courage and determination of counterprotesters, violent white supremacists were not able to roam the streets of Sacramento attacking unsuspecting families or pedestrians, and they were shut down.

Following the fascist assault, the police immediately launched a witch hunt against anti-fascists, with California Highway Patrol officers interrogating and harassing injured protesters in their hospital beds, while not pursuing charges against the Nazi stabbers. Within twenty-four hours, the police released unsubstantiated public statements blaming anti-fascist protesters, actively covering for the Nazis.

The day after the Sacramento rally, Nazi and racist Trump supporters made violent threats against me and students and staff at my school, demanding that I be fired.

Instead of defending me, the neoliberal BUSD administration attacked me and began their own witch hunt. Four days after I was stabbed, the district issued me a formal discipline, then later, on August 31, 2016, they took my entire August paycheck out of my bank account. On Wednesday, September 21, 2016, three weeks into the school year, the BUSD administration removed me from a faculty meeting, escorted me to my classroom to collect my personal belongings, made me turn in my keys, and then marched me out of the school. I was placed on administrative leave.

Every witch hunt includes a shameful roundup, and Berkeley was no exception. I found out that the same day I was placed on administrative leave, several of my immigrant and English Literacy Development students were removed from class and questioned about me by the school district's lawyer, without their parents being notified or present. They were also questioned about their off campus, outside of school political activities and activism. They were forced to answer questions in English, which is not their native language. My other immigrant and international students, and only my immigrant and international students, were rounded up and questioned while I was on administrative leave. Even Latina students whom I had taught years earlier but who had spoken out in my defense at school board meetings were interrogated by district officials. And just when it seems like it couldn't be more shameful, students were told by BUSD lawyers and administration to keep their "interviews" a secret and to "*tell no one.*"

The initial shock and fear that I and my students experienced from this victimization soon gave way to anger, and that anger galvanized us to take action. Before I left the school on the first day I was suspended, I asked my coworkers to announce what happened to the rest of the staff and to urge them to get to the school board meeting that evening. Teachers, school support staff, students, and parents filled the school board meeting to speak out in my defense, and even shut down the meeting to demand the right of one the parents to speak. The following school board meeting, we had twice as many people there and shut down the meeting again. Teachers, school employees, students, parents, and community members joined me to attend every school board meeting during the time I was on leave. We held mass organizing meetings where we voted on demands and a plan of action from week to week. Students, in particular, were incredibly courageous and inspiring—making speeches at school board meetings, writing and circulating their own petition, wearing stickers and buttons, even organizing internationally for students to call in to the school board meetings from Mexico City to make speeches. I spoke to the media every chance I got. And even though there were days when the pressure and uncertainty certainly took their toll on me, the movement sustained and bolstered me far more than anything else could have. I knew that I had to speak up, because if I didn't, other great teachers would get run out of teaching. Students would have learned a lesson in demoralization and cynicism rather than the strength of their own courage and leadership. There was no way I could allow that to happen.

I am a union and civil rights activist. I am a member of the Berkeley Federation of Teachers (BFT) executive board, a founding member of the Equal Opportunity Now/By Any Means Necessary (EON/BAMN) Caucus in both the National Education Association (NEA) and the American Federation of Teachers (AFT). As I mentioned above, I am also a national organizer with the Coalition to Defend Affirmative Action, Integration, and Immigrant Rights and Fight for Equality By Any Means Necessary (BAMN). If not for my experience as a political organizer and the support of my national organizations, I would have felt too isolated to fight the way I did. Thanks to EON/BAMN and to teachers in my school and others who supported me, I got my union to file a grievance to restore my pay and to also advocate for my swift return to my classroom. My lawyers in BAMN also filed lawsuit on my behalf against BUSD for discrimination, violations of free speech, due process, and academic freedom, and they filed a lawsuit on behalf of my students and their parents for discrimination, racial targeting and intimidation, and for violating the students' freedom of speech.

Six weeks after I was removed from my classroom, I was returned to my classroom and to my students and school community. Our movement won. I also got back the money that the district took from me months before. Despite the best efforts of Trump's racist and neofascist supporters, the concerted and direct action of teachers, students, and the community defeated them. And while we utilized the union court system, we didn't make the mistake of relying on them. By far, credit for our Berkeley victory goes to the movement that spread nationally, and even internationally, with each passing day. My students, in particular, learned to stand up for themselves through the course of my defense campaign. They gained confidence and clarity in the strength of their understanding and of putting it into practice. Building that movement would not have been possible without the backing and movement organizing methods of EON/BAMN.

ONGOING LEGAL DEFENSE CAMPAIGN

A week after I returned to my classroom, the electoral college made Donald Trump president. And though I did not know it at the time, only a few months after Trump was elected, the California Highway Patrol

(CHP) collusion with the fascists went into high gear. Over a year after the protest, in the summer of 2017, and only three weeks before fascists murdered Heather Heyer in Charlottesville, Virginia, Sacramento District Attorney Anne Marie Schubert officially joined the police collusion with the Nazis in a new witch hunt. She charged me and two other anti-fascist protesters, Mike Williams and Porfirio Paz.

The police and the DA's policy of allowing Nazis to get away with attempted murder in Sacramento and pursuing charges against the anti-racists who were injured by and stood up to them set the stage for the lynch mobs and murder in Charlottesville in the summer of 2017. The blood of Heather Heyer is on the hands of the California Highway Patrol, the Sacramento Police, and DA Schubert.

There is ample evidence of police collusion with the Nazis. The police have the names and pictures of every white nationalist with their knife out on the capitol grounds on the day of the protest, yet have arrested none of them. Despite a mountain of paperwork and hours of video footage CHP submitted as "evidence" against the anti-racist defendants, they included not a single police report or any police video footage from the day. The police dossiers written after the fact were authored by a single police officer who wasn't even present on the ground at the protest. Yet they reveal open political targeting of the anti-fascist counterprotesters who were present. Stab victims were visited in their hospital beds by police who harassed them about those who opposed the white supremacists. The police showed little interest in pursuing an investigation of the fascists. Taped phone interviews conducted by the police reveal their willingness to cover for the Nazis, providing assurances to some of the most violent Nazi aggressors that they were not being investigated, and that they were being treated as the victims by law enforcement. Black journalist Cedric O'Bannon, who was stabbed and seriously wounded at the protest, was then profiled and subjected to police recommendation for charges based on pictures obtained from his social media page with his fist in the air and excerpts from Wikipedia of the "black fist" or "anti-fascist salute." The SIM card from his camera, which showed footage of the Nazis who stabbed him, was taken and destroyed by CHP officers, who showed more interest in obtaining O'Bannon's knowledge and opinion of me than of pursuing an investigation into the Nazis who almost killed him. Transcripts and photos obtained by my legal team showing the damning evidence of the police witch hunt are available on bamn.com/ defendyvettefelarca.

The legal defense of "The Sacramento 3" (Mike Williams, Porfirio Paz, and me) continues. We have appeared in court multiple times, with supporters picketing the courthouse and packing the courtroom demanding that the charges against us be dropped. All the support that we have received has been incredibly good for our morale. If we go to trial, the continuation and expansion of that support will be vital to ensuring our freedom. I fervently believe that defeating the growth of fascism in America and across the globe is a duty and an obligation. It can only be done through building a mass anti-racist movement committed to taking direct action. Thus far, we have succeeded in stemming their growth and have scored crucial victories against them in California, providing a model for the anti-fascist movement everywhere. But we still have work to do.

It is apparent to millions of people in the U.S. and across the globe that Donald Trump is capable of creating a tyrannical authoritarian regime. Every day brings a new example of Trump's assault on democracy: kidnapping and ripping immigrant children from the arms of their parents, terrorizing immigrants and Muslims to enact a racial purge, empowering police to target and brutalize Black and Latina/o communities, encouraging the rape and sexual assault of women, the active discrimination of LGBTQIA+ people, and obstructing justice, to name a few. In this situation, the groups that call themselves Nazis, KKK, and neo-Confederates are the equivalent of the fascists who followed Mussolini in Italy and Hitler in Germany. Their alt-right counterparts share the same politics without the identifiable costumes. Thanks to Trump, white supremacists and fascists have become bolder and more dangerous. They back Trump because of, not in spite of, his racist and misogynistic attacks. That is why forcing Trump out of office by making him resign or by otherwise removing him is central to defeating fascism now.

We are living in a period of the biggest threat to democracy that many people can remember. In Sacramento and the Bay Area, fascist and alt-right thugs have been shut down and defeated time and again by mass militant direct action. The resistance movement to Trump is capable of victory, as long as we remain committed to maintaining our political goals and taking action untethered from the cynical electoral maneuvers of politicians. We teach our students about concepts of freedom and democracy and to stand up to injustice and despotism. Today, our commitment to those freedoms is being tested on a historic scale. The active mobilization and defense of bold anti-fascist activists can ensure that the tragedies of history are not repeated. "Never again" is now.

In August 2005, the incredible devastation of Hurricane Katrina struck the Gulf Coast. While the hurricane itself was destructive, the real damage and high death toll came during Katrina's aftermath, particularly in the city of New Orleans, where the forces of exploitative capitalism and a total failure of governance came together to create a truly monstrous outcome.

Showing how little we learn and how deeply racism is embedded in the American system, in 2017, Hurricane Maria resulted in another horrific catastrophe on the American colonial territory of Puerto Rico. Maria started a chain of events that eventually resulted in over three thousand largely preventable deaths as the result of a wholly inadequate federal government response, one that contrasted sharply with the quick and overwhelming response in whiter, politically better connected parts of the United States, such as Texas. As we continue to watch the fallout from Maria spread, the specter and lessons learned from Katrina loom large in every analysis and give us a ghastly partial preview of what lies ahead.

Originally written in October 2015, the following chapter details how the legacy of Hurricane Katrina created a wide opening for the corrupt forces of education privatization, in the form of largely unregulated charter schools, to effectively commandeer the public education system in the most impacted areas—predominantly communities of color plagued by persistently high levels of poverty.

Writing from New Orleans, Roburt Knife has been working with young people for thirteen years and is in his seventh year as a full-time classroom teacher. He has taught history and English at different alternative, public, private, and charter high schools in Chicago, Houston, and New Orleans.

The Big Takeover of New Orleans

by Roburt Knife

> America; America is killing its youth.
> —Suicide, "Ghost Rider"

There's no place like New Orleans. This is a statement I've heard repeated endlessly and one I've made. It can be made as a compliment. It can also imply or infer a smear. It just depends on who's doing the speaking and who's doing the listening. New Orleans, Louisiana, is home to almost 370 thousand people, nearly 100 thousand less than in 2004, before Hurricane Katrina hit the Gulf Coast. That notorious event changed the future of New Orleans in far-reaching ways.

The history of New Orleans is tumultuous: steeped in corruption, the largest incarcerator on the planet [2019 update: Oklahoma now leads in incarcerations], a longtime capital of the United States slave ports, murder, extreme political seediness, and white supremacy (David Duke), police abuse, intense poverty, racism, class struggle, and home to the largest slave revolt in United States History. The Crescent City is also home to the American foundations of jazz music, Creole culture, the first free Black residential neighborhoods, and a long-running tradition of incredible integration amidst stark segregation. Regardless of where citizens may land on these spectrums, the people of New Orleans retain a resiliency and a level of hustle that is so incessant that outsiders often wonder how it's possible to stay so positive and hopeful amid so much overtly official deceit and plunder.

In 2004, the dropout rate in New Orleans was 70 percent, and until recently it led the world in incarcerations. This city and its poorer working class have never received love from the status quo or the powers that be, even though the majority of U.S. drilled oil comes from off the banks of the Gulf of Mexico. For those who look to Louisiana for their shadowy business, be they from the state or not, Katrina and its complicated aftermath brought perfect opportunities for "the shock doctrine," disaster capitalism, and the Chicago School of Economics financiers spearheaded by Milton Friedman's philosophy. Friedman was a Nobel Prize winner and high-level economist in the United States whose philosophy wreaked havoc on the poor and working class, leading to some of the most intense, thorough, and violent societal coups and take-overs around the world throughout the second half of the twentieth century, particularly in Latin America. Given his legacy, he can arguably be defined as a war criminal, as millions suffered when the programs he designed were implemented.

After the storm, regular Chicago dartboard target American Secretary of Education Arne Duncan made the now infamous statement that the "best" thing to happen to the New Orleans educational system was Hurricane Katrina. It was obvious to most working-class and poor citizens that this statement was made out of salivating opportunism and glaring greed. Despite Duncan's shiny smiles and his promises of education for all based on Race to the Top and No Child Left Behind, most thinking people were fully aware that the wolf was in the henhouse.

Since Hurricane Katrina, thousands of younger, whiter, less experienced, and alternatively accredited teachers have replaced the 7,500 predominantly Black and unionized teachers who were illegally fired right after the storm. At the time, many in the media argued that the firings were the result of a failing system that was being reorganized so it could be rebuilt correctly—in a new way that could show results through data. According to so-called experts like Arne Duncan and the lobbying group the American Legislative Exchange Council (ALEC), a privatized charter school system with fewer oversight regulations could help in such a situation. Unions could be turned away, and the people who own the charters could be freed of limitations on how they spend their money.

Since the inception of charter schools decades ago, spaces have been mindfully built with ideas of community and arts integration, making good use of all-inclusive educational philosophies. It wasn't until fairly recently that the world of privatized business interests started to use the methodology of charter schools as a practice for their business models. After 2005, charter schools began to pop up all over the Gulf Coast, taking over public forums of education. After only a few years of study, many of the unsavory details of the mishandling of school funds that has accompanied privatization have become increasingly traceable and apparent. Nonetheless, the shift marched ever forward. Despite a billion-dollar class action law suit and legal victories for some of fired teachers, most would not be invited back. A swift takeover was occurring in New Orleans on the tail end of the storm. In many ways, New Orleans has been a petri dish for the privatization of education experiment.

Companies like Teach for America (with financial ties to the Walton family), among countless others, are examples of corporate entities that have invested in the idea of "alternative" certification in an effort to quickly transform recruits of their programs into certified "teachers." Ninety-six thousand three hundred people became teachers in the U.S in 2012–2014. Nearly one-tenth of them were recruited by TFA, and the majority of TFA recruits get planted in lower-income communities and lower performing schools. There are 619 entities in the U.S. that provide alternative, fast-track certification, allowing people with little to no experience to enter the classroom as full-time teachers.

Typically, a recruit in an "alt-cert" program can be officially certified after a six to eight week in-service, teaching in a school for a year, and being rated favorably by superiors (within the school and within the respective programs). All recruits are required to pay a large tuition fee. Conversely, most highly qualified, veteran, career educators go through a full four-year education program, including a student teaching practicum, where they observe for a number of months before they are allowed to teach under the guidance of their mentor. Beyond that, the majority of them complete a master's program, while still continuing regular certifications and accreditations throughout their teaching careers. Ironically, an alt-cert recruit only needs a bachelor's degree to qualify. The contrast in preparation for the future teacher in these two scenarios is overwhelming.

Recruits in alt-cert programs often sign contracts that allow them to be farmed out to new locations that are mostly determined by the overseeing program. Some alt-cert programs require a recruit to stay in teaching for a very short time, often one to two school years. Then, they are allowed, if they wish, to completely leave the teaching profession.

However, we are beginning to see recruits fulfill their initial time requirement in the classroom and, rather than quitting, getting pulled up into an administrative position (sometimes tripling their salary) by a colleague from their alt-cert group. This is not an exceptional practice—it is becoming the norm. In less than seven years, a novice teacher with little to no experience can become a full-fledged principal, overseeing an entire school.

Another major issue with this overall scenario is that recruits are, more often than not, sent to states, cities, schools, and neighborhoods where they do not know the culture or the people, and they are not expected nor prepared to become involved in any other way than to show progressive data that "proves" student achievement. Are these recruits sent to affluent areas or predominantly white environments? No. To be clear, though, some teachers go through alt-cert programs after years of teaching in alternative or private schools, where a state certificate has only been required more recently, but they make up a small number. Conversely, some recruits fulfill their requirements from their alt-cert programs, staying in the teaching profession for countless years, having a tremendous impact on scores of young people. Unfortunately, these types of recruits are also few and far between.

Efforts by companies with these recruits are superficially set up to "save" "underprivileged" populations under the false philanthropic banner: "Every student can learn." These types of charters often trickily refer to themselves as "No Excuse Model" schools, allowing "no excuses" for data that does not show student growth. If a school does not show enough growth, it can be closed and another charter can be written.

Despite philanthropic involvement, many charters allow their boards to disburse funds however they see fit. This opens the door to staggering financial corruption and fund misallocation. When misallocated fund scenarios abound in the schools due to corruption, who feels the negative effects most? Students, teachers, their families, and the future of working society at large. Many teaching recruits fold under the pressures that are created by such scenarios. If a recruit quits for any reason, they still must pay off their tuition debt. Millions are made by the alt-cert companies every year on thousands of new recruits entering the teaching force around the U.S., only to quit due to lacking resources, inadequate preparation, and/or a lack of support, often leaving students with no teacher at all and a "failed" recruit in serious debt.

So who are these programs *really* serving? Neighborhood schools are a thing of the past; they no longer exist in New Orleans. Millions are spent out of budgets every year to bus students out of their neighborhoods and all across the city to different schools filled with other students in exactly the same set of confusing social and sometimes dangerous logistical circumstances. Many students are waiting for the school bus at 5:30 a.m., only to start class hours later. By the time they arrive, many are already exhausted, with the obvious effect in the classroom. So more pressure is put on the teacher to show favorable results, regardless of how or why a student may be struggling, or they can be fired. After all, Louisiana is a right-to-work state;[1] no excuses. Programs designed to address anti-poverty conditions to an *actual*, effective degree are still vastly overlooked for a system that seems to have access to tremendous amounts of funding, thereby making the philanthropic label sound hyperbolic at times. Subsequently, student achievement is directly related to almost *any* in or out of school circumstance. If recruits move to completely unknown areas that they are indifferent or insensitive to, working with groups of kids that they know nothing about, how will that affect the overall learning and educational environment? Quite simply: negatively. More often than not, this equation will come out positive mostly for disaster capitalism investors and their shareholders. There are reasons that oil companies like BP and Exxon have gotten involved in education. There are reasons that banks like Chase and Capital One have gotten involved in education. Think it's the overall well-being of young people? Every year, the U.S. spends about five hundred billion dollars on education for young people aged five to eighteen. In 2011, a single year's profits for investors in K-12 (kindergarten through twelfth grade) education reached 389 million dollars.

The overall data for New Orleans has shown quite clearly that when 80 percent of the schools in New Orleans were charters (about three years ago), 56 percent were graded D or F ("failing") schools. Since Katrina, only 4 of the 107 schools taken over could report operating above the state's average. Statistics show that most New Orleans high school seniors have not been able to meet the American College Testing (ACT) state college acceptance requirement, meaning that new college students have to pay for remedial classes that do not count toward their

---

1   A right-to-work law prohibits security agreements in union contracts.

graduation. Since 2010, the New Orleans Recovery School District (RSD) has closed more than 20 schools. In fact, only a minority of charter schools around the nation outperform district schools. This clearly exposes, with its own data, that the corporate charter monopolization of the public school system *is not proving effective*.

2018 AMENDMENT/UPDATE

In the three years since this article's original publication, the subjugation of New Orleans to the disaster capitalist vision of "education" has grown larger, shiftier, and even bolder in many respects. The press "epiphanies" in recent years, detailing corruption around schools suffering under systems of poverty, show traits that are ubiquitous and "business-as-usual" across the entire system of schools in New Orleans. The "New Orleans Takeover" is the largest school reform-takeover in the history of the United States. In longevity, these "philanthropic-educational" systems are affecting multiple generations and hundreds of thousands if not millions of children. It is arguably one of the largest metropolitan crises on the mainland United States in the last hundred years. The truth may never really surface, as it is being implemented in a city that is mostly Black and working class, where 83 percent of students are considered "disadvantaged." National media often paint a picture of post-Katrina education in New Orleans as a "new" system that put an old model to bed—and good riddance. The data is often touted as showing growth in numbers, progress from jockeyed movement, advancement toward graduation, and as a model that has benefited the majority of the city. The simplest word I can think of to define the entire macrocosm is *fraud*.

Disaster capitalist liaison (and outright dipshit) Arne Duncan hosted a Honduran military coup leader in post-Katrina New Orleans and bragged about the operative capabilities of its system in such a climate (i.e., post-shock), nearly raising evil genius Milton Friedman from the dead. Close examinations of the data show that around 40 percent of the city's charter schools are at "D" or "F" grade status and plenty are working within transitional statuses.

Truth be told, there are ways to manipulate the data to make it appear as though the system is successful, when, in reality, the practices, numbers, vernacular, and statuses being moved around in so slickly serpentine a manner that they become hard to chase, difficult to analyze, elusive to clarify, and arcane in scope. For example, a continuously failing charter school could arguably be closed (not that *that* is a good thing), but it could alternatively be given a "T" grade and achieve a transitional status, allowing it to remain open until the next interval of its assessment, keeping the machine charging ahead like a junkernaut, despite flagrant corruption. Unfortunately, I believe that is the overall point: to keep anyone watching confused and in an information chasing loop, to allow the new design, step, or transition to continue to generate profit for those who benefit, while keeping the people of the city trapped, underserved, repressed, and oppressed. It is a literal microcosm of the long history of New Orleans, where systems touted as beneficial for marginalized communities are, in actuality, tools for control and debasement.

Two years before the storm, the state government created the infamous Recovery School District, which took over about two-thirds of the city's schools. The other third would be controlled by the Orleans Parish School Board (the local school district), in essence, creating a two-tiered system. In 2018, between 98 and 100 percent of the city's schools are chartered, meaning nearly all of those under the Orleans Parish School Board are operating with a similar model. OPSB was recently found in noncompliance by the state for mismanaging and underproviding services and documentation for basic, moderate, and special-needs learners. In this scenario, many local schools have also been found noncompliant by the same state government that's cited the district, and then rolled out Act 35 after the storm, effectively opening the door for this type of negligence to develop. Twelve years later, the state wanted to know what happened. This is truest definition of paradox, until you realize that it's a smokescreen for the state to cover its tracks since the storm.

Charter schools are something that many companies and large-scale corporations have invested in. If an affluently powerful entity is interested in creating its own charter, the chances are that it can. With the right team of lawyers, the guidelines can be met and the loopholes can be examined for profitable utilization along myriad pathways. Manipulating data and utilizing marketing strategies to not only sell a product but to sell an idea (and the data of their design) is commonplace for many of the parties involved. It was an aspect of their business model before they set their sights on education. In New Orleans, it has changed the shape of what education will look like forever. The neighborhood school no longer exists. The business of contracts in the city is an extremely lucrative one that runs like backdoor Chicago nepotism to the nth power. From immensely widespread school bussing to uniform vendors to building cleaning crews to textbooks and standardized testing to teacher contracts with Teach for America and Teach New Orleans, the system is a maelstrom of a business model.

A popular statistic trickling through mainstream media recently is 100 percent graduation rates for many New Orleans high schools, lauding how well they prepare their students for the post-secondary world. The Cowen Institute for Public Education Initiatives had to retract its study, which fudged figures in regards to test scores and graduation rates. Pro-charter research and reporting agencies are openly lying about the data in hopes to normalize this type of system in the age of Betsy DeVos. It is relevant to note that in 2014, under DeVos, post-bankruptcy Detroit was the American city ranked number two in its privatization, with charter schools comprising about 55 percent of its schools (compared to New Orleans at 98–100 percent). The aristocrats are pushing the New Orleans model nationally.

In this model, many schools are making retention a thing of the past. Where a student shows academic deficiency in the realm of skill or credit acquisition, that student will assuredly be pushed along through the slippery advancement process, all the way to graduation, often being promoted through simpler and simpler tasks. Teachers are regularly coerced to alter large swaths of grades, intimidating them into undermining instruction and compromising their professional ethics. Of course, all students need to graduate, but if the primary goal is to make sure that the data reads 100 percent, then the focus is not on an ethical concern about the educational interests of the student; it is on the marketing of the school and the system and ensuring their essential continuation, regardless of *why* a student may be struggling. Scores do not equal learning, and this type of practice does the child absolutely no justice. Situations like these require closer attention to the student, with educational/behavioral and/or life interventions in an ethical effort to get to the root of why their learning may be suffering.

There is a clichéd line from multiple high school youth rebellion films that goes something like, "How could a kid get all the way through school and be a functional illiterate?" The question assumes that one child here or there slips through the cracks as an absolute travesty and testament to the broken school system à la the American Reagan 1980s media archetype. However, the modern snapshot of this same concern shows the entire system of New Orleans schools headed in this exact direction for the majority of its children in all grades for at least the last thirteen years. The magnitude of the problem is more than tremendous.

The economic model that is superimposed over New Orleans charters is one that is thoroughly life draining and leads to frequent burnout among not just students, teachers, and personnel but within the actual school climate itself, with many schools plagued by crumbling structures and/or infrastructures. Many charters require their teaching recruits to work incredibly long hours for a set salary, so the idea of overtime is nonexistent. Most of the system exists within a paradigm that is predominantly post-union, despite what one finds in local news reports. Louisiana is a right-to-work state, and New Orleans schools are under a near monopoly of privatization. After 7,500 teachers were illegally fired thirteen years ago, many of the remaining veteran staff members are now burning out or being pushed out, so turnover is high and morale is low. Nonetheless, the jobs are consistently filled by young recruits; they are constantly restructured, making it possible for extremely unqualified teachers to climb the ladder toward administration, where the paychecks triple for keeping the system moving.

Over time, the stories begin to seem unreal: one New Orleans principal was outed as a white supremacist after being spotted at last year's rallies against the removal of the local statue of Confederate General Robert E. Lee. There are principals who have retired after years of salaries exceeding three hundred thousand dollars, at a time when many schools in the city struggle with pest infestations and unaddressed black mold and asbestos contaminations caused by the storm. Often, new "teachers" with little to no background in education teach for three to five years in the classroom (hardly enough time to become seasoned), get assisted tuition from their respective charter(s) to acquire a masters in educational leadership, and get moved into administration by a personal friend or professional cohort. Consider the implication: a twenty-five- to thirty-year-old principal who oversees more than one thousand kids, with three years teaching experience and a salary of six figures. Conversely, teachers often enter the profession at between thirty and forty thousand dollars a year. Big philanthropy is not interested in paying a seasoned teacher a reasonable salary, especially if a position is only expected to last two years (as is the case for the majority of post-Katrina, non–education background recruits). To the corporate mind, with turnover so high, doing so would establish a dangerously unlucrative pay scale.

The configuration of oversight here is also notoriously and confusingly decentralized, something that even this pseudo-anarchist finds insane. No *one* entity is necessarily in charge of, responsible for, or accountable for all students. It is certainly shocking in magnitude and a phenomenal ethical concern, especially if one could potentially reimagine what *could* be done with a charter system that was actually based around revolutionary, restorative, social justice, anti-poverty, and anti-exploitative principles. Unfortunately, in New Orleans, that type of sentiment is wishful thinking that merely takes away precious time from campaigns of direct action. The whole concept of wiping an education system clean to start over again has been a marketing line regularly pushed by regional philanthropists to cover up how much damage they have actually done. What they are actually praising is privatization, a concept utilized widely outside of education, but which is indicative of the same nefarious methods and goals that were behind the hostile coups in numerous countries around the world during the twentieth century (read your CIA and School of the Americas history).

This flagrant underinvestment in said oversight has its worst effect on our young students who are constantly shuffled around the system, sometimes culminating in essential life skill deficiencies in foundational areas like literacy and employability. Disproportionality (the excessive targeting of Indigenous, Black, and Brown young people for clinical diagnoses, behavioral referrals, and economically quantifiable services)[2] has helped the entire region become a boon for the prison-industrial complex through the school-to-prison pipeline, by way of No Child Left Behind's zero tolerance and No Excuses cultural implementations. These, in turn, show language that is egregiously synonymous with the Clintons' Tough on Crime legislation used to ramp up the aforementioned private prison boom of the 1990s.

Beautiful New Orleans lost more than twenty thousand students to the storm. The average ACT score in the city is approximately 16.4,

---

2   Such as premature tracking into special education programs—ed.

frustratingly lower than required to be admitted to many local universities. However, these numbers do not reflect an inherent deficiency in young people. Make no mistake: they represent a population that has been taken advantage of by disaster capitalists, politicians, and professionals in exploitation, who had literally been waiting for an excuse to take over the organization of education in the city. Systems and cycles of poverty have always exploited their respective populations; that is the nature of the violence that houses these ostensible human rights violations. On the other hand, there are scores of teachers and other staff members who work tirelessly to educate young people and to find ways to serve the youth of New Orleans with equity, restorative justice, and respect. They abound in the buildings after hours and can be found up late at home, planning, studying, and working, spending their own money for supplies, providing kids with meals and precious time, offering some kids the only positive aspect of their entire day. These are not the types of folks that are often remembered by history, and there are a lot of them in New Orleans right now making miracles happen one interaction at a time.

Over 831 million dollars were funneled into New Orleans charters in 2014–2015. Taxpayers have invested billions since the storm in an arrangement built for opportunists. What does that investment look like for students? Nothing like justice. They continue to live in stark segregation, with the violence of a system that sees kids in seats as dollar signs. Negligence in education trickles all the way down to the student, driven by the greed at the top, where designer suits, slick cars, and inflated bank accounts accompany the claim to know exactly what the students of New Orleans need. This scenario coagulates and exacerbates while our kids navigate mismanaged funding, sit at broken desks, and eat D-grade food, often provided by the same companies that service regional jails. Their futures have been tossed to aristocratically ambitious predators. The system is kept in constant, confusing motion so that no one watching closely will be able to get a handle on it long enough to stop it or get a law applied to it in the hope of controlling its corruptibility.

The Big Takeover of New Orleans has become a petri dish model for the rest of the country, and in some cases other countries, to extrapolate from when devising methods of control, manipulation, and profiteering at the expense of the working people of the region. The shock doctrine is real, and direct action is *still* a threat to it. Bleak as it seems, all of this *proves* that educational literacy for the Indigenous, Black, Brown, and marginalized communities of the world is still something that scares the absolute shit out of the powers that be. They know that if we all get it together, they are finished. Find your strengths and apply them in the struggle to bring direct action to the problems that marginalized people face most. Sacrifice and work to serve those who struggle more than you do. All power to the people.

SUGGESTED READING

Michelle Alexander. *The New Jim Crow: Mass Incarceration in the Age of Colorblindness*. New York: The New Press, 2010.

Mark Andersen. *All the Power: Revolution without Illusion*. Chicago: Punk Planet Books, 2004.

W.E.B. Du Bois. *Black Reconstruction: A History*. New York: Free Press, 1999 [1935].

Paulo Freire. *Pedagogy of the Oppressed*. New York, Continuum, 1992 [1970].

Eduardo Galeano. *Open Veins of Latin America: Five Centuries of the Pillage of a Continent*. New York: Monthly Review Press, 1997 [1973].

Naomi Klein. *The Shock Doctrine: The Rise of Disaster Capitalism*. Toronto: Alfred A. Knopf Canada, 2007.

Malcolm X and Alex Haley. *The Autobiography of Malcolm X*. New York: Ballantine Books, 1992 [1965].

Huey P. Newton. *Revolutionary Suicide*. London: Penguin Classics, 2009 [1973].

Diane Ravitch. *The Death and Life of the Great American School System: How Testing and Choice Are Undermining Education*. ReadHowYouWant. com, 2010.

Joel Augustus Rogers. *Sex and Race* vols. 1–2. New York: Helga M. Rogers, 2011/2014 [1941/1944].

Bobby Seale. *Seize the Time: The Story of the Black Panther Party and Huey P. Newton*. Baltimore, MD: Black Classic Press, 1991 [1970].

Assata Shakur. *Assata: An Autobiograhy*. Chicago: Chicago Review Press, 1999 [1987].

Harriet A. Washington. *Medical Apartheid: A Dark History of Medical Experimentation on Black Americans from Colonial Times to the Present*. New York: Doubleday, 2006.

Howard Zinn. *A People's History of the United States*. Harper, 2016 [1980].
2005 Act 35 State of Louisiana/Letter by Attorney General Eric Holder
Leon Waters's work on the Destrehan Rebellion

For decades, unions—including teachers' unions—have been steadily in decline across much of the United States, following relentless legislative and judicial attacks from a wide variety of right-wing and neoliberal political forces. Nationally, this culminated in the U.S. Supreme Court's Janus decision in June 2018, which prohibited the compulsory collection of dues from nonunion members who benefit from union negotiated contracts, a move that was designed to fiscally disembowel union organizing and political advocacy for the foreseeable future. As mentioned, however, this grim new reality of weak or nonexistent unionization—which culminates in depressed wages, fewer workers' rights, reduced benefits, and isolation in the workplace—has been in place for many years in quite a few states, rendering the teaching profession increasingly less attractive for new recruits and leading to severe teacher shortages in many areas.

In an explosion of resistance during mid-2018, teachers in a large number of these anti-union states (West Virginia, Arizona, Kentucky, North Carolina, Colorado, and Oklahoma) decided they had enough of their stagnant wages and poor working conditions and went on a series of wildcat strikes that shut down schools for weeks, while bringing their concerns right to the steps of the state legislatures. Though fiscal support for striking teachers ended up being provided in part by national teachers' unions (which have far less money to spend following the Janus decision), these massive statewide strikes were organized using new and often decentralized methods that hold a great deal of promise for future labor struggles in an increasingly hostile national climate for organized union activity (and workers, in general). The newly awakened power and organizational innovations of the teachers in these politically hostile states should come as no surprise to anyone familiar with labor history in the United States. Going back well into the nineteenth century, this history is full to the brim with workers (often immigrants) who started their resistance to power in the most difficult and seemingly inauspicious circumstances and concluded their struggles having effected lasting positive change. Sometimes these gains came at terrible personal cost to individual workers, but those fighting have long been aware that the people who are the most dangerous to the status quo are often the ones who have the least to lose and everything to fight for.

The author of the next piece, **Taylor McKenzie**, is a punk now in his third year of teaching German at a secondary (middle and high) school in Oklahoma City. In the following reflections on his teaching, written in March 2016 and August 2018, Taylor honestly addresses some major issues and big questions about teacher training, practice, and the labor struggle in the U.S., including the very important fact that *where* one teaches will strongly impact exactly what and how that teaching is going to go down. Taylor can be contacted directly at iresignhc@gmail.com.

Letters from the Educational Battle Lines in Oklahoma (AKA Everywhere, USA)

by Taylor McKenzie

> No asylums for the crazy
> No churches for the godly
> No rules for the ruled
> —The Outcasts, "Just Another Teenage Rebel"

MARCH 2016

Hi, everyone, I just started teaching middle school and high school German at a combined middle/high school in Oklahoma City. I'd like to say that before I started six weeks ago I had no official training. No teaching degree or certification. No actual plans to teach. To explain, I was working at my uncle's screen printing shop. One day I made a tee shirt delivery to my former secondary school, and I decided to say "Hello" to the German teacher that I had throughout middle school and high school. She said, "Hey! Oh man, can you come outside for a minute?" Once outside, she told me that the school desperately needed a full-time German teacher. I was shocked and overwhelmed and told her that I definitely would have to sleep on it before I made my decision. Regardless, she took me downstairs to meet the principal and got things rolling. The next day, I got in touch and told her I would take the job. After winter break, I became a substitute teacher for the classes that I'm currently teaching, and then I began the "emergency certification" process (a process in which the district starts and then streamlines the teaching certification process while you are teaching under a temporary contract).

You may be asking yourself, "Why would they desperately need someone like me, who has no prior experience or training or anything of the sort, to fill this position?" I have studied the language for over ten years and lived and worked in Berlin for two years, but that doesn't mean I know how to teach it to kids ranging from the seventh to the eleventh grade. In short, you could say that Oklahoma has been waging a war against education for some time now. Just within the past week, the state legislature voted to ban the AP U.S. History Exam, because it does not teach "American exceptionalism" (this is a direct attack on Indigenous identities, a push to further silence any discussion about the atrocities that the U.S. has perpetuated—and so blatantly!). Teachers are also sick of meager pay in comparison to bordering states, where salaries are at least ten thousand dollars more a year, so many have left Oklahoma to live and work in Texas. To sum things up, Oklahoma is in a state of emergency when it comes to public education.

So here I am, winging it like a baby bird taking first flight. Even though I'm a new teacher and sometimes I feel like I'm just treading water in the middle of the ocean, with no land in sight, it's a wonderful job, in that you get to be around raw, "still not so beaten down and molded by society" bundles of energy all day. It's exhausting, but learning all of today's new dance moves and slang from teenagers sure as hell beats listening to adults groan about their miseries. And most of the time they're honest, and if they do try to lie to you, they're usually pretty bad at it.

But even though the students are mentally fresher than many of the adults in their lives, that does not mean that they are immune to opinions, biases, and rhetoric, regardless of whether these are humane or inhumane, open-minded or narrow-minded, considerate or anti-social, worldly or nationalistic, critical or blind. When I think of teaching resistance, I ask, "How do you accomplish this objectively without just teaching them your own opinion and cleverly convincing them your way of thinking is right?" What I've tried to do in these past couple of weeks, when larger, difficult questions come up in class, is to respond with questions that guide them to even more questions. I hope to, even if ever so slightly, instill a habit of constantly questioning everything, to not be afraid to ask both authority figures and yourself questions that might shake any foundations you previously thought to be unshakeable or off-limits. One of the hardest things about this is coming up with the extemporaneous, simple questions as answers to their difficult questions. I know there are some resistance teachers out there reading this who have experience with this type of Socratic nudging, urging young people to keep questioning their peers, parents, family, and every other adult with an opinion out there. If so, how do you make this process effective? Do you have an arsenal of responses that you have at hand to use when these types of situations present themselves? I've found myself thinking about tangential conversations that I've had with the students these past couple of weeks, and then only after the fact thinking of better, more open and accessible ways to frame an idea or a simple question that would have gotten their mental gears cranking.

A conversation that has stuck with me throughout all of the everyday chaos so far (teachers, you know what I'm talking about) is a brief back-and-forth about U.S.-erected, Japanese internment camps that I had with a student. We were reading a novel about the rise of the Nazis in Germany and the simultaneous, steady decline of Jewish civil rights leading up to the Holocaust. The student made some comment about concentration camps. I felt compelled to derail the class discussion a bit to focus on the political history of the U.S. and make some comparisons. Students in the U.S. are often taught about the big, bad Nazis, but this can allow for the other Western powers of the twentieth century to catch a break when it comes to criticism of their warring strategies, crimes, or policies. I asked them if the United States had ever done something similar, for instance, the Japanese internment camps. I pointed out that the internment camps and the concentration camps existed at the same time and used similar methods of exclusion and isolation. The student did not want to recognize any comparison between the two countries' actions. It was as if the fact that an entire people's civil liberties were directly targeted and violated, with the uprooting of families and forced internment, was pushed aside in their minds, or at least less critically analyzed, just because there was not a calculated genocide taking place within the Japanese concentration camps erected by FDR.

Is this a product of historical whitewashing in the U.S.? Of living in a state where the legislature, in 2016, for chrissakes, voted to ban the AP U.S. History Exam, because it exposes the historical lies, genocide, and bigotry of the U.S. government? Absolutely. So maybe that student still thinks I'm wrong, or maybe they think I'm just a lefty with an overly one-sided view. All in all, none of that matters if they managed to ask themselves at least one question regarding their opinion of the topic. Teaching resistance is teaching how to question. But it's important to remember that questioning your own beliefs and opinions is just as crucial as questioning those of others. As teachers, we have to remain open to new cultural developments, trends, and ways of thinking and perceiving the world, and we should hold the students in our classrooms to the same critical expectations. But we also have to help guide them to their own personal avenues of self-questioning and questioning factors in their environment. Pushing them to question themselves is one of the first steps, if not the first step, to teaching them how to resist injustice.

P.S. Teachers! If you have any wisdom to share, any good, simple questions to get students thinking and questioning on their own, please email me at iresignhc@gmail.com. I would love to meet any teachers out there who might be reading this.

FOLLOW-UP, AUGUST 7, 2018
A lot has happened since John so graciously asked me to contribute to *Teaching Resistance*. Rereading this feels like reading a diary entry from two years ago, with all of the questions addressed to myself. I have found a few possible right answers to some of these questions. Having a couple years of experience under my belt, I can confidently say that the start to this school year feels better than ever. I know what I am doing a bit more. I have the lesson plans from the last two years to work with, and I can now go back and tweak everything to be better than it was the first couple go-arounds.

I mention the fact that teaching gets better with a couple years of experience for two reasons. The first is to encourage other new teachers, for whom this year is their first in the classroom. Know that it does get easier, but you have to personally find out whether this is good for you or not. The second reason is that now that the actual teaching comes a little easier, I can see more clearly how the whole game of education in the U.S. is played.

So much about our own jobs and the state of local politics was illuminated for so many teachers in Oklahoma by the teacher walkout that happened this past April (Oklahoma followed West Virginia's example, and Arizona, Kentucky, North Carolina, and Colorado also had similar protest movements around the same time). First of all, allow me to generalize. Okies are not known for saying "no" or for being confrontational. They would rather overwork themselves and let that be their source of pride than stir things up for a better endgame. But what everyone saw at the walkout could give anyone goosebumps.

There were roughly seven thousand people at our capitol building every day of the walkout (one day there were an estimated thirty thousand). It was packed. One in, one out, all day. It was a festival outside. Almost every public school was closed for almost two weeks. Teachers were bussed in from all over the state every morning. Gymnasiums were opened up for sleeping quarters for teachers. Buses drove out to their route stops to feed students. There was an actual community effort unlike any I have ever seen in my whole life of living here. There were moments where the whole capitol rotunda would swell with a couple thousand people just screaming out of raw frustration, sometimes even without slogans. Just imagine a couple thousand teachers screaming and booing and yelling at once. I will never forget that.

I will also never forget how many of the politicians treated everyone who came to their office doors. Some were very open and understanding, but some berated everyone, saying, "Get back to work!" Being inside Oklahoma City's capitol every day and seeing how the local government functioned, the boy's club, the bro politician culture, was a real eye-opener for so many teachers. The walkout came to a disappointing conclusion when the largest teachers' union here pulled the plug. In retrospect, after feeling upset and bitter about not being able to dictate the terms of our own walkout, I realize that the huge disappointment at the end only strengthened the teachers' movement in Oklahoma.

Right after the bitter end, more people applied to run for political office than in previously recorded Oklahoma history, hundreds of them being teachers. My cousin went to one of the training sessions for new candidates, and she told me that the lady teaching the class had no idea what to do with that many newcomers. There was not a glorious, happy victory at the end of this walkout, unlike in 1990, the last teachers' strike in Oklahoma. That four-day walkout ended with a clear victory, the passing of House Bill 1017. But did teachers remain politically active after they got what they fought for? Obviously not on a large enough scale. Anti-education, pro-oil politicians have been successfully cutting funding for the past two decades. When a majority of the state's public school teacher body felt the degree of the house and senate disregard for education, something switched on. And when the walkout ended as a dud, it stayed on.

Yes, we got a raise. But the house and senate are fooling themselves if they think that 175 dollars more a month is all teachers are interested in. A teacher I met at the walkout said, "One of the things that makes us good teachers is the fact that we are bad at self-advocacy." And I think that is true for many teachers, but teachers in Oklahoma learned how to say *"no!"* in a different context this year. We came out not only advocating for ourselves but advocating for an understanding that education is a living, breathing body. We know that it takes smart and empathetic administration, healthy and comfortable students, and teachers treated decently to foster a brighter future. If members of the house and senate do not know that already, well, they will just have to hear it from the hundreds of teachers running for office this political season, because thanks to a bitter end we have not forgotten the nasty way this game can be played. Don't worry, though, we can teach you the rules—we're teachers!

>> In the introduction of this book, I touched briefly on Dick Hebdige's idea that there are hierarchical, authoritarian structures built directly into our educational institutions and systems. Pressure to adhere to the contours of society's underlying power structures is established in a multitude of ways in schools, from the layout of the campuses and design of the buildings to the teacher-centered arena of the classroom itself. The traditional instructional strategy involves a teacher standing in a position of central focus, often behind a podium in front of an audience of students, and transferring knowledge directly to them in a largely one-way stream. The students then store, or "bank," this knowledge for later regurgitation and some measure of processing, a method Paulo Freire critiques at length in his classic book *Pedagogy of the Oppressed*.[1] In this manner, the power structures and hierarchies that our educational institutions were built to reflect effectively "naturalize" and reproduce themselves, generating unconscious acquiescence to an established order whether the teacher-sourced ideas being "banked" by students are radical in theory or not. A core tenet of radical teaching is deconstruction: radically rethinking the classroom environment, disassembling hierarchies of all kinds, and fundamentally critiquing "school" in general. The traditional, teacher-centered "banking method" of instruction has proven itself to be totally insufficient in generating genuine student literacy, engagement, and comprehension beyond the surface level in most subjects, particularly with students whose identities and socioeconomic statuses are not implicitly privileged within the dominant systems that generated the educational institution—systems that are, more often than not, grounded in colonialism, white supremacy, patriarchy, and a host of other oppressions.

By necessity, given the diversity of population, information "banking" has been challenged many times at the primary and secondary levels in public schools, to varying degrees of success. However, this deeply flawed method is still predominant on college campuses, where actual teaching is often thought of as drudgery by prestigious, tenured professors who would

---

1   Paulo Freire, *Pedagogy of the Oppressed* (New York: Continuum, 1992 [1970]).

much rather get a lecture over with so they can return to their individual research and writing tasks. This makes the rare tenured professor who embraces radical pedagogy and puts it into practice in their own classroom especially valuable, plus a bit revolutionary, given the low-key institutional pressure to not "rock the boat." It also makes for someone whose class I would definitely like to attend.

The following essay is written by **Ron Scapp**, the founding director of the Graduate Program of Urban and Multicultural Education at the College of Mount Saint Vincent in the Bronx, where he is professor of humanities and teacher education. His books include *Teaching Values: Critical Perspectives on Education, Politics and Culture* (New York: Routledge, 2003) and *Living with Class: Philosophical Reflections on Identity and Material Culture* (New York: Palgrave MacMillan, 2013), coedited with Brian Seitz. He has collaborated with others on different projects, including with cultural critic and writer bell hooks, another person whose class I would definitely like to attend.

Notes on an Anarchist Pedagogy

by Ron Scapp

Oh I believe in miracles
Oh I believe in a better world for me and you
Oh-oh-oh, I believe in miracles
Oh I believe in a better world for me and you
I close my eyes and think how it might be
The future's here today
It's not too late
It's not too late, no!
Oh I believe in miracles
Oh I believe in a better world for me and you
Oh-oh-oh, I believe in miracles
Oh I believe in a better world for me and you, you, you
—Ramones, "I Believe in Miracles"

To enter classroom settings . . . with the will to share the desire to encourage excitement, was to transgress. Not only did it require movement beyond accepted boundaries, but excitement could not be generated without a full recognition of the fact that there could never be an absolute set agenda governing teaching practices. Agendas had to be flexible, had to allow for spontaneous shifts in direction.[1]
—bell hooks

---

1   bell hooks, *Teaching to Transgress: Education as the Practice of Freedom* (New York: Routledge, 1994), 7.

INTRODUCTORY NOTE: ON BEING REASONABLE—OR NOT

Soon after the 2016 U.S. presidential election, my book *Reclaiming Education: Moving Beyond the Culture of Reform* was published.[2] I believe it to be a well argued, cogent, and evenhanded critique of the deleterious influence and impact that neoliberalism has had on the United States generally and on (public) education specifically. The book is, to my mind anyway, a hard-hitting, clear, and persuasive reaffirmation of education understood as a transformative process—understood as what Paulo Freire calls "education as the practice of freedom." Such an understanding and affirmation of education stands in stark contrast to the way neoliberals construe and promote education, that is, education viewed as a "product." I believe *Reclaiming Education* to be a very reasonable book informed by the important work of Henry A. Giroux, bell hooks, Stanley Aronowitz, and Angela Davis, among many others. Unfortunately, it strikes me that the circumstances that made *being reasonable* reasonable have drastically changed. As a result, something that might typically be considered less reasonable, even much less reasonable, may be required of us, *by* us. Of course, I say this at a time that is approaching the end of the Trump administration's second year, a time during which we have witnessed (on a daily basis) one unreasonable assertion or action after another. At such a moment, it thus seems reasonable to reconsider, rethink, and reassert the claim that education is a process of transformation—that, however unreasonable it may seem to some, education ought to be fully embraced by us as the practice of freedom, just as Freire asserted. We may now need to acknowledge and accept that *being reasonable* under the current assault on education has its limits and, in fact, may prove to be unreasonable. The assault on education, after all, is an assault on freedom, and how can we *reasonably* stand by and allow such an assault to go unchallenged? Thus, to embrace education as the practice of freedom is, as bell hooks asserts, "to transgress," that is, to engage in *teaching resistance*.

I say this not so much as some kind of "tit for tat" response to the frightening display of blatant disregard for reason forwarded by Trump and his many spokespeople (shout-people?) but as an attempt to break away from the numerous strictures of trying to maintain "being

---

2   Ron Scapp, *Reclaiming Education: Moving Beyond the Culture of Reform* (New York: Palgrave Macmillan, 2016).

reasonable" in this moment of unreasonableness.[3] So what follows is more or less a compilation of notes on what might be considered an *anarchist pedagogy*. I want to advance (as I and others have done before) a pedagogy that articulates and advocates a stance (*resistance*) against the fascistic moves to (further) control and constrict education as the practice of freedom. But here, in these notes, I want to present this stance in an abridged manner and to offer those reading a brief argument and means for liberating teaching and learning, in and out of the classroom, in the ever strangulating age of Trump. These notes are inspired by and loosely modeled on David Graeber's musings, *Fragments of an Anarchist Anthropology*,[4] as well as drawing influence from Robert Haworth's anthology *Anarchist Pedagogies: Collective Actions, Theories, and Critical Reflections on Education*.[5] But unlike Graeber's and Haworth's bold efforts to lay out and forward anarchy, my efforts here are far more modest in scope and ambition. I also suspect that I express a certain tentativeness regarding anarchy as such. My goal here is to consider, in a very cursory and provisional but honest manner (in this, Graeber and I are very much on the same page) how educators might approach and "deploy" anarchy methodologically in the classroom. I want to offer something concise, clear, and useful to help those so inclined to resist and overcome the stultifying rigidity that has imbued itself throughout education on all levels of instruction—a rigidity that has been championed by neoliberals and social conservatives alike in the name of reform (in this, I believe that Haworth and I are on the same page).[6] I want to make a move here, a move that many may well perceive as somewhat (or very) unreasonable, a move to explicitly embrace anarchy methodologically as a means to purposefully reconsider the dynamics of education under siege and to promote "education as the practice of freedom." Now, it may just be the case that embracing anarchy methodologically is tantamount to embracing it ideologically. But for my purposes, in what I am attempting to sketch out, I want to

---

3   Ron Scapp, "Of PomoAcademicus Reconsidered," *Humanities* 5, no. 3 (Summer 2016): 66–77.
4   David Graeber, *Fragments of an Anarchist Anthropology* (Chicago: Prickly Paradigm Press, 2004).
5   Robert Haworth, ed., *Anarchist Pedagogies: Collective Actions, Theories, and Critical Reflections on Education* (Oakland: PM Press, 2012).
6   Ron Scapp, *Reclaiming Education: Moving Beyond the Culture of Reform* (New York: Palgrave, 2016).

simply note that whatever an anarchist pedagogy might prove to be, it may not provide us an argument for advancing anarchy universally—and doing so is not my purpose here. I am aiming to offer a short and straightforward example of (and rationale for) embracing education as the practice of freedom and using "an anarchist pedagogy" to help achieve this.

NOTE 1: WHY AN ANARCHIST PEDAGOGY?

When I was growing up, anarchy had pretty much one and only one possible meaning: utter chaos and a total disregard for any notion of the rule of law. The term anarchy evoked fear and was identified with those who were unpatriotic and represented a threat to the promise and security of the United States. This was, after all, during the Cold War and the Vietnam War and fears over the security of the nation and the world itself ran deep, as they do once more (whether real or imagined). As Justin Mueller notes in his essay, "Anarchism, the State, and the Role of Education":

> Anarchism has had a rather bedeviled career, maligned by many, misunderstood by most, and marginalized even by erstwhile theoretical allies. In the popular imagination, it is often seen as simply synonymous with chaos, disorder, or violence; more likely to evoke the image of a smashed Starbucks window than a nuanced philosophy based upon principles of economic and political equality.[7]

I believe that Mueller's summation of the attitude and general perspective regarding anarchy here in the United States is pretty much spot on and explains why it will lead many to question my desire (rationale) to in any way employ "an anarchist pedagogy" in the name of education.

In his introduction to *Fragments of an Anarchist Anthropology*, David Graeber titles the first fragment: "Why are there so few anarchists in the academy?"[8] My impulse is to respond "duh!" and then "duh!": first, I would never ask that question, for many reasons; second, "duh!" how

---

7   Justin Mueller, "Anarchism, the State, and the Role of Education," in Haworth, *Anarchist Pedagogies*, 14–15.

8   Graeber, *Fragments of an Anarchist Anthropology*, 2.

could anyone "inside the academy" not instinctively know why?[9] And, of course, Graeber does know why. But he is much more optimistic (?) than me. And he is certainly not naive about *the academy.*

I suppose my question would be/is, "But why are there so many authoritarians and even fascists in the (U.S.) academy?" And my impulse is to respond simultaneously to my own question: "duh!" and then "duh!" First, why ask such a question given the history of education in the United States. Second, "duh!" given the documentation of the various abuses of power historically throughout our school systems and the current vexed nature of education in our nation, what other response is there than "duh!"? There are many scholars and activists who have called our attention to this history and current state of education in the United States, but Joel Spring's work comes readily to mind, and his book *Deculturalization and the Struggle for Equality: A Brief History of Dominated Cultures in the United States* should offer even those resistant to accepting such a history enough evidence and analysis to at least acknowledge that schooling has never been free of politics (oppressive values and forces) and, specifically, a politics of devaluation and domination of nonwhite peoples. As Spring rightly notes:

> Unfortunately, violence and racism are a basic part of American history and of the history of schools. From colonial time to today, educators have preached equality of opportunity and good citizenship, while engaging in acts of religious intolerance, racial segregation, cultural genocide, and discrimination against immigrants and nonwhites.[10]

So actually, my question (note) is: Given the history that Spring and many others have documented and the current state of education, how can we not consider "an anarchist pedagogy"? That is, how can we not demand "education as the practice of freedom"? Once again, the response must be: "duh!" this is so because those of us of committed to education as the practice of freedom must reenter our various educative

---

9   Gayatri Chakravorty Spivak, *Outside in the Teaching Machine* (New York: Routledge, 2003); Pierre Bourdieu, *Homo Academicus* (Stanford, CA: Stanford University Press, 1998).

10   Joel Spring, *Deculturalization and the Struggle for Equality: A Brief History of Dominated Cultures in the United States* (New York: McGraw-Hill Education, 2012), 2.

spaces and locations and be prepared to advocate for and enact the liberatory and transformative power of education (once again).

NOTE 2: SELF-CRITIQUE, YET AGAIN

Like many Americans (and many others around the world), I have been attempting to process (and resist) the Trump election and his presidency, if in modest ways. Of course, this is difficult on many levels, in part because he has quickly and loudly begun to do things (sign "executive order" after "executive order," as well as appoint questionable individual after questionable individual to his cabinet and the Supreme Court) that will have and have already had important consequences. One such action/appointment has been the successful installation of Betsy DeVos as secretary of education.

This is certainly not the first time that a secretary of education has been so openly hostile to public education and to education as the practice of freedom. One need only remember Ronald Reagan's secretary of education, William Bennett, and his explicit charge to dismantle the Department of Education and to upend public education in the process. Since the Reagan era, the impact and effect of neoliberalism (and its push to privatize everything, including public schools by way of the charter school and "choice" movement) have done real harm to students, teachers, administrators, and entire communities. And now Betsy DeVos is poised to continue the assault on education in a manner that is nothing less than the (patho)logical next step in the corporatization of education.

That the corporatization of education is already well underway—one could even argue that it is already achieved—doesn't mean that all hope is lost. I believe that the work of Michael Apple, bell hooks, Henry A. Giroux, Kenneth J. Saltman, Paulo Freire, Angela Davis, Alex Molnar, and the many other theorists and critics who have identified and confronted the influences and consequences of neoliberalism have also pointed to numerous ways for achieving education as the practice of freedom.

But, at this particularly dark moment in our nation's history, I feel the need to act inside the classroom in a manner that more readily and visibly embodies the important and insightful critiques and guideposts of critical pedagogy, perhaps in a manner inspired by Graeber and Haworth that rejects and abandons (education) policy and more demonstratively and communally embraces the liberatory and transformative power of education itself, free from the bondage of neoliberalism (in other words, *teaching resistance*).

Early on in *Fragments of an Anarchist Anthropology*, Graeber offers us: "against policy (a tiny manifesto)." He tells us:

> The notion of "policy" presumes a state or governing apparatus which imposes its will on others. "Policy" is the negation of politics; policy is by definition something concocted by some form of elite, which presumes it knows better than others how their affairs are to be conducted. By participating in policy debates the very best one can achieve is to limit the damage, since the very premise is inimical to the idea of people managing their own affairs.[11]

And as the people I have identified in these notes thus far all document, policy (education reform) is little more than a "governing apparatus which imposes its will" on teachers, students, administrators, and entire communities with high stakes testing, the deskilling of teachers, the cuts to and diversion of funding for public education, and the imposition of the corporate model to direct and control all "outcomes." Following Graeber's pushback to "policy," I want to enact, to whatever degree possible, "an anarchist pedagogy" to acknowledge, confront, and overcome the very dominating and authoritarian dynamics at work in the classroom today from kindergarten right on through to graduate school.

I want to evoke and provoke the issue of anarchy as a counterforce and impulse to the "governing apparatus which imposes its will on others." I want to methodologically engage education as the practice of freedom, and not *just* ideologically (of course, I would agree that a *genuine* embracing of education as the practice of freedom ideologically would axiomatically mean to embrace it methodologically as well—as I believe Paulo Freire and bell hooks demonstrate and many others also successfully participate in such engaged pedagogy).

But for my musings here, I want to consider *enacting* freedom directly and in totality throughout the classroom. This is the case, in part, because I want to challenge myself and, to some degree, many of my colleagues to once again consider and reconsider how we "are" in the classroom, living and embodying education as the practice of

---

11 Graeber, *Fragments of an Anarchist Anthropology*, 9.

freedom and, in part, to accept the need to acknowledge, confront, and address the reality that we "operate," however critically, within the very "governing apparatus which imposes its will." As a result, I am, for the sake of these notes, forcing myself to fully embrace freedom and, to whatever degree possible, attempting to reimagine and re-comport myself toward promoting education as the practice of freedom.

As good a "critical" pedagogue as I believe I am and have been, for me these notes are a call to identify my beliefs, habits, and pedagogy, not unlike Descartes' *Meditations on First Philosophy* were for him. These notes are a consideration of how I embrace and enact those beliefs and habits and that pedagogy and a challenge to improve upon my pedagogy. I have decided that rethinking my own pedagogy in light of an anarchist pedagogy might prove the most challenging, informative, and constructive mediation on pedagogy I could contemplate and enact at this moment.

NOTE 3: A SHORT TAKE ON EDUCATION AS THE PRACTICE OF FREEDOM

In addition to taking the time and space for self-reflection and self-critique, another purpose of these notes is to offer someone who hasn't read bell hooks or Paulo Freire a sense of the look and feel of such teaching in a short form, like some kind of field guide. I also want to offer those who do engage with the work of such critical pedagogues, and who do such good work themselves, a discussion that they can have to hand to disseminate to students, colleagues, and even "policy makers" to help drive home the importance of resisting the disastrous effects of "the banking system" of teaching. I also want to offer them an argument that emphasizes and promotes the many possibilities of the transformative power of education when embraced as the practice of freedom. And just as I am using these notes as an opportunity to challenge myself, perhaps these notes can be of similar use to those who regard themselves as critical pedagogues and who engage education as the practice of freedom. It is from this very respectful and humble position that I believe we all always need to rethink, reconsider, and reclaim our pedagogies from the "governing apparatus which imposes its will."

At this moment I am particularly interested in rethinking the pedagogy I bring to the classroom and hopefully help to create in the classroom, because there has been a very palpable recoiling due to the gush of emotions since Trump's election. Students, colleagues, and just about everyone I meet are pushing hard to explain, resist, and (sadly) even in some cases to justify and defend Trump's agenda and manner. If, as I have already noted, politics has always been at play (at work) in our education systems, our schools, and our classrooms, it appears that we are currently experiencing an intensification of the polarizing impact of (bad) politics on education and, along with it, an intensification of the scrutiny over what is being taught and by whom. The various moves to impose a corporate model on education and to specifically limit education as the practice of freedom that have unfolded over the past thirty years have proven to be successful in numerous ways.[12]

We have encountered the ongoing assault on academic freedom: from the imposition of "standardized syllabi" that "inform" the consumers (the students) what to expect from the product (the course) to the influence of "for-profit" schools promoting "marketable skills and degrees" that continue to undercut and otherwise call into question the "value" of the humanities and fields of inquiry such as Ethnic Studies, LGBT Studies, and so on, and from the ever increasing demand for educators and students to adhere to the corporate benchmarks of productivity, efficiency, and accountability, buying in to the belief in the authority of the market itself to the continued devaluation of the "labor" of educators as educators and to the promotion of educators as merely distributors of useful information (that is, to be more useful in and to the labor market).

These notes are intended to take a simultaneously reflective break from the ever-growing authoritarian reach of the state and of "the market" and, at the same time, to suggest some decisive actions to promote and reassert education as the practice of freedom. This is why

---

12 Michael Apple, *Education and Power* (New York: Routledge, 1982); Stanley Aronowitz, *The Knowledge Factory* (Boston: Beacon Press, 2000); Angela Davis, *The Meaning of Freedom* (San Francisco: City Lights, 2012); Paulo Freire, *Pedagogy of the Oppressed* (New York: Continuum, 1992 [1970]); David A. Gabbard, "Education Is Enforcement: The Centrality of Compulsory Schooling in Market Societies," in *Education as Enforcement: The Militarization and Corporatization of Schools*, ed. Kenneth J. Saltman and David A. Gabbard (New York: Routledge, 2003); Henry A. Giroux, *On Critical Pedagogy* (New York: Continuum, 2011); hooks, *Teaching to Transgress*; Peter McLaren, *Critical Pedagogy and Predatory Culture* (London: Routledge, 1994); Alex Molnar, *School Commercialism* (New York: Routledge, 2005); Kenneth J. Saltman, "Introduction to the First Edition," in Kenneth J. Saltman and David A. Gabbard, *Education as Enforcement*.

I have said that I would like these notes to serve as a kind of field guide to education as the practice of freedom.

As many of us directly involved in the "field of education" (working as teachers and administrators from kindergarten through twelfth grade, or those working in schools of education and on various education initiatives and in policy think tanks) have witnessed (and sometimes promote and/or confront), there is much emphasis on a "best practice" approach and on "evidence-based" support for said practices. As a result, so much of education, research, and teaching is "data-driven," even when the data is suspect (or just wrong). And still more harmful, there exists a prejudice against "theory" and against a theoretical approach to teaching within a social/political/cultural context that emphasizes other aspects and dimensions of teaching and learning (such as the history and legacy of racism, sexism, class elitism, homophobia, and biases against those with abilities and disabilities that render them "problematic" or outside the mainstream of education concern). All of this leads to an obsession with "information," to the detriment of teaching and learning.[13] We also wind up with no vision or mission—education becomes little more than a "jobs preparatory program" and a competition in the marketplace. This is what leads us to the litany of reform programs (from the Bush administration's No Child Left Behind to Obama's Race to the Top, never mind the practically innumerable local initiatives attempting to "fix" education). The results are proving disastrous for all.

At the same time, even though someone may employ a theoretical stance and perspective, this doesn't guarantee a successful classroom dynamic. We need to remember that *how we are* (a concern of these notes from the very start) is just as important as what we are presenting and even why. We need to establish trust and a sense that students have the freedom to explore, challenge, work together, and even be wrong. Of course, I recognize that the classroom dynamics will look different in elementary school than in a graduate seminar, but for the sake of this meditation on pedagogy, I would like to posit that while acknowledging the differences that exist at different levels of instruction, the essential character of "education as the practice of freedom" ought to be manifest

---

13   Scapp, *Reclaiming Education*, chapters 5–6.

at every level and at every turn. The hard and important work of good teaching is helping to create and establish that freedom.

NOTE 4: AN EXAMPLE FROM THE FIELD

As I mentioned in the previous note, of course I believe that age and level of instruction bring with them genuine differences to the learning environment, so part of the goal of these notes is to provoke more and different explicit engagements toward embracing and enacting education as the practice of freedom at each level—by those teaching at each of those different levels of instruction. In addition, as Haworth's *Anarchist Pedagogies* acknowledges and discusses, anarchy itself is multifarious and is differentiated depending on any number of circumstances and "localities." As Allan Antliff puts it in the afterword to Haworth's anthology, "I was struck again by the diversity of approaches and perspectives within anarchist pedagogy, as well as the many avenues awaiting further development."[14] So I very much acknowledge the many different layers, levels, and dynamics of teaching and learning (whether in state-run schools—i.e., public schools—or with homeschooled children and private institutions of all stripes), as well as acknowledge the complexity of "anarchy" itself and of anarchist pedagogies. What I want to offer here is just one example of how, at both the undergraduate and graduate levels, we might attempt (or at least entertain?) an anarchist pedagogy—in part, to challenge and push ourselves as educators and to promote education as the practice of freedom.

In my introductory note, I indicated (or at least suggested) that I am not a self-described anarchist and may have reservations regarding a politics predicated on anarchy. (I will say more about that later.) I am much more allied and associated with those who typically get identified as "critical pedagogues" and with critical pedagogy itself. But, as I also remarked in the introductory note, I feel compelled to push myself in an *anarchist* direction (action) precisely because of the particular moment in which we find ourselves. And while I have always practiced what bell hooks calls "an engaged pedagogy," one that honors and respects education as the practice of freedom, I feel that it is necessary to explicitly embody *acts* of resistance against "a state or governing apparatus which imposes its will on others" and simultaneously to explicitly embody *acts*

---

14   Allan Antliff, "Afterword," in Haworth, *Anarchist Pedagogies*, 326.

of liberation in the classroom. While I do believe that critical pedagogy strives for this and demands strategies for achieving an engaged pedagogy, I feel it necessary to consider more fully an anarchist engagement as a means of considering and reconsidering my own "critical" pedagogy. What follows is just one modest example of an attempt to disrupt the stultifying status quo while struggling to engender greater freedom and student participation in teaching and learning.

Just as there has been increased monitoring and deskilling of K-12 (kindergarten through twelfth grade) educators, those teaching in higher education have also encountered the impact of the "state or governing apparatus which imposes its will." This type of imposition comes in many forms and varieties, just as is the case with K-12 education, but, regardless of the form or type, this imposition is consistently both mandated by the state and manipulated by the many corporations (educational entrepreneurs) now "dedicated" to improving education, with their alleged innovative tests and other instruments that better "measure" student success and teacher productivity. At the college and university level, there is an ever-increasing attempt to control and restrict (academic) freedom in and out of the classroom. This is also achieved by different means, but one major factor is through the *conformity* (and concomitant rigidity) demanded (dictated) by all sorts of accreditation bodies, both at the department and program level. The accrediting organizations get to make such demands before placing their imprimatur on an "approved" program. And this is also done at the university level as a whole (for example, by regional accrediting agencies and associations that cover different sections of the United States, through which each institution "gets accredited"). What is interesting (that is to say, depressing and oppressing) is just how readily and willingly so many professors and (I suppose a bit more understandably) administrators accept, adopt, and require these "impositions" (the establishment of very specific criteria regarding "learning objectives and outcomes," as well as the "collection" of vast amounts of data all required to get accredited or reaccredited). One consequence of these mandates has been the steady transformation of course syllabi from what was once an expression of academic freedom and (often) a somewhat idiosyncratic articulation of an individual professor's "take" on a subject, theme, or discipline to what is now an almost uniform publication that pronounces, in advance, everything required by the regional accreditation organization. In addition, these accreditation organizations more and more frequently not only tell you that you must collect this data, they also tell you what are the "acceptable" categories, terminology, and objectives. Thus, any given college course syllabus now looks almost identical to all other syllabi, even those from a different discipline, all, to my mind, in an attempt to regulate teaching and learning and bring them under the control and watchful eye of the "state or governing apparatus which imposes its will."[15]

Now, there are many unfortunate consequences to such conformity and uniformity, but what I would like to focus on here is how such an imposition contributes to working against education as the practice of freedom and how in the name of "rigor" we allow rigidity to set in and control our classrooms. By requiring that professors reproduce a syllabus from a universal template, to ensure clarity, student responsibility, due dates, and all course requirements, departments and universities impose a form and structure on all courses and rigidly demand conformity. Please understand that I very much appreciate clarity and the articulation of responsibilities and so on, but what gets sacrificed in the process is something I believe is essential to education as the practice of freedom, namely the freedom to encounter each class as a community of active participants in teaching and learning and not just the passive recipients of information and instruction. To some, the "syllabus issue" may seem a relatively minor one, but for me it indicates and creates the very opposite to the educative space that I attempt to offer and negotiate with each and every class I teach. And my refusal to perform accordingly, specifically to distribute a syllabus on the first or second day of class (if at all), is both an act of resistance (however minor in the grand scheme of things) and an important act of invitation and welcome to those students in the class. In essence, I am, with the effort and contribution of the class, attempting to create a different educative space from the one that is expected to be uniformly implemented via the "universal syllabus."

There is a long tradition of attempting to create such an "other space." Feminist pedagogy has argued for and provided such other spaces, at times at grave personal and professional cost (denial of tenure or promotion, as well as ridicule). So too have disciplines and

---

15 Scapp, *Reclaiming Education*.

perspectives as diverse as Ethnic Studies, Queer Studies, Environmental Studies, and Performance Studies offered challenges to the constrictive traditional learning environment (space) and also offered new possibilities of reconfiguring those spaces (in and outside the classroom). In his essay "Spaces of Learning: The Anarchist Free Skool," Jeffery Shantz rightly notes that:

> Social theorist Michel Foucault used the occasion of his 1967 lecture, "Of Other Spaces," to introduce a term that would remain generally overlooked within his expansive body of work, the notion of "heterotopia," by which he meant a countersite or alternative space, something of an actually existing utopia. In contrast to the nowhere lands of utopias, heterotopias are located in the here-and-now of present-day reality, though they challenge and subvert that reality. The heterotopias are spaces of difference. Among the examples Foucault noted were sacred and forbidden spaces which are sites of personal transition.[16]

It is precisely this effort to help create another kind of space, a "heterotopia," that leads me to disrupt the distribution of the syllabus as the first gesture of the semester and to solicit and elicit contributions and participation from the class toward this end.

Part of the reason that complying with the "syllabus edict" is problematic is that it fully initiates and substantiates "the banking system" of teaching that Paulo Freire so astutely identified and named and so thoughtfully and thoroughly criticized (as oppressive). Participating in the automatic act of handing out the syllabus (hard copy or electronic) constitutes the very first "deposit" within the banking system and renders students passive from the very start: "This is what you will need to know!" So the very modest and simple gesture of *not* distributing the syllabus initiates instead the very first activity for the entire class, specifically, a discussion of what the class will be.

Of course, such a stance, such a gesture, doesn't mean that I would not have thought through the course beforehand. Certainly, I envision a course that would be meaningful and connected to their program of study. But what I do not do is "decide" everything in advance and leave

---

16 Jeffery Shantz, "Spaces of Learning: The Anarchist Free Skool," in Haworth, *Anarchist Pedagogies*, 124.

no room for input, suggestions, and contributions to the syllabus that we create, to enhance the course *we* create. This offers students a (new?) way of interacting in the class with each other and the teacher, a way of engaging in social and educative interactions that are mutual and dialogic from the very start. As Shantz claims:

> Anarchist pedagogy aims toward developing and encouraging new forms of socialization, social interaction, and the sharing of ideas in ways that might initiate and sustain nonauthoritarian practices and ways of relating.[17]

I am claiming that the simple and modest gesture of extending a welcome to participate goes a long way "toward developing and encouraging new forms" of teaching and learning, new forms of mutual and dialogic interaction that are both respectful of the subject matter and of the students and, if successful, create the very "heterotopia" Foucault and Shantz describe.

I also ask students about the ways we might be able to evaluate their work and the course itself, evaluate the success of the teaching and learning and my ability to help facilitate successful teaching and learning. The results vary, but students always come up with interesting and innovative ways to evaluate and consider their work and the value of the course.

I suspect that someone who feels very obligated to teach "required material"; i.e., for a biology or math course, might say that such "flexibility" and "student input" are unacceptable, because it is not doable in their classes and is even detrimental to staying "on pace" with the course—that they don't have even one class "to waste" on such a gesture, such an invitation to contribute to the dynamics of the class. I respectfully disagree, and I have worked with colleagues who teach such "rigid" courses and helped them experiment with inviting student contributions to the making of the course (in some cases it is only the first class, but in others that "activity" extends well into the semester).

I fully understand the concerns some may have regarding *not* distributing the course syllabus and having students directly contribute toward its creation. But it is truly amazing to witness the levels of involvement and responsibility by all. And this first gesture is a genuine

---

17   Ibid., 126.

one. It allows both the teacher and students an opportunity to create a different kind of educative space and to embrace education as the practice of freedom.

NOTE 5: ANARCHY MEANS NO RULERS, BUT CAN WE STILL HAVE LEADERSHIP (IN THE CLASSROOM)?

Justin Mueller, in his essay "Anarchism, the State and the Role of Education," is again helpful when he notes:

> The word "anarchy" comes from the Greek, "an" meaning "no" or "without," and "archos," meaning "ruler" or "authority." In this sense, the concept does not mean "chaos" but rather an opposition to hierarchical power relationships, which are the corporeal embodiment of the notion of "opaque" authority. Thus opposition to the State and capitalism are appropriately features of anarchist theory, but they are incidental byproducts of this primary rejection of hierarchy, of divisions between those who command and those who are compelled to obey. This simple principle of opposition to hierarchy and imposed authority, taken seriously, logically extends to an opposition to all dominating and exploitative social, political and economic power relationships, including not just capitalism and the State, but patriarchy, racism, sexism, heterosexism, war (and by extension, imperialism), and any number of other manifestations of power disparity as harmful to human development.[18]

I quote Mueller at length here because he offers us a succinct and useful description of anarchy and touches upon some important issues that I want to connect specifically to classroom dynamics, following up on my "syllabus example" in the previous note.

As exaggerated or melodramatic as it might strike some, *not distributing the syllabus* is for me, the students, and my colleagues a bold act indeed. It not only indicates that "we" share the important task of laying out the course, but it is also a blatant disruption of business as usual, one that can and does have consequences (from very good pedagogical

---

18 Justin Mueller, "Anarchism, the State, and the Role of Education," in Haworth, *Anarchist Pedagogies*, 15–16; see also Ron Scapp, "Taking Command: The Pathology of Identity and Agency in Predatory Culture," in Saltman and Gabbard, *Education as Enforcement.*

results to some vexed administrative and programmatic reactions). And, in essence, I see it as a moment of anarchist pedagogy, but one that, in fact, taps into and invites the expression of solidarity and *leadership* at the very moment that the expected authoritarian gesture is abandoned. The action of not distributing the syllabus sets off reactions and concerns, but they are now reactions and concerns of the entire class (including me). I suppose that there are any number of other gestures (nonactions) that could also disrupt the *class as usual* modality (again, one can think of numerous strategies emanating from feminist pedagogies to the techniques of the late controversial psychoanalyst Jacques Lacan). But I believe that offering students the possibility (and the responsibility) to participate (differently) provides an opportunity for genuine solidarity and leadership in the class.

I know that Mueller notes that "anarchy" means without a ruler or authority, but I want make a distinction between a "ruler" and an "authority." I do not mean to split hairs here or in any way undermine my own (attempt at an) anarchist pedagogy by reinscribing "leadership" and "authority" in the now "syllabus-less" class. But, perhaps as a consequence of the influence of critical pedagogy, I still want to believe (hope) that when presented with such opportunities, students do work collectively (in solidarity) and guide (lead) each other and themselves, precisely because they tap into their own expertise and knowledge (authority) and their natural desire to learn.

As I have previously acknowledged, I view myself very much in the tradition of "critical pedagogy," but I also acknowledge that these notes are very much a genuine expression and reconsideration of that pedagogy, of my pedagogy. I am guessing that if anyone has read this far, they have either "tolerated" my "critical" perspective and leanings and my commitment to "education as the practice of freedom" or have continued to read on just to compile more evidence of my naive "progressive" view of education as "transformative." I admit to all of this, but with an important caveat: my "critical pedagogy" is neither unexamined nor a "blind" (naive) buying in to what Richard Kahn would identify as the "industrial strivings of modernity" or "the ideology of progress."[19] While

19 Richard Kahn, "Anarchic Epimetheanism: The Pedagogy of Ivan Illich," in *Contemporary Anarchist Studies: An Introductory Anthology of Anarchy in the Academy*, ed. Randall Amster et al. (New York: Routledge, 2009), 125–33.

I do employ and deploy Freire, I come to him with the strong influences of feminism (specifically bell hooks), ethnic studies, and postmodernism. As a result, I am well aware of the language and ideology Kahn warns us about but believe my own work and disposition help prevent me from falling prey to such dangers—these notes are, for me, another example of not remaining fixed or (self-)satisfied with my pedagogy.[20]

So my modest attempt at engaging an anarchist pedagogy strikes me as no less challenging to myself or the students, if we consider the notion of liberatory pedagogical engagement as an opportunity to express and further develop their own expertise and authority. I see this as an important example of how knowledge, expertise, and authority typically get co-opted by individuals and institutions, converted into "authoritarian" positions and stances, and denied to students, save on the performance of complying to this or that task or requirement. For me, this is similar to confusing ambition with greed—I want students to be ambitious, to desire and yearn for knowledge and wisdom, and they need to be ambitious to do so. But, alas, in our sorry state (literally), ambition is only understood (known) as greed.

A FINAL NOTE: OF COURSE MORE NEEDS TO BE SAID, BUT WHAT I'VE SAID WILL COST ME

Beginning with the introductory note, I have acknowledged that these notes should be very much considered a "cursory and provisional but honest" attempt at rethinking my own pedagogy at this particular dark moment in U.S. history. I also know that much more needs to be worked out, and much more has been worked out by others. But this was intended to be a moment of honest reflection on my own pedagogy and an attempt to continue mapping out new directions and strategies to engage education as the practice of freedom.

The syllabus action is just one of many such actions and nonactions taken by me each and every class. I also, whenever and wherever possible, attempt such actions and nonactions during committee meetings and other gatherings where the typical hierarchical authoritarian rule is at play. This involves many gestures, many comments, many risks. I

---

20 Ron Scapp, "The Subject of Education: Paulo Friere, Postmodernism, and Multiculturalism," in Paulo Friere, with James W. Fraser, Donaldo Macedo, Tanya McKinnon, and William T. Stokes, eds. *Mentoring the Mentor: A Critical Dialogue with Paulo Freire* (New York: Peter Lang, 1997).

have purposely spoken about one particular act and not about many others. I have done so to avoid (or at least minimize) the backlash from many quarters that even these modest notes will no doubt provoke.

Even contemplating an anarchist pedagogy these days is risky business, and I know that even what little I have considered in these notes will cost me, as it has cost others. As we know, people in charge don't even like the "suggestion" that the order of things is subject to debate and possibly being *disordered*. My work, in and out of the classroom, has always been a struggle to have that debate and to create such disorder (not chaos and violence), to create "heterotopias" wherever possible, however modestly.[21] My own background in philosophy, education, and ethnic studies has led me to act in certain ways; it seemed appropriate to consider *acting* even more—even if it turns out that what I am doing should be continued.

In her essay "Anarchism, Pedagogy, Queer Theory and Poststructuralism: Toward a Positive Ethical Theory, of Knowledge and the Self," Lucy Nicholas claims:

> Many anarchist pedagogical practices and perspectives can be understood alongside poststructuralism and queer theory because they are concerned with subjectivity, in terms of shaping individuals according to maximum possible "autonomy." This is a process that both perspectives tend to consider as fundamentally situated and collective. As such, anarchist approaches to pedagogy can easily be allied with poststructuralist ideas about the subject as nonfoundational and, therefore, while not predisposed to any particular way of being, having the potential to be fostered according to a particular ethic.[22]

What I have attempted to begin here is to understand my own postmodern perspectives and pedagogy in light of what an anarchist pedagogy might be (for me). I wanted to push myself (however far I could), to take a "particular way of being" (my way of being in and out of the classroom) and to consider "a particular ethic," an anarchist ethic and pedagogy.

---

21 Ron Scapp, *Managing to Be Different: Educational Leadership as Critical Practice* (New York: Routledge, 2006).
22 Lucy Nicholas, "Anarchism, Pedagogy, Queer Theory and Poststructuralism," in Haworth, *Anarchist Pedagogies*, 242.

DEFEND PUBLIC EDUCATION

Art by John Fleissner

So what the fuck are you going to do, kid?
Still ratting at the chains of the gates of the world. . .
But you can't quite pretend.
Still tasting youth's bitter exile here in your empty generation's
  wasteland. . .
Where all the things that you've been clinging to are being ripped
  from your hands.
—Modern Life Is War, "The Outsiders"

>> Since its inception in 2015, the "Teaching Resistance" column in *Maximumrocknroll* has frequently featured guest authors who have addressed the many problems with so-called public school "reform" efforts. In the United States, a prime example of this has been the proliferation of for-profit (and so-called "nonprofit") charter schools, privately run institutions (often with corporate backing) that operate outside the public school system yet draw fiscal and classroom resources directly from it. As a force of privatization, charter schools are generally nonunionized and are often staffed with overworked, inexperienced teachers, many of whom are there solely to take advantage of a government program (Teach for America) that provides recent four-year college graduates with little to no teacher training an opportunity to relieve their debt in exchange for two or three years of service in these schools, which don't require teaching credentials—a process described at length by Roburt Knife in "The Big Takeover of New Orleans," earlier in this volume.

Meanwhile, the administrations of charters frequently take advantage of parental desperation in struggling public school districts to cherry-pick the most well supported students, while freely ejecting students with greater personal challenges (who end up back in the public schools), all in order to gin up charter school aggregate standardized test scores and appear "better performing" than public schools in the same area. This "evidence" of higher student test performance—an incredibly dubious method of measuring student learning that has roots in white supremacy—is then used to apply political pressure to increase charter school funding, while reducing concurrent funding for public schools. It also puts increased pressure on public school teachers' unions to accede to political (generally right-wing and neoliberal) demands for greater fiscal austerity, increased class sizes, and significant reductions in hard-won benefits, resulting in a significant quality of life impact for teachers—who already labor in what is arguably the lowest compensated of the major postgraduate professional fields.

However, it is important to remember that the rise of charter schools in the U.S. is just one example of the ways in which hypercapitalist and neoliberal forces have pushed teachers to defend themselves, their profession, and their students from disempowerment worldwide. In Mexico, the teachers of Oaxaca are in a state of open conflict with the government over its efforts to privatize the public school system, while reducing the ability of Indigenous communities to have a say in how their own local schools are run. This ongoing conflict, which turned openly violent in 2006—with the violence generally inflicted by the state—has flared into the global news cycle a few times, most notably with the murder and "disappearing" of scores of teachers and their supporters in several waves of brutal government oppression. While attention from the rest of the world comes and goes, the violence and repression by capital in full collusion with the Mexican state continues unabated.

The next chapter is by **Scott Campbell**, a radical journalist, writer, and translator based in California. He previously lived in Mexico for several years, including in Oaxaca. His pieces appear frequently on El Enemigo Común and It's Going Down. He can be found online at fallingintoincandescence.com and @incandesceinto on Twitter. Solidarity to our Mexican colleagues and power to the people everywhere against capitalism and imperialist hegemony over public education.

The People and Teachers Unite against the State and Neoliberalism in Oaxaca

by Scott Campbell

> Los caídos en esta guerra
> No se han ido, siguen luchando
> Siguen viviendo en nuestra memoria
> Mucha sangre se ha derramado
> Siguen viviendo
> No hay miedo, ya no hay miedo
> No hay miedo, no existe el miedo
>
> (The Fallen in this war
> They are not gone, they are still fighting
> They continue to live in our memory
> Much blood has been spilled
> They keep living
> There is no fear, already there is no fear
> There is no fear, fear doesn't exist)
> —Tercer Mundo, "Caídos"

In the fall of 2008, while in the city of Oaxaca, I walked with David Venegas in the plaza in front of the Santo Domingo Cathedral, a massive four-block church and former monastery whose construction first began in 1572. We were returning from the courthouse nearby, where Venegas had to report every fifteen days. A prominent member of the Popular Assembly of the Peoples of Oaxaca (APPO) and the antiauthoritarian group Oaxacan Voices Building Autonomy and Freedom (VOCAL), Venegas was arrested, beaten, and tortured in April 2007, held for eleven months on charges of "possession with intent to distribute cocaine and heroin, sedition, conspiracy, arson, attacks on transit routes, rebellion, crimes against civil servants, dangerous attacks, and resisting arrest," and eventually conditionally released. Until he was found innocent in April 2009, one of those conditions was his semimonthly presentation at the courthouse. As with any trip he made in public, Venegas had at least one person accompany him to provide some security against being arrested or disappeared.

During this walk, he recounted a story from July 2006, about a month after the people of the southern Mexican state of Oaxaca rose up in open rebellion against the state government. From the plaza in Santo Domingo, which served as the center of the social movement in 2006 after it was forcibly removed from the city center—the Zócalo—one can see an auditorium on a nearby hill called Cerro del Fortín. This auditorium was built by the state government specifically for the annual celebration of the Guelaguetza. Guelaguetza is both an event and a concept. It is an Zapotec word meaning reciprocity or mutual aid, an important tenet of communal Indigenous life. It is also a state-run occasion that brings dancers from Oaxaca's seven regions to perform "traditional" dances, modified from Indigenous festivals that marked the beginning of the planting season. The state's biggest tourism draw, tickets to the annual July Guelaguetza cost around four hundred pesos (at the time around forty dollars), beyond the means of the average Oaxacan, thereby excluding them from a celebration of their own culture.

Just before the state-run Guelaguetza was to be held in July 2006, Venegas told me, "During those days of freedom, I was walking here in front of Santo Domingo and saw people up in the auditorium painting '*Fuera Ulises*' in huge letters on the seats" ("Ulises Out," referring to then governor Ulises Ruiz Ortiz). Opposition was so great that the state ended up canceling the commercial Guelaguetza, while the APPO organized its own free People's Guelaguetza.

The above anecdote of an anecdote serves as a microcosm for a story still unfolding—a story told by a survivor of state repression, while standing in the shadow of a building that serves as a reminder of the five hundred–year legacy of colonialism, about a social movement not only fighting against a despotic regime but at the same time working to reclaim and reimagine life and culture outside of the structures of an authoritarian state and an impoverishing neoliberal system. While the 2006 Oaxaca Commune was crushed by Federal Police and military force five months after running the state government and police out of power and administering affairs via popular assemblies, the embers that led to that rebellion continued to smolder. Fast forward a decade, and the resistance in Oaxaca has wrapped up the celebration of its Tenth Annual Teachers-Peoples Guelaguetza. For good measure, blockades were also set up around the Cerro del Fortín at 6:00 a.m. the morning of the second of two commercial Guelaguetza performances, causing the festivities to occur in front of a largely empty auditorium.

Just as in 2006, what started this year's revolt was a teachers' strike. Teachers belonging to the National Coordinator of Education Workers (CNTE), a more radical faction of about 200 thousand inside of the 1.3 million–strong National Union of Education Workers (SNTE, the largest union in Latin America), went on indefinite strike on May 15, 2013. Their primary demand was the repeal of the "educational reform" initiated by Mexican President Enrique Peña Nieto.

A neoliberal plan based on a 2010 agreement between Mexico and the Organization for Economic Cooperation and Development (OECD), the reform seeks to standardize and privatize Mexico's public education system, as well as weaken the power of the teachers' union. Publicly supported in his efforts by pro-business lobbying groups, such as Mexicanos Primero and the Employers Confederation of the Mexican Republic (COPARMEX), Peña Nieto set out to implement the OECD agreement and then some, changing articles 3 and 73 of Mexico's constitution. Together, they create a standardized system of teacher evaluation, as well as granting schools "autonomy"—that is, autonomy to raise funds from the private sector—or, in other words, to privatize.

A standardized evaluation system that is imposed from above without the input of teachers, while at the same time placing the fault for low scores solely on teachers' shoulders, is extremely problematic. The attempt to create a monoculture, "one size fits all" education system that produces a certain type of student, as Gallo Téenek noted, "doesn't, knowing the cultural diversity that exists, take into account the reality and local conditions of each of the regions, municipalities, communities, and states in the country, as well as the inequality and poverty that prevail throughout the nation—for example, in regions of Oaxaca, Chiapas, Guerrero, contrary to the better conditions that exist in cities such as Monterrey, Guadalajara, and the Federal District."

The second major aspect of the reform, making schools "autonomous," opens up each school to the direct influence of capital. As CNTE Section 22 from Oaxaca explained in a letter to parents, "Parents will have to pay for the education of their children, since the federal government has disowned its responsibility to maintain schools, meaning it will not send funds to build, equip, or provide teaching materials for schools. It also clearly states that parents and teachers will manage the financial resources to maintain the operation of the schools, which will lead to the establishment of compulsory monthly, bimonthly, or semiannual fees."

CNTE Section 9 in Mexico City pointed out that by forcing schools to continually fundraise in order to exist, in the name of autonomy and with the pretext of involving parents in the management and maintenance of the schools, the legislation "opens the door for the de facto legalization of fees, allowing the entrance of businesses into schools and turning the constitutional provision guaranteeing free public education into a dead letter. This has a name: privatization."

The teachers also demanded more investment in education, freedom for all political prisoners and prisoners of conscience, truth and justice for the forty-three disappeared students from Ayotzinapa, and an end to neoliberal structural reforms in general.

While the CNTE has been fighting against the educational reform for the past three years, a teachers' strike in and of itself is fairly uneventful. It occurs annually in Oaxaca as a tactic used by the union leading up to the beginning of the school year in the fall. Usually, the strike happens, followed quickly by negotiations with the state, a compromise is reached, and everyone goes home. In 2016, however, the CNTE upped the pressure by announcing a national strike instead of striking on a state by state basis. And, in 2016, like in 2006, the state refused to even talk to the union, instead deploying thousands of Federal Police and gendarmerie to areas where the strike was strongest—primarily Oaxaca, Chiapas, Michoacán, and Mexico City, though also in states such as Guerrero, Tabasco, and Veracruz.

In another echo of 2006, it was a brutal act of state repression that turned a labor dispute into a widespread revolt. Ten years prior, it was the predawn raid and destruction of the teachers' encampment in the Zócalo of Oaxaca on June 14. Following the beginning of the strike in 2016, there were several police actions against teachers in Oaxaca,

Mexico City, and Chiapas, as well as the arrest of the Oaxacan union leadership.

In response to police attacks, teachers in Oaxaca began setting up barricades and highway blockades around the state. By mid-June 2016, the CNTE controlled thirty-seven critical spots on highways throughout the state, blockaded in part with fifty expropriated tanker trucks. The blockades were so effective that ADO, a major first-class bus line, indefinitely cancelled all trips from Mexico City to Oaxaca, and Federal Police began flying reinforcements into airports in the city of Oaxaca, Huatulco (on the coast), and Ciudad Ixtepec (on the Isthmus).

Given the climate of escalating state repression, in a statement released on Friday, June 17, the Zapatistas posed the following questions:

> They have beaten them, gassed them, imprisoned them, threatened them, fired them unjustly, slandered them, and declared a de facto state of siege in Mexico City. What's next? Will they disappear them? Will they murder them? Seriously? Will the "education" reform be born upon the blood and cadavers of the teachers?

On Sunday, June 19, the state answered these questions with an emphatic "Yes." The response came in the form of Federal Police machine-gun fire directed at teachers and residents defending a highway blockade in Nochixtlán that for a week had been successful in preventing hundreds of federal forces from reaching the city of Oaxaca.

Initially, the Oaxaca Ministry of Public Security claimed that the Federal Police were unarmed and "not even carrying batons." After ample visual evidence and a mounting body count to the contrary, the state admitted Federal Police opened fire on the blockade. In total, eleven were killed that morning in Nochixtlán. Fourteen were murdered by the state in Oaxaca during the course of the conflict, including Salvador Olmos García, aka Chava, a community radio journalist and pioneer of the anarchopunk movement in Huajuapan, who was kidnapped, beaten, run over, and left for dead by police on the streets of that city on June 26.

Following the Nochixtlán massacre, the struggle took on an increasingly popular dimension through 2016. This took the form of direct actions, marches, material support, and expressions of solidarity from across Mexico and beyond, in numbers far too large to count. By way of example, here are some of the actions that occurred in the aftermath. Parents and teachers took over tollbooths in both Mexico City and Durango for a day, allowing cars to pass through for free. On July 3, an explosives device was detonated at the headquarters of business associations in Mexico City that were lobbying the government to crush the uprising. There were three days of intense mobilizations from July 5 to July 7 in Mexico City. On the first day, there were at least seventy simultaneous blockades and marches, followed by four mass marches on July 6 and at least ten blockades on July 7.

The Zapatistas continued releasing statements in support of the teachers' struggle, on one occasion stating, "To say it more clearly: for us Zapatistas, the most important thing on this calendar and in the very limited geography from which we resist and struggle is the struggle of the democratic teachers' union." They also went further and announced that they were suspending their participation in the July 17–23 CompArte Festival for Humanity, which they had called for earlier this year. Instead, they sent delegations from all the Zapatista caracoles to donate the food they would have eaten during the seven-day festival to the teachers in resistance in Chiapas. This amounted to 290,000 pesos (15,600 USD) worth of food.

In recognition of the contribution of the people to their struggle and the fact that the people have demands that extend beyond the immediate concerns of the union, on July 9, Section 22 of the CNTE in Oaxaca called for a gathering of teachers and Indigenous leaders to "build a peoples' agenda against structural reforms." The union met with authorities from ninety municipalities in the state. It is important to note that these authorities are selected as the moral leadership of their communities not through a vote based on political party but by nomination, discussion, and agreement reached in community assemblies. A second such gathering was held in early August 2016.

Also that month, teachers in Chiapas blockaded the international airport in Tuxtla Gutiérrez for the second time on August 1, also shutting down Torre Chiapas, a skyscraper housing private and government offices in the state capital on August 2. Emiliano Zapata's birthday, August 8, saw upwards of a hundred thousand teachers and farmers march together in Mexico City. A day later, farmers, teachers, and civil society groups took over a toll plaza on the Nayarit-Sinaloa highway, allowing cars to pass for free, asking that instead of paying the toll drivers donate to the struggle. Teachers, civil society groups, and prominent academics gathered in Mexico City on August 10 for a twelve-hour national forum to discuss what a democratic and holistic education project would look like. At the same time, for five days in a row, teachers in Chiapas blockaded and shut down businesses belonging to transnational corporations and companies that are part of the neoliberal business association Mexicanos Primeros. The Guatemalan teachers union also expressed their support, shutting down an international crossing with Mexico for the second time on August 13.

These actions clearly had an impact. On August 3, major business associations held a press conference urging the government to take the "difficult actions" necessary against the "impunity" of the CNTE and claiming they would take legal action against the union for "human rights violations." They also hinted at halting payments to the government's health care and housing programs. On August 8, with no appreciation for irony, business owners in Oaxaca attempted to hold a strike to demand the use of government force against those on strike. Solidarity among capitalists didn't materialize, and most businesses remained open.

While all of these actions were occurring, the CNTE and the Interior Ministry were holding negotiations—negotiations that the state agreed to following the massacre. They met more than ten times, addressing political, educational, and social issues. At each meeting the teachers came prepared with specific proposals and asked the government to do the same. However, the end result of every meeting was the same: no progress on the core issues.

On August 22, the day classes were supposed to start, frustrated in their attempts to crush or wear down the teachers, Mexican President Enrique Peña Nieto announced, "There will be no more dialogue; education first." A day later, Public Education Minister Aurelio Nuño stated, "With complete clarity, we say there is no possibility of returning to any negotiations until all children are where they should be, in a classroom. And precisely because the future of Mexico is nonnegotiable, the educational reform will continue." The defense minister got into the act, declaring armed forces support for the reform and saying that soldiers intended "to serve as an example for others." Not coincidentally, that same day three airplanes full of Federal Police arrived in Oaxaca to join the thousands of state forces already stationed there, an indication that Peña Nieto might make good on his statement that "the government has no qualms about the use of force" as a means to resolve the teachers' strike. At least 1,500 more Federal Police were in Oaxaca by Wednesday, August 24, and helicopter flyovers of the city had resumed for the first time since the Nochixtlán massacre.

After the first week of school came and went with the strike still on, the government retaliated by announcing it would begin fining and firing teachers. Fines were issued to 43,231 teachers, most from Chiapas, while 1,225 were slated to be fired in Oaxaca, 570 in Chiapas, and 80 in Michoacán. Despite the legal and military machinations unleashed against the union, the CNTE still appeared firm. A Section 22 assembly in Oaxaca on August 26 agreed to continue the strike, threatening that if the government didn't negotiate seriously, "activities will be carried out that will generate countrywide ungovernability." They pledged to put permanent highway blockades in place on August 29 and to prevent governor-elect Alejandro Murat from taking office on December 1.

Shortly thereafter, however, the strike began to fall apart piece by piece. All of a sudden, on September 3, 2016, Section 22 announced it would be returning to classes on September 7. It said this decision was made during the state assembly, yet no record of it is present in the publicly available notes of that meeting. Rather, that record says the union agreed that the national strike would continue.

On September 12, teachers in Chiapas blockaded the state capitol building, the state congress, the city hall of Tuxtla Gutiérrez, the state offices of the Ministry of Housing, and the post office, giving the appearance that the teachers' movement remained steadfast in the southeast corner of Mexico. Yet that same day, Luis Miranda Nava, the minister of social development, flew to Chiapas on the presidential plane to meet with the governor and several high-ranking state and police officials, as well as the leadership of CNTE Sections 7 and 40.

Following that meeting, the teachers held an assembly and decided to seek "a political exit" from the strike. The next day, on September 13, teachers from Guerrero, Chiapas, and Michoacán withdrew from the national CNTE encampment in Mexico City, leaving behind only a small group of teachers from Oaxaca. In a subsequent assembly on September 15, the Chiapan teachers voted to end the strike and return to classes on September 19. With teachers in Oaxaca already deciding to return to classes and the teachers in Michoacán also voting on September 15 to end the strike, the strike can be considered to have ended on that day. In total, it lasted 124 days.

What was the result of four months of struggle? What went right and what went wrong? A critical analysis of events is beyond the scope of this essay, but a few initial reflections can be offered. Those who came out best in the struggle are the teachers in Chiapas, where the government, if it keeps its word, has pledged not to implement the educational reform for the remainder of Enrique Peña Nieto's term [which ended on November 30, 2018—ed.], to unfreeze the union's bank accounts and pay back wages, rescind outstanding arrest warrants against movement members, and invest tens of millions in school infrastructure. In Oaxaca, the teachers started negotiations with the government again on September 20, 2016, but no agreements have yet been reached. As for Guerrero, Michoacán, and Mexico City, it's not clear if negotiations or government concessions occurred.

At the end of the day, the educational reform remains in place. Its repeal was the primary demand of the strike. The fact that different states arrived at different arrangements with the federal government in what started as a national strike speaks to a lack of cohesion among CNTE sections. And just when public sympathy and mobilization in support of the teachers was at its peak following the massacre in Nochixtlán, the teachers accepted the carrot of negotiations offered by the state. Entering into weeks of fruitless negotiations brought the struggle off the streets and behind closed doors, deflating the momentum it had acquired, just as the government hoped it would. When the CNTE finally had enough of talking in circles, the school year was about to start and the government had thousands of federal forces in place in Oaxaca and Chiapas. Faced with the threat of physical force and the loss of popularity, as the strike meant children went without education, one by one the sections returned to class.

Lastly, the CNTE stayed true to its roots. First and foremost, it is a teachers' union, not a revolutionary movement. While the CNTE adopted more populist rhetoric, calling for the repeal of all neoliberal reforms, and the street responded in support, the street also urged the teachers not to abandon the struggle and to keep in mind the demands and sacrifices of the people. Throughout its history of often impressive struggle, the CNTE has consistently, like a moth to a flame, been demobilized by offers of access to power. To actually endeavor to repeal all neoliberal reforms would essentially mean overthrowing the existing social, economic, and political order in Mexico. The CNTE is not built for that nor as it is currently constituted and functions would it be a desirable vehicle for revolutionary change.

Despite its flaws, with the support of many sectors of society, the CNTE displayed tremendous fortitude in maintaining a four-month national strike in the face of a massacre, widespread police violence, an intransigent government, powerful business lobbies, firings, fines, and imprisonment, and a media apparatus whose sole mission was to defame it. It consistently brought hundreds of thousands of people out into the streets, coordinated national actions, and effectively shut down interstate commerce in Chiapas and Oaxaca at will. The union displayed a willingness to listen to the people, holding countless meetings and assemblies with parents, workers, farmers, local authorities, Indigenous communities, and civil society organizations. It presented an analysis of the educational and economic crises facing Mexico and offered alternative proposals through collaboration with communities. And from the start, the CNTE's demands went beyond issues of wages or working conditions, including opposition to neoliberalism, justice for Ayotzinapa,[1] freedom for political prisoners, and more. More impressively, teachers did this without getting paid for four months and with all union bank accounts frozen. For all it may lack, the CNTE also offers important lessons when it comes to confronting capitalism and the state. To truly challenge the neoliberal narco-state in Mexico would require social movements with comprehensive analyses and representation to mobilize with the determination, discipline, and support that the CNTE is capable of mustering and providing from and for its members. Despite the end of the strike, the conflict is far from resolved, and the peoples of Oaxaca have shown they will not be silenced in the face of the weapons of power, ten years later providing another lesson in dignified resistance. As the popular slogan goes, "A teacher fighting is also teaching."

2018 POSTSCRIPT

In the two years since the 2016 teachers' strike, much has happened in Mexico, but little has changed. With regards to the struggle of the CNTE, the educational reform remains in place but is far from being

---

1   On September 26, 2014, forty-three male students from the Ayotzinapa Rural Teachers' College were forcibly removed from campus and disappeared.

universally implemented. In states where the CNTE is the strongest, such as Oaxaca and Chiapas, lower profile tugs of war have been occurring over the past two years between the CNTE and the state and federal governments over teacher involvement in state education policy and access to positions on the state boards of education. In Oaxaca, teachers have been targeted for these efforts, suffering at least three assassinations and an acid attack on one of their encampments.

Along with the more direct struggle, we can see the impact of 2016 in other recent events. Last year, Mexico was hit with two devastating earthquakes in under two weeks. The first wrought destruction on large sections of Chiapas and Oaxaca, while the second hit Mexico City and the surrounding areas. Not even waiting for the government to fail to respond, civil society mobilized immediately following both quakes—autonomously organizing rescue, clean-up, and rebuilding efforts, and collecting and distributing aid. In Oaxaca, in particular, the CNTE played an important role in collecting and delivering aid and supplies to impacted communities in the Isthmus region. The connections, coordination, and capacity to mobilize developed over the course of the struggle in 2016 surely assisted in the people's response to the 2017 quakes and made a tangible difference in the lives and well-being of those affected.

Another event latent with the echoes of 2016 is the passage of the national Internal Security Law at the end of 2017. The law increases the domestic policing and surveillance powers of the Mexican military and legitimizes "the use of force" to "control, repel, or neutralize acts of resistance." It also allows for the suspension of "human rights protections" and ensures state forces may act with impunity. Critics of the law rightly claim that rather than being used as a tool against the cartels that the government itself is in cahoots with, the new law is much more likely to be deployed against social movements, making the state's preference for repression all the more likely when it is faced with the next uprising. Well aware that they are in the government's sights, the CNTE organized several statewide and national mobilizations against the new law.

In the summer of 2018, the CNTE again attempted a national strike, but it failed to gain much momentum or attention, especially as it occurred in the midst of a presidential election. In the eyes of many, those elections, won decisively by Andres Manuel López Obrador, will open up new spaces for contesting the neoliberal and repressive policies of the Mexican state once he takes office later this year. López Obrador, a populist and ostensibly a leftist, comes into power largely due to the unmitigated disaster that was the Peña Nieto presidency. In addition to the repression mentioned above, the past six years in Mexico have seen dramatic and tragic increases in violence, corruption, impunity, inflation, and privatization, deservedly earning Peña Nieto the honor of being the most unpopular president in modern Mexican history.

While López Obrador made the plight of the average Mexican the theme of his campaign, he simultaneously formed a coalition with the far-right Social Encounter Party, filled his cabinet and down-ticket candidates with former members of Peña Nieto's PRI party, and met with banking and multinational corporations to ensure them of his commitment to neoliberalism. Thus, it seems as unlikely as ever that change will come from above. We have certainly not heard the last of the CNTE or the many popular and Indigenous movements organizing around Mexico. As we in the United States mobilize to fight our own battles, it is crucial we pay attention to, understand, and build links of solidarity with our comrades fighting different versions of the same beast next door.

Maximumrocknroll Radio's "Teaching Resistance" DJ Slot

by John Mink

The following piece is the playbook of a 2017 segment on Maximumrocknroll Radio on the theme of radical teachers in punk, with a focus on songs from people who happen to be teachers and play in bands. These people also combine their teaching practice, radical principles, and the aesthetics and ethics of punk (the smart kind) into a deliciously flammable cocktail to lob at the nearest cop car or shitty administrator, all while simultaneously teaching students how to make a similar cocktail to lob at whatever they like. Here's a breakdown of some details on the songs selected. There will be more of these in the future!

—You can download or stream the MRR Radio broadcast featuring Teacher Punks (co-hosted by John Mink, editor of the "Teaching Resistance" column) right here: http://www.maximumrocknroll.com/mrr-radio-1522/.

1. SEEIN' RED: "RESIST" (FROM THE *MARINUS* SEVEN-INCH, ON EBULLITION RECORDS, 1996)

Probably the most obvious choice of bands to lead this compilation off with, Dutch hardcore legends Seein' Red are the first band punks usually think of when they imagine teachers in bands. Jos from Seein' Red is a teacher in Holland and has been since before Lärm morphed into Seein' Red in the late eighties. Radical politics are woven deeply into their music and life practice. Seein' Red continued to be really good through the nineties, which is when "Resist" was recorded.

Though I didn't play it on the show (and it was a tough choice), the song "It Must Fall," from the same period, is also great and was on the crucial *Critical Pedagogy* twelve-inch compilation put out in 2000 by longtime teacher punk Athena K. (singer for The Dread) on her label Six Weeks Records—a worthwhile record indeed. In the booklet that comes with this compilation, Seein' Red's Jos C-Red had the following to say about why he got into teaching:

> If we want to have a better world, then we have to start creating some alternative for the ones who are taking part in that world "tomorrow." The ones I am talking about are children, and it is very important to show them alternatives and to tell them that there is no absolute truth, especially not the truth they see on television every day. Being a teacher, for me, is one of the ways I can resist and I encourage others to do the same."

2. THE OVENS—"BUREAUCRATS KNOW BEST" (FROM *SETTINGS*, A CASSETTE- AND BANDCAMP-ONLY RELEASE, 2012)

The Ovens (from Chicago, different from the Bay Area Ovens) are a queercore band who play early KRS-influenced, distortion-saturated punk with catchy vocals. This song also has the distinction of being the only song in this set that is actually about specific issues that teachers face in our line of work. Both Heather and LB from The Ovens are public school teachers in Chicago, and LB also writes the excellent, radical teaching–focused zine *Truckface*. Chicago became one of the most embattled school districts in the country under neoliberal overlord Mayor Rahm Emmanuel (a former Obama administration official, natch). Under Rahm's forceful attempts to privatize public education, dozens of schools deemed to be "underperforming" in standardized tests, mostly in the poorest districts, were closed. This policy has forced students from these closed schools to either travel huge distances to go to the nearest public schools or to attend private charter schools, where profit motive is the main administrative priority, and students can get kicked out for pretty much anything if they are threatening to bring down the school's test score or behavioral metrics. Here is some writing from LB in *Truckface*, talking about what was happening:

> Today I spent 8 class periods in the library, dressed as a zombie for our world war z book festival. Over 600 students came to the

festival to play games about the book (bingo, zombie musical chairs, jeopardy) and get their faces painted. We dressed as zombies while other schools heard their sad fate.

We will survive, while other schools will not. Though we have received repeated threats this year and have begun to wither due to the excessive stress, our school was spared. We still remain on probation, an arbitrary designation when our test scores are higher, our attendance levels are higher, and graduation rates continue to move upwards, we still have that label affixed to our beloved school as a way to scare us, threaten us and control us.

Five years ago, i got a job at a school that will be spared while thousands of other hard working teachers, just like me, will no longer have jobs, and thousands of students out there will no longer have passionate teachers. It was luck to get a job at a higher performing school. And as many words that the politicians will spill about resources and test scores, they are unwilling to admit that they are driving good teachers away either through school closings or excessive bureaucratic control.

To say it plainly, businessmen and women are destroying public education.

After an exhausting day of celebration with my students, I mourn the losses around the city and know that anyone of us could be next if we don't do something first.

3. STRANGE FACES—"NO PEACE" (OFF THEIR 2016 DEMO, ALSO ON THE *FREQUENCY OF THE TRUEWAVE VOLUME II* TAPE COMPILATION FROM NERVOUS INTENT RECORDS *SHAMELESS PLUG*)

Ben, from this killer Bay Area darkwave band (he also plays in Screaming Fist, formerly in Kapital and New Flesh), is a social worker in a San Francisco public school, and the singer, April, is a homeless youth outreach coordinator. They also played a benefit for the striking teachers in Oaxaca, Mexico, who have come under extreme government repression (including murder) for standing up for their own rights and those of their students as they battle exactly the same neoliberal forces of public school privatization and related "accountability" issues (i.e., union-busting) that we are dealing with as teachers in the U.S. The violence and repression that these teachers have faced, however, is markedly worse, and solidarity right now is super important. See the piece "The People and Teachers Unite Against the State and Neoliberlaism in Oaxaca" in this book, which examines the teachers' revolt in Oaxaca using firsthand perspectives and reports.

4. DIAMOND GLAZE—"DIAMOND GLAZE" (STREAMING ON BANDCAMP, 2015)

Nani, who lives in London, is a teacher who has worked at a school for students with severe learning difficulties for thirteen years. She focuses on expressive arts, helping students figure out a way to express themselves via art and music. She also works with Richard Phoenix (with whom she plays in the raging teacher-centric punk band Kichigai). Recently Nani and Richard helped students (all high school and junior high ages) form and record two band projects, Rock Penguins and Diamond Glaze—this track is a powerful, snotty, and noisy early post-punk jammer from Diamond Glaze (à la Raincoats or Kleenex)!

5. SCHOLASTIC DETH—"KILLED BY SCHOOL" (FROM THE 2002 *KILLED BY SCHOOL* SEVEN-INCH, ON 625 THRASHCORE)

You really can't fuck with short-lived thrashcore legends Scholastic Deth, who formed in 2002, put out a bunch of music, and broke up that same year because B (of the crucial Jud Jud) was going off to graduate school—thus the song "Killed by School," duh. B came back after a bit and has played in numerous innovative hardcore combos since, including Conquest by Death, No Statik, Replica, and Convenience. Members of the latter two combos Julianna and Alicia are both public school teachers in Oakland, B is now a philosophy professor at a state University, and Dharma just schools everyone anyway. Just gonna go ahead here and say it's a crime that I didn't also include the teacher-centric Bay Area modern band Replica on this playlist, but I will get them in on the next one.

6. LOS CRUDOS—"TIEMPOS DE LA MISERIA" (FROM THE 1993 *LA RABIA NUBLA NUESTROS OJOS. . .* SEVEN-INCH)

Martin of Crudos, Limp Wrist, etc. has been a teacher for many years. As is evident from this Crudos song and many others, just because you work as a teacher does *not* mean you have to act as an agent of a fucked-up government and structurally racist, capitalist system. If you are a teacher, you can *resist* that system and help your students acquire the tools to do the same.

>> Among the various subcultures that pockmark the Western (and to an increasing extent global) social landscapes, the more than forty-five-year-old punk movement has defied all odds and internal contradictions to remain stubbornly, multigenerationally resilient and insurgent; a magnet and haven for outsiders of many stripes. While this book emphasizes the radical, often intellectual side of punk, there's nothing implicitly radical in something that was born of a culturally reactionary moment, and much of the subculture is also deeply apolitical, nihilistic, or even embracing of openly reactionary ideals and symbolism; unexamined fixations that some punks "get over" and some don't. The latter represent the side of punk that the culture at large is most familiar with, and while this has been eclipsed in many ways within the subculture by politically and socially aware insurgents (such as those contributing to this book), that sometimes reactionary under-current is still an aspect of punk that has long presented a barrier to entry for many people who otherwise might be interested.

All that said, inside the reflexively rebellious adolescent impulse and space that gave birth to punk can also be found the seeds of radicalism. Those who are cultivated by this "side" of punk and stick it out in the subcul-ture while growing intellectually, personally, and spiritually often display a distinct resilience and incisiveness that leads to a unique manner of existing in and interacting with the world that isn't easily come by otherwise (you could call it "an attitude"). These punks are survivors, tough, smart, and often very empathetic.

The introduction to the first "Teaching Resistance" column in 2015 (and the introduction to this book) lays it out like this: "Although the institutions of education are historically problematic and often oppressive, students who have experienced them as 'outsiders' understand the importance of learn-ing from teachers who have developed radical notions of what education is and how it works. Sometimes these students become teachers themselves, helping subvert the educational institutions or finding alternatives outside of them."

Given that much of punk (such as that usually covered in *Maximumrocknroll* magazine) embraces idealism, strong personal ethics, and intellectualism, it makes sense that so many radical punks have become teachers while remaining punks—it is one of the few "professions" that potentially leaves room for radical expression and empowerment. The personal journeys made by these teachers can help them to have a strong degree of empathy and connection to marginalized and nonconforming students, those who don't fit in to the neat boxes that dominant culture demands and strongly encourages through its institutions (very much including schools).

The next essay is by **Christiana Cranberry**, the guitarist and singer for Sister Rat, and a public school educator presently located in Kansas.

Who Punk Forgot

by Christiana Cranberry

> You can't turn around,
> It's too late for that now,
> Don't expect to see your friends waiting on the ground,
> Don't expect to see them on the ground,
> Friends are only friends when you're around
> —J Church, "Waiting on the Ground"

I watched the movie *Suburbia* when I was eleven years old, so 1984.[1] It was overflowing with sexism and violence. It was exploitative, but with a clear eye for how it actually is in real life—toxic from day one (earlier). Director Penelope Spheeris also focused her camera lens on these attitudes toward women in the revealing documentary *The Decline of Western Civilization*.[2] I was willing, as a male-presenting young punk rocker, to overlook most of the misogyny. It came off as silly and reactionary. *Suburbia* was a drama, a movie; *Decline* was an honest exposé of the friction that existed in the highly charged beginning days. Then there were the women in *Decline*—they seemed anything other than weak or passive to me. In fact, I immediately saw my role models in these women. Exene Cervenka takes up the entire stage, larger than life and full of heart. The women of the punk movement were kicking against these pricks and winning.

---

1   Penelope Spheeris, *Suburbia* (Atlanta, GA: New World Pictures, 1984).
2   Penelope Spheeris, *The Decline of Western Civilization* (Los Angeles: Spheeris Films, 2016).

For all the macho posturing, punk men often wore makeup and dyed their hair. Punk men cared about the way their clothes fit; how they expressed their internal mood. Punk was feminine. It seethed underneath the surface, rising sporadically to growl and hiss at the bourgeoisie. Punk brought blaring attention to the reality of child abuse, sexual abuse, and broken homes; most often our own. The cycle of abuse and the toxicity of strict gender roles was apparent in the seventies on television shows like *Happy Days*. Mass media latched onto the spectacle of punk, usually focusing on safety pins, colored and charged hair, and makeup (best portrayed in "The Day My Kid Went Punk").[3] The early eighties were the golden age of punxploitation, but it can still be found today. This was, of course, a step behind the times. Media, classically, couldn't keep up when punk was at its first fork in the road, definitively split between new wave and hardcore.

New wave picked up the more colorful elements of punk rock, while hardcore honed in on the aggression. It mirrored the polarizing times of the Reagan era. Reagan: a showman and war hawk who pushed politics back to the far right. His addled presence at the end of the eighties was analogous to the tenor of the country: angry, misguided, and rapidly more militant. The nation would learn about shadow wars in Latin America—conversations about Nicaragua that were being had in the lyrics of punk songs would make their way into the living rooms of the middle class. Punk rock was acting as a pragmatic political tool, but it wasn't immune to the burnout that often leads to meandering, nebulous retrospection. New wave, beginning as a dadaesque, perfectly valid artistic rebellion, was quickly picked over by the media; its corpse left to slowly decay in gay dance bars. While punk rock's macho expression often feels tempered by irony, it is an expression of a strength and will to power that is far too aware of itself. Hardcore punk is not Mick Jagger's puckish swagger, but more often a drill instructor in the war of poor white blues. [I agree with the author that this broader image and public perception of hardcore as such has remained stubbornly persistent despite the long (foundational, in fact) and vital history of people of color punks in the scene—ed.]

---

3   *ABC After School Special*, Season 8, Episode 7, "The Day My Kid Went Punk," directed by Fern Field, aired October 23, 1987, accessed June 11, 2019, https://www.youtube.com/watch?v=MXGn4We3AbM.

In punk music, whether it be hardcore, new wave, proto-punk, or beyond, there are those whose main impetus is to entertain, and another strain that strives to teach: anarchy, peace, social libertarianism. Mostly, the social became political, as we tried to understand our place at the end of the millennium. We wandered, subconsciously aware that we were at the beginning of some great experiment. The fifties image of a relationship was clear male domination, but it was also propaganda employed to quash the undeniable movement of liberation that was seeded during the anarchist and labor movements; post-suffragette women were heading toward a reckoning. The parents of the punk rockers grew up with the Civil Rights Movement that feminism forgot, and they comported themselves accordingly. Free love was code for sexual recklessness and the skewed psychosexual power dynamics of suburban key parties. The cracks in the youth movement of the sixties became rills of ego posturing in the seventies, carving out canyons of rock and roll excess in the eighties. Punk's reply to this entrenched male domination was incapable of including trans people and the neurodivergent community. Punk tokenized the hell out of the fringes of these groups but never fully incorporated them. Unfortunately, punk can be as elitist as it is populist. Still, it pushed into the nineties, and the scrappy underdog of a subculture shifted and rearranged through the relatively mild Clinton era into the emerging world of everlasting war.

Punk is best understood through zines—they brought a real cohesion to the worldwide community. I read about kids hanging out in parks, a sort of early Occupy movement. I grew up reading about punk in my dad's issues of *High Times* from 1978 to about 1983. There were often short articles and letters from punks and the parents of punk rockers, and though, given the source, I took it with a grain of salt, I feel like it was a fairly unfiltered look at the era. Besides being students of counterculture, my father and I also shared a physiological trait that made us feel dimorphically opposed, mind and body. My dad, incapable of facing ridicule and lowered status as a trans woman, hid it nearly his entire life. I do not begrudge him this, as I witnessed the shaming when any signs of his transsexual yearnings bubbled to the surface. My mother openly hated him for it and equated him with me. Punk rock got me out of that house, several years after my father and brother made their exodus. Homeless the day I graduated high school, I was dependent on my gang. We were a very disparate group of people, all looking for the perfect balance of independence and family. As a trans woman, I was properly armed with female role models, but desperately few trans. I found myself despondently scouring *Maximumrocknroll*, *Profane Existence*, *Slug and Lettuce*, etc. for any sign of life from trans punk rockers. What I found were very bold crossdressers, brilliant and funny drag queens, the self-hating Jayne County, and several others from the same generation.

The founding punks who dared to cross gender lines, to fuck gender roles entirely, were very inspiring but seemed trapped in the mores of the seventies and eighties, unable to fathom the future movement of transgender and transexual folks. The trans kids today tend to lean way farther to the far left than the trans population of these generations and older. They are the children of punk and metal, removing themselves from its sexism and misogyny. The internet has taken the conversations we had in *Maximumrocknroll* and run with it, thanks to trans punk rockers. Early twenty-first-century punk has been revitalized in the Trump era. Kevin Seconds, Ian MacKaye, Dave Dictor, and many more seminal punk singers challenged strict male gender roles in the eighties, paving a way for men in these last few years of the two-thousand-teens to give me hope for a better future. Because, while I didn't see the representation and alliances with trans women and men and the neurodivergent community then, these communities could only truly coalesce in the internet age. In this time when information is key, and conversation both dialectical and myopically social, we are finally freed from the yoke of upper-crusty gatekeepers.

Social justice and freedom of speech are not anathema; they can work together to expose hate. Without being able to see the problem, how can we fix it? I refuse to believe that trans and queer punks bringing the notion out of the safe space of the riot grrrl movement is an admission of defeat. I believe that when marginalized people are allowed to gather together they can heal emotional traumas and set about doing the larger work of economic and other reforms. When people are under attack, they tend to group together and are wary of those who offer comfort when they don't appear to be suffering in the same ways.

Today, I look around and I see the hardcore kids are mostly adults. I see my crust punk friends sobering up. My friends are taking jobs in social work. Some of us learned these concepts at youth shelters like P.H.A.S.E. in Austin, where I heard it in the lyrics of Jeff Ott's Fifteen. I gained emotional intelligence and considered socialism through the lyrics of Lance Hahn. Punk taught us to be better humans. Even the most macho hardcore guy is often someone I trust a little more than your average Joe (not always, though). I'm happy that there is still hardcore music. I miss melodic hardcore, but there have been some solid whisperings of a return to intelligent pop punk. This makes me happy, because while I love hardcore, crust, d-beat, powerviolence, I also love pop punk, roots punk, and, at the risk of being exiled, a lot of music that isn't punk. In the nineties, this wasn't a very popular place to be.

Growing up in the Bible Belt was far from easy. Being transgender only added significant weight to the load. I couldn't be open about being trans, but at least there was a decent punk scene when I started going out in 1987–1988. Unfortunately, hardcore punk was heading toward crossover, and metal attitudes were the exact thing I was desperate to get away from. There were plenty of metalheads at my junior high willing to add to the daily torture of being different in the center of the Bible Belt, and there was nothing punk about that. Another example of my early disenfranchisement became evident in the difference between the first Agnostic Front album and the extremely conservative second album. My earliest memory of punk was the deep excitement I felt from the urgency and pure energy, and, conversely, the revulsion I felt from the sexism, macho attitudes, and growing nationalism.

Fast forward to long after the days of crossover, which retrospectively produced a few fucking great albums. In the late nineties, the men around me started claiming they never were punk, and I found myself surrounded by metalheads with no discernible politics. While homeless, I'd often find myself in very frightening situations, because I was clearly feminine. I had knives pulled on me; I was kicked in the face repeatedly. Fortunately, I was able to sober up sixteen years ago and transition fifteen years ago. It took getting off the streets—I had to have my baseline needs met before I could even consider transitioning. Without the support I received from my wife and the lyrics of Fugazi, Stiff Little Fingers, and Fuel, I would probably be dead. I had a broken femur and a splenectomy to prove it was possible, if not imminent.

When I was getting thrown into cars by boneheads in high school, I was armed with words, set to driving music, that expressed nearly exactly how I felt inside. When the ignorance that surrounded me tore down all my defenses, I would grow strong by the lyrics. It was the most powerful elixir in the world. "Thanks for telling that joke to me, I have a name for that." When singer Sarah Kirsch came out as trans, I finally felt like there was someone in the world who was similar to me. I finally felt like I would be able to talk to someone who explicitly understood my pain. We would bond over what we hid, how it harmed us, and the hope we had for our futures. I dreamed of these things as I sent all the money I could to try to alleviate her suffering. I had to do that because, tragically, weeks after I found out she was transitioning, I learned she had a rare disease: fanconi anemia. I wished over and over she would pull through. I needed a sister who was born out of punk rock. I needed her to tell me that we would be okay. When she died, I felt more alone than ever.

Laura Jane Grace bravely came out of the closet to a massive audience. The internet had for several years been making it easier for young transitioning trans, nonbinary, and gender fluid kids to find each other. They were building a revolution. They used social media platforms to get their voices out. They shared videos highlighting their changes, and they didn't need the counterculture the seventies built to get there. Gender exists outside of that, and punk is a side note, but hardcore music is life-affirming. We know how well it can instill resilience, something trans people need. There is a growing, tight-knit underground of trans punks keeping each other alive. It makes me feel sixteen again. I feel like I did when I just found punk rock. We all absolutely should be screaming for the rights of these kids.

What punk got right was its social justice, its dedication to harm reduction. Matty Luv (of Hickey) and his girlfriend Ro started the San Francisco Needle Exchange, for example. I was homeless, I was an alcoholic, I hit rock bottom and moved in. It took a long time to heal from that. While floating helpless as a plastic bag caught in the wind, I learned what organizations were doing the work to keep homeless people alive. Government has provided nearly no safety net for when your life goes down the tubes, and punk rockers are often the ones sewing these gaping holes shut. We, the egalitarian intelligentsia, have to take care of one another first, so we can have the energy to fix everything else. Right now, I do my part as a paraprofessional educator at a high school in Kansas. My only hope is that the presence of a punk rock trans woman in the halls shows teens the power of survival.

Trans rights are part of the modern era, and there is much work left to do there. It is no fault of zine editors to have excluded or mocked trans people in the past. We have been one of the most acceptable punching bags forever. What is new is being used as a wedge issue in politics—we are under attack, in actual danger, and definitely could use the strength of punk. We struggle to take it, to be seen, to walk together with culture warriors. A cursory glance of older issues of punk rock zines will turn up the word "retard" used for almost every single slightly frowned upon subject. In reviews, letters, columns, the neurodivergent weren't seen as humans with something to offer the world. Things have improved, though. There is an incline in education and understanding in punk that these communities deserve humanizing and protecting. When I was a teen, I met some skinheads at a show. This was 1988, and though they intimidated me, this was before the Metzgers radicalized them into white nationalism. They described themselves that night in Oklahoma City as "the big brothers of the punks, there to look out for the weaker ones." I actually thought that was noble—it made me feel like life was working the way it should. I don't know how truthful they were being, honestly, yet I still believe the strong should care for the weak. Punk, through its revolutions, might have not been equipped to help some groups, but it did create generations of people prepared for the task to come.

>> Adult Education and ESL (English as a second language) teachers in the U.S. have a unique privilege and responsibility in working with the students they teach. All of their students are people who have been marginalized under the American system in a wide variety of ways—in mid-sized to major cities almost all the students are people of color, many (a clear majority) are immigrants (including undocumented immigrants), and economic disadvantage is the norm. Additionally, the students are generally adults who have to juggle work, children, and other family responsibilities with school, which is often held at night. As a result of such high experiential diversity among students, their teachers face some pedagogical challenges—but these same challenges also present a unique opportunity to incorporate their students' widely varied perspectives into classroom teaching and practice. Teachers in these institutions often find, as I personally have as an adult school teacher, that their students have a powerful work ethic, deep and focused curiosity, and a keener understanding of how fucked the system is—and why—than the teacher and other school authorities ever could.

Ruth Crossman, who wrote this chapter of *Teaching Resistance*, teaches English as a second language in the community college system. A writer and activist who has always held that the pen is mightier than the sword, Ruth sees ESL instruction for immigrant communities as a path to empowerment. She works to create a supportive and student-fronted classroom environment where students can draw on material from their own lives in order to improve their English skills. In this chapter, she describes a specific instance in which she used images to generate open discussion and develop descriptive skills in her adult ESL classroom. She also includes an excellent lesson plan based on the lesson she described.

Problem Posing in the ESL Classroom

by Ruth Crossman

> I memorized what the teacher said
> No one ever asked what was in my head
> I learned to color in the lines
> I learned to spit back all the lies
> Their values and their history
> Were deposited in me
> —Alice Bag, "Programmed"

> No pedagogy which is truly liberating can remain distant from the oppressed by treating them as unfortunates and by presenting for their emulation models from among the oppressors. The oppressed must be their own example in the struggle for their redemption.
> —Paolo Freire

I was teaching night school when I found out about Trump's election. It was a noncredit ESL class in the Mission District of San Francisco, a rapidly gentrifying Latinx neighborhood, and over the course of the night we had heard the atmosphere at the nearby bars and restaurants go from loud and boisterous to deadly quiet. My students had been dutifully working with me on a lesson about how to fill out job applications, but it was getting harder and harder to keep up a pretense that everything was normal. I realized there was probably no point in continuing the lesson at about 8:30 p.m. Pacific Time. Everyone in the room, including me, was surreptitiously checking their phones to see which states had been called and which were still in play. I wasn't sure how to address it, but I decided that it was important to be authentic: I needed to step out of teacher mode and talk to the class as my heartbroken self and not as their grammar teacher. I told them that it looked like Clinton was going to lose, that I was sorry, and that I loved them and worried about them. I also said that I understood if they wanted to end class early that night. I was on the verge of tears, but my students were stone-faced. In fact, they looked grimly determined. Karena,[1] a Venezuelan woman who always sat in the front row, shrugged her shoulders. "It's okay, teacher," she said. "Tomorrow is a different day." Then someone else asked me a grammar question, and we went back to the lesson. The tone was subdued and there were a lot of muttered side conversations going on in Spanish, but the class continued.

Over the rest of that semester, there were a lot of conversations in the teacher's room about how to address "what was happening" with our students, but the sense I picked up during class was that it wasn't something they wanted to talk about at school. Sometimes a student would bring up "Mr. Trump," but whenever that happened I noticed there were other students who would look uncomfortable or shut down. I thought of myself as I had been in elementary school—a stoic, studious child growing up in a neighborhood ravaged by the crack epidemic—and remembered that the teachers I had always loved best were the ones who made the classroom into a literal sanctuary: a well-ordered, highly structured place where I could forget about what waited for me at home and lose myself in books and math problems. I decided to take the same approach with my students now. We talked about how to give directions and how to describe work experience using past tense verbs. We talked about how to compare prices for vegetables and how to read medicine labels. We didn't talk about politics.

Nevertheless, the experience I had on election night was nagging at me. I wanted to find a way to bring the issues of the outside world into my ESL class, but I needed a way to do it without making my students feel uncomfortable and without making the conversation about me. As I turned these questions over in my mind, I remembered a book that impressed me in graduate school, but which I had pretty much ignored ever since: *Pedagogy of the Oppressed* by Paolo Freire.[2] A radical

---

1   All of the students' names have been changed in this piece.
2   Paulo Freire, *Pedagogy of the Oppressed* (New York: Continuum, 1992 [1970]).

activist from Brazil, Freire had developed his own pedagogical theory while teaching literacy to farm workers. The biggest prick to my conscience during this period was Freire's warning that education is never neutral and that students must be put at the center of their own learning process. The *why* of using Freirean pedagogy with my students seemed pretty self-explanatory, but I was less clear about the *how*. That was when I remembered one of his key techniques: generative imagery. Freire would present his students with a "generative" image, a picture suggesting a scenario which they could recognize from their own lives. Using this picture, he would elicit their ideas and help them transcribe the words from speech into text. In this way, rather than being mere "banks" for meaningless sets of words, the students could be actively engaged in their own learning. They would be in control of how their minds opened. Something told me I had to try this with my students, but the thought of actually designing a lesson centered around the activity was daunting. I knew that students came to my class exhausted from long days of work, and I wasn't sure how much emotional energy they would have for talking about social issues in class. What right did I have to start talking about mass deportation in the presence of students who might themselves be undocumented? Was it worth it to devote an entire class period to talking about what to do when the cops pulled you over if many of my students seemed more interested in improving their spelling skills? Still, the idea nagged at me.

The semester came to an end, and in the spring I found myself working with a group of beginning English students who were not so different from the class I was with on election night. I wanted to try using generative images, but I was unsure how far I could go into sensitive topics. Many lower-level ESL books have picture prompt activities which ask students to generate a story based on an image, but I felt torn about introducing my own. I saw my opening when we began a unit on health and dealing with emergencies such as car accidents and fires: if we were going to talk about calling 911, we might as well talk about calling the police. The ICE raids in California were well underway at this point, and every day my social media was filled with warnings about immigration sweeps happening in the Bay Area. I knew my students were affected by this, but I also suspected there were other issues that would color their perceptions. They might have experienced brutality or coercion at the hands of police in their home countries, but they might also live in neighborhoods with high levels of gang violence or drug dealing, as I had when I was a child.

I decided see my generative image activity as a way of exploring the theme of police interactions without imposing any particular role on them or making assumptions about what experiences were most significant to them. I wanted an image that related to the police but would not be unnecessarily traumatic: no men kneeling in cuffs, no ICE agents raiding factories. The picture I eventually chose was simple: a handcuffed man being led down a flight of stairs by a police officer as his neighbors watch in the background. I started class by projecting the photo and asking them two simple questions. *What is happening? Why?*

"The police are arresting a suspect," a young man in the front row said, and everyone nodded their heads.

"Teacher, how do you say it, those things around his hands?" another student asked. I wrote the word *handcuffs* on the board.

"Why is he being arrested?" I asked.

"Assault," someone said, and many other students nodded their heads.

"Selling drugs," someone else suggested.

"Murder!" a guy in the back shouted out. Then Amanda spoke up. There were only a few women in the class, and she was by far the most vocal.

"Domestic violence."

I noticed several of the men in the room look down at the table. Together, we made a scenario. The man had been drinking and using drugs. He was jealous of his wife. He thought she had another boyfriend. He started hitting her. Their neighbors were scared and called the police. Now the man is going to jail. I gave the students time to copy the story down, then moved on to the next phase of the Freirean dialectic.

"What are all the problems you see in this story?"

"Drugs," one person said.

"Mental problems," called out another.

"Alcoholic," a third said.

I was fascinated as the conversation unfurled. In the end, the main issues students wanted to know about were the difference between a therapist and a psychologist, how to say support group in English, and how to get help if you have a drinking problem. We ended the activity by giving the man and his wife advice and talking about how to go to Alcoholics Anonymous. There was also a lively discussion about how sometimes women hit people too. I had anticipated none of it, but it turned out that being willing to cede control of the discussion opened up a space in which the students could talk about something important to them without feeling judged.

In that moment, I realized that what had felt uncomfortable for me to address as a lecturer began to feel more normal if I made myself a facilitator instead. With the generative image, the students could project their ideas and worries onto a fictional character. They had control over how much they felt comfortable sharing. More importantly than that, I was calling on their own, often extensive, life experience as a resource for discussing the situation. In a political climate where many of them were reminded daily how little power they had and how little their voices were heard, Freirean problem posing had become a source of empowerment within the classroom.

LESSON PLAN: USING GENERATIVE IMAGES IN CLASS

This lesson is inspired by the generative image method used by the Brazilian educator Paolo Freire, but the methods have been modified to suit the needs of low beginning to low intermediate ESL students learning in an American adult school context. The students in my class were above the literacy level, but it can be used in literacy classes with some minor modifications.

Schema Building

Select an image that is related to a theme the students are familiar with, preferably something they have talked about in class. It is best to do this as part of a thematic topic such as nutrition, emergencies, or housing, and to give the students several days of practice with relevant vocabulary so that they feel confident speaking about the picture in English.

Present the Generative Image

Choose an image that is suggestive but open-ended, preferably a photograph. Examples might include a family moving out of a house, someone looking inside a refrigerator, or a person looking at a stack of bills and looking concerned. Project the image for the students, and/or pass out enough copies for each student to have one. Explain that you are going to write a story together about the photo. Give students five to ten minutes to discuss the photo in pairs or small groups and circulate to answer questions or supply vocabulary. After this group work, elicit ideas from the class about what is happening in the picture. There will probably be a variety of ideas, but after some discussion you should be able to get a sense of what the most popular theory is. Listen to the students and then reiterate their ideas for them orally (e.g., okay, so the family is moving because they don't have money, right? They are moving to another city).

Write the Story
Transcribe the narrative you and your students have generated onto the whiteboard, underlining any new vocabulary presented. Give the class a chance to copy it into their notebooks. Have the class read the story out loud together. If you are working with a LESLLA (Literacy Education and Second Language Learning for Adults) population, you may find it helpful to recycle the text in subsequent classes as a way of practicing reading and writing.

Critique the Story
Ask the students what problems the people in the story have and write down their answers on the board. Then ask them to think of ideas for what the people in the story can do about these problems. You can model this as much as you need to in order to make sure the students understand the prompt. Either let the students discuss it in groups or have them suggest ideas, and write their solutions on the board. You may be surprised at how creative their solutions are.

Extension Activities
There are several ways to build off this lesson, depending on what resources you have access to and what level your students are at. The following are some ideas.

- *Role-Play.* Take one of the possible solutions suggested by the students and help them write and act out a role-play between two people (for example a landlord and a tenant), and then perform it for the class.
- *Writing Assignments.* Have students write a letter to the person in the picture giving them advice. Or if the solutions they suggested

involved a writing component, such as a letter of complaint, give them a model and help them write letters of their own.

- *Community Research.* As a homework assignment, ask students to research any resources that exist in their community to help with the problem you talked about and present the information to their classmates. If possible, see if you can find a guest speaker who is willing to talk to the class and give them more information.

The following lesson plans were conceptualized in December, 2016, at a time when the ongoing traumas for marginalized people in the United States were growing ever more acute and the future looked bleak. That pattern has continued and intensified into the present, and it seems like vigilance and active resistance will be necessary for the foreseeable future. If there is one thing I would emphasize in implementing a lesson plan like this, it is the note that I included after step 7—make sure you, the teacher, are engaged enough in this process and have a sufficient working knowledge of the subject (you can learn it!) to be able to quickly assess/vet any resources that students find on the internet. It is vital to understand the powers that be are adept at deceit and have doubtless laid many traps. So be alert—your students' safety and that of others may depend on it.

Lesson Plans for Community Self-Defense in a Time of Resurgent Neofascism

by John Mink

> I get so sick of the fashion and the fascism,
> Makes me crazy, wanna try a little smash-ism!
> —Screamers, "Anything"

It is near the end of the second decade of the twenty-first century. Unbridled neoliberal capitalism holds total hegemonic sway over the vast bulk of the world's population, including those living under ostensibly "communist" economies, such as China's. In the absence of a deeply organized and united radical opposition, reactionary neofascist ideologues have been gaining increasing prominence in world governments, especially in Europe and the United States. The ideas underlying this neofascist resurgence is not by any means new, of course, and in the United States they have been present to varying degrees in our government, economy, and society at large for centuries. However, the election of Donald Trump in 2016 came with an open embrace of neofascism and hate-based politics that had been slightly more subsurface in the past. This open resurgence of bigoted right-wing extremism has unquestionably resulted in a great deal of trauma for the marginalized people Trump and his ilk target and has created an overall version of reality that is several degrees bleaker. This is a reality we have to fight tooth and nail, and we can start in our own communities.

    I have worked as a social studies teacher at an adult school (Adult Equivalency Diplomas/GEDs/ESL) and in high school as well, in both cases in the Oakland/Berkeley/Alameda area. As a teacher in the aftermath of the 2016 election, it seemed ever more urgent to make an effort to help get the ball rolling on new ideas for self- and community empowerment among my students. As often radical thinkers surviving against incredible odds, many of these students, especially in the adult school, had already been pushing that ball hard and had rolled it quite a distance. As marginalized students who had (have) been living in an increasingly dangerous macro reality, it seemed that finding full-class solidarity, pooling collective knowledge, and sharing resources was a good way to start addressing the freshly sharp problems of the traumatic present.

The following essay is a basic lesson plan for anyone who is in a position to help teach and collaborate with others (it does not have to be restricted to a classroom). There are many documents to be found on the internet (and otherwise) that contain a breakdown and list of legal and community-based resources that marginalized people in the United States can turn to for support and advocacy during these difficult years of drastically increased state, economic, and street-level oppression.

In the endnotes of this lesson plan/column are a few resource bases/documents that I have been pointed to, and I'm sure you can find many others—and *please* share them with me at teachingresistance@gmail.com, so I can share them as well. These documents (and ones like them) could have potentially be useful in many situations, including workshops/community spaces/etc. Please consider lending your skills to the development of these resources or beginning new ones. As an educator, my lesson plan with these documents (or similar materials) is the following:

1. Prior to class: print the entire document (with a link to the original document at the top and email it to all students—they will need to access it online to use the hyperlinks).
2. Briefly introduce the general concept of legal and community-based advocacy resources to students—ask them first if they know what these things are, because student-centered instruction is always better, and someone might have a way better answer than the teacher! Then have the whole class do a silent brainstorm/quickwrite on what some of these resources (or functionally similar institutions, formal or otherwise) are that they can think of in their communities/neighborhoods and what they do (if they know). Make sure everyone has a chance to write down their ideas, then do a five-minute small group/pair share discussion on what they came

up with, followed by a structured but student-centered full-class discussion on what community and legal advocacy is and can be.

3. Pass out the document. Flip through it together and introduce different topics—when taking questions, give students a chance to answer them first, in case someone has a better/more personal understanding of the topic than the teacher. If students are working on reading/comprehension skills, have them do read-alongs for first couple of numbered items on each section before moving on to next topic.

4. Go into independent or small-team research time. Have students do more in-depth research on at least one of the topics of interest or pertinence to them or to other people they are connected to. Ideally, distribute laptops or other online electronics (if available—chromebooks are available at my adult school and many high school worksites), so they can investigate links. If the school does not provide (or provides only limited) electronic resources, encourage students to use their cell phones and/or team up and pool their information technology resources with other students to work together (if this is relatively comfortable for them—a previously established strong classroom community helps in this). The teacher can also look up stuff with students on their own computer/laptop. Circulate and help students with legal and academic language as needed.

5. Have students write a brief summary of the specific resources they researched and how these can be accessed in their community. If these resources cannot be accessed in their community, they can write about what *is* available as an alternative (if anything) and/or what they think can be done to help make these resources accessible to them—make sure they know that there are no right or wrong answers! Also, let students know they can talk/write about why they chose their particular topics if they wish, but that they don't have to—everyone has the right to privacy.

6. If there is time, have a structured full-class discussion on what they came up with, especially their ideas for helping to make legal and community-based advocacy resources available in their own communities—let them build on each other's ideas, but the teacher should not be afraid to lend their own expertise or applicable guidance as is appropriate. Try to compile a good list of these ideas for future sharing in broader online community building.

7. *Revisit* and *repeat* this at least once every couple of months to build a broader resource base, then share it!

One more thing that is crucial: vet the resources being explored before having students contact them and/or adding them to the online list, develop a strong, working knowledge of various trusted organizations and groups, and/or rely on others who have a good index of knowledge about them. There have long been fake radical advocacy groups that are fronts for actors with bad intentions, i.e., "Free Legal Aid for Undocumented Migrants," which is run by ICE (Immigration and Customs Enforcement). Be careful that your students are not looking into a trap, and if they are, remember that showing them exactly how you figured that out is a vital educational opportunity as well!

ENDNOTES
Here are a few of the resources that students and other educators shared with me thus far. All these web addresses were successfully accessed on June 12, 2019. Sorry for the lengthy web links in print, but no one said data entry in the service of justice was going to be easy:

Concrete Suggestions in Preparation for the January 2017 change in American government, a broad and highly-descriptive list of advocacy resources assembled by Kara Hurvitz (and the document I originally designed this lesson plan around): https://docs.google.com/document/d/17Rj40_i39gTuo4hMNNmhToLo_NnJnzjnr3Tx9onTPfE/preview

Resources for Intervention and Deescalation, a resource base of bystander intervention and deescalation strategies separate from the oppressive state, assembled by Mimi Thi Nguyen http://deescalationandintervention.weebly.com/

Programs and Initiatives from the National Network for Immigrant and Refugee Rights http://www.nnirr.org/drupal/programs

INCITE!'s Resources for Organizing—INCITE! works to produce educational resources that support grassroots organizing to end violence against women of color and create safer, more liberatory communities. https://incite-national.org/resources-for-organizing/

As previously mentioned, please share any other resource bases that you know of with me at teachingresistance@gmail.com. (You will definitely be given credit for any shares I make!)

Being a radical thinker and/or a punk as well as a public school teacher is a delicate balancing act. To remain true to our ideals and put them into regular practice in the classroom, realistically, takes some measure of compromise, plus a lot of 3D chess playing and subtle subversion within and around the institutions where we work. In the final analysis, as we navigate these complex spaces, we must weigh the costs of such adaptations against the potential impact of the radical practice we are trying to bring to the table. Over time, we may see if our many collective subversions and episodes of open resistance add up to a revolution, big or small.

As *Teaching Resistance* comes to a close (at least as far as this book goes), it is easy to feel a bit overwhelmed. The obstacles facing radical teachers are daunting, and figuring out how to effectively push back against the overwhelming structural power that forces of oppression and injustice bring to bear on marginalized people takes a lot of trial and error, a lot of self-critique and revision, and a lot of work—all while we try to stay kind to ourselves and be good to those we love.

The following short essay is a rumination on the nature and connections between radical punk/DIY culture, teaching, and the complications and possibilities of using non-radical (even antiradical) platforms to spread radical ideas. It is a previously unpublished work by **Mike Friedberg**, who wrote one of the very first "Teaching Resistance" columns in early 2015. Mike teaches seventh grade science and eighth grade language arts at a public school in Chicago. Like many of the contributors to this book, Mike is still an active member of the DIY/DIT punk community—he has run a record label and distributor, booked shows, was in a band (Kontaminat), and still produces the zine *No Thanks*. A punk, a teacher, a radical, a parent, and more, a bio shared at least in part by all contributors to this book, who, like most teachers in general, wear many hats and give themselves entirely to the things they love.

Navigating Spaces

by Mike Friedberg

Grow your hair, shave your head, can't please 'em all
If I can't please everyone I won't try at all.
—Artificial Peace, "Outside Looking In"

I

The lines between educator, activist, punk, and political affiliations may appear to be ambiguous. Navigating these boundaries is a task that every radical teacher must face continuously throughout their work.

There is a myriad of perspectives on how we, as punk educators, can make the greatest impact—in the classroom, in the school, in the community, or toward research and best practices. Every punk teacher has likely pondered these questions.

While I hesitate to make blanket statements on the abilities of a group, I firmly believe that every teacher should be a strong writer. In the words of an author who I have criticized, "Reading is *the* skill" (emphasis added). I couldn't agree more with this statement. Literacy skills are the foundation for every content area. Regardless of its flaws, education is the key to upward mobility for many of our students—as it has been for many of us.

In punk, we learn to create, we learn DIY. We repudiate conspicuous consumption in the name of art—fliers, zines, writing music, releasing records, etc. For many punk educators, our classrooms become an extension of the DIY philosophy. And for many, writing becomes one as well.

I first gained confidence in my own writing by receiving some recognition for my blog posts. In 2016, I was granted a graduate assistantship for a master's program in Community and Teacher Leadership at Northeastern Illinois University. The assistantship paid for my tuition (as well as a small stipend).

I was forced to not only generate quality writing for a research board but also work with my professors to publish their work. This was an extremely overwhelming task. I was used to blog posts, which were written almost like columns or articles. Academic writing is a whole different beast. Additionally, I had a year to complete a research proposal and then execute a mixed-method study, with the goal of publishing it in a peer reviewed academic journal.

For those unfamiliar with this arduous task, in peer reviewed research, every single sentence essentially fits into one of two categories: A) research states X, and this is what we can infer; B) I'm making this inference/extrapolation, and here's the research to support it. I had gone from writing for my own zine, to blogging, to a territory that was radically ambiguous to me.

I reached out to punk professors for guidance: Michelle Gonzalez, Mike Amezcua, and Rich Booher. I am eternally grateful to these people for their patience and encouragement. They empowered me and showed me that these seemingly overwhelming tasks could be completed. By the end of my first year, I was not only proud of the work I had done for my professors but also of my sixty-seven-page research proposal. After receiving harsh criticism on my writing, I worked diligently to produce the document that would guide me through my first study. Hearing immense praise on my final work from the same professors who had been so relentless was incredible. It was akin to pouring your blood, sweat, and tears into a record and hearing amazing feedback from punks you respect.

II

On November 30, 2018, Anna Nessy Perlberg passed away at the age of eighty-nine. She had witnessed the Nazi youth march through Berlin, as well as the Gestapo trying to capture her father. She was just nine years old when she fled Prague, days before Hitler invaded. She was also my grandmother.

Processing my grandmother's death was challenging. In perhaps a moment of catharsis, I wrote a piece dovetailing my Grandma's emphasis on not being complicit on issues of injustice to speaking out against racist teachers. A friend of mine suggested I submit it to an education site with a large following.

I was extremely hesitant. The site has a large focus on "school choice" and "reforms," euphemisms for things I do not agree with at all. There is much I disagree with on the site. Was this an appropriate venue?

After talking with fellow union members, I came to several conclusions. First, any venue to get my writing out would be worth pursuing. Writing is something I wanna do, and I will gladly take some promotion, even if it's from a site that I don't totally see eye to eye with. Second, perhaps this was an intrinsic act of subversion. Maybe writing a radical piece for an organization I didn't see eye to eye with was "throwing a spanner in the works," as Zounds put it. This does not mean being an apologist or defending views that aren't mine. But publishing a piece I was proud of for a website that I disagreed with wasn't an act of betrayal. It was a way to get my writing out there without preaching to the choir.

Punk educators often debate how to navigate spaces. Many of us want to publish what we find, whether it be in a fanzine or in an academic journal. We work with peer reviewed research and want to share our findings, often in the name of social justice. How do we do this? What are "best practices"? And how do we stay true to our DIY ethics within a system that we often have fierce disagreements with. The answers are often ambiguous, and the paths are not always clear.

All punk teachers have multifaceted identities that we have reconciled. We know the system doesn't work, and we teach within it in the name of working for justice and a better world. The light in the darkness often comes in navigating spaces where we are forced to come to terms with difficult questions. There is no one way, no perfect answer. The DIY ethic taught us to create, share, and work for justice. And that is what drives each of us every day, regardless of where we share our work. Classrooms, bands, academic journals, or fanzines—these are the venues where we fight.

About the Authors

Jessalyn Aaland is an interdisciplinary artist based in the San Francisco Bay Area, working across social practice, painting, and sculpture to explore how the K-12 (kindergarten through twelfth grade) education system functions, both as a site for conformity and of resistance. Through her project Class Set, she has provided over four thousand Risograph printed, artist designed posters featuring social justice quotes to schools, libraries, and nonprofits nationwide. A former public high school English teacher, Aaland has been an artist in residence at SÍM in Reykjavik, Iceland, and at Facebook's Menlo Park Headquarters, and is a 2018–2019 Political Power fellow at Yerba Buena Center for the Arts.

Natalie Avalos (Chicana/Apache descent) is an ethnographer of religion whose research and teaching focus on Native American and Indigenous religions in diaspora, healing historical trauma, and decolonization. She received her PhD in Religious Studies from the University of California Santa Barbara and is currently a Chancellor's Postdoctoral Associate in the Religious Studies department at University of Colorado Boulder.

Alice Bag (sometimes known as Alicia Velasquez) is a singer/songwriter, musician, author, artist, educator, and feminist who was also a devoted, radical public schoolteacher in California and Arizona for decades. Alice was the lead singer and cofounder of The Bags, one of the first [and best—ed.] bands to form during the initial wave of punk rock in Los Angeles. The Alice Bag Band was featured in the seminal documentary on punk rock, *The Decline of Western Civilization*. Alice went on to perform in other groundbreaking bands, including Castration Squad, Cholita, and Las Tres. She is the author of the critically acclaimed books *Violence Girl* and *Pipe Bomb for the Soul.*

Scott Campbell is a radical journalist, writer, and translator based in California. He lived in Mexico for several years, including Oaxaca. His pieces appear frequently on El Enemigo Común and It's Going Down. He can be found online at fallingintoincandescence.com and @incandesceinto on Twitter.

Mike Corr (aka Mike Noonan) is an activist and mercenary educator, teaching World and Middle East History at various Bay Area community colleges. With his Irish roots and internationalist principles, the Palestinian struggle has been an inspiration and motivation for him in both activist and academic pursuits since watching the Second Intifada unfold in 2000. For Mike, it is an honor to be a conduit for the voices of Palestinians in struggle he had the privilege to work with during his academic research.

Christiana Cranberry was born and lived twenty years of her life in Oklahoma City, Oklahoma. She has been in punk bands since she was fourteen; her current band is called Sister Rat. After high school she spent six years as a homeless traveler. She currently resides in Lawrence, Kansas. Christiana is a high school level para-educator but has spent over a decade making shirts for her favorite bands. She is also a baker and chef.

Ruth Crossman is a writer and educator who currently lives in Oakland. Her political writings have appeared on the website Poets Reading the News and in the anthology *11/9: The Downfall of American Democracy.*

dwayne dixon is the writer of the zine *Astronaut Etiquette.* He is an anthropology professor at University of North Carolina, where he is widely noted for his powerful, conversational, student-centered teaching practice. dixon is also an active member of Redneck Revolt (https://www.redneckrevolt.org/), an anti-racist, anti-fascist community defense formation that advocates for broad working-class solidarity and very explicit rejection of structural racism/white supremacy.

Yvette Felarca is a teacher and civil rights activist, national organizer with the Coalition to Defend Affirmative Action, Integration, and Immigrant Rights and Fight for Equality By Any Means Necessary (BAMN).

John Fleissner is an artist, organizer, and public school art teacher in Milwaukee, Wisconsin. You can find his art on picket lines, on the walls of the city, and wheat pasted around town. He is a rank-and-file member of Milwaukee Teacher Education Association and has spent years before entering the classroom as a field organizer for public sector labor unions.

Mike Friedberg has booked shows, run a label, and most recently played in Kontaminat. He started working with youth at a community center in 2007 and has been teaching middle school science since 2012.

Michelle Cruz Gonzales, the author of *The Spitboy Rule: Tales of a Xicana in a Female Punk Band*, is a former preschool teacher who writes a lot. She has been in many influential punk and hardcore bands including Spitboy, Instant Girl, and Bitch Fight. Michelle teaches English and creative writing at Las Positas College, an open-access community college where nobody has to take a standardized placement test and where anyone can now take transfer-level English and math during their first semester.

Roburt Knife, writing from New Orleans, plays music in his mutant new wave/punk band Room 101. He has been working with young people for thirteen years and is in his seventh year as a full-time classroom teacher. He has taught history and English at different alternative, public, private, and charter high schools in Chicago, Houston, and New Orleans.

Frankie Mastrangelo is an educator living in Richmond, Virginia. She's working on a PhD dissertation that looks at how neoliberal buzzwords, like innovation, circulate through and influence various cultures and communities.

Ian McDeath is a teacher, an anarchist, and an artist [and excellent punk musician—ed.], in no particular order. For him, education, freedom, and creativity are inextricably linked. Each of these things requires the others, and each of these things produces the others, so he tries to bring all of them to everything he does.

Taylor McKenzie has been a part of the Oklahoma City punk scene for roughly fifteen years, playing in various bands and booking shows. His current projects are American Hate, Karger Traum, and DJing under various monikers, mostly techno. He lived in Germany for a year on two separate occasions and has been teaching seventh to twelfth grade German at Classen School of Advanced Studies in Oklahoma City since February 2016. CSAS being his alma mater, he finds himself teaching German in the same classroom in which he began learning German.

Lindsay McLeary is the academic coordinator for the Upward Bound program for low-income and/or first-generation college students in Berkeley. Lindsay spent his formative years knee-deep in SoCal's survivor-heavy punk/hardcore scene and now has the peculiar distinction of being the most heavily tattooed person in University of California Berkeley's Department of Equity and Inclusion. He has worked in education and educational outreach for well over a decade, including stints as a lecturer at University of Southern California and Stanford and as a classroom teacher in Oakland and Richmond, California, public schools.

Kadijah Means was born and raised in Oakland, California. She is the former Berkeley High School Black Student Union president and Amnesty International chapter president. She has been featured in *USA Today* and other publications in recognition of her role as an organizer of the thousand-strong Black Lives Matter protest in December 2014. Kadijah is the former communications department chief of staff for the Afrikan Black Coalition (ABC), which successfully pressured the University of California regents to divest twenty-five million dollars from private prisons. Kadijah interned for both Congresswoman Barbara Lee and the East Bay Community Law Center's Clean Slate practice in 2015, was the recipient of the Princeton Prize in Race Relations that same year, and was interviewed on noted podcast *This American Life*. Kadijah currently attends University of California Santa Cruz, where she has written the cultural competency curriculum for the campus-wide diversity training for the past two years and participated in the reclamation of Kerr Hall, resulting in guaranteed housing for African Black and Caribbean-identified students on campus.

Melissa Merin (she, her, hers, or they; cis) has been writing since she could hold a crayon. She is established as a parent, a lover and partner, a queer, an antiauthoritarian, and a consistently retiring punker. She is too Black to ever be considered a snowflake. Melissa believes in utilizing a diversity of tactics to build the world we need; one of her favorite tactics is writing. Melissa is a longtime educator and agitator and has never been able to get it together to "publish," though many zines and many blogs tell the story of trying.

Jessica Mills is a punk lifer who has played sax and bass for quite a few very well-known bands from the early nineties into the present. She is a former *Maximumrocknroll* columnist and author of the punk parenting memoir/guide *My Mother Wears Combat Boots*, current MRR book reviewer, intrepid copy editor for this volume, and English instructor at Central New Mexico Community College in Albuquerque.

John Mink (editor) is a social studies teacher who has worked at the high school and adult school levels, and who refuses to hide his political radicalism from his students. He has been a contributing writer and editor for underground publications and zines including *Slingshot*, *Absolutely Zippo: A Fanzine's Anthology*, and *Collapse Board*. He is editor and founder of the *Maximumrocknroll* magazine monthly column "Teaching Resistance" and is a vocalist/bassist for several internationally recognized punk bands. John lives in Berkeley, California, with his partner Megan March, who is also his bandmate in the truewave/punk group Street Eaters.

Mimi Thi Nguyen is still punk, despite threatening to quit eight times. She is also associate professor of Gender and Women's Studies and Asian American Studies at the University of Illinois Urbana-Champaign. Her first book is *The Gift of Freedom*. Her upcoming project is called *The Promise of Beauty*.

Sarah Orton, born in Oakland, is thirty years old and has been an educator, advocate, and activist in interpersonal violence and social justice movements for seven years. She has a background in sexual health and human sexuality studies and believes that sexual violence is a public health and human rights issue. Please email her directly with any ideas, inquiries, or for access to specific lesson plans, as she also believes that education and the exchange of ideas and information should always be free and accessible.

Steven Raser is a punk and a special education teacher in Oakland, California, who is deeply invested in the radical, proud inclusion of his students into the greater student body.

Ron Scapp is the founding director of the Graduate Program of Urban and Multicultural Education at the College of Mount Saint Vincent in the Bronx, where he is professor of humanities and teacher education. His books include, *Teaching Values: Critical Perspectives on Education, Politics and Culture* and *Living with Class: Philosophical Reflections on Identity and Material Culture*, coedited with Brian Seitz. He has collaborated on different projects with others, including with cultural critic and writer bell hooks.

E. Schmuse is a political radical and teacher in the German state of Bavaria. E. Schmuse is a pseudonym used by the author due to harsh Bavarian state policies about the personal political ideologies (to say nothing of actual activism) of teachers.

Frederick Schulze is an active member of the Koko Lepo youth solidarity program in Belgrade, Serbia. His scholarly work concerns racism, the state, and political economy in Belgrade. Before he received his doctorate in anthropology on these themes, Freddie worked a lot of odd service and education jobs in Texas, where he developed his anti-capitalist and anti-etatist politics.

Martin Sorrondeguy is a queer, Latinx punk. He is the singer for well-loved, influential punk and hardcore bands, including Limp Wrist, Los Crudos, and Needles, runs the record label Lenga Armada, is a longtime shitworker for *Maximumrocknroll* magazine, directed the 1999 classic punk film *Beyond the Screams: A U.S. Latino Hardcore Punk Documentary*, and is a top-notch photographer who has authored three books of amazing photos he shot of bands from all over the world. Martin also happens to be a dedicated teacher who has been involved in radical education for decades and is noted for putting as much passion into his classroom work as he is known for in punk.

Miriam Klein Stahl (cover artist for this book) is a Bay Area artist, educator, and activist and the *New York Times* bestselling illustrator of *Rad American Women A–Z* and *Rad Women Worldwide*. In addition to her work in printmaking, drawing, sculpture, paper cut, and public art, she is also the cofounder of the Arts and Humanities Academy at Berkeley High School, where she has taught since 1995. As an artist, she follows in a tradition of making socially relevant work, creating portraits of political activists, misfits, radicals, and radical movements. As an educator, she has dedicated her teaching practice to addressing equity through the lens of the arts. Her work has been widely exhibited and reproduced internationally. Stahl is also the co-owner of Pave the Way Skateboards, a queer skateboarding company formed with Los Angeles–based comedian, actor, writer, and skateboarder Tara Jepson. She lives in Berkeley, California, with her wife, artist Lena Wolff, daughter Hazel, and their dog Lenny.

Lena Tahmassian is assistant professor of Spanish Cultural Studies at the University of South Carolina in Columbia. Discovering punk as a somewhat maladjusted, first-generation youth in Arizona provided her with an early critical language of rejection of oppressive social norms. After several formative years in the San Francisco Bay Area, she has now carried that initial discovery to its logical conclusion as a teacher and researcher in humanities and critical theory.

Murad Tamini is currently a teacher in the classroom after spending many years as an official in the General Union of Palestinian Teachers (GUPT). In addition to this experience, he was and remains an activist against the occupation, from the time of the First Intifada in 1987 to the nonviolent popular resistance movement initiated by the villagers of Nabi Saleh in 2009.

Ash Tray played in Frau and Good Throb, among London's best punk bands of the 2000s, and spent a lot of time and energy to help make some pretty amazing things happen in the London and UK punk scene. Ash teaches children with autism in England, where she makes even more amazing things happen.

Acknowledgments

Thanks to Jessica Mills, Aaron Elliot, and Michael Ryan for their crucial editorial eyes, Steven Stothard and PM Press, Peter Rodrigues for being a great teaching mentor, the tireless editors and shitworkers at *Maximumrocknroll*, all the punks who fight for a better world, the incredible educators who contributed to this book and wrote columns, and every student and teacher who is uncompromisingly radical in the classroom and beyond.

ABOUT PM PRESS

PM Press was founded at the end of 2007 by a small collection of folks with decades of publishing, media, and organizing experience. PM Press co-conspirators have published and distributed hundreds of books, pamphlets, CDs, and DVDs. Members of PM have founded enduring book fairs, spearheaded victorious tenant organizing campaigns, and worked closely with bookstores, academic conferences, and even rock bands to deliver political and challenging ideas to all walks of life. We're old enough to know what we're doing and young enough to know what's at stake.

We seek to create radical and stimulating fiction and nonfiction books, pamphlets, T-shirts, visual and audio materials to entertain, educate, and inspire you. We aim to distribute these through every available channel with every available technology—whether that means you are seeing anarchist classics at our bookfair stalls, reading our latest vegan cookbook at the café, downloading geeky fiction e-books, or digging new music and timely videos from our website.

PM Press is always on the lookout for talented and skilled volunteers, artists, activists, and writers to work with. If you have a great idea for a project or can contribute in some way, please get in touch.

PM Press
PO Box 23912
Oakland, CA 94623
www.pmpress.org

PM Press in Europe
europe@pmpress.org
www.pmpress.org.uk

FRIENDS OF PM PRESS

These are indisputably momentous times—the financial system is melting down globally and the Empire is stumbling. Now more than ever there is a vital need for radical ideas.

In the years since its founding—and on a mere shoestring—PM Press has risen to the formidable challenge of publishing and distributing knowledge and entertainment for the struggles ahead. With over 300 releases to date, we have published an impressive and stimulating array of literature, art, music, politics, and culture. Using every available medium, we've succeeded in connecting those hungry for ideas and information to those putting them into practice.

Friends of PM allows you to directly help impact, amplify, and revitalize the discourse and actions of radical writers, filmmakers, and artists. It provides us with a stable foundation from which we can build upon our early successes and provides a much-needed subsidy for the materials that can't necessarily pay their own way. You can help make that happen—and receive every new title automatically delivered to your door once a month—by joining as a Friend of PM Press. And, we'll throw in a free T-shirt when you sign up.

Here are your options:

- **$30 a month** Get all books and pamphlets plus 50% discount on all webstore purchases

- **$40 a month** Get all PM Press releases (including CDs and DVDs) plus 50% discount on all webstore purchases

- **$100 a month** Superstar—Everything plus PM merchandise, free downloads, and 50% discount on all webstore purchases

For those who can't afford $30 or more a month, we have **Sustainer Rates** at $15, $10 and $5. Sustainers get a free PM Press T-shirt and a 50% discount on all purchases from our website.

Your Visa or Mastercard will be billed once a month, until you tell us to stop. Or until our efforts succeed in bringing the revolution around. Or the financial meltdown of Capital makes plastic redundant. Whichever comes first.

Anarchist Pedagogies: Collective Actions, Theories, and Critical Reflections on Education

Edited by Robert H. Haworth
with an afterword by Allan Antliff

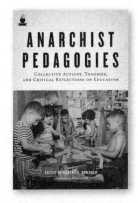

ISBN: 978-1-60486-484-7
$24.95   352 pages

Education is a challenging subject for anarchists.
Many are critical about working within a state-run
education system that is embedded in hierarchical, standardized, and authoritarian
structures. Numerous individuals and collectives envision the creation of
counterpublics or alternative educational sites as possible forms of resistance,
while other anarchists see themselves as "saboteurs" within the public arena—
believing that there is a need to contest dominant forms of power and educational
practices from multiple fronts. Of course, if anarchists agree that there are no
blueprints for education, the question remains, in what dynamic and creative
ways can we construct nonhierarchical, anti-authoritarian, mutual, and voluntary
educational spaces?

Contributors to this edited volume engage readers in important and challenging
issues in the area of anarchism and education. From Francisco Ferrer's modern
schools in Spain and the Work People's College in the United States, to
contemporary actions in developing "free skools" in the U.K. and Canada, to
direct-action education such as learning to work as a "street medic" in the
protests against neoliberalism, the contributors illustrate the importance of
developing complex connections between educational theories and collective
actions. Anarchists, activists, and critical educators should take these educational
experiences seriously as they offer invaluable examples for potential teaching and
learning environments outside of authoritarian and capitalist structures. Major
themes in the volume include: learning from historical anarchist experiments
in education, ways that contemporary anarchists create dynamic and situated
learning spaces, and finally, critically reflecting on theoretical frameworks and
educational practices. Contributors include: David Gabbard, Jeffery Shantz,
Isabelle Fremeaux & John Jordan, Abraham P. DeLeon, Elsa Noterman, Andre
Pusey, Matthew Weinstein, Alex Khasnabish, and many others.

*"Pedagogy is a central concern in anarchist writing and the free skool has played
a central part in movement activism. By bringing together an important group of
writers with specialist knowledge and experience, Robert Haworth's volume makes an
invaluable contribution to the discussion of these topics. His exciting collection provides
a guide to historical experiences and current experiments and also reflects on anarchist
theory, extending our understanding and appreciation of pedagogy in anarchist
practice."*
—Dr. Ruth Kinna, Senior Lecturer in Politics, Loughborough University, author of
Anarchism: A Beginners Guide and coeditor of *Anarchism and Utopianism*

Out of the Ruins: The Emergence of Radical Informal Learning Spaces

Edited by Robert H. Haworth and
John M. Elmore

ISBN: 978-1-62963-239-1
$24.95   288 pages

OUT OF THE RUINS
*The Emergence of
Radical Informal Learning Spaces*

Edited by Robert H. Haworth & John M. Elmore

Contemporary educational practices and policies across the world are heeding the calls of Wall Street for more corporate control, privatization, and standardized accountability. There are definite shifts and movements towards more capitalist interventions of efficiency and an adherence to market fundamentalist values within the sphere of public education. In many cases, educational policies are created to uphold and serve particular social, political, and economic ends. Schools, in a sense, have been tools to reproduce hierarchical, authoritarian, and hyper-individualistic models of social order. From the industrial era to our recent expansion of the knowledge economy, education has been at the forefront of manufacturing and exploiting particular populations within our society.

The important news is that emancipatory educational practices are emerging. Many are emanating outside the constraints of our dominant institutions and are influenced by more participatory and collective actions. In many cases, these alternatives have been undervalued or even excluded within the educational research. From an international perspective, some of these radical informal learning spaces are seen as a threat by many failed states and corporate entities.

Out of the Ruins sets out to explore and discuss the emergence of alternative learning spaces that directly challenge the pairing of public education with particular dominant capitalist and statist structures. The authors construct philosophical, political, economic and social arguments that focus on radical informal learning as a way to contest efforts to commodify and privatize our everyday educational experiences. The major themes include the politics of learning in our formal settings, constructing new theories on our informal practices, collective examples of how radical informal learning practices and experiences operate, and how individuals and collectives struggle to share these narratives within and outside of institutions.

Contributors include David Gabbard, Rhiannon Firth, Andrew Robinson, Farhang Rouhani, Petar Jandrić, Ana Kuzmanić, Sarah Amsler, Dana Williams, Andre Pusey, Jeff Shantz, Sandra Jeppesen, Joanna Adamiak, Erin Dyke, Eli Meyerhoff, David I. Backer, Matthew Bissen, Jacques Laroche, Aleksandra Perisic, and Jason Wozniak.

Anarchism and Education: A Philosophical Perspective

Judith Suissa

ISBN: 978-1-60486-114-3
$19.95   184 pages

While there have been historical accounts of the anarchist school movement, there has been no systematic work on the philosophical underpinnings of anarchist educational ideas—until now.

Anarchism and Education offers a philosophical account of the neglected tradition of anarchist thought on education. Although few anarchist thinkers wrote systematically on education, this analysis is based largely on a reconstruction of the educational thought of anarchist thinkers gleaned from their various ethical, philosophical, and popular writings. Primarily drawing on the work of the nineteenth-century anarchist theorists such as Bakunin, Kropotkin, and Proudhon, the book also covers twentieth-century anarchist thinkers such as Noam Chomsky, Paul Goodman, Daniel Guérin, and Colin Ward.

This original work will interest philosophers of education and educationalist thinkers as well as those with a general interest in anarchism.

"This is an excellent book that deals with important issues through the lens of anarchist theories and practices of education . . . The book tackles a number of issues that are relevant to anybody who is trying to come to terms with the philosophy of education."
—*Higher Education Review*

Anarchist Education and the Modern School: A Francisco Ferrer Reader

Francisco Ferrer
Edited by Mark Bray and
Robert H. Haworth

ISBN: 978-1-62963-509-5
$24.95   352 pages

On October 13, 1909, Francisco Ferrer, the notorious
Catalan anarchist educator and founder of the Modern School, was executed by
firing squad. The Spanish government accused him of masterminding the Tragic
Week rebellion, while the transnational movement that emerged in his defense
argued that he was simply the founder of the groundbreaking Modern School of
Barcelona. Was Ferrer a ferocious revolutionary, an ardently nonviolent pedagogue,
or something else entirely?

Anarchist Education and the Modern School is the first historical reader to gather
together Ferrer's writings on rationalist education, revolutionary violence, and the
general strike (most translated into English for the first time) and put them into
conversation with the letters, speeches, and articles of his comrades, collaborators,
and critics to show that the truth about the founder of the Modern School
was far more complex than most of his friends or enemies realized. Francisco
Ferrer navigated a tempestuous world of anarchist assassins, radical republican
conspirators, anticlerical rioters, and freethinking educators to establish the
legendary Escuela Moderna and the Modern School movement that his martyrdom
propelled around the globe.

*"A thorough and balanced collection of the writings of the doyen of myriad horizontal
educational projects in Spain and more still across the world. Equally welcome are the
well-researched introduction and the afterword that underline both the multiplicity of
anarchist perspectives on education and social transformation and the complexity of
Ferrer's thinking."*
—Chris Ealham, author of *Living Anarchism: Jose Peirats and the Spanish Anarcho-
Syndicalist Movement*

*"This volume brings together for the first time a comprehensive collection of Ferrer's
own writings, documenting the daily life and aims of the Escuela Moderna, alongside
reflections, often critical, by contemporary anarchists and other radical thinkers.
Together with the editors' thoughtful Introduction, the result is a fascinating collection—
essential reading for anyone keen to go beyond the image of Ferrer the martyr of
libertarian education and to understand the perennial moral and political questions at
the heart of any project of education for freedom."*
—Judith Suissa, author of *Anarchism and Education: A Philosophical Perspective*

Punk Rock: An Oral History

John Robb
with a foreword by Henry Rollins

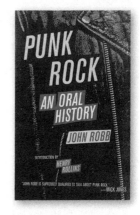

ISBN: 978-1-60486-005-4
$19.95   584 pages

With its own fashion, culture, and chaotic energy, punk
rock boasted a do-it-yourself ethos that allowed anyone
to take part. Vibrant and volatile, the punk scene left
an extraordinary legacy of music and cultural change.
John Robb talks to many of those who cultivated the
movement, such as John Lydon, Lemmy, Siouxsie Sioux,
Mick Jones, Chrissie Hynde, Malcolm McLaren, Henry Rollins, and Glen Matlock,
weaving together their accounts to create a raw and unprecedented oral history
of UK punk. All the main players are here: from The Clash to Crass, from The Sex
Pistols to the Stranglers, from the UK Subs to Buzzcocks—over 150 interviews
capture the excitement of the most thrilling wave of rock 'n' roll pop culture ever.
Ranging from its widely debated roots in the late 1960s to its enduring influence on
the bands, fashion, and culture of today, this history brings to life the energy and
the anarchy as no other book has done.

"Its unique brand of energy helps make it a riot all its own."
—*Harp* magazine

*"John Robb is a great writer . . . and he is supremely qualified in my opinion to talk about
punk rock."*
—Mick Jones, The Clash

"John Robb is as punk rock as The Clash."
—Alan McGee

The Day the Country Died: A History of Anarcho Punk 1980-1984

Ian Glasper

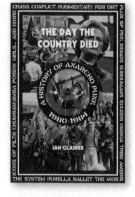

ISBN: 978-1-60486-516-5
$24.95   496 pages

The Day the Country Died features author, historian, and musician Ian Glasper (*Burning Britain*) exploring in minute detail the influential, esoteric, UK anarcho punk scene of the early Eighties. If the colorful '80s punk bands captured in *Burning Britain* were loud, political, and uncompromising, those examined in *The Day the Country Died* were even more so, totally prepared to risk their liberty to communicate the ideals they believed in so passionately.

With Crass and Poison Girls opening the floodgates, the arrival of bands such as Zounds, Flux of Pink Indians, Conflict, Subhumans, Chumbawamba, Amebix, Rudimentary Peni, Antisect, Omega Tribe, and Icons of Filth heralded a brand new age of honesty and integrity in underground music. With a backdrop of Thatcher's Britain, punk music became self-sufficient and considerably more aggressive, blending a DIY ethos with activism to create the perfectly bleak soundtrack to the zeitgeist of a discontented British youth.

It was a time when punk stopped being merely a radical fashion statement, and became a force for real social change; a genuine revolutionary movement, driven by some of the most challenging noises ever committed to tape. Anarchy, as regards punk rock, no longer meant "cash from chaos." It meant "freedom, peace, and unity." Anarcho punk took the rebellion inherent in punk from the beginning to a whole new level of personal awareness.

All the scene's biggest names, and most of the smaller ones, are comprehensively covered with new, exclusive interviews and hundreds of previously unseen photographs.

"The oral testimony assembled here provides an often-lucid participant's view of the work of the wider anarcho-punk milieu, which demonstrates just as tellingly the diversity as well as the commonality by which it was defined. The collection hints at the extent to which—within a militant antiwar, anti-work, anti-system framework— the perception and priorities of the movement's activists differed: something the movement's critics (who were always keen to deride the uniformity of the 'Crass punks') rarely understood."
—Rich Cross, *Freedom*

The Spitboy Rule: Tales of a Xicana in a Female Punk Band

Michelle Cruz Gonzales with a Foreword
by Martín Sorrondeguy and Preface by
Mimi Thi Nguyen

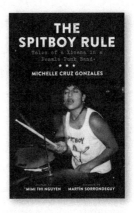

ISBN: 978-1-62963-140-0
$15.95   160 pages

Michelle Cruz Gonzales played drums and wrote lyrics
in the influential 1990s female hardcore band Spitboy,
and now she's written a book—a punk rock herstory.
Though not a riot grrl band, Spitboy blazed trails for women musicians in the San
Francisco Bay Area and beyond, but it wasn't easy. Misogyny, sexism, abusive fans,
class and color blindness, and all-out racism were foes, especially for Gonzales, a
Xicana and the only person of color in the band.

Unlike touring rock bands before them, the unapologetically feminist Spitboy
preferred Scrabble games between shows rather than sex and drugs, and they
were not the angry manhaters that many expected them to be. Serious about
women's issues and being the band that they themselves wanted to hear, a band
that rocked as hard as men but sounded like women, Spitboy released several
records and toured internationally. The memoir details these travels while
chronicling Spitboy's successes and failures, and for Gonzales, discovering her own
identity along the way.

Fully illustrated with rare photos and flyers from the punk rock underground, this
fast-paced, first-person recollection is populated by scenesters and musical allies
from the time including Econochrist, Paxston Quiggly, Neurosis, Los Crudos, Aaron
Cometbus, Pete the Roadie, Green Day, Fugazi, and Kamala and the Karnivores.

"The Spitboy Rule *is a compelling and insightful journey into the world of '90s punk
as seen through the eyes of a Xicana drummer who goes by the nickname Todd. Todd
stirs the pot by insisting that she plays hardcore punk, not Riot Grrrl music, and inviting
males to share the dance floor with women in a respectful way. This drummer never
misses a beat. Read it!"*
—Alice Bag, singer for the Bags, author of *Violence Girl: East L.A. Rage to Hollywood
Stage, a Chicana Punk Story*

Parenting without God: How to Raise Moral, Ethical, and Intelligent Children, Free from Religious Dogma, Second Edition

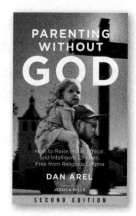

Dan Arel
with a Foreword by Jessica Mills

ISBN: 978-1-62963-708-2
$15.95   176 pages

Children inevitably turn to their parents for more than just food and security; equally important are assurance, recognition, and interpretation of life. A child develops best in an environment where creativity and discovery are unimpeded by the artificial restrictions of blind faith and dogmatic belief. *Parenting without God* is for parents, and future parents, who lack belief in a god and who are seeking guidance on raising freethinkers and social-justice-aware children in a nation where public dialogue has been controlled by the Christian Right.

Dan Arel, activist and critically acclaimed author, has penned a magnificently practical guide to help parents provide their children with the intellectual tools for standing up to attempts at religious proselytization, whether by teachers, coaches, friends, or even other family members. *Parenting without God* is also for the parent activist who is trying to make the world a better place for all children by first educating their own children about racism, sexism, and all forms of discrimination that continue to serve as a barrier to the fundamentals of human dignity and democracy. It's for parents who wish for their children to question everything and to learn how to reach their own conclusions based on verifiable evidence and reason. Above all, Arel makes the penetrating argument that parents should lead by example—both by speaking candidly about the importance of secularism and by living an openly and unabashedly secular life.

Parenting without God is written with humility, compassion, and understanding. Dan Arel's writing style is refreshingly lucid and conveys the unmistakable impression of a loving father dedicated to redefining the role of parenthood so that it also includes the vitally important task of nurturing every child's latent human impulse for freedom and autonomy. This second edition has been expanded with new material from the author.

"*Parenting without God is not just about the absence of religion—it's about the glorious space that opens up for secular parents and their lucky kids once the clutter and smoke of religion is gone. Dan Arel's voice is clear, smart, and a welcome addition to the growing chorus of parents taking the hands of their children and running at full speed into the real world.*"
—Dale McGowan, author/editor of *Parenting Beyond Belief* and *Raising Freethinkers*

This Is How We Survive: Revolutionary Mothering, War, and Exile in the 21st Century

Mai'a Williams

with a Foreword by Ariel Gore

ISBN: 978-1-62963-556-9

$17.95   224 pages

In *This Is How We Survive: Revolutionary Mothering, War, and Exile in the 21st Century*, Mai'a Williams shares her experiences working in conflict zones and with liberatory resistance communities as a journalist, human rights worker, and midwife in Palestine, Egypt, Chiapas, Berlin, and the U.S., while mothering her young daughter Aza.

She first went to Palestine in 2003 during the Second Intifada to support Palestinians resisting the Israeli occupation. In 2006, she became pregnant in Bethlehem, West Bank. By the time her daughter was three years old, they had already celebrated with Zapatista women in southern Mexico and survived Israeli detention, and during the 2011 Arab Spring they were in the streets of Cairo protesting the Mubarak dictatorship. She watched the Egyptian revolution fall apart and escaped the violence, like many of her Arab comrades, by moving to Europe. Three years later, she and Aza were camping at Standing Rock in protest of the Dakota Access Pipeline and co-creating revolutionary mothering communities once again.

This is a story about mothers who are doing the work of deep social transformation by creating the networks of care that sustain movements and revolutions. By centering mothers in our organizing work, we center those who have the skills and the experience of creating and sustaining life on this planet. *This Is How We Survive* illuminates how mothering is a practice essential to the work of revolution. It explores the heartbreak of revolutionary movements falling apart and revolutionaries scattering across the globe into exile. And most importantly, how mamas create, no matter the conditions, the resilience to continue doing revolutionary work.

"Mai'a's ongoing journey is about mothering as a daily revolution, brought into focus by living and loving at major revolutionary sites of our contemporary world. From Palestine to Egypt, Chiapas, Berlin, and especially the U.S. Midwest, Mai'a shares her experiences of navigating the intimate intergenerational impact of a constant state of political and personal war with detail and a crucial side-eye. This book is an opportunity to see the life you are living, and lives you would never see otherwise, in new and interconnected ways."
—Alexis Pauline Gumbs, author of *M Archive: After the End of the World*

Rad Families: A Celebration

Edited by Tomas Moniz
with a Foreword by Ariel Gore

ISBN: 978-1-62963-230-8
$19.95 296 pages

Rad Families: A Celebration honors the messy, the painful, the playful, the beautiful, the myriad ways we create families. This is not an anthology of experts, or how-to articles on perfect parenting; it often doesn't even try to provide answers. Instead, the writers strive to be honest and vulnerable in sharing their stories and experiences, their failures and their regrets.

Gathering parents and writers from diverse communities, it explores the process of getting pregnant from trans birth to adoption, grapples with issues of racism and police brutality, probes raising feminists and feminist parenting. It plumbs the depths of empty nesting and letting go.

Some contributors are recognizable authors and activists but most are everyday parents working and loving and trying to build a better world one diaper change at a time. It's a book that reminds us all that we are not alone, that community can help us get through the difficulties, can, in fact, make us better people. It's a celebration, join us!

Contributors include Jonas Cannon, Ian MacKaye, Burke Stansbury, Danny Goot, Simon Knaphus, Artnoose, Welch Canavan, Daniel Muro LaMere, Jennifer Lewis, Zach Ellis, Alicia Dornadic, Jesse Palmer, Mindi J., Carla Bergman, Tasnim Nathoo, Rachel Galindo, Robert Liu-Trujillo, Dawn Caprice, Shawn Taylor, D.A. Begay, Philana Dollin, Airial Clark, Allison Wolfe, Roger Porter, cubbie rowland-storm, Annakai & Rob Geshlider, Jeremy Adam Smith, Frances Hardinge, Jonathan Shipley, Bronwyn Davies Glover, Amy Abugo Ongiri, Mike Araujo, Craig Elliott, Eleanor Wohlfeiler, Scott Hoshida, Plinio Hernandez, Madison Young, Nathan Torp, Sasha Vodnik, Jessie Susannah, Krista Lee Hanson, Carvell Wallace, Dani Burlison, Brian Whitman, scott winn, Kermit Playfoot, Chris Crass, and Zora Moniz.

"Rad dads, rad families, rad children. These stories show us that we are not alone. That we don't have all the answers. That we are all learning."
—Nikki McClure, illustrator, author, parent

"Rad Families is the collection for all families."
—Innosanto Nagara, author/illustrator of *A Is for Activist*